# What people are saying about

# The Journey Across Forever

Throughout his writings, Wayne Saalman interlaces real occurrences that challenge the entire notion of pure materialism. Whether you accept or deny the reality of these astonishing events, they do happen. Anything that does happen, can happen. The challenge laid out by Saalman is for you, the reader, to become hyper aware of your surroundings and take advantage of the extraordinary gifts that are presented to you in this work.
**John B. Alexander, Ph.D.**, author of *The Warrior's Edge, Reality Denied* and *UFOs: Myths, Conspiracies and Realities*

Wayne Saalman in *The Journey Across Forever* presents the reader with a book of challenges, and responding to them will change your life. Saalman traces the idea that consciousness is causal and fundamental through the centuries from ancient spiritual teachers to modern physicists and shows the inadequacy of materialism. He addresses why understanding the primacy of consciousness is so important in understanding reality and your place in it.
**Stephan A. Schwartz**, author of *The 8 Laws of Change and Awakening*

This wonderful journey through light-years and mysteries will inspire and motivate the reader to look deeper into the world around us. It frees the mind to wonder, and that is a beautiful thing.
**Whitley Strieber**, author of *Communion, Transformation, A New World*, and other works.

*The Journey Across Forever* is a phenomenal experience. It is a book that dares the reader to push past the veil and explore the

realms of possibility. A must-read!
**G.L. Davies**, author of *Harvest: The True Story of Alien Abduction*

*The Journey Across Forever* is a terrific read, full of brilliant ideas and insights. It may well be the best book you'll read this year.
**Ken Bruen**, bestselling author of the *Jack Taylor* series

# The Journey Across Forever

A Magical Provocative Odyssey through the Ages, Around the World and into the Great Beyond.

# The Journey Across Forever

A Magical Provocative Odyssey through the Ages, Around the World and into the Great Beyond.

Wayne Saalman

Foreword by John B. Alexander, Ph.D.

BOOKS

Winchester, UK
Washington, USA

JOHN HUNT PUBLISHING

First published by O-Books, 2023
O-Books is an imprint of John Hunt Publishing Ltd., 3 East St., Alresford,
Hampshire SO24 9EE, UK
office@jhpbooks.com
www.johnhuntpublishing.com
www.o-books.com

For distributor details and how to order please visit the 'Ordering' section on our website.



ISBN: 978 1 80341 170 5
978 1 80341 171 2 (ebook)
Library of Congress Control Number: 2022930120



A CIP catalogue record for this book is available from the British Library.

Design: Stuart Davies

UK: Printed and bound by CPI Group (UK) Ltd, Croydon, CR0 4YY
Printed in North America by CPI GPS partners

# Contents

**Books by Wayne Saalman**

**Fiction**

*The Dream Illuminati*

*The Illuminati of Immortality*

*Dragonfire Dreams*

*Crimson Firestorm Mars*

**Nonfiction**

*The Journey Across Forever*

This book is dedicated, in memoriam, to **Robert Anton Wilson,** my spiritual and literary mentor, whom I had the honor of meeting only once, but whose writings have influenced me in too many wonderful ways to count.

# Acknowledgments

I wish to thank Colonel John B. Alexander at the outset here for his exclusive Foreword and support during the writing of this book. I initially contacted the Colonel after reading two of his amazing books: *UFOs: Myths, Realities and Conspiracies* and *Reality Denied – Firsthand Experiences with Things that Can't Happen, but Did,* for it was clear to me that our interests and viewpoints were profoundly similar and harmonious. I have found that the Colonel's writings are elegant, extremely intelligent in scope and exhibit a total grasp of the issues. They also radiate, to my way of thinking, total credibility and genuine integrity, which is priceless when one considers the themes we are concerned with here. It is for these same reasons that I chose to quote him in my novel *Crimson Firestorm Mars,* a fictional thriller about what might potentially transpire if the race to be the first to colonize the Red Planet should turn deadly before any group of astronauts even gets the chance to blast off.

The Colonel's credentials are impeccable. He was a founding member of IRVA, a former SSE councilor and a past president of the International Association of Near-Death Studies. He is also retired from the Los Alamos National Laboratory and has served on studies with the National Research Council, the Army Science Board, the Council on Foreign Relations, NATO, and was a senior fellow at a Department of Defense university.

The topics in his book, *Reality Denied,* are numerous and include personal stories about telepathy, psychokinesis, fire walking, remote viewing, "otherworldly" adventures with psychoactive plants, the near-death experience and a myriad of other intriguing subjects. In his book *UFOs: Myths, Conspiracies, and Realities,* the Colonel offers us what I think is the most credible review of the many conspiracies tied into the "Phenomenon" that I have ever read. After all, he spent most of his life on the "inside" as regards this topic, by which I mean a lifetime in the army, engaging with countless military and government officials. He was thus in the unique position over the years of being able to follow up on conspiratorial leads about things like secret government programs, government coverups and the like, in order to determine what was genuinely true and what was mere hearsay. He strongly advocates that both military officials and scientists be allowed to openly pursue the matter of UFOs and be given the privilege of not having their careers and reputations smeared for daring to do so. "There is little doubt," he writes, "that some unidentified flying objects are real, three-dimensional solid objects, which are physically present and observable." There is hard data to back this statement and the Colonel pursues and shares that data with meticulous, indeed forensic, intensity. Nevertheless, he also wrote that, "The extraterrestrial hypothesis is but one possibility, and probably not the best fit with the facts." This leaves us with a mystery still and only time will tell if that mystery gets solved.

Personally, I see the Colonel as an extremely rare military figure. He is a man who has actually fought for and promoted, at the highest levels of the "Establishment", the use of nonlethal weaponry and has understood for decades now that the first goal of a true warrior is to protect life. In my novel *Dragonfire Dreams*, which I published several years before encountering the Colonel's books, I quoted Morihei Ueshiba who wrote in his book, *The Art of Peace*, "The way of the warrior has been misunderstood… To injure or destroy is the worst sin a human being can commit. The true way of the warrior is to prevent slaughter – it is the art of peace, the power of love." What a laudable and noble statement that is. It is the kind of enlightened stance that one does not generally associate with virtually any military figure, but Colonel Alexander is definitely the exception and what is most remarkable about him is that he has never been one to just talk the talk. He has taken action over the years, for as well as the two books cited above, the Colonel has published three other books which are highly significant to humanity: *The Warrior's Edge* in which he discusses such topics as meditation, intuition, visualization, biofeedback, psychokinesis and the martial arts as researched by the U.S. Military. *Future War: Non-Lethal Weapons in Modern Warfare* (with a foreword by Tom Clancy) and *Winning the War: Advanced Weapons, Strategies, and Concepts for the Post-9/11 World*. It should be noted that Colonel Alexander has conducted nonlethal warfare briefings at the highest levels of government, including the Executive Office of the President, the United States National Security Council, senior Department of Defense officials, members of Congress and the Director of Central Intelligence.

The great human dream is surely to have many more – countless numbers, in fact – of hero warriors like Colonel Alexander. What a better world this earth would be if there were millions of military personnel who thought like him and sought to preserve life in any way they could rather than being gung-ho to take lives, drive people from their homes and make a shambles of cities and rural environs. In the extensive Foreword the Colonel has written for this book, readers can learn a great deal more about this fascinating and incredible man, a military figure who has fought his whole life for the preservation of democracy, human rights and the privilege of being able to freely express oneself. In my view, Colonel Alexander stands as a role model for future warriors and I believe he is an icon and a legend for that reason. This is why I contacted him and why I hope his legacy will be known and appreciated by millions for the message it sends.

Most philosophers have known, at least since 500 BCE, that the world perceived by the senses is not the "real world" but a construct we create – our own private work of art.
**– Robert Anton Wilson**
*Cosmic Trigger*

The process of creation is infinite and eternal, and we are part of how this creation happens. There is an old saying that our lives are gifts *from* God, and that what we make of them are gifts *to* God. A diamond sparkles through the diversity of its many facets, so perhaps our lives, ultimately purified through the realms of form and formlessness, become analogous to these facets, each with its individual contributions to make to the whole.
**– David Fontana**
*Life Beyond Death*

When one sees that everything exists as an illusion, one can live in a higher sphere than ordinary man.
**– Gautama Buddha**

The soul that is attached to anything, however much good there may be in it, will not arrive at the liberty of the divine.
**– St John of the Cross**

# Foreword

## By John B. Alexander, Ph.D.

HEREIN LIES AN INCREDIBLE SYNTHESIS of the wisdom of the Masters of the Ages. It will challenge all readers to initiate an inner search while providing many guideposts through an eclectic mixture of experiences of the body, mind and soul. Choose from it what you wish. Disagree if you wish, but know that Saalman presents a panoply of deeply personal ventures, profound thoughts, and powerful speculations, that may trigger a yearning to explore what lies beyond. Know that the boundaries of consciousness are truly unlimited. Contrary to the materialistic thinking of so many, the brain and the mind are not synonymous. At its core, the universe is consciousness, and you are perfectly integrated into the cosmos. Be prepared to push the envelope and your self-induced boundaries, even if it makes you uncomfortable. Especially if it makes you uncomfortable.

To fully comprehend the meaning of life requires serious consideration of things spiritual. That contemplation will take many lifetimes. Currently you are experiencing but one, and the illusion of separateness, at times, can be overwhelming. A central theme of this book is exploring our/your spiritual nature, and how the evidence and signs to follow are ubiquitous.

In the western/developed world, with the predominant belief system steeped in materialism, many people are reluctant to acknowledge their inner spiritual feelings. Note that *spiritual* and *religious* are not necessarily synonymous. As illustrated in the following chapters, many people fail to recognize that there are competing belief structures in the world. The dominance of technological advances in some cultures does not necessarily mean they have moral superiority, though many of them tend to think so. Saalman, an intrepid global explorer and spiritual surveyor, details cross-cultural experiences that will challenge the reader, possibly activating unplumbed yearnings, especially if they lie dormant in the veiled recesses of the mind.

As he and I have both learned, there are other cultures, ones in which spirituality is preeminent and permeates all aspects of life. Based on ancient teachings, some extraordinary travelers forsake the physical altogether, but at a price incomprehensible to most humans. Then, too, there are a few sagacious individuals who successfully integrate the competing domains of spirituality and materialism and provide a path towards balance that is sustainable both individually and collectively. It is that balance we wish for all of you to find. Deeply personal, there is not one true path, and ultimately many mansions.

Life constantly affords everyone a wide array of challenges and opportunities. Not all of these are pleasant or desirable, especially while one is enmeshed in them. However, when viewed in hindsight, many of the experiences that were thought to be negative at the time, turn out to be positive in the long run. As an example, loss of a job can be quite devastating. Most often, however, that leads an individual to pursue new avenues that would have been unavailable under the original set of circumstances.

Repeatedly, such incidents have manifested in my life. Even after 32 years associated with the U.S. Army, I was not looking for retirement. It was a dispute with the Colonel's Assignment Branch of the U.S. Army Military Personnel Center that led me to request retirement in lieu of an undesirable assignment. Had my decision not happened, I might never have had the opportunity to join Los Alamos National Laboratory (LANL), which allowed me to interact with some of the most brilliant scientists in the world such as my friend, Edward Teller (father of the Hydrogen Bomb & his two daughters). Without retiring and going to LANL I would never have participated with the

Army Science Board, been assigned to various NATO studies or been in a position to influence senior politicians and captains of industry. It was because of the unanticipated career shift that I became involved in the development of the nonlethal weapons field for the military. Commensurate with the theme of this book, the emphasis was on conservation of life while offering necessary alternatives for application of force in a world that has yet to embrace its true spiritual nature.

It was specifically because I retired at what I thought was a premature time that I was afforded the opportunity to study at the Kennedy School of Government at Harvard University, the Sloan School of Management at MIT, and to participate with the Council of Foreign Affairs that led to the Department of Defense creating the Joint Nonlethal Weapons Department. If I could've had the career path that I imagined I wanted, I would never have become friends with Tom Clancy, who provided forewords for two of my nonfiction books.

The point is, what you think you want, is not always in your best interest. What appears to be disheartening at one moment, may well lead to great enjoyment at a later one. Obviously, these most often occur when you least expect it. As will be explored in this book, consciousness is preeminent, and functions in ways we cannot understand. As a believer in reincarnation, I have come to think that there is a prenatal contract that each of us has made, and there are guiding forces that create the opportunities for each of us to fulfill our predestined assignment. The conundrum, of course, is the inevitable controversy between free will and predestination.

Throughout my life, I have always been interested in a wide range of phenomena. That is germane here as you will be introduced in Wayne Saalman's book to many extraordinary events that stretch the imagination. While I was in the U.S. Army, I had unusual opportunities to explore fields not normally associated with the military. Today, few people remember just how broken the Army was coming out of the Vietnam War. It was based on that recognition by certain senior leaders, such as four-star generals Bernie Rogers, Edwin (Shy) Meyer, and several others, that had the foresight to allow some of us to explore techniques that were associated with what was then known as *New Age* thinking. At that time, the antics of the *flower children* were also thought of as the *dawning of the Age of Aquarius*. For traditionalists, it was about as far from conventional military comportment as one could get.

Both generals Rogers and Meyer rose to the pinnacle of the U.S. Army, namely the Chief of Staff. It was under their leadership, and, importantly, protection, that we were able to create one of the most innovative organizations ever to grace the American military, Task Force Delta. For the record, this is not to be confused with Delta Force, the U.S. Army's premiere counterterrorism organization. Rather, TF Delta, led by Colonel Frank Burns, was the equivalent of civilian think tanks, but operating with very few of the constraints normally found in the military. The mission was to search out emerging concepts and technologies that could be brought back and incorporated into the Army structure to make it better. The motto was "What is the difference that makes a difference?"

Participants involved were all volunteers. That also included many civilians who were not employed by the Department of Defense, but rather people who had become so intrigued with the activities that they chose to join in. Amazingly, these people paid their own expenses for the privilege of playing. At the administrative core of TF Delta, there were only five people actually assigned to the element. The rest of us in the military had regular assignments and balanced our activities between our day job and the think tank.

As an example of what was accomplished, we were some of the first participants to employ ARPANET, the forerunner of what we know today as the Internet. The U.S. Army was, and is, distributed globally. In 1980, to coordinate a paper on any given topic traditionally would take several weeks, as the material generally moved through the postal system. At the time we operated over phone lines at about 60 bod per second. That is incomprehensible with today's Internet speeds of megabytes. That meant you could literally watch each letter being typed out. However, we were able to reduce the time to staff a paper from weeks to a single day. Along with the *New Age*, the *Information Age* was just being born, and we were surfing on the leading edge of the tsunami that was to come.

But it was exploring philosophies and institutional concepts that were at the heart of TF Delta developments. Neurolinguistic programming (NLP) had just been conceptualized and written about in the book, *Frogs into Princes.* That was key to NLP gaining popularity. Through both TF Delta and my conventional assignments, I actually had the NLP creators, Richard Bandler and John Grinder, under contracts, albeit separately. One of the key projects also involved Tony Robbins, who went on to become world renowned as an inspirational consultant.

One such project stands out in my mind and is exemplary of what you can do if you put your mind to it. That was *Project Jedi,* named after the famous Jedi Masters of the *Star Wars* movies. The primary effort had to do with improving pistol shooting by creating an NLP model based on the best marksman in the world. But we also explored other capabilities that are of more direct relevance here.

Psychokinesis is quite controversial. Scientists fret that, if psychokinesis is real, the *law of conservation of energy* is violated. At some point around that time in my life, I heard about an Israeli entertainer named Uri Geller who was making quite a name for himself by bending spoons, ostensibly with the power of his mind. Of course, skeptics believed it was all a trick, but an aerospace engineer, Jack Houck, who worked at McDonnell Douglas, had developed a process in which psychokinesis metal bending (PKMB) could be taught to the general public. These became known as *spoon bending parties*. Shortly before we initiated *Project Jedi*, I had invited Jack Houck to hold one of those spoon bending parties at my apartment in northern Virginia. Also in attendance was Major General Bert Stubblebine, the commander of U.S. Army Intelligence and Security Command (INSCOM), who was my boss at the time. Among the other attendees was Ted Rockwell, who had been Admiral Rickover's technical director in the development of the nuclear Navy, Andrija Puharich, who was responsible for bringing Geller to the United States, Anne Gehman, a renowned medium, and several others.

For those in attendance, this spoon bending party would have profound implications. The group was seated on the floor, more or less in an oval. Serendipitously, MG Stubblebine was directly across from Anne Gehman. As the event progressed, we moved to what Jack called *the graduate session*. That meant that each of us would hold two forks and that no physical force would be allowed. Suddenly, without warning, one of the forks in Anne Gehman's hand drooped over a full 90 degrees. While we were aware of some other minor bending, such as fork tines moving, this was the first time we had personally observed such a significant spontaneous bend.

This was proof positive that psychokinesis was real and could interact at a visible macrolevel. Based on that information, we integrated the concepts in the future INSCOM meetings. The real focus was not to bend metal; it was to admonish commanders to not ignore reports of unusual activity, simply because they didn't believe something was possible. Using Houck's process, we were able to inculcate the information to a much larger audience. Applicable here is for readers to follow that advice. Just because you can't immediately explain an event, that doesn't mean that you should offhand reject it. Compare the information against ground truth, such as in this case that the spoons or forks actually bent.

Returning to my interaction with Tony Robbins, one day he and I took a small group of military personnel who had not been exposed to the work we were doing, either with NLP or the psychic field, and offered them a unique opportunity. In the morning, we had each of them learn how to break boards karate style. That afternoon, we held a successful spoon bending party. Then, the crowning event took place that evening at a small farm near the Maryland suburbs. It was there that we all engaged in firewalking. While skeptics will again attempt to postulate rational explanations, they do not hold up. Yes, the fire is hot and if you do not follow the instructions, and note a shift in consciousness, there is a high probability that you will get burned. None of the participants in this event received any burns.

Closely associated with the efforts of TF Delta was the creation of the *First Earth Battalion* by my friend, the late Lt. Col. Jim Channon. Some readers may be aware that the notion was popularized in the George Clooney movie, *The Men Who Stare at Goats*. The movie called it *The New Earth Army*, but the storyline was derived from Channon's brainchild. While many of us were embodied in composite characters in the movie, Channon was depicted one-for-one by actor Jeff Daniels, who sported an unrealistic ponytail while nailing many of Jim's attributes.

An old soul, Channon was an amazing Imagineer and fantastic artist. While assigned in Hollywood, both formally and informally, he was involved with exploring many of the Aquarian New Age concepts that were prevalent on the West Coast at that time. *The First Earth Battalion* was purely conceptual, and literally owned by Channon. He called it, *The Natural Guard*, and, *A Force of Hearts*. Adeptly, he translated much of the Aquarian New Age thinking into practical military applications that were designed to reduce the potential for violence and save the planet. His concepts were eco-friendly and decades ahead of his time. Understanding global consciousness, and seeing us as *warrior monks*, he portrayed traditional military tasks in a manner that would be coincidental with the philosophies of the Masters you will read about in this book.

It was hard to imagine many of his concepts actually being inculcated into the U.S. Army. He addressed such things as ethical combat, evolutionary teamwork, omnidirectional thought, that structure could be derived from spirit and that there might even be an *Army of Light*. Directly applicable was his concept that *God is evolution,* and that personal evolution was the purpose for being. Channon's manuals are available, which means that you can read them for yourself. Jim, with his war-cry, *Go Planet*, is missed.

For the record, while goats did die, none of those deaths was caused by staring. Jon Ronson, who wrote the book by the same name, grossly distorted reality; and then they made the movie. From that you might understand the accuracy of the details. The reason for addressing both TF Delta and the First Earth Battalion is to point out that you may find evidence of consciousness interactions in the most unexpected places. They happen in your life consistently. The trick is to have awareness of your situation and the environment, and to integrate your spiritual nature into your daily life.

Importantly, Saalman also reinforces this theme of human responsibility for stewardship of the Earth. Far too much emphasis has been placed on the Christian concept of "man's dominion over..." and too little on our obligation for protection of the planet to ensure continuance of our existence. As noted by *The Moody Blues*, and espoused in indigenous cultures, it is *A Question of Balance*. Nothing speaks more significantly to the problem than the anthropogenic origin of the current global impact of climate change and the ever-increasing extreme weather events that are now ravaging us. Consider that since 2005, the earth has marked ten of the hottest years ever recorded. While the Antarctic is losing 200 billion tons of ice per year. Meanwhile, the Artic Ocean is becoming navigable for the first time in human history. The oceans are rising and inundating low-lying communities, many of which are extremely poor and without viable options. Out of balance and unsustainable.

"De" Nile is not only a river in Africa, denial is an insidious form of thought that is employed to block progress by those fearful of change and who generally embrace the illusion of separateness. We appear to have entered a *post-truth era*; one in which facts are too often deemed irrelevant. There are numerous significant examples. Certainly, those denying the reality of global climate change are among the most obvious. This, despite the vast amount of evidence that Gaia is providing us in abundance, such as hurricanes, floods, droughts, and ever-increasing aggregate temperatures. Similarly, the Covid-19 pandemic produced incomprehensible denial of the severity of the virus among many despite documented hospitalizations and deaths. Further, such people tended to deny the long-term effects, the totality of which will not be known for years or possibly decades. In the U.S., the majority of Republicans at the time of this writing continue to deny the legitimacy of the current president. Categorically proven to be false, some leaders continue to foster the *Big Lie*, that the election was stolen due to massive fraudulent ballots, this despite 61 court cases being summarily dismissed due to a lack of evidence. There is little doubt that fear is a motivating factor.

Counterintuitively, many of today's political leaders deny the scientific evidence of the horrendous impact of global climate change. Intriguingly, for decades if not centuries, it has been the scientific community that most frequently has denied the reality of many of the events captured in this book. Too often, the few serious scientists who have dared to enter contentious fields such as studies of psychokinesis, remote viewing, postmortem communication, and other consciousness fields, have been chastised by their peers. It is known, however, that a majority of people have had some personal experience with psychic phenomena. Some choose to ignore it. Many, including scientists, choose to observe from the shadows. Nevertheless, there are some brave souls who have dared to step forward and acknowledge reality, torpedoes be damned. Saalman's message to readers is basically to encourage everyone to stand strong and to be among those who step forward and follow both their instincts and the data wherever it happens to lead.

Decades ago, while working on my doctoral thesis, my mentor, Dr. Elisabeth Kübler-Ross (known for her landmark book *On Death and Dying*), wisely instructed me to revise one recurring word. Based on the literature available, I had addressed *religiousness*. At her direction, we changed that to *spirituality*. While I had placed limits seemingly imposed by others in the research literature, she could see a reality that was far greater. This seemingly minor change had a profound impact on the outcome of the survey I was conducting. At the time, I was surveying changes in participants in Kübler-Ross's *Life, Death and Transition* workshops. When asked about their beliefs, I was surprised at how many respondents noted their connection to a spiritual concept. Some rejected the "dogma of the church," while others appreciated the form and ritual of traditional religions, but still embraced the concept of a spiritual relationship. While I was surprised, Elisabeth was not.

This was in the late 1970s and the concept of near-death experiences (NDEs) was being brought to the fore for the very first time. The book, *Life After Life*, by Dr. Raymond Moody, was just beginning to receive public attention. With Raymond, Elisabeth was one of the very first medical doctors to actually discuss NDEs. Previously there were rare books, such as *Return from Tomorrow* by Dr. George Ritchie. As a soldier during World

War II, he had twice been pronounced dead, only to be revived. Isolated reports go back millennia, the earliest being reported by Plato who wrote about a soldier named Er who awoke on his funeral pyre and spoke with amazement about what he had experienced. For the vast majority of cases, however, they remained untold or known only in family folklore.

Now, more than four decades later, NDE's are often looked upon as spiritually transformative experiences or STEs. As Dr. Bruce Greyson elucidates in his recent book, *After: A Doctor Explores What Near-Death Experiences Reveal about Life and Beyond,* one of the central messages derived from these experiences is a *reduction in fear of death*. We now know that there are millions of people who have had NDEs, as they occur in all cultures around the world. Historically, they have occurred for millennia, though rarely discussed for fear of ridicule and rejection. Through expanding exposure of the concepts via mass media, many of the people who have had such experiences are now prepared to talk about them openly.

There seems little doubt that consciousness continues beyond physical death, although we are not quite certain of the form. Serious studies suggest that reincarnation is one of the most plausible concepts, and with that, the notion of karma becomes prevalent. Here, in *The Journey Across Forever,* Saalman postulates that it is possible for human beings to move well beyond violence and killing as a primary means of conflict resolution, for the human spiritual journey goes on both within and without oneself.

There are certainly complicating factors, especially as we seem to have entered a *post-truth era;* one in which facts, only occasionally are deemed relevant. But ground truth is critically important. When it comes to physical death and the continuation of consciousness, one must follow the facts wherever they take us. Unfortunately, when it comes to researching such issues the paucity of funding is startling. While materialists spend billions searching for the *God Particle*, it is a pittance that is allotted to the ultimate question of life after death. It is my view after studying phenomenology that we are tackling a topic that is at least as complex as cancer. While the *God Particle* may be of interest to a few theoretical scientists, continuation of consciousness should be of concern to 100% of the population. If you consider research funding in total, our priorities as humans are totally incongruent.

There are many other areas of research of phenomena that yield tantalizing clues. It is the intrepid explorer who will follow the trail, even at the risk of one's personal reputation. The telltale suggestions are everywhere. Hopefully, by reading this book you will become more sensitive to the seemingly extraneous tidbits that are, in fact, tracks for you to follow.

Yes, there be shamans. For decades, my wife, Victoria, and I have visited with shamans all over the world from the Amazon to the Himalayas, across Central Asia, Latin America, Turkey, and of course here in the United States with our Native American colleagues. There were voodoo ceremonies in West Africa in which we saw shamans defy the laws of thermodynamics. Worshiping fire, they could stand in it, sit in it, and walk away without a hair on their heads being singed. In Mongolia we had apports precipitate out of nothingness. In Brazil, during Umbanda ceremonies we repeatedly saw discarnate entities seemingly possess the bodies of willing subjects. Then, of course, there was ayahuasca.

Relatable here, is the worldview of most shamans. In the West, many people think of the *real world* and the *spirit world* as things that are separate and distinct; that is, of course, if one with materialistic views even entertains the possibility of a spirit world. Conversely, shamans tend to move back and forth seamlessly between these ultimate domains. All reality is simply a continuation of consciousness and possibly similar to the transition between life and whatever comes after. For millennia, mystics and shamans have transited these etheric domains, often leaving markers for the next intrepid adventurer to follow. Here, Saalman has collected many of those oft obscured indicators, dusted them off, and presented them for the intuitively sensitive reader to follow. He writes that he, "even took the Bodhisattva Vow which, in brief, is to help all sentient beings become enlightened." This book is part of his promise. Now, the challenge is yours to accept or reject.

There is no doubt about the physical reality of some UFOs, but at the conclusion of my book on that topic I stated, "In the end it is clear that the universe is far more complex than we ever imagined. We are not close to solving the enigmas posed by UFOs, rather we are still at the front end of defining the fundamental issues and boundaries." The sentiment of complexity permeates all aspects of the incredible phenomena that have been observed.

Throughout his writings, Saalman interlaces real occurrences that challenge the entire notion of pure materialism. The events that I have here affirmed support both the physical reality of the firsthand experiences reported, as well as the extraordinarily high probability of realms beyond our commonly accepted human senses. Whether you accept or deny the reality of these astonishing events, they do happen to every individual. *Anything that does happen, can happen*. The challenge laid out by Saalman is for you to become hyper aware of your surroundings and take advantage of the extraordinary gifts that are presented to you.

What is the destiny of humanity? Saalman recommends thinking globally as a necessary effort to save the planet. There has been far too much denigration, even demonization, of the inevitable concept of *globalization*. We all live on the same planet and its health is paramount for continuance of human existence. Expanding on the notion, I have stated, "If you are thinking globally, you are thinking too small." The interconnectedness extends beyond the planet as consciousness permeates and is universal. We certainly agree that the nationalists, though they be very vocal, clearly fail to recognize that globalization is not foreign intervention or a plot against their present situation, but rather continuance of a natural order that cannot be ignored.

The fundamental flaw in the materialist's world is the illusion of separateness, be that of self, family, clan, or country. Acting in one's self-interests is often counterproductive and, in the end, detrimental to the wellbeing of those individuals or groups. The Covid-19 pandemic has proven time and again that there are other aspects of consciousness (I'm referring to the virus itself) as it, too, chose its path, thereby disrupting our daily lives. For many, medical mitigation methods were met with disdain, and too frequently viewed as infringements on personal liberties. The protestors often thought the wearing of masks was merely to protect themselves and they seemingly cared not about the safety of others. Foolishly, national borders were considered impenetrable, even as the virus continually mutated presenting ever more virulent strains and taxing many medical systems to breaking point.

However, because of legal and administrative requirements, national borders are of significance. The responses of each country were important, first to curtail the spread of the disease and then as to how to allocate medical resources. Finally, as vaccines became available, there was great disparity between rich and poor countries. While Covid-19 vaccines were created in record time, distribution became quite contentious. Isolationists tended to believe in an insular approach, while realists understood the physical interconnectivity of the economies in most countries where extensive travel for business, science, and recreation are undeniable norms. The virus continues to mutate at the time of this writing, thus requiring ever ongoing global vigilance. While the interconnectedness of consciousness is even broader, the pandemic provided everyone with a physical example of just how interrelated we all are. Denial of this reality, while present in some circles, is to the detriment and peril of all.

While assigned in Hawaii nearly half a century ago, I was discussing acupuncture with my native Hawaiian Executive Officer, Rich Haake. He was an adept practitioner of Aikido, with remarkable understanding of ki/chi. Following Nixon's inaugural visit to China to reestablish diplomatic relations, this was a time when Western doctors were just getting their first serious glimpses of the application of acupuncture. Amazingly, it was being used in lieu of chemical anesthesia for major surgery and many other uses. To be successful this meant the Chinese doctors had an intrinsic understanding of a human energy system not even acknowledged in the West. Application of this form of treatment requires complete knowledge of meridians inherent in the flow of Chi throughout the body and even beyond. That includes organs, such as the triple heater, that have no physical correlate. As Rich explained to me, "They (Western Science) are just learning what we (Asians) have known for thousands of years."

Adroitly here, Saalman has brilliantly marked a path. Read further, and you too will be exposed to wisdom both new and ancient. Guides, incarnate and discarnate, daily provide clues. It is up to you, the reader, to recognize these hints, subtle though some may be, and act accordingly. There lies within us all a moral compass. While sometimes muted, or overwhelmed by competing agendas, if followed, it will keep you on track and lead you on to your destiny. It will not fail you. Listen.

"The choice is yours. With, or without your consent, you play a role in the drama unfolding before us. Entering into the fray consciously has advantages, seen and unseen. The implications of the events we have all witnessed are awe-inspiring. *Yes, you are your brother's keeper, for you are a spiritual being having a human experience.*"

Confronted with high strangeness, Hamlet correctly states, "There are more things in heaven and earth, Horatio, than are dreamt of in your philosophy."

So mote it be.

## Introduction

# Fast Times, Fiery Dreams & the Race Against the Clock

*THE JOURNEY ACROSS FOREVER* is a collection of essays and personal stories intended to inspire. It is offered in a spirit of positivity to all who are questing for answers to the most compelling and profound questions a human being can ask.

Are there easy answers?

No, there are not. We know this for certain, for despite struggling our way through millenniums of toil and often deadly violence in the pursuit of those answers, we humans have yet to reach consensus on any of the numerous existential mysteries which surround our lives and often haunt our minds. For most people, unfortunately, fighting for mere survival and dealing with forms of hardship and tragedy have been challenge enough, never mind taking the time to figure out the "meaning" of life.

Only, yes, there have been wondrous pleasures for countless people along the way, as well. Millions have enjoyed tremendously exciting times and many a happy and loving day in their lives. Some have even managed to acquire phenomenal riches, achieve unmitigated success in various careers or have won fame, acclaim, and the devotion of admirers worldwide.

Even so, every person not currently walking upon this earth has died, no matter their wealth, their achievements, their place in society or anything else.

Maybe, just maybe, however, the Essential Self – the "psychospiritual complex" or "soul" does live on in some "Great Beyond" as many of us have come to believe and as so many spiritual teachers and wisdom masters throughout the ages have insisted is actually the case.

We hope so, of course. Most of us do want to live on. The question is where do we go when the soul "slips the mortal coil"? Where is this "otherworld" we hear about and is there really a "heaven" and a "hell"?

Christians worldwide certainly believe that the answer to that last question is an absolute yes.

Quite intriguingly, Eastern sages are inclined to agree, but in a very different way. Buddhists and Hindus believe that as the poet John Milton once put it: "The mind is its own place, and in itself can make a heaven of hell or a hell of heaven."

The consensus seems to be, then, that there is indeed a heaven and a hell of sorts and, of course, we all want to arrive, post haste upon our earthly exit, into the former and definitely to avoid, at all costs, the latter. We want to enjoy lives of the purest pleasure, not lives of suffering and pain.

Fortunately, it is entirely possible to achieve such an objective as many a wisdom master has made quite clear. To do so, one does not need to become a perfect saint, however, nor live a life of strict adherence to any particular religious creed, nor set of doctrines. One need only do good in the world and, ideally, become spiritually liberated, which is to say free of the chains and shackles of the kind of delusory thinking that is so often imposed upon us by "authority" figures who are themselves mired in distorted thinking. Quite possibly the word *enlightenment* is simply a label for learning to think for oneself and gaining control over one's own life.

What do I know to speak out on such a topic?

The best answer to that question is quite illuminating. As the Zen master Suzuki Roshi once put it (and ever so succinctly): "Strictly speaking, there is no such thing as an enlightened person. There is only enlightened activity."

What that means is that we can say anything we wish but it is what we do that counts, and not just in our better moments. This is about what we do over and again. In biblical terms this accords with the aphorism that by our fruits are we known. In my particular case, those metaphorical fruits are the ideas and insights offered on the following pages. These must speak for themselves.

All I will say at this point, therefore, is that after decades of probing the mysteries and enigmas of life as we perceive them here on this earth, I know that the soul seeks its secrets and the body its amusements, its perfect fleshly miracles and its shameless naked amazements. I know that we humans love our pleasures and loathe our pains; that not only do most of us want to live long lives, we want to live *forever*.

The bad news, of course, is that we quite obviously do not live forever; not physically.

The good news is that the Essential Self, which each of us *is* in all reality, may indeed be eternal in nature.

What is the difference? The word "forever" is a time-based concept, whereas when we speak of the "eternal", it refers, in essence, to a dimension that is beyond, or outside of, time. The way to understand life in its fullest measure, therefore, is by delineating what belongs to the physical realm and what transcends physicality. This means that we must make a choice every time the path we are on comes to another split in the road. Either we go the way that remains, ever and always, focused solely on material ends in a world of flesh and bone, of steel and stone, hoping that it might lead at last to some form of physical immortality instead of oblivion, or we choose to go the way that opens out into the more ambiguous, subtle domain of the metaphysical realm, placing our hope of continuance in what is known as "spiritual immortality".

Either way, we stake our very future on that choice, but only one of the two choices holds real promise, I believe, despite the astonishing advancements made in our genetic sciences in recent decades.

I came of age in the Sixties and the Seventies, which was

a highly charged, beautifully liberated and genuinely positive era. It wasn't that way for everyone, of course. Many people experienced tumultuous and tragic events. The Vietnam War had America deeply divided over whether it was a just conflict or quite the opposite. As a young man in the prime of my life, however, I was under the spell of surging hormones, a natural predilection for expanding my horizons in every possible way, not to mention beneath the sway of a countercultural attitude that came to me courtesy of certain writers, artists and rock stars whose books, paintings and music were irresistibly influential. Astrology was also popular at the time and there was a great deal of talk about a New Age being born: the Age of Aquarius.

Taken altogether, these enchantments were so compelling at the time that I was fully convinced that a New Age was indeed in the offing. As if to make the argument even more convincing, there was mass cultural upheaval and spectacular displays of defiance against the old order out on the street and in the news on an ongoing basis. I will speak more about these events on the pages that follow, suffice it to say at this juncture, therefore, that certain seeds were planted within me at that stage of my life that have continued to grow over the decades and are still growing. Along the way, quite fortuitously, they have enriched me immeasurably. That growth, I believe, has delivered up a myriad of ambrosial fruits that to me have acquired the taste of nothing less than the nectar of the gods.

I understand that this could be perceived as pure hyperbole or rank exaggeration on my part. Then again, this perception might well be founded on insights of genuine authenticity, in as much as words can express concepts which ultimately transcend words and labels.

The problem for all of us, of course, is that even after some five thousand years of civilization, humanity has yet to reach any form of unanimous agreement on what actually constitutes "truth".

One can only try one's best, therefore, to ask the right questions and make the most informed decisions of which one is capable. This is precisely what these writings attempt to do. As the author of this work, I will look at what orthodox religion and scientific materialism have bequeathed us over the centuries, as well as many subjects which fly in the face of these twin cultural skewers; namely, the enigmatic nature of consciousness and spirituality, the possibility that we are all "psychic" to some extent and the fact that "paranormal" events do indeed happen, even though conventional thinking tells us that such events are impossible. Then there is the UFO to ponder as it flashes past us with its mysterious occupants. Now often known as UAPs – Unidentified Aerial Phenomena – these strange vehicles sometimes defy the very laws of physics and thereby force us to ponder the imponderable and broaden our horizons to a fantastically astronomical level. Finally, and crucially, we will look at the implications of those reports which come to us from the realm of the Near-Death Experience and consider what we might reasonably expect once we pass from this world into the dimension known as the "Afterlife".

We shall not look at any of these topics in a dry, academic manner, however, for the dynamic phenomenality of life stimulates me too much for that. What I shall attempt to do on these pages, therefore, is carry the quest for insight onto a higher level of contemplation. The effort here will be to tease out the meaning of the human experience in its fullest potential, for what I presently perceive is that we live in a multidimensional spectrum of reality that is so profoundly rich in nature that one can only approach it with the most magical, poetic prose one is capable of conjuring. Virtually every aspect of our vast universe astonishes, from the microscopic to the macrocosmic, when we look deeply enough into it. To me, life is electrifying and is meant to be explored with eyes wide and minds amazed. The mundane and the miraculous, the profane and the sacred, in my view, are complementary aspects of life and what distinguishes them from each other is simply one's personal perception and the subsequent interpretation of that perception.

That interpretation, by the way, can mean the difference between living one's life with a sense of clarity, joy and positivity or in a state of obliviousness and delusion.

What I am offering the reader of this book, therefore, is a ride on what I call the "firewheel of wonder"; a magic carpet ride if you will. The attitude here is that if a person can transmute the mundane into the miraculous, then one has already become the ultimate magician. If one succeeds in becoming such a thing, epiphanies and revelations are sure to emerge.

The intent, again, is to inspire, not convince, for conviction should not come from what others say. It should come from one's own life experience. The answers are ultimately within, after all. They are within each of us. The stories and insights which others offer us can, at best, only fascinate. As a result, we must take our chances and seize the proverbial day, make mistakes along the way and learn from them. We must enjoy victories where we can but hold fast to that pivotal point within by carefully observing the enchanting profusion of curiosities before us. These will ultimately prove to be illusory according to many a wisdom master, but beautifully so. After all, it is what we make of them that determines our lot in life.

Know, however, that virtually everything is at stake as we proceed: our bodies, our minds, our souls, our very place in the greater scheme of things and, crucially, the future of humanity itself and the fate of the very planet upon which we live. As we humans face a "brave new world" of technological sophistication, it is obvious that we are clearly not medieval in our sciences, yet millions of us are still medieval in our spirituality. Why is that? Why are so many people still caught up in the strains of religious bias, nationalistic fervor, and the racial prejudice of our forebears when these biases so often bring violence and death in their wake? Is the dopamine rush which so often results from this way of thinking that powerful and pleasing? Should these strains not have been left behind centuries ago?

I believe so. Humanity, after all, is now on the cusp of going interplanetary as these words are being written and the technology already exists for creating a habitable base on the Moon and sending an exploratory expedition to Mars for the purpose of setting up a colony there. Meanwhile, there are countries on this planet with sectarian and tribal peoples still throwing stones and rocks at each other and beating each other over the head with sticks and clubs. Tragically, there are people starving to death in many countries, while others sit in royal splendor in majestic mansions enjoying culinary feasts and sipping the finest wines on the market.

We need to do better, therefore, and we *can* do better. It all begins with an evolution in thinking and an "Aquarian revolution" may certainly be pursued if we choose to make, and call, it that. All it takes is enough people to redefine the times and humanity's place within them. This, by the way, is precisely what so many young people in the Sixties and early Seventies sought to do and it succeeded in one respect, however short-lived its overt presence on the world stage. It planted the seed in millions of minds that our higher ideals can indeed turn into a cultural movement of great magnitude and scope.

We might well be at a pivotal, transitional time of positive, seismic change once more, which is encouraging, especially when we consider the present state of what some are calling the "apocalyptic" politics of the day, especially in conjunction with the cataclysmic challenges of climate change we now see in the form of torrential rains, floods, tsunamis, typhoons, hurricanes, earthquakes, tornados and massive, unbelievably catastrophic wildfires. We have nothing to fear by breaking free of the past, though, and moving on into more enlightened times. The planet needs us to do that, our children especially. We adults must lead by example, not by preaching and pontificating, and using the disturbing language of those who are still wrestling with the demons of the Dark Ages. We must do this even if we feel at times as if we are flying by the light of a planet going up in flames. As Mahatma Gandhi suggested so wisely and to the point: "Be the change that you wish to see in the world." To these words of wisdom, I would simply add that being the change you want to see in the world involves a choice and that choice is to pursue your change in a spirit of love or with a sense of fear. Does the choice promote inclusion or exclusion, kindness to self and others or greed and self-interest only? The former ultimately leads to positivity and beneficence, while the latter leads to detriment and a dystopian future for humanity.

On the positive front, there is every reason to believe that death is not the end for any of us and that our lives will continue in bountiful ways if we can but learn to be kind and compassionate to each other. Those reasons fill the pages ahead and have the potential to bring a smile to every face. Perhaps, as the poet-mystic Walt Whitman once wrote: "All goes onward and outward, nothing collapses, and to die is different from what any one supposed, and luckier." Whitman tells us that it is just as lucky to die as to be born and "I know it" he says. Almost universally, yogis, mystics, metaphysicians and those who have returned to this earth from some "otherworld" after a near-death experience agree wholeheartedly with this perspective. They cease to fear death. It is my hope that the reader of this book will, as well, for time flies and all our fiery dreams are ever and always in a race against the clock. The sooner we deal with the issue of our own passing, therefore, the better. The reality is that our lives on Earth end. There is no way around that. There are ways, however, to *know* beyond the shadow of a doubt that life goes on in bold and beautiful ways.

So let us proceed now and do so with boldness ourselves,

remembering along the way to keep a keen sense of humor at all times, for we must foster a lightness of being within if we are to succeed in raising ourselves up. What is to be gained is a sense of liberation, illumination and spiritual immortality here and now, which is precisely what humanity needs in order to activate the next phase of its own history in a loving and positive way.

# 1

# The Cosmic Fun House Mirror of Fools

LIFE IS A FREE-FOR-ALL. No one knew that better than the late Robert Anton Wilson whose many brilliantly satirical and profoundly hilarious books carried the idea of spiritual liberation to delusion-busting heights. For me personally, he became the model of the sagely cosmic provocateur I wanted to become. To my way of thinking, he was the best, bar none, at weaving together the widest possible discourse on both science and spirituality. He explored the historical roots of these two approaches to life with an unflinching eye, offered stark assessments of their presence in the world today and then made a mental quantum leap when painting a picture of the direction the two might go in the future. To Wilson, science and spirituality were like the twin strands of DNA which spiral around each other and the breadth of his insights in regard to both proved nothing short of staggering to me.

In fact, so fascinated was I, and so taken, by Wilson's tales of the "Illuminati" when I was young that once I had won a contract with New Falcon Press, which published Wilson, I ended up putting the word Illuminati in the titles of both of my first two novels: *The Dream Illuminati* and *The Illuminati of Immortality*. Wilson, to my eternal gratitude, wrote extensive introductions to each.

Now, here again, I have turned to Wilson for the opening chapter of this book, the title also inspired by his ground-breaking tome, *Cosmic Trigger*. In that volume, Wilson explained how his own interest in the "Illuminati" eventually led him "through a cosmic Fun House featuring double and triple agents, UFOs, possible Presidential assassination plots, the enigmatic symbols on the dollar bill, messages from Sirius, pancakes from God-knows-where, the ambiguities of Aleister Crowley, some mysterious hawks that follow Uri Geller around, Futurists, Immortalists, plans to leave this planet and the latest paradoxes of quantum mechanics. It has been a prolonged but never boring pursuit," he said, "like trying to find a cobra in a dark room before it finds you."

What one easily gleans from this challenging description is that life is, indeed, a free-for-all with a spectacular array of possible intrigues for the intrepid explorer, as well as many a dark danger, but he made it an appealing challenge and essentially insisted that if one was willing to chance his or her arm to uncover truth, one could indeed succeed.

What he was perhaps ultimately saying is that only a fool would hide in his or her room, cowering in fear from life's myriad challenges, for that is totally defeatist. On the contrary, he insisted again and again that one should boldly go forth, for this is really the only way one may solve any of life's curious and compelling mysteries.

One might even conjecture that pursuing the myriad mysteries of life is precisely *why* we are here in this world, a notion that shall be explored in greater detail on the pages that follow.

None of this is to say, by the way, that at the end of it all there is some "cosmic joke" at play. After all, the suffering in this world is undeniable and, from what one may decipher from the writings of yogis, mystics, psychics, seers, sages, wisdom masters and those who have had near-death experiences, for many, suffering in the Afterlife is undeniable there, as well. This fact, if true – and I suspect it is – offers many a compelling reason to take urgent action now in order to prevent such an outcome later for oneself and for those we love.

From this author's perspective, if we do not take the time and make the monumental effort to see through the illusions and delusions of this, our deeply troubled world, when will we do what is necessary to find truth and understand the reality in which we find ourselves?

Life is short, after all, and the next phase of our lives is looming. If anyone refuses to believe this particular assertion, simply consider how quickly the months, seasons and years come and go. Do we not say as much every New Year's Eve? There is simply no time for complacency, not if we really want to reach even the most rudimentary level of spiritual enlightenment, which is more than sufficient, I believe, for finding one's way forward in this world and in the Great Beyond itself. It is a doable proposition, in other words, if we keep our minds and hearts open to every possibility and cultivate compassion at every opportunity for the sake of bolstering our karmic imprint.

If we humans are immortal – as Wilson and so many wisdom masters suspect we are – then we have every reason to live in hope that great and exciting wonders await us in the Hereafter, but only if we choose to be true to ourselves and live our lives wisely here and now.

This is a very exhilarating notion, indeed, and to my way of thinking, it is profoundly electrifying. It keeps me seeking spiritual insight with ever greater urgency.

To this precise point the Tibetan wisdom master Padmasambhava once stated: "If you want to know your past life, look into your present condition; if you want to know your future life, look at your present actions." Indeed, let us do that and live out our lives with a sense of truth, love, laughter and lightness of being, such that we might ourselves become "Beings of Light", fully and completely, in the Hereafter. What are Beings of Light? They are those advanced spiritual entities we hear about repeatedly in what is known as the "Near-Death" literature. I shall have much more to say about them as we proceed. In fact, numerous aspects associated with those who have had a near-death experience will be explored here, for what returnees have to say offers us some of the most compelling and important insights that humanity has ever had the great good fortune of learning.

At the outset, however, we must wisely admit our own ignorance and our sometimes-foolish behavior in order to humble ourselves for the learning curve to come. By doing so, we may see the world from a fresh perspective, open up our lives anew and – this is crucial – laugh off our past mistakes, for it is laughter that brings bliss in abundance and lifts one's spirits like nothing else. As a Japanese proverb puts it: "Time spent laughing is time spent with the gods."

When we find ourselves laughing so hard that tears are streaming down our faces, we cannot but know exactly what that expression is all about and just how "godly" wonderful such moments are. They are moments of sheer ecstasy, precious moments that we never forget.

Even better than spending one's time laughing with the gods, however, is the idea of becoming *as a god*. How do we do that? According to the first book of the Bible, Genesis, in which we learn that Adam and Eve had been told by God not to eat of a certain tree "lest" they should "die", a serpent who was somehow able to speak in secret to Eve told her that she would *not* die if she ate of the fruit of the tree. He then further revealed why Yahweh had fibbed about that. It seems this deity had an ulterior motive and in Genesis 3:5 we discover what that motive was. "For God doth know that in the day ye eat thereof, then your eyes shall be opened, and ye shall be as gods, knowing good and evil."

The takeaway here is crystal clear. It is in knowing good and evil that we may become as gods. This is a major revelation if we really stop to think about it, but most people don't, probably because humanity has known good and evil since time immemorial and the two have seemingly never turned anyone into a "god".

While there is nothing essentially funny about good and evil, Wes "Scoop" Nisker in his book *Crazy Wisdom* did manage to find a humorous angle on another aspect of Genesis; to wit: "The Bible says that God looked at his creation and 'saw that it was good.' Some crazy wisdom observers," he writes, "think this could be the first recorded use of irony."

Irony, indeed.

Irony, fortunately, can wring a laugh out of almost any topic of human interest nowadays, save for those of the most evil, unspeakable and murderous magnitude.

In fact, irony and satire have been the saving graces of humanity over the centuries as it has struggled across the millenniums simply to survive. Humanity, after all, has had to endure constant hardships and random outbursts of pure savagery in order to keep the species going. The word *irony*, by the way, comes from a Greek word meaning, "dissimulation or feigned ignorance". An expression is ironic if it has an underlying meaning which differs from that which is stated, but only if the statement is taken at face value. At times, it can even allude to precisely the opposite of what is being said.

Satire is basically a visual or literary device which people use in order to hold various and sundry activities up for ridicule, usually just for a laugh, unless what is being shown or stated devolves, as often happens, into some harsh level of sarcasm of a more vicious nature.

The point here is simply to say that the wiser souls among us have gotten quite clever over the centuries in the way they have learned to handle dissent and disagreement with those who are less advanced in their ability to understand complex issues and who take offense much too easily and are, therefore, prone to angry outbursts which sometimes lead to violence and death.

As Friedrich Nietzsche once stated: "The growth of wisdom may be measured exactly by the diminution of ill temper."

The wise do not commit acts of violence; they do not get

angry because they know better. They *know* good and evil. They know that we reap what we sow, and they especially know that evil can only gestate in the minds and hearts of those who cannot comprehend that it is their own thoughts, words and deeds that lead to acts of violence, aggression, envy, jealousy, vengeance and every other low-level quality of human emotion, some of which are seriously malevolent in constitution.

Evil, in short, is committed by those who cannot understand that what they think, say and do is, in fact, the root cause that brings about that which they fear the most.

The wise also know that every aspect of life as we experience it here on Earth is always going to manifest in some form of duality. Even good and evil are just another instance of duality among many such facets. Each of us instinctively knows this, for we all experience or witness positive and negative activities, light and dark, illness and health, old age and youth, people who are rich or poor, moral and immoral behavior, things attractive and things repulsive, acceptance and rejection, feelings of happiness or sadness, selflessness and greed, and so on. Such polarities may seem forever in opposition to one another, but the fact is that for either aspect to exist, the other must exist also. This makes every such pair complementary in nature and what this ultimately means is that neither end of the spectrum will ultimately eradicate nor conquer the other. We must, therefore, live with this fact and make the best of it in whatever way we can.

While we are all able to think and feel to varying degrees, either of these two qualities can be dominant within us. This is why some people can be so coldly intelligent and calculating or, conversely, much too sensitive and empathetic for their own good. This is also why there is great truth in the wise words of one Horace Walpole, an eighteenth-century English writer, politician and keen observer of humanity, who once wrote: "The world is a comedy for those that think and a tragedy for those who feel."

Given the doom, gloom, greed, thievery, corruption, murder, war and general horror we see on our TV news shows nowadays, not to mention the rancorous rhetoric which flickers across our social media platforms, a sensitive soul could be forgiven for not wanting to *feel* too deeply, simply for his or her own good.

As for *thinking*: what are we to make of what we see going on in this day and age? From all appearances, humanity seems nothing short of maniacal for putting up with the profiteering of the few ahead of the health and welfare of the species and the planet itself, which is *why* there is global warming, contaminated oceans, depleted soils, raging wildfires, deadly droughts and a sky seething with pollutants.

Governments tell us that making the necessary changes to turn the tide on our cascading woes if done too abruptly would bring about an economic downturn so severe that millions of people would be put out of work and mass starvation would surely follow in its wake. Never mind that the ultra-wealthy could solve that problem in no time at all if only they were generous enough to offer the funds needed to get humanity through the transitional period required to move, for example, from a global, fossil fuel-based, economy to one based on clean energy.

All things considered, therefore, it is damn lucky that we humans are immortal.

By that I mean that it is our great good fortune that we are, first and foremost, spiritual entities having a physical experience and not simply finite mortals destined inexorably for oblivion.

What this implies, if such thinking is correct, is that even those who believe themselves to be *merely* human are, in essence, sacred celestial beings and eternal in nature.

Quite amusingly, this makes us all, quite literally, Holy Fools.

After all, who isn't fooled by appearances? Reality certainly seems to be contingent on our five senses and surviving physically does seem to be what this life is all about.

That humans are fooled by appearances, however, is not an accident, wisdom masters tell us. They say that such a state of perception is an evolutionary necessity inherent in nature so that the psychospiritual complex – the "real I" we all are – will be challenged by our physical existence in a genuine way. Without the soul losing itself within the material realm, they explain, the Essential Self could never rise to the more profound levels of understanding it is possible for the soul to experience.

We need our earthly illusions, in other words, in order to put the soul to the ultimate test, for without having to physically cope within a life and death context, the psychospiritual essence could not grow in magnitude and scope. It could not discover the immeasurable magnificence of love, kindness, compassion, charity and the many other values of a sublime nature.

When metaphysicians call this a "test", what they mean by that is that the challenges of life *test one's mettle*. This viewpoint is in contradistinction to the notion that "God" created us to be "His" loyal minions and is ever testing our love for "Him", not to mention testing how obedient we are to "His" commandments and so on, so that "He" can determine if we are worthy of eternal life in "His" presence or if we should burn in Hell, instead.

A truly loving God, metaphysicians say, would never condemn a soul to such a place as Hell forever, although a temporary spell in a state of purgation might well feel like it. (There are definitely ways to avoid this altogether, however, as we shall see.)

What wisdom masters say is that the "Genetrix" – the creative force – of the cosmos, call it God, the Tao, the Akasha, Brahman, the Great Spirit, the Matrix or whatever name you wish to assign, creates this earthly experiential situation for its own enrichment and that this process is intensified by the vicissitudes the soul must inevitably confront as life goes on over the years.

What this implies, quite fortuitously, is that life has a purpose and that we are fooled by appearances in order for that purpose to be actualized.

The Vedic traditions of India call this *vilas*, the "play" of Brahman, the Supreme Essence of All of Creation, or *lila*, a "game" that "God" plays.

The thinking here is that Brahman, the Godhead, goes out of itself in order to perceive its own existence. Brahman objectifies itself so that it can subjectively experience itself. In stark contrast, if no objective domain existed, then the subjective essence of "God" would forever remain unconscious. Bifurcation or the splitting in two of the One Essence into a subjective / objective scenario is what allows conscious awareness to arise and become concretely actualized.

This, in turn, means that we are all in this situation together no matter what we believe about virtually anything. It means that we are all Holy Fools, together and forever, whether we know it or not (and most do not), but that is, quite intriguingly, a beautiful and enthralling thing, for it makes of life a challenge of epic proportions. After all, anything that is *enthralling* includes every kind of experience imaginable from the most ecstatic to the most dangerous and evil. This is why human experience is made to run the gamut from a direct perception of the most mind-blowing and electrifying sort to the very opposite end of the spectrum in the form of tragic and torturous traumas which can literally break our hearts and scare the life out of us.

What we make of these multifarious adventures subsequently determines the quality of our lives. For some, such experiences lead to highly advanced states of being and levels of bliss that are beyond words. For others, they prove to be either simply mundane or so awful that the unfortunate person might well plummet downward into a depressive state of mind from which he or she may never recover.

Either way, the spectrum is replete with delusion at every level.

This is why Shakespeare noted all those centuries ago that, "There is nothing that is either good or bad but thinking makes it so."

One definition of enlightenment calls it a state of being where one is always in control of one's own thoughts. Controlling our thoughts is what allows us to grow in a positive way and helps us to avoid falling into a pit of despair over events that are upsetting or unsettling.

There are no guarantees how any event will go, of course, but by controlling what *can* be controlled in our lives, we at least have the chance to get past most of our delusory notions and attain fulfilment, peace and contentment in our mortality, but only so long as we understand that at a deep subconscious level we are, in truth, immortals.

Understanding that we are immortals is the secret knowledge that sets the soul free. It is the ultimate truth that liberates us in every way.

When the soul is set free of delusion, the multitudinous illusory appearances become a magical drama, not events that fool us any longer. When the soul is no longer lost in a cloud of delusion, there is clarity of mind and life no longer appears to be distorted like those images which one may encounter in a fun house mirror.

In fact, the cosmic fun house mirror is the great equalizer because we all see ourselves reflected in a distorted reality there. When we fully get it that we are immortal beings who have been fooled into believing that we are "mere mortals" for a spiritual purpose, that mirror becomes an amusement instead of a tragic nightmare, which is not to say that one no longer weeps for the many tragedies that so many ultimately suffer. The great hope here, however, is that – possessed of such knowledge – one might lend a hand and help to alleviate misfortune in some way.

The prescription for happiness, then, is knowing that you are at one with the sublime force which becomes all phenomena in the cosmos. You are a part of the Supreme Essence which goes out of itself in order to experience and know itself. In that sense, this life is pure illusion, but ultimately in a good way. Indeed, it is positive in such an amazing way that one might well find oneself saying as the sage Long Chen Pa once did that, "Since everything is but an apparition, perfect in being what it is, having nothing to do with good or bad, acceptance or rejection, one may well burst out into laughter."

Knowing that we are immortal means that we understand that we live countless lives and always will, for reincarnation is a genuine phenomenon and this is also a critical and crucial part of the secret knowledge that helps to set the soul free. Mystics, yogis, seers, sages, wisdom masters and metaphysicians have been telling us this for millenniums.

Today, however, the most compelling argument for immortality comes from those who have been medically resuscitated and have returned from the dead. We shall have a deep look at that phenomenon as we proceed, but first let us consider the matter of time.

## 2

# An Aquarian Quantum Leap

THE PLANE OF THE EARTH'S ORBIT projected outward forms a great circle in the celestial sphere. This projection is known as the ecliptic. Ringed about the ecliptic in the starry heavens all around our home planet are what came to be called the constellations of the Zodiac. That name means "cycle or circle of little animals", although the constellations are anything but small. In fact, they are astronomically huge in a "connect the dots" kind of way, but what is significant about them is that in the most ancient of times, these symbolic figures allowed the wisest of our ancestral stellar observers to chart a certain cosmic order and keep track of calendrical time in a way that eventually gave humanity insights and knowledge at a very advanced level of thinking.

While these astronomers were the first to use the Zodiac for very practical time-keeping purposes, it was astrologers who over the course of the centuries came to utilize those figures the most, mainly for finding psychological and spiritual insight into humanity as a whole and into individual people's personality traits and propensities at a personal level.

Astronomers today call astrology a "pseudo-science", but even so many of us who make every effort to adhere to factuality find that these same zodiacal figures somehow speak to a certain "spirit" of the times. This could be for the very simple reason that the so-called Age of Pisces is considered by astrologers to be on the wane, while a promising fresh new age, one called Aquarius, is said to be coming into prominence more and more. This transition is gradual, rather than abrupt, we are told. It is not like what happens with a clock that ticks down time in exacting increments.

If we are openminded observers, it does seem as if a transitional era is in progress and, to my way of thinking, it is as easy to call this era the "Age of Aquarius" as anything else.

I believe that the feeling that one era is passing and that a new one is steadily and gradually arising has the power to make many of us look to the future with renewed hope that a better, more enlightened, epoch is in the making because, quite frankly, the Piscean era was a catastrophically violent, malicious and murderous epoch if ever there was one.

To say that this new era is "in the making", however, is misleading. To phrase it this way implies that a power beyond humanity is bringing the new epoch to fruition, but it is doubtless truer to say that humanity itself must be the power that brings anything new into fruition for itself.

In other words, each of us must take responsibility for every aspect of the world in which we live because wishful thinking certainly isn't enough to bring about a more enlightened age. Such a transformation will and does take work. It takes determination. It takes mindfulness at an Olympian level, which is to say that awareness and the attentiveness of each of us must be ramped up to a superluminal degree. One's efforts, as it were, cannot be hit or miss. We cannot do the right thing simply here and there, while making a mighty effort only on the rarest of occasions. This is especially true considering the state of the world at this time.

If this sounds like a troubling amount of effort, it is, but only at the beginning when one is kickstarting the process, so to speak. If we are persistent with our mindfulness, in time, quite intriguingly, a superior form of expanded consciousness takes over and an epiphenomenon occurs: the everyday mind quantum jumps to a higher level of awareness. When that happens, observational prowess increases dramatically and the power of what we will here call "radical magical mindfulness" becomes the everyday norm. The result is that appearances cease to be deceiving and one enjoys what the Buddha called a "higher sphere" of living. The "magical" aspect of it comes with understanding and appreciating how astronomically fortunate it is for each of us that conscious awareness exists at all.

A consequence of the gratitude such a perception generates is that life can then seem profoundly miraculous and inspire endless awe within us.

What may happen concurrently is that we become spiritually liberated by living in this higher sphere. That is, we no longer reside in a narrow "reality tunnel" sourced in but one particular religious viewpoint. With the quantum leap, we are lifted above all provinciality and experience a way of seeing and experiencing the world that is universal in nature. Rather than taking the position of the "part", we become the "whole" and perceive in a ubiquitous manner. When that happens, we become a "syncretist", a person who can recognize the good in all religions and all spiritual traditions and appreciate the positive qualities on offer. At that point, one generally finds many of those qualities worthy of emulation.

While what I call "radical magical mindfulness" (more on this anon) is a way of perceiving that takes extraordinary attentiveness at the outset, spiritual liberation cannot come about unless one cultivates it in a more intellectual manner. For starters, one should seek to know the historical roots of the religion of which one happens to be a part due to familial and cultural ties. From there, one should make a concerted effort to seek out the historical roots of other religions. By deeply pursuing a comparative viewpoint of the various religions which populate our planet, we educate ourselves and expand our intellectual capacity to understand other peoples and cultures. In the process, we learn a lot about how a certain religious viewpoint grew from out of a certain milieu and this, too, is critical to our intellectual expansion and the freeing of our mind from biases and prejudices. By keeping a journal and writing down our thoughts on these matters, we accelerate the process considerably, for writing structures thought and clarifies one's insights enormously.

Once we go fully universal, then, we are free in a way that is difficult to imagine when we are still very much viewing life from a provincial perspective, but that freedom brings bliss in its wake and it lends a radiant beauty to our every thought, word and deed. It also carries us to new heights in terms of our sensitivity to the plight of others and we become infinitely more compassionate and empathetic to the challenges and vicissitudes which others face. Our heart goes out to everyone in the whole world, so to speak, and that can make for a better world, indeed.

It is with such an end in sight and in such a spirit that we go forward here. Hopefully the effort will hasten the process of transforming as many people as possible into living in a better, more spiritually enlightened, manner.

Wisdom masters tell us that we came into this world in order to experience life in a concrete, physical way. Scientific materialists will balk at this notion and insist that the universe came into being purely in some random manner and that life is totally meaningless. That's not all. Scientific materialists also say that there is no such thing as spirituality. "That is all crazy thinking," many a hard-core materialist has insisted. "It's a delusion, so get real. Life just is and that is all there is to it, so quit making a fool of yourself."

It is for each of us to decide whether subscribing to a spiritual view of the world or to that of the scientific materialist makes a fool of us, however. One is well advised, therefore, to pursue knowledge in both arenas in order to understand what is different about them and what is the same. After all, neither approach is as absolute as many an exponent of either of the two views would have people believe.

This is a crucial point to get to grips with as we go forward here. Neither science nor spirituality can prove what they contend in absolute terms, but this is actually good, for it means that it is up to each of us to make up our own minds. It means that we have a choice. It infers that we possess free will.

Only how *free* is the free will we possess if we are not willing to challenge the veracity of it? That is the question, and it is a major question. In fact, it is the most important question we can ask ourselves if we are genuinely serious about pursuing the truth of our existence.

This question determines how daring we are and how honest we are willing to be with ourselves and our loved ones, for no one lives or operates in a vacuum. Integrity and belief have a knock-on effect with those around us.

Nevertheless, if we are true to ourselves, we will speak that truth and live that truth and do so with love. That is what the most revered wisdom masters down through history have always done.

Gary Zukav, writing in his book *The Seat of the Soul*, asks "What is truth?" His answer is this: "Truth is that which does not contaminate you but empowers you." He also writes that "We are coming to the close of a grand cycle astrologically" and goes on to remark that "The negativity of the last two-thousand-year cycle is being collected now so that it can be discharged and transformed…"

The writings here are about that very thing: the discharging of the Piscean horror show and the transformation that can and must follow on from it.

To that end, we might consider the old proverb that warns about learning from history or being doomed to repeat it, for this is a truth that haunts humanity at this juncture in the evolution of our species. If we do not learn from history events will do more than just repeat themselves. They will keep spiraling further and further out of control in shockingly repetitious patterns until humanity itself crashes or explodes in some form of final apocalyptic lunacy.

The far better approach, indeed, is for humanity to collectively take a quantum leap skyward on the metaphorical wings of spiritual wisdom and escape the devolutionary downward spiral which leads inexorably to a dystopian future, or worse, to oblivion.

There is every reason to believe that we can make that spiritual quantum leap to a Brave New Age if only enough people choose to do what the ancient wisdom masters have done for millennia: play the long game. After all, one does not come to know that it takes over twenty-five-thousand years for the Earth to circle the galaxy and arrive back where it started unless one subscribes to the longest game imaginable and in wise collusion with equally intelligent individuals over many, many generations.

Still, we must wonder how the ancients *did* figure this out all of those thousands of years ago and how they understood it well enough to inscribe that knowledge into stone megaliths around the globe.

That is a mystery and will probably remain a mystery, but it is a *magical* mystery, which is a beautiful thing, for there is no magic without mystery; and without humanity seeking to answer such mysteries, there is no pursuit of truth; and without the pursuit of truth there is no spiritual quantum leap to higher knowledge; and without accessing higher knowledge, we humans can never be greater than we are now and we will not manage to save our species, nor the flying orb upon which we find ourselves: namely our wondrous, now polluted, Planet Earth.

Nevertheless, we are where we are, and the climate situation is dire. What this means is that, at last, everything is truly at stake.

That is the formidable challenge with which we must contend now, but there is a way forward and it is through quantum expansion, or to put it another way: through the recognition of our psychic multidimensionality, with its incredible, virtually miraculous, prospects for each and every one of us.

# 3

# Daring to *Really* Think Outside of the Box

WHILE STROLLING ONE of the quaint, ancient streets of Galway, Ireland one day with the brilliant, prolific *Noir* author Ken Bruen, I spotted a tall young man coming our way with a box on his head. Ken and I had been talking about his latest book, *The Galway Reflections,* and we were essentially lost in our discussion as we strolled along. Then Ken noticed the man, as well, and we cut quick glances at each other and broke stride.

The box the man was wearing appeared to have been painted with a kind of wash of gold and it covered the top of his head to his mouth. Other than this single, unlikely feature on his head, I noticed that the man was dressed quite sharply. In fact, he was attired in fine clothes and wore polished black patent leather shoes, the whole of which made for a very odd juxtaposition indeed.

As we neared the man, Ken and I looked at each other once more, this time with no small amount of bafflement. After all, Halloween had come and gone the week before and certainly no one else on the street that day was out and about wearing a costume, which meant that we had no idea what was up with this confounding figure. Ken, however, quickly nailed it. "I guess he literally prefers to be thinking *inside* of the box!"

Later, I had my own Galway reflections (so to speak!) about this particular topic and thought how the proverbial "box" which we, the public, are so often encouraged to "think outside of" by various inspirational writers and speakers is generally of a dynamic, but decidedly "worldly" nature; namely, how we might be more creative in our efforts to expand our business horizons and thus achieve a better position for ourselves in life by obtaining a more lucrative portion of some market share and "getting rich".

Nowadays millions of individuals have taken this brand of positive thinking onboard with great zeal and are even practicing advanced levels of visualization for the express purpose of activating the so-called "law of attraction". The underlying hope, of course, is that by doing so one will bring one's greatest dreams to fruition, no matter what those dreams happen to be.

Many, I believe, can claim true success with the law of attraction to some extent, but I have to ask if that success is, in all actuality, not simply down to concentrating one's focus. After all, as a particular saying has it, "Where attention goes, energy flows."

Eventually, I thought, *Why stop only at the level of "worldly" enrichment with such concentration?* How about daring to *really* think outside of the proverbial box in the pursuit of experience, only in this case, "otherworldly" experience? How about daring to seek super advanced levels of knowledge, wisdom and insight in this way? After all, we are only on this earth for a century at best and most people fall far short of that. This is not to say, of course, that fame, acclaim and wealth are less than fantastic in their own right. They clearly are, but to trot out that oldest of lines about money: "You can't take it with you."

No, you cannot.

What I am speaking about here, then, is the possibility of not just thinking outside of the proverbial box, but outside of the body itself. If one's immediate reaction to this notion is instant dismissal that is not surprising for several reasons. For starters, those of us raised in Western society on a steady stream of scientific materialism and Judeo-Christian religious dogma are taught nothing about such a possibility. In fact, we westerners are told that in scientific terms there is no proof whatsoever that a "soul" even exists. Our religious leaders, in contrast, insist that the "soul" *does* exist, but it only leaves the body at death and goes to some form of heaven, purgatory or hell depending on how commendably or horribly one has lived one's life. We are also instructed to never question the validity of the doctrines we have inherited from the faith into which we happened to be born, which is essentially a threat.

What if there is, however, every reason to question the validity of conventional paradigms?

Consider the words of the highly respected psychologist, Abraham Maslow, in his book *Religions, Values and Peak Experiences*. "The very beginning, the intrinsic core, the essence, the universal nucleus of every known high religion… has been the private, lonely, personal illumination, revelation, or ecstasy of some acutely sensitive prophet or seer."

This statement can scarcely be disputed. Abraham, Moses, Jesus, Muhammad, Buddha, Rama, Krishna, Confucius, Lao Tzu, Zoroaster, Mithra, Apollonius and virtually all other figures around whom a religion was, or has been, founded speak earnestly and reverently of otherworldly beings, be these entities "gods", "angels", "demons", "saints", "dakinis", "devas", "nagas", "beings of light" or "God Almighty" himself. Needless to say, millions upon millions of people over the centuries have believed absolutely in the truth of these encounters and experiences and hold them in the highest of regard.

Yet, few of us think that any such similar encounters or experiences in contemporary times are equally valid or equally of value. So complete is humanity's general cultural indoctrination that most people believe that only "religious authorities" may speak of these encounters and experiences, and only in the context of a clearly defined religious tradition. Custom dictates, in other words, that we label these encounters and experiences in a very specific way and that only certain persons are sanctioned to speak of them.

In brief, as with all humanly created contexts and labels, these encounters and experiences are put into very specific "boxes" and are to remain there. Political, scientific and religious institutions especially stigmatize anyone who disregards conventional orthodoxy and they generally ostracize anyone who dares to challenge them. Why? Because these notions have been in force for centuries and millenniums and the institutions know that enforcement ensures their survival.

Fortunately, in today's world, there are now millions of people in the West who are braving a particular activity that arose in the East: namely, meditation; and while meditation may have its origins in certain religious traditions, the psychological and health benefits of meditation are by now well documented by western science. In these more progressive times, in fact, many westerners are so proficient at achieving deep states of meditation that they are having some pretty remarkable experiences. Some practitioners are actually reporting out-of-body experiences in which they find themselves in other dimensions entirely.

If one studies the various ancient, western wisdom traditions, which began millenniums ago, one discovers that most of the masters were affiliated at that time with what were called "Mystery Schools" and subscribed to the idea that there are many dimensions in the cosmos. The ancients called these dimensions "heavens". This is why, for example, even now we still hear the expression, "I was in seventh heaven". Seven heavens, or dimensions, was precisely what the wisdom masters claimed were real.

Early Christians like St Paul were well versed in the teachings of the Mystery Schools and long before him the ultimate Hebrew religious leader, Moses, had grown up deeply immersed and initiated into the wisdom traditions of the Egyptians. Likewise, in the Middle East, the Sufis held to this same notion about multiple heavens, while yogis in the Far East have always stated and quite unequivocally – based on firsthand experience – that the multidimensionality of human spirituality is genuine.

For westerners in the Middle Ages, however, these notions fell into disrepute owing to the manner in which the Catholic Church exercised its "authority" and control over the European peoples. The idea that there was "forbidden", or "occult" (hidden), knowledge altered virtually everything in the western world. Eventually, only those who had direct knowledge of the "soul" or "spirit" and had experienced out-of-body moments themselves understood fully what was being suppressed and how real the metaphysical side of life actually is.

A firsthand experience of any nature, it should be noted, is always the most convincing of any and should be the preferred approach to knowledge, for to "know" a truth is far more valid than merely "believing" something based on second or third hand information. Spiritual masters in the various mystery schools knew this and made it a tenet of their tradition that gaining firsthand knowledge alone was the way to true "gnosis", true knowing.

Such experiences, perhaps, won't make anyone wealthier in worldly terms, but, on the positive side, they will most assuredly leave one feeling richer in spirit and less afraid of death, not to mention giving one a truer taste of one's own immortal nature. Such an insight, we might add, is an inexpressibly powerful way for learning how to *really* think outside of the proverbial box.

# 4

# The Truth That Sets the Soul Free

IN THE BEGINNING was the *Word* and the Word was with us. It slipped from its dark chrysalis of mystery like no other thing in history. The Word is what makes us or breaks us. It is what frees us or enslaves us. It is what *defines* us.

So we *think*... So we *tell* ourselves. So the *Word* would have us believe.

What is anyone to believe, however, when we consider how the human species has acted over the course of the last few millenniums? Namely: abominably. After all, the "Age of Pisces" came and went with a haunting and horrific crucifixion, with an innumerable series of murderous, rampaging conflicts and crusades, with countless "holy wars" and pogroms, with a torturous Inquisition, burnings at the stake, rampant political upheaval, revolution by the blade and bullet, multiple cases of genocide and, finally, all-out war on a scale so immense, deadly and explosive that only the blowing of two atomic bombs at Hiroshima and Nagasaki could finally bring the Age to a shuddering close.

What now for the shell-shocked ranks of humanity in the raw "Aquarian" dawn after all of that?

This is a big question, of course, and one must wonder... Is the worst of what so many have suffered over the span of human history even over? It hardly seems so when we read the daily paper, listen to newscasts on television or pursue reports over the internet. What we see and hear these days are endless tales of betrayal, murder and war; tales of greed, thievery and scandal occurring at every level of society, including corruption at the top and preventable starvation at the bottom.

It appears that the acid vat of history is nothing more than a seething, roiling cauldron of lives in turmoil; a fetid, flesh-eating brew as dark as the dead of night, a potion so potent and powerful that, time and again, it boils over and scalds absolutely everything in its path. As a result, one may be forgiven for thinking that life is perhaps nothing but a curse; a harrowing gambol across a threatening landscape as one makes one's way inevitably to the edge of an abyss, then plunges.

Only wait a second...

The events known as "history" aren't *only* about the harrowing and the horrific, however. They are not only about war and death, about barbaric behavior, destruction, disease and disaster. They are simultaneously – almost miraculously – brimming over with the sweet smell of wondrous things too: love, laughter, kindness, compassion, charity and friendship, as well as the magnificent and moving creations that are to be found in the arts and architecture of human culture and in our many amazing scientific, medical and technological inventions, our ethics and morals, and in our near-universal desire by peoples across the globe to live together in peace. Millions of us celebrate our existence in virtually any and every way we possibly can, which we are free to do if we live in an open society with liberal, democratic values.

So, indeed, the acid vat of history is a troubling and tumultuous brew certainly, but within it, in colorful serpentine streaks amid the murky, viscous sludge of the churning waters of the cauldron, swirl nothing less than the mysterious, metaphorical elixirs of the gods...

Or if one prefers, we might call these intriguing and compelling streams "God's luminous liquid undercurrents". Or perhaps we should just call them the rippling cream of humanity's purest essence bubbling up to the surface like the finest of alchemical distillations, like the most perfect blend imaginable of the higher human values known to us.

In brief, we humans live in a world rooted in dualism: in

attraction and repulsion, in good and evil, in right and wrong, in a cultural milieu that argues over what is true and what is false. At a fundamental atomic level this dualism also prevails, for the universe itself and all material things, including our very bodies, are rooted in positive and negative energies.

Human experience, however, is rarely clear-cut in terms of these dualisms. There is an entire spectrum of activity which predominates alongside these concepts and there are multiple ways of looking at any particular issue. This is why there is so much confusion in the world and so many conflicting notions on what is true.

One of the great minds of the Renaissance, Francis Bacon, the English philosopher and statesman, captured this point perfectly when he said, "Man prefers to believe what he prefers to be true."

This short and simple insight is stunningly spot on. Millions, if not billions, of people on this earth have always chosen to believe what they prefer to be true, rather than what the facts make so vividly and abundantly clear to anyone who is willing to follow the facts where they happen to lead.

Threading through any set of facts, however, is difficult, for what one may discover is that over the centuries, details and realities have been routinely altered and they are still being altered by those whose self-interests are threatened by whatever details and truths might go against them. This has led to countless historical inaccuracies, to cover ups, to government whitewashing, to religious brainwashing and, tragically, to general cultural delusion on a scale that flat out astonishes.

I am acutely aware that this may seem like a form of conspiracy thinking, but in essence it is not. That is because if one is diligent and honest in his or her pursuit of truth, what one may ultimately discern is not one huge, colossal cabal plotting against the masses in breath-taking unity, but thousands upon thousands of tiny cliques and factions seeking an advantage over other cliques in a particular tribe, fiefdom, village, community or nation.

After a single decade of youthful intuitive skepticism, I vividly remember how I began to question the religion of my birth, the Roman Catholic Church. For the record, I have always loved the beautiful sayings attributed to Jesus and the love he showed for everyone, but the dark side of the Church, with its bizarre and contradictory doctrines and dogmas, never made sense to me and, to be perfectly honest about it, I never did accept that those doctrines and dogmas were actually true. This is not to say that I didn't find the rituals mesmerizing because I did. I was dazzled by the silken vestments, the golden ornaments, the stained-glass windows, the pillars, and the paintings and never tired of hearing inspirational sermons extolling the virtues of love, charity, kindness and compassion, and always enjoyed the ethereal music I heard in the various churches I attended over the decades. To this day, I am spiritually moved by the many images of Jesus, not of his crucifixion, but of his divine, Sacred Heart.

Hellfire and brimstone, however, simply never cut it with me and never will.

Thanks to the Vietnam war, which was highly unpopular among the youth of my day, I was similarly led to begin questioning my government. Being naturally predisposed to philosophical and metaphysical musings, I went on to instigate a form of academic analysis of my own mindset in my early twenties. What I discovered was that virtually every belief, prejudice, bias and preference I held needed to be put on the table for inspection. These mental constructs were then subjected to a raw and utterly merciless forensic examination that eventually left me in tatters.

Only not forever.

I subsequently began reading the works of wisdom masters the world over and it soon changed everything for me. I grew spellbound by the notion of spiritual liberation, illumination and the curious potential of what we call enlightenment.

What I eventually learned was that no serious seeker of "truth" should ignore the possibility that "spiritual liberation" and "illumination" comes, not from uncovering any form of "absolute" truth, but instead from threading one's way through as many contending viewpoints as possible and ultimately transcending the lot.

As the Zen master Seng Ts'an once stated. "It's no use to seek truth, just let false views cease."

How elegant and simple this sounds. In reality, however, identifying and letting go of false views can take decades of unbiased, open-minded contemplation, persistent rumination on the meaning of any particular perspective and a profound review of the significance of that which is being assessed. It certainly took me one hell of a long time to achieve this owing to the complexity of the challenge, but that did serve to prove to my satisfaction, in shockingly stark terms, how deeply rooted a belief system actually is.

The Buddha, ever resourceful and wise, once stated: "Do not believe in what you have heard. Do not believe in traditions because they have been handed down for many generations. Do not believe anything because it is rumored and spoken by many. Do not believe merely because the written statement of some old sage is produced. Do not believe in conjectures. Do not believe merely in the authority of your teachers and elders. After observation and analysis, when it agrees with reason and it is conducive to the good and benefit of one and all, then accept it, and live up to it."

In stark contrast to following such genuinely sensible and openminded advice, most of us living in the current century still choose to believe what we *prefer* to be true rather than what the facts make clear. Many people further prefer to believe that those who do not agree with them are against them, which is far from the case in most instances. Viewpoints are relative, after all, and do not need to be perceived as threatening in any way if one is wise enough to keep to the high ground and think the best of one's fellow planetary citizens. Unfortunately, there has been such an escalation in the ability of individuals and organizations to loudly and repeatedly flog a particular viewpoint in the name of a certain self-interest these days that this perspective has tumbled into the gutter in way too many public forums. As a result, the political and religious divide has grown so wide in recent times as to beggar belief.

Of course, humanity has always been under the sway and power of opinion and self-interest. This is certainly nothing new. One could name names, of course, but to do so would only serve to set up yet more divisiveness. Nevertheless, perhaps – just perhaps – a massive number of us are ready for a new era in which we understand just how relative truth is and can, therefore, help our fellow human beings rise above the various platforms which promote uncompromising authoritarian agendas or agendas rooted in some form of arrogant righteousness. Perhaps, as the Buddha suggests, we might use observation and analysis, and see what accords with reason and common sense before deciding on how our myriad social and cultural issues should be structured.

It is a common biblical aphorism that "truth" is what sets the soul free, but what is this notion of "truth" if it is rooted in a particular religion and is, therefore, culturally relative? How do we separate this truth from its provincial origins? How do we get to the level of a universal truth that transcends such an origin when we live in a world which seems to thrive on dogmatism, exclusion and religious righteousness?

I would say that common sense alone can certainly take us a long way toward achieving that end. Throw in a measure of skepticism (without bias), a compromising attitude, valuing wisdom over fear and guess what? Setting the soul free might well happen as naturally as the exhalation of one's next precious breath. We should, therefore, heed the words of those tens of thousands of people who have had a near-death experience and report that no religious tradition prevails over any other in the Hereafter. This means that regardless of what claims we may hold about the religion to which we subscribe, a divine power is with even those who do not share that view.

As the Sufi mystic, Kabir, put it: "Friend, hope for the divine while you are alive. Jump into experience while you are alive! Think…and think…while you are alive. What you call salvation belongs to the time before death. If you don't break your ropes while you're alive, do you think that ghosts will do it after?" He also said: "When the Divine is being searched for, it is the intensity of the longing for the Divine that does all of the work." Clearly, Kabir was a man who had become spiritually liberated and his powerful, telling words offer potent inspiration, indeed.

# 5

# Our Looming, Inexorable Journey Onward

TO PARAPHRASE THE TIBETAN wisdom master Milarepa: "Without being mindful of death, whatever spiritual practice we take up will be superficial." Death is the great bugaboo of the world, and the Grim Reaper is its chief agent. Tibetan Buddhists call this figure Yama, Lord of Death.

No one wants to die, of course. No one wants this wonderful earthly life to end, despite how so many have experienced such wildly fluctuating ups and downs and trials and tribulations, unless one happens, of course, to be suffering from such severe mental distress or physical pain that death is seen as one's sole relief.

As every religious and spiritual tradition on the earth makes clear, however, death is not the end. It is, of course, the end of the physical body, but it is not the end of the "I", the "real me". The soul lives on with full consciousness in an "afterlife" of some nature with the ability to sense and feel quite intensely.

According to those who have had a near-death experience, the only difference at the outset will be that one sees oneself as disembodied – or more correctly put – embodied in an extremely subtle energetic form. In fact, to our own eyes at that point, we will probably seem completely the same, they say. When we look down, we will see the hands we have always known, and we will be wearing clothes with which we are familiar. That is due to a subconscious impulse we all apparently have to make ourselves feel comfortable as we come to terms with an altered reality.

Taken altogether, these truths present a very good reason not to fear death. As Ian Curry, author of a book entitled *Visions of Immortality*, writes: "Death is far more likely to be experienced, not as a descent into darkness, but as an ascent into light." That means that most of us will be welcomed into a positive, loving, forgiving situation, while only truly evil people – abusers, torturers, and murderers – will be made to face a dim, grim realm of suffering, for after all what goes around, does indeed come around.

Quite intriguingly, wisdom masters in the Far East tell us that the mind's ability to comprehend reality is increased sevenfold at the outset of one's transition into the more subtle planes of existence. (This just may be a way of saying "many times over".)

Usually, according to most near-death returnees, one travels through a long, dark tunnel of some sort at an amazing speed before eventually emerging into a realm of light. There, the newly departed soul may find him or herself greeted by loved ones or by a more highly evolved being whose presence may be like that of a large orb of pure radiant light. These beings, whether familiar or not, will comfort us and welcome us into their domain. What may be seen all around these kind spirits is a beautiful meadowland with a brilliant blue sky and flowing rivers. Some returnees report seeing hundreds or even thousands of souls floating about or wandering through a wondrous, bucolic scene, smiling and laughing, and enjoying themselves as if rapturously happy. (For greater detail on all of this the books of the late Michael Newton are recommended. Newton held a doctorate in counselling and was a state-certified Master Hypnotist in the state of California. Quite intriguingly, he could take his subjects so deeply down into the subconscious layers of their minds when he hypnotized them that they would reach a "super conscious" level of perception and describe amazingly coherent scenes of life in alternative dimensions. The titles of his major works are, *Journey of Souls*, and *Destiny of Souls*.)

Quite interestingly, most loved ones which returnees met in the Hereafter were pretty much seen to be in the prime of their lives again. That is, they were youngish and bursting with robust health. After this initial meeting, many have reported that what followed was a great feast where everyone ate of the finest cuisine and imbibed the most delicious elixirs imaginable.

If this all sounds a bit like the legendary Avalon of the ancients, where endless feasting and eternal youth is said to reign, it might well be so. It could be one and the same place, in fact.

While Avalon was the paradise of the Celts, the Vedic yogis spoke of a very similar place, as well. For example, Swami Muktananda, in his spiritual autobiography *Play of Consciousness*, tells how after years and years of deep meditation, he found himself in a celestial land known as Tandraloka one day. He was greeted by a god who came for him on a jeweled chariot and, once the god whisked him away, he was taken to a city of such beauty that he was left in awe. He writes: "All of the people of the city were young, healthy, and free from sadness. Although their bodies were slim, they were strong, and they all glowed with a remarkable radiance."

The yogi was then taken into an exquisite palace full of gold and fabulous jewels and it turned out to be the home of Indra, the very god at his side. At once, there was beautiful music to be heard and Swami Muktananda realized that he was now in "the world of the virtuous, where sensuous desires are fulfilled, and because it grants enjoyment, it may also be called Sakamaloka, the world of the satisfaction of desires."

The astonished yogi, however, was not allowed to linger for long and he was soon put back upon Indra's chariot and returned to his meditation chamber, but not before seeing hell, as well. This should not surprise us. The descent into Hell seems to be part of every truly profound shamanic or spiritual experience. Even Jesus was made to experience Hell, as were so many of the pagan gods and heroes that populate the Greek and Roman literature. In fact, these latter figures were quite often forced to travel into the Underworld or Hades. The reason for this is no mystery: there is no deep understanding of the heavenly dimensions of celestial pleasure unless one also gains a direct perception of how shockingly awful the realms of suffering actually are. In any case, it was through this thoroughly overwhelming experience that Swami was given his most powerful insight into the reality of the Vedic scriptures. He knew at that point for certain, he says, that the gods exist and so, too, other realms, which left him ecstatic with joy.

As fabulous as those "lokas" sound, one of the holiest of all the Vedic scriptures, the Rig Veda, states that, "Although my spirit may go far away to distant realms, let it come back to me again so that I may live and journey here." In other words, this Earth is pretty special too. The Buddhists believe that there is no better place for gaining Supreme Enlightenment than on this very planet we inhabit while experiencing life in a human body.

Buddhists tell us that there are six realms:

1. The realm of the gods.
2. The realm of the demi-gods.
3. The human realm.
4. The animal realm.
5. The realm of hungry ghosts.
6. The hell realm.

All of these realms interpenetrate with each other, Buddhist wisdom masters say, which is why one may travel into other dimensions in a subtle body either via a deep meditative rapture or a full-blown out-of-body experience.

The Vedic yogis have also noted that one may travel to these realms through the utilization of a psychotropic substance which takes one's consciousness down to a molecular level, such as the sacred elixir known as soma in the ancient times. Once there, one may meet denizens of the astral domain and communicate directly with them. Likewise, those who dare to indulge in an ayahuasca ceremony, smoke dimethyltryptamine (DMT) or ingest a large quantity of *Psilocybe cubensis* ("magic mushrooms") have also reported similar encounters with various nonhuman entities.

It should be emphasized, however, that ultimately upon one's passing from this earth one will only go where one's karma essentially forces or allows one to go. If it is to a higher realm, then what is generally reported is that one will at first experience familiar forms with which one can identify. A Westerner may see religious, saintly or angelic figures and people who look, speak and act in ways that seem little different from the culture in which one resided while alive on earth. An African, Middle Eastern or Oriental person would likewise experience familiar people he or she knew while alive and also encounter various holy figures from their own culture.

So long as one's actions were of a more virtuous and beneficent nature, we are told, our karma will carry us through to a positive realm full of love and beauty. If, on the other hand, however, one's karma was not so good, then – depending on how selfish, ignorant, unkind or evil one's actions were – such a person may experience either a murky, ghostly realm where he or she might wander for an indeterminate time with few, if any, satisfying encounters or one might well be carried straight away into a truly dark and horrible hell realm for what is said to feel like eons, which fortunately will not last "forever".

No realm, wisdom masters tell us, is forever. One does not suffer in hell for all of eternity as Christianity would have it. Nor does one wander about as an earthbound ghost, forever lost and lonely in a spooky land of lethargy and confusion, trying fruitlessly to enjoy the pleasures one once knew. Near-death returnees tell us that if one cries out sincerely for help that plea will eventually be answered by a kindly, angelic Being of Light who will explain why the person is where he or she is and then aid the person in his or her efforts to move on. Many of these souls are sent back to be reincarnated on earth, often into a life with many hardships and challenges which will allow the person to make amends for their erroneous or less than noble behavior.

While the Abrahamic faiths generally do not openly subscribe to reincarnation nowadays, their ancestors in the more ancient of days did accept and believe in such a doctrine. In fact, the Jewish religion still holds such a belief. Several Gnostic sects in the early centuries of Christianity held a belief in reincarnation, as did Origen, one of the most respected of the Church fathers.

In any case, it was the Emperor Justinian who rejected the concept of reincarnation in 553 CE after convening the Second Council of Constantinople. It is interesting to note here that it was a Byzantine emperor who declared the belief "anathema" at that time, not the reigning pope, though the Church was happy to go along with this edict for it made its control over people even more secure. There were to be no second chances allowed where salvation was concerned!

Socrates, Plato and other Greek sages also believed in reincarnation, as did members of the Orphic Mystery Cult, and likewise the Celtic and Germanic pagans.

While Christianity these days forbids any belief in reincarnation, a concept that postulates that there is a realm where the deceased reside until they are either sent, or choose, to go back to life on Earth, the religion does espouse an absolute belief in the existence of other dimensions in the form of Heaven, Purgatory and Hell.

In short, there is no question that in the minds of most human beings, East and West, there is a belief that there are other dimensions to existence and that they are for real. Likewise, shamans all around the globe have had a solid belief in the reality of other dimensions for millenniums, as do the many millions of people who have experienced ghostly encounters and those mysterious, shapeshifting beings who have been labeled "extraterrestrials".

Jim Marrs, in his book *Alien Agenda* lists three main types of so-called extraterrestrials, namely the "grays", the "humanoids" and the "Transcendentals". It is this last group that is likened to the angels of yore and what the late researcher came to finally believe is that these beings are not physical in the same way as human beings. Quite intriguingly, the humanoids and grays may not be strictly physical either, since both groups are known to appear and disappear quite inexplicably, not to mention float about and pass-through solid walls. (Jesus, too, was said to be able to pass through solid walls once he was seen again after his crucifixion. These encounters were precisely what led his followers to believe that he had been resurrected from the dead.)

Controversial author Whitley Strieber tells us in his book, *A New World* that he saw a deceased friend of his inside a spacecraft that was being piloted by "alien" figures, which directly ties extraterrestrials into the dimension of the afterlife.

The famous *Tibetan Book of the Dead* goes into great detail about the "bardos" or ethereal dimensions that one will experience upon one's death. It is from such ethereal planes that one eventually returns to the earth to begin a new life or ascends into higher realms of being altogether. In a similar vein, *The Egyptian Book of the Dead* gives extensive detail about what a soul encounters in the afterlife.

Metaphysicians believe that what the soul experiences once it departs the body is the astral realm. From there, depending upon one's depth of understanding of the purpose and meaning of life, one may advance into further realms beyond. Altogether, there are said to be seven heavens or dimensions where the more highly evolved among us may go. If true, this is precisely why we must pursue knowledge of a metaphysical or spiritual nature with great vigor while we are yet upon this earth, for we are given the opportunity to grow and expand ourselves in a very real way in this environment.

Ultimately, metaphysicians believe that the purpose of life is spiritual enrichment. This is true for the singular soul, as well as for the benefit of the Godhead itself, which seemingly seeks to experience all things and all possibilities unto infinity.

In brief, such a colossal goal requires an entire cosmos in order to bring such a purpose to full fruition. The staggeringly brilliant inference which may be made about such a purpose is that each and every one of us is a contributor and a co-creator of this infinitely vast eternal universal drama, which makes it a very personal situation, indeed.

One would be wise, therefore, to review his or her life on an ongoing basis in order to assess how one is doing *before* one departs this Earth. This allows for what might be called a "course correction" if one is deemed necessary, for near-death returnees say that one of the most profoundly unsettling events in the afterlife occurs when one sees one's entire life flashing before his or her mind's eye. That event is known, quite simply, as the "life review", but the intensity of it is apparently anything but simple or humdrum, for we are made to feel exactly what we made others feel and super intensely at that. In fact, the event can be so overpowering and overwhelming in scope and magnitude, some insist, that it generally proves life-altering to those who experience it and return to tell the tale.

To that end, delving deeply into one's own personal narrative, as I shall do here now, is to find the proverbial devil in the details.

# 6

# Atom Bombs, Battling Cabals & the Rise of the Aquarian Counterculture

SEVEN YEARS AFTER ATOMIC BOMBS blew Hiroshima and Nagasaki to near-oblivion in Japan, and Adolf Hitler allegedly blew his own head off in a bombproof bunker in Berlin, I was born onto this mad planet in the midnight hour on a New Year's Day as snowflakes swirled and the earth grew positively covered in the lovely, though illusory, appearance of perfect purity.

Little did I know, nor even begin to suspect, what I was in for by being born into this world of form and substance. Like everyone else, though, I soon found out. What I discovered was that I had arrived in the midst of a wickedly violent habitat where *millions* of my fellow inhabitants were attempting to recover – physically, mentally, emotionally and spiritually – from the most catastrophically destructive conflict in global history.

The controversial Harry S. Truman was still in the White House that year, but not for long. Soon Dwight D. Eisenhower, the former Supreme Commander of the Allied Forces in All of Europe during World War II, assumed the mantle of President of the United States. What did any child in America know at that point? Our land had gone untouched for the duration of the conflict, which meant, as far as we were concerned, that war had been totally unreal and we were living in a veritable paradise.

Indeed, for me, life was utterly bucolic. I had joined a family of five near a small city in Northwest Ohio to begin my life as any child does. My father, still fairly fresh from the war himself, had secured a job in a factory and he had built a new home for his growing brood of children. My mother, with her hands quite full, stayed at home to raise us. There was not much money, but life proceeded. Gardens were sown and fruit trees planted.

As far as I was concerned, I was living in the Garden of Eden. There was room to run, land to roam, brothers and sisters with which to play. I can still see the lush green lawn in my mind's eye, see us all playing our games there amid the bright yellow dandelions which grew in vast, radiant profusions in the brilliant sunlight. There were copious quantities of flowers all around the grounds and huge gardens full of healthy vegetables. There was a fruit orchard with apple, peach, pear and plum trees. There was a thorny hedgerow of blackberries. There was raspberry bramble and a small vineyard loaded with huge, succulent grapes which one could eat straight off the vine.

In short, we ate well, we played hard, we laughed long and loud. Like every working-class family at the time, we accepted our lot and the years simply rolled on in an utterly ordinary manner with one final sibling, a sister, joining us eventually and then the family was complete.

Europe, meanwhile, was slowly rising from the carnage which had engulfed it; its cities still essentially smoldering, its inhabitants continuing to clear away the rubble from all around them. The survivors were traumatized; many in fact like the walking dead. Reality for them had become a thing to be feared and "truth" a thing to be cursed.

In Washington DC, meanwhile, in the myriad backrooms and privileged corridors of power, the elite of our nation were going about their secret machinations with the stealth of a medieval cabal of crusaders plotting to take over everything. The same was going on in London, Moscow and most of the other capitols on the planet, as well. The second Great War had brought out the worst in everyone. After all, killing on an industrial scale could not but trigger desperation, greed and insecurity in people everywhere.

Meanwhile, the Gestapo's tenacious survivors, the most

resilient of men, supposedly crushed and gone, were on the run underground in unknown numbers. They were speeding off to far-flung lands all around the globe, hiding out where they could and plotting their next moves. Intelligence agencies knew that and acted swiftly to co-opt as many of these men as they could for their own selfish ends. Agencies such as the CIA, MI6 and the KGB were secretly hiring more than a few of these former enemies in order to extract their knowledge, employ their skills and gain technological advantages thereby.

At the same time, the millionaire financiers, owners of the banks and the largest multinational corporations history had ever known were busy with their own machinations. Competition for resources and land, and for Machiavellian and Orwellian control, was soon reaching a feverish pitch as nuclear contaminants ate into the upper stratosphere of the earth, the atomic radiation itself raining down like a misty black plague, though few spoke of that as the testing continued.

Indeed, ever more powerful and lethal bombs were being developed in the secret laboratories of the scientific genii: not just atomic bombs, but nuclear bombs, hydrogen bombs and bombs with the power of a thousand exploding supernovas. The conventional weapons factories, for their part, eagerly continued to spew forth their eerie smoke and soot like something out of Dante's horrific, unexpurgated *Inferno*, providing a brutal portrayal of Hell itself. There was money to be made in weaponry in those days, by God, and there still is.

Meanwhile, the religions of the world, as ever, were paying lip-service to peace on Earth and goodwill toward men, but there was blood on their scriptures, though few dared to even think it. History had locked in the veracity of it long before, however. Between the violent Crusades, the terrible and torturous "Holy Inquisition," the various *jihads* and pogroms, the Holocaust and other genocidal assaults by one sect, denomination or peoples against another, there was ample proof that the religious institutions of this earth were not what they were being made out to be. Some of the greatest leaders of these organizations, in fact, were saying that the "Final Conflagration" of all time was absolutely imminent for this was what their doctrines and dogmas stated. Tales of Armageddon, I was to learn, would only increase as the years rolled on.

Entrenched in medieval thinking, the same as the cabals within many of the world's governments, such religious institutions had amassed property and holdings of incalculable worth by then. Theologians, promulgating notions written in stone so ancient, cracked and moss-laden that they could barely be deciphered in their original forms anymore, had – with very few exceptions it seems – lost the plot as completely as had the world's political leaders and everyone else.

Humanity, nevertheless, was getting on with the business of living after the war and, yes, hope was springing eternal as ever. In fact, an era of technological innovation was charging forth from the many laboratories across the land, creating amazingly clever gadgets of every conceivable type and brand. With fresh thinking percolating at a heady pitch in both the scientific and the liberal arts establishments everywhere, the modern world was, as it transpired, being spawned with electrifying bravado. Revolutionary communication devices such as telephones, radios and television sets were getting better by the day and in the medical field stupendously inventive machines were being deployed for the *benefit* of people, which was a welcome change indeed. The automotive industry, too, had begun to reach new heights of success in design and cars were becoming affordable to even the average wage-earner.

My father, like so many, bought his first car about this time and eventually purchased the family's first television set. Into this environment, I slowly came of age and, as the conformist Fifties gave way to the incandescent intensity of the Sixties, Western civilization, as a whole, went *ultra-modern*. It metamorphosed into one huge, insatiable, consumerist giant of commerce.

Unfortunately, greed escalated astronomically in the process as well, but the Powers That Be were more than pleased by that. People were working harder than ever and keeping their bony shoulders to the wheel. Prosperity was blossoming beautifully upon the land and the elites thought it perfect as they continued to reap the lion's share for themselves.

With the assassination of President John F. Kennedy, however, all hell started to break loose in America and I watched with eyes wide as it unfolded live on television. It was not only the death of a president that hit those airwaves. There was a second murder two days after the president was gunned down, this time his alleged assassin. On that day, I saw – and the whole world witnessed – the murder of a man in real time, live on TV, and it took us profoundly by surprise to say the least.

We were soon to see many more people die on television, for the war in Vietnam was stealing across our screens on a daily basis and the killing was growing relentless. Bombs were raining down from the sky and poisons too: military strategists were clearing the jungle with something called Agent Orange. Nevertheless, America did not rid the world of the Communist "hordes." America, as history now notes, was eventually forced to give up the fight in Vietnam and retreat. Public opinion simply went against that war and for good reason. It was based on the notion that the Western powers were fighting to bring democracy to the Vietnamese people and save them from falling prey to a communist dictatorship, when really it was about keeping a military presence in the region and controlling resources. The same could later be said of the Afghani and Iraq wars and so little changed.

Fortunately, back in the day, there was a positive side to the era and it had everything to do with rock 'n' roll. The Beatles had come along to lift Americans from their gloom after the

Kennedy assassination with music that was irresistibly melodic and rapturously exuberant. Millions of us were swept up in that exuberance and it lit up our minds like nothing before it.

What followed on from The Beatles made every young person in America feel as if something monumental was occurring. A whole new era seemed to be under way and the songs of Bob Dylan definitely added to that perception, for his songs had a depth never before heard in popular music. Dylan sang that "The Times They Are A-Changin'" and how the answers to life's many conundrums were "Blowin' in the Wind." He once said in an interview that "It was like a flying saucer had landed... that's what the Sixties was like." For his own part, he showed no mercy whatsoever to the "Masters of War" and was determined to stand over their graves until he was sure they were dead. Dylan was like an Old Testament prophet who had come in from the wilderness and he dared to warn the political, military-industrial complex that "A Hard Rain's A-Gonna Fall". We were all going to be swept away by the deluge if their warring ways did not cease.

Dylan wasn't alone in this, of course. Other artists were putting their fears and social concerns into song lyrics at the time, as well. For example, Barry McGuire had a chart topper called the "Eve of Destruction". It hit number 1 in September of 1965. Its lyrics implied that an exchange of nuclear ballistic missiles might well be unleashed at any moment and destroy virtually everything and everyone on the planet. As an added shocking twist, the lyrics (penned by P.F. Sloan and Steve Barri), made it quite clear to listeners that there was no way to hide from those deadly fireballs once they started flying back and forth, which sent an ice cold shiver up my young spine. Indeed, as a 13-year-old, I took that notion very seriously and still do.

Such were the times. With their piercing insights into war, racism and injustice, artists such as Dylan, The Beatles, the Rolling Stones, the Doors, Jimi Hendrix, Jefferson Airplane, the

Grateful Dead, Crosby, Stills, Nash and Young, and numerous other bands created a powerful, united antiwar front and the combined influence eventually gave rise to a counterculture known as the "Love Generation", which rose like a magical, spellbinding collective against the steamrolling ways of the "military/industrial complex". When America finally retreated from the Vietnam War it seemed as if that collective effort had not been in vain. As incense and cannabis smoke wafted through the air, the books and lyrics of the Love Generation's New Age heroes spoke of an era of transcendence, of an astrological Aquarius, and it was to supplant the murderous Age of Pisces and birth a new world entirely.

Behind it all, however, the Powers That Be thought otherwise and made sure that such notions were ridiculed and eventually stopped dead in their tracks. The status quo needed to be maintained and as the Sixties gave way to the Seventies the Aquarian dream began dying a slow death. By 1977, there was little left of the dream thanks to the so-called "punk" movement, with its thrashing guitars, angry lyrics and nihilistic disdain for "peace and love." In fact, Johnny Rotten of the Sex Pistols stated unequivocally that he had no interest whatsoever in "all that hippie shit of peace and love." (Though to be fair, Elvis Costello, in 1979, did give us a powerful rendition of the Nick Lowe tune "What's So Funny 'Bout Peace, Love & Understanding?") In any case, by 1980 the Conservative factions had swept into power with Ronald Reagan as their hero and that was that. Hippiedom was consigned to the dustbin of history.

So, there we have it. The "Powers That Be" won the day and the bloody offensives of the Great War Machine continued, especially in the Middle East where the oil which lubricates the war machine itself is on tap in barrels by the millions. Profits have soared in the Oil industry along the way as have sales in the Armaments industry.

Perhaps, looking for peace and love across the whole of the

Earth really was pie in the sky thinking when one looks back on it all now, for to overcome the survivalist impulses which have haunted humanity for hundreds of thousands of years is a pretty tough challenge to overcome. Still, as our species contemplates the possibility of flying off to Mars and setting up the first ever permanent interplanetary colony there, we would all do well to keep asking ourselves when we will finally become a more enlightened species instead of a race of barbaric savages who just happen to be extremely clever at designing complex forms of technology.

Our instincts and impulses are, of course, absolutely natural to us and because of that they are, to paraphrase the Immortal Bard in *The Tempest*, such stuff as dreams are made on. This is how and why we can glamorize violence and war, and easily convince our young bucks that a "real man" fights tooth and nail for the causes of his elders. In doing so, he can become a hero himself, but only if he triumphs on the battlefield.

Clearly, from a higher perspective, glamorizing violence sends the wrong message to our young and it has brought about not just the stuff of unrealistic dreams and fantasies, but the stuff of nightmares. Because of that, it is riskier than ever these days to stand up for one's principles and appeal to reason with those who are ready and willing to throw a fist or let blaze with a gun at the slightest provocation. History has taught us many lessons, indeed; to wit, speaking truth to power can get one murdered. So can daring to question a radical extremist with a fundamentalist ideology. Nevertheless, it is possible for humanity to bring a much better world to pass if it chooses. We could, for example, glamorize the kind of mental and emotional strength it takes to exercise restraint when dealing with combative people, for this is the proper role of the warrior.

Finally, just to say, the brief era of peace and love in the Sixties and early Seventies need not be seen as simply an aberration. Instead, it can be seen as a foreshadowing of the world we are yet capable of creating. There is a popular inspirational affirmation going the rounds these days. It says, "If it is to be, it is up to me." Indeed, it is up to each of us.

We can't all be historical figures, of course, but we can all figure into history in our own small way, even if we only influence but a few others over the years. Fortunately, occasionally, ideas can multiply exponentially, however, so who knows? What goes around, comes around and inspiration can be such stuff as paradise is made on if enough people choose to think and act with loving positivity instead of its horrid opposite.

# 7

# Strawberry Fields Forever

## *The Beatles & their Magical Mystery Tour de Force*

TO DELVE MORE DEEPLY into the phenomenon of The Beatles, I believe, is both instructive and significant for reasons we shall explore as we proceed here, but like millions of teens and pre-teens in 1964, I witnessed a cultural event such as the world had never before seen. It was called Beatlemania. It began in America when their song, "I Want to Hold Your Hand", went to Number 1 on the Billboard Hot 100 chart. This was followed by the arrival of the band into New York City in February of that year and their appearance on the Ed Sullivan Show, complete with countless screaming, crying, hysterical female teenage fans. The intensity of that hysteria was off the charts. No one had ever seen anything like it. Apparently, The Beatles themselves were as surprised by it as anyone.

"I Want to Hold Your Hand" remained at Number 1 for seven weeks and was followed at Number 1 by another of their songs, "She Loves You". This latter tune remained at Number 1 for two weeks and was then followed at Number 1 by "Can't Buy Me Love", which held the top spot for five weeks. No one before or since has had three number one singles in a row.

When "Can't Buy Me Love" hit Number 1 a unique constellation of hits occurred on the Billboard Hot 100: The Beatles held the top five places. This unique charting was as follows: 1. "Can't Buy Me Love". 2. "Twist and Shout". 3. "She Loves You". 4. "I Want to Hold Your Hand" and 5. "Please Please Me".

In addition to holding the top five places on the Billboard chart – an achievement which Billboard itself says will probably stand for all time – The Beatles had 14 entries in the Hot 100.

Again, like millions of others, I was thoroughly astonished by the unprecedented level of excitement that The Beatles were generating. I found their brand of rock 'n' roll utterly exhilarating and irresistible. What continues to amaze me is that even when I play their early hits nowadays, some fifty years later, I still get a rush of exhilaration and delight that never fails to put a smile on my face. I usually achieve this end by creating my own playlist and cranking up the volume while driving in my car. The first surge of elation usually begins with "I Saw Her Standing There". After that I kick the action into even higher gear with "She Loves You". Then I segue, for memories sake, into "I Want to Hold Your Hand" and follow that with the Lennon screamer, "Twist and Shout", after which the action rockets off into my personal all-time McCartney favorite: "All My Loving".

I could easily continue on here raving about masterpieces like "Strawberry Fields Forever", "A Day in the Life", "Hey Jude", "Let It Be" and "Yesterday" (the most covered song in pop music history) or express my heartfelt love of the albums *A Hard Day's Night, Rubber Soul, Revolver, Sergeant Pepper's Lonely Hearts Club Band, Magical Mystery Tour, the "White Album", Abbey Road* and so on, but suffice it to say that the influence of this band, which dominated the rock and pop music world for a mere 10 years, had a lifelong effect on me.

Their music was just one part of that total effect. The lifestyle of these and other musicians influenced millions of us during the band's stay at the top and it is common knowledge that The Beatles' collective experimentation with psychoactive substances had millions of us doing likewise. While the "Fab Four" did not spark the so-called "hippie" movement itself (it began in San Francisco's Haight-Ashbury district), their adoption of the hippie look was obvious for one and all to see.

While I was still too young to join in on that movement at its outset, I nevertheless purchased my first guitar at 13 and by the time I was 15 years of age I was in a rock band called The New London Rebels. Indeed, I found myself mesmerized by what I was seeing on TV. The Beatles weren't the only show in town, so to speak. There were scores of great bands around in those days, from the Animals to the Zombies, but I was fantastically inspired by the way the music of The Beatles evolved over the years, especially after they took special note of, and interest in, the uniquely powerful lyrics of Bob Dylan. Once they met the artist in Manhattan's Hotel Delmonico and Dylan "turned" them "on" to marijuana, virtually everything changed.

Rock 'n' roll in conjunction with cannabis and LSD essentially catalyzed the whole Aquarian movement. First up came the explosive psychedelic outrageousness of Jimi Hendrix's album *Are You Experienced*, then the proto-heavy-metal music of bands like Cream, the Doors and Iron Butterfly, as well as the more celestial offerings of bands like Pink Floyd and the Moody Blues. Later, the stage show *Hair*, came along. This was a theatrical production that really sent the whole notion of the "Age of Aquarius" into the global heavens and later gave the band The Fifth Dimension a number one record with "Aquarius / Let the Sunshine In" in April of 1969.

When I was 15, however, it was The Beatles' iconic appearance and their talk of expanded consciousness that really set my world on fire. When *Sergeant Pepper's Lonely Hearts Club Band* came out in 1967, it helped to spur on what became known as the "Summer of Love". At that point, I had yet to smoke marijuana. Nevertheless, I decorated my entire bedroom in colorful collages and placed – on its own – a large, framed, full-page photograph of the Maharishi Mahesh Yogi on my back wall. I even put a spotlight on the smiling, bearded guru whose countenance seemed utterly sublime and cosmic in the extreme to me. As sitars jangled and other exotic Indian instruments droned and thumped on *Sgt. Pepper*, I read an article about meditation and dove straight in with it as if born to it.

Perhaps I was.

Eventually, I would travel all through the Far East with my companion at the time: to Kathmandu and the Himalayas of Nepal where we had the stupendous pleasure of trekking through the Annapurna Range. Then it was on to the exotic plains of India and the Taj Mahal; onward again to the banks of the Ganges in that country's holiest of cities, Varanasi, where we encountered a "gold-medalist" astrologer who altered the dynamic of our relationship and, in time, our destinies completely, but we accepted that with surprising equanimity. After all, we were the freest of free souls at the time and so we simply pressed on together to Calcutta and Darjeeling where we enjoyed spectacular views of Mount Everest, K2 and Kanchenjunga, then traveled on again through what was then known as Burma, wandering the streets of Rangoon and Mandalay, and walking at length through the astonishing Valley of a Thousand Temples. Finally, we arrived in Bangkok, Thailand, where countless golden stupas were to be seen, all gleaming with preternatural luminescence in the hot, tropical sunshine like sacred, otherworldly wonders from another dimension entirely.

*A long and winding road?* Indeed. A *magical mystery tour?* Absolutely.

Mesmerized more than ever with the idea of liberation and enlightenment, my companion bade me a gracious farewell on the island of Koh Samui and I flew off to Hong Kong and Tokyo on my own, then took up refuge within the sacred temples of Kyoto. The whole of the experience, I must say, proved captivating enough to have lasted me a lifetime, but there was still so much more to come.

In retrospect, I am completely humbled by the great good fortune I had of going around the world by the time I was 30 years of age. In fact, I still cannot believe how those travels were down to certain fortuitous synchronicities over which I had no control. When we meet the right person, I learned, there is magic. (It may not last forever, but it does open one to the reality, power and numinosity of synergy in a way one cannot otherwise know.) One might say, of course, that the whole of it "just happened", but I have to wonder as I look back, was it pure luck or did karma from a previous life play into this? I only ask the question because it all seems so improbable as I look back on it with a heart full of gratitude.

The Buddha would probably say "yes" to the idea that it was karma that propelled me along. The Dalai Lama would probably say "yes", as well.

What this implies, I like to think, is that my love of music carried with it a sacred connection, a divine link no less, which is pretty cool, indeed.

Now as I sit here writing at my desk in the west of Ireland, peering out my window and gazing appreciatively across the silvery waters of Galway Bay, I can only think how lucky I am to have lived the life I have lived. After all, many of those I knew over the years who lived through the same time frame did not fare so well. Many died along the way in tragic circumstances. I had friends die in Vietnam, for example, or who came back from the war suffering from injuries or post-traumatic shock syndrome. One close friend of mine made the foolish mistake of getting hooked on heroin and died of an overdose at a mere 22 years of age. Another close friend got carried away with his partying and in a drunken moment of madness climbed up on a moving vehicle and was subsequently thrown from it, smashing his head against the road and dying instantly.

Life can be brutal that way. It is not all fun and fascination. Nevertheless, as I sit here looking out my window, I can see the stony hills of County Clare on the far shore of the bay where the Burren sits with its magical, mysterious, megalithic dolmens and other wonders. The Cliffs of Moher are there, too, ever ready to hold viewers spellbound by their majestic height and ragged, dangerous precipices. Recently, a young teen fell off one of the cliffs there and plunged to his death. My point is that we make choices in life and sometimes people make very bad choices. They go where they should not go. They do what they should not do. Nothing is sure, of course, so we must stay vigilant at all times and proceed with caution and care.

Then, again, perhaps one thing *is* sure: Music is sacred.

As the late molecular biologist, Darryl Reanney, put it in his book *The Death of Forever – A New Future for Human Consciousness*: "Music is the most powerful alchemy we know, the magic agent of transcendence that lifts consciousness into a more perfect state. When we lose ourselves in music, *we become more real.*" (His emphasis.) By the way, the title, *The Death of Forever*, alludes to the fact that "forever" is a concept rooted in time. Sadly, John Lennon, who wrote the lyrics to "Strawberry Fields Forever", one of The Beatles' most loved songs, was at best offering up a wistful wish. In his song "Across the Universe", he similarly sang how nothing was going to change his world, but his life *did* change and tragically so; in fact, all lives change and on a constant basis. (By the way, when I "imagine" a world with no religion as Lennon sang in his most anthemic song, I cannot see this particular utopian ideal as making for a better situation for humanity. Without at least some exposure to a spiritual tradition with a measure of emphasis on love, charity, and compassion, most, I fear, would worship money and fame even more than they do now and pay scant attention to anything other than their own self-interests.)

The good news is, of course, that the music plays on and that there are all types of music to be enjoyed. Great bands and artists today carry on the musical traditions of yesteryear with equally wondrous skill and talent, and some innovative artists are inventing new forms of music entirely.

Fortunately for us, music is everywhere nowadays, on our

radios, television sets and streaming services; in every mall, store and restaurant. Nothing seems to make people happier than delighting in a live performance by one of their favorite artists or dancing the night away to whatever type of music most appeals. No matter what era one is born into one can discover transcendent expressions of the soul in the music of one's choice just as I did in the tunes of The Beatles and with so many other great artists and bands. I have personally reached profoundly transcendent heights with the music of countless artists. All it takes is immersing oneself with an enthusiastic ear. After all, enthusiasm itself is entheogenic, which is to say it can carry one to divine heights if one makes it one's sole focus. This is not just hyperbole.

As Professor David Fontana wrote in his wonderfully insightful book *Life Beyond Death*: "Not surprisingly, music has always been regarded as akin to magic, and there does appear to be something supernatural about its ability to alter the consciousness of the listener. It can arouse deep emotions, evoke memories, create associations and, at its most profound, inspire transcendental states similar to those experienced in deep meditation. Music can take us into the formless inner realm beyond words and concepts..."

That it can. Many of those who have returned from a near-death experience say that there are dimensions in the Great Beyond which are filled with heavenly music. It is as if angelic choirs and ethereal orchestras are conjuring the most uplifting, celestial melodies imaginable and purely for the joy of one and all.

We might remember here, as well, what Beethoven once said. "Music is the mediator between the spiritual and the sensual life."

That is certainly true in the case of rock 'n' roll, which is why we might further remember here that it was Chuck Berry, one of the founding fathers of the genre, who first wrote and recorded the song, "Roll Over Beethoven". The Beatles also recorded a great cover version of this song for their first album. I suspect that Beethoven himself would have been both amused and pleased by these tributes, for the music of all ages give us, perhaps, the greatest expressions of the soul that we humans can know. Music can exhilarate us, or it can soothe us. It can give us maestros like Bach, Beethoven and Mozart. It can give us Rock "gods", pop idols and magical rides into the inner realms like no other art form.

While I don't expect to hear Rock classics brightening the already brilliant emerald meadows of "Summerland" in the Hereafter should I get there, I do, however, expect to hear every song I have ever heard while living in this world at least one more time. That is during my life review. Quite intriguingly, returnees from the Hereafter tell us that we may move forward or backward in time while that review is going on. They also say that we may linger on any scene we wish for as long as we like, which should make for some very interesting and exhilarating moments, indeed. Personally, I might just choose to linger on many an aural masterpiece for untold ages!

In the meantime, though, at the flip of a switch, millions of us have access to every form of recorded music that has ever been made. So let the music play, I say, and ride it with joy to the very last day. "The beat goes on..." and in more ways than one as we shall see.

# 8

# Taking Back the Hijacked Mind

THE GREATEST OBSTACLE to uncovering the deeper truths in life is primarily down to the self-delusion that one already knows everything that one *needs* to know or *can* know. To think that you cannot really know more than you already do, nor learn anything of substance beyond what you have learned by a certain point in life, however, is to preclude yourself from higher, more profound, streams of information.

It is unfortunate that so many prefer to adopt a know-it-all attitude and dismiss topics of study, or subjects of inquiry, which don't fit within the rigid parameters of a limited worldview, rather than taking the time to look into and explore the wealth of possibilities that can expand one far beyond those parameters.

What many don't realize is that, in all probability, they arrived at their point of stasis quite unwittingly. The reason for this likely lies with our educational systems which staunchly promote rote learning in contrast to the more creative approach of allowing intrigue to take its natural course and letting the mind chase whatever topics are of keen interest.

It's understandable, of course, that a great deal of rote learning is necessary for a technology-driven culture to flourish. We need mathematicians, physicists, engineers, and architects, to name but a few of the vital professions required, and we would likely not fill those ranks if we let children study only what they found agreeable, interesting and easy to understand.

Nevertheless, imaginative exploration should receive equal time. After all, motivation is always down to interest. Only how much intellectual interest in various forms of knowledge can one conjure if one chooses to abdicate his or her free time to passively watching television or idly surfing the internet and scrolling endlessly through inane social media platforms?

In his book *Neuropolitique* Timothy Leary notes how, "The charismatic, self-appointed Voice of God appears on the television screen skillfully producing an altered state of consciousness, seducing the audience into classic voodoo trances. Inciting in hypnotized brains fierce religious-tribal fanaticisms." Elsewhere in the book, he writes, "Brainwashing is happening to all of us all of the time. Knowledge of brain function is our only protection against it. The solutions to our predicament are neurological. We must assume responsibility for our nervous systems."

Indeed, we must.

Neuroscientists today speak of left brain / right brain activities and the consensus is that each hemisphere of the brain has certain processing capabilities which are dominant. The left brain primarily works with linear information and logic, while the right brain is spatially oriented and processes information in a more holistic fashion. This is not an absolute division, however, and studies show that the prefrontal cortex, where most of our day-to-day thinking takes place, certainly draws from both hemispheres.

Emotional intelligence, meanwhile, is an area of knowledge that gets almost no attention in our educational systems, and this may be a greater problem still. If children were to learn about the "molecules of emotion" and how to control them via mindfulness and meditation, the world would likely be a much more peaceful and harmonious place. If children learned the power of cooperation over competition on a global scale, we might possibly never have violence or war.

Meditation offers the most direct way in which to access higher brain wave states which are conducive to holistic thinking and the control of our emotions. Such states can result in increased creativity and insights of a magnitude that are sometimes so profound in scope that they are life changing.

Beta is the brain wave of our ordinary, everyday mind in which we communicate with one another. It is a necessary state for societies to function. To access no other states, however, can eventually drive a person into a life that is brimming with mental stress and multiple problems of a physical nature. This is why meditation is so important. It allows a person to cultivate states of mind which help one overcome problems related to mental and physical forms of stress and it can even relieve disease.

The alpha wave, in contrast, is slower in frequency and it tends to give a person significant relief from the incessant mind chatter that goes with the beta brain wave. Beta can make one feel nervous and irritable, whereas alpha can calm the nerves. It can result in feelings of peace and tranquility and allow rationality to prevail over emotional turmoil.

A deeper state, one beyond alpha, is called theta and reaching it results in experiencing slower brain waves still. While the delta brain wave is the slowest of all, resulting in sleep (and unconsciousness), theta is known for generating access to a twilight state that exists between the conscious and unconscious realms, where a greatly expanded mental state can be known; one associated with healing and transcendence.

One might call this greatly expanded mental state "nonlocal mind" or "mind at large", for it is here that all minds have their source and continue to be connected throughout life. Jung called this mental realm the "collective unconscious" (which means that our most common mental brain wave state – beta – could rightly be labelled "collective consciousness").

Mind at large – MAL – is a level of mind that can be characterized as oceanic in scope, while the unit of consciousness we humans usually experience via the beta brain wave state can be likened to but a single drop in that ocean.

One cannot access MAL, however, without reaching deep states of consciousness that are only available in meditative repose. To meditate is to cultivate access to MAL.

What may be experienced when one *does* access MAL are expanded levels of insight into one's personal life and life in general. The answers to important questions or creative resolutions often emerge from entering this mental state. Many scientists and artists attest to the reality of MAL. (Poets famously refer to this state of mind as accessing the "muse".)

The important thing about experiencing MAL is that it allows one to be aware of, and experience, a reality of significantly vaster proportions than the one we experience in our mundane, everyday world.

When one accesses MAL on a regular basis, one's worldview begins to change for the better. The sense of oneness with "all that is" comes naturally to the fore via theta brain waves. When one reaches this state of mind, over and again, one may even find oneself sensing the kind of subtle, eternal, infinite attributes that go with the concept of God, or the Tao, the Akasha, the Pneuma, the Ka, the Great Spirit, the Cosmic Mind or the Matrix. (However one wishes to characterize it.)

The ultimate, elevated perspective, perhaps, is the state known as gamma and it is at the opposite end of the scale from delta, for gamma brain waves are the fastest of all. Gamma, however, is believed to perform an integrative function, to process information from all of the regions of the brain. When one considers that we experience millions, billions and trillions of bits of stimuli on a daily basis, it is easy to recognize the importance of such an integrative function.

The vital point here is that absolutely anyone can learn how to access MAL and that it can be done easier than most people imagine. Even ten or fifteen minutes of meditation in the morning can start the process. Simply take a comfortable seat and let go of all thoughts, while taking deep breaths in and out. Thoughts will spring into the mind unbidden, but one should simply ignore them and focus on sensing the energy that can be felt flowing through the body and filling every fiber of one's being in every cell of which one is physically composed.

MAL is on offer to everyone in this way and it infuses all of us, whether we know it or not.

Accessing it on a regular basis eventually results in experiencing moments of supraconscious insight, which may sound very uppity, overstated or unreal, but to wade into even the shallowest waters of the oceanic mind is to sense the potential that is there.

Take no one's word for it, though. Each of us is free to seek it out for ourselves and prove its existence to our own liking. We are free to take back the hijacked mind we have had stolen from us by those who have forced their views and thinking on us over the years, especially when we were young and vulnerable. To do so can and will invariably alter one's life for the better, for there is magic to be found in MAL. After all, MAL is the field of energy that organizes absolutely everything in the universe, which means that it is the ultimate miracle in and of itself.

# 9

# Blood on the Tracks

## *Dylan's Powerful Lyrics & His Electrifying Impact on All of Humanity*

BOB DYLAN'S GENIUS is something that never ceases to mesmerize me and not only when I play his recordings and grow inspired beyond all measure by the profound depth of his lyrics, but even when I am not playing his records. Dylan is in my heart now like some supreme western guru who is head and shoulders above everyone else, even those who are considered the wisest in our culture.

Dylan famously balked at being called "the spokesman of his generation", for he knew damn well that he was more than that: he was and is the embodiment of the conscience of Western civilization.

This, too, I suspect is a perception that he would, likewise reject, for Dylan is such a bright, "freewheelin'" soul that he has, over the decades, simply refused to be burdened with the expectations of his fans. His sole goal is to make music and let his music speak for him. He certainly did not want to be leading movements and shouting his objections about injustice over megaphones and microphones when he was young. His songs spoke of civil rights and the unconscionable nature of war. He wanted only to be left to his own devices to pursue his artistic visions. He wanted to write lyrics that rang out like poetry and to make music that possessed, what he called, "that wild mercury sound". (No substance on earth is more slippery and difficult to contain than mercury, a substance also known as quicksilver!)

Dylan wasn't a politician, after all. He was just a pure-hearted singer of the soul. He was a minstrel, and he still is.

Rolling Stone magazine in the first decade of the 21st century named Dylan's song "Like A Rolling Stone" number 1 of the 500 Greatest Songs of All Time.

That was no small deal. When we think of all the incredible songs that have moved us over the years and this one tops them all, that is a stunning achievement.

Dylan, with a canon of hundreds of songs, agreed in one interview that "Like A Rolling Stone" is indeed his best of all time. The magazine acclaimed its "revolutionary design and execution" and explained that the song received its initial start when one of Dylan's closest of friends at the time asked him to sing a verse from "Lost Highway" by Hank Williams, a tune which broods with grave agony about the trials and tribulations of being a rolling stone and living a life of sin. Dylan put precisely that kind of grit and pain into the singing of his own song and, at just 24 years of age, it was a phenomenal feat.

One of the greatest rock 'n' roll bands ever, The Rolling Stones, had already been down that rogue highway, as well, and were deep into the blues at their inception. However, when they chose their name, they took it from a composition by the Hoochie Coochie Man himself, Muddy Waters, a song called, "Rollin' Stone".

Perhaps, then, no other title better suits what "rock" music is all about than the idea of being out on the road, daring to break free, seeing the world on one's own terms and taking one's chances. To do that one had to become a "rolling stone" oneself.

As someone who hit the highway at a very young age myself, I could relate to all of that and I fairly exulted in being a rogue of the road with destination unknown for quite a number of years.

Dylan, of course, inspired the band The Byrds to take up his songs and electrify them. Their first major hit was "Mr. Tambourine Man". The jangling 12 string guitar of Jim McGuinn perfectly captured what soon became known as Folk Rock.

One of the most magical and exhilarating moments in all of rock history followed a few years later. It was when Jimi Hendrix recorded Dylan's "All Along the Watchtower". His version is so incendiary and sizzling, so absolutely apocalyptic and moving, that I still get goosebumps when I hear it, especially when I listen to those lines about not talking falsely now and how the hour is getting late.

The hour is indeed getting late; now more so than ever.

The guitar solo in the middle of that tune, by the way, is one of the most hair-raising, breath-taking, electrifying virtuoso performances ever recorded and when Hendrix lets blast with the final lines of the song, the attentive listener cannot but explode from the thunderous power and fury of the recording. "All Along the Watchtower" is Dylan at his most prophetic best. The only thing that could have made the song even more staggering would have been if Dylan had had the "Four Horsemen of the Apocalypse" approaching the figure in the watchtower instead of just two unnamed riders.

One of my personal favorite Dylan albums is *Blood on the Tracks*, which arrived in the early Seventies. It is a very different kind of record. The title, in my opinion, is the most revelatory in the entire history of rock music. It perfectly captures truth in two ways: as we all know, a song on any album is called a "track" and we also know that it is a wounded animal in the wild that leaves blood on its own tracks, especially as it laboriously drags itself off in an effort to flee from whatever predator has inflicted the damage and wants to kill it. (Usually a human being nowadays, unfortunately, with a high-powered rifle.) The animal, of course, seeks to save its own skin.

Dylan was a very wounded man during that particular time frame, it seems, for he had just gotten divorced from his wife, Sara, and he was hurting. He was hurting badly.

We're all wounded likewise at one time or another in our

lives. After all, each of us suffers the vicissitudes of this world to some degree and that means that we all have blood on our own tracks in one way or another. No life is perfect, not even those of the rich and the famous. Obviously, some people suffer more than others, but I can personally identify with many of the emotions behind Dylan's rage and hurt on that album, for I've been down that dark road myself. I know the pain, I know the agony. It makes one feel as if a colossal stone has rolled over you; and not just a stone, but a big, bone breaking boulder that leaves you in a bloody heap.

So, yes, once you pick yourself up and hobble off, there is blood on the tracks. Oh, indeed, there is blood on the tracks.

And maybe that's good. Consider the wise words of Rumi in this regard: "You have to keep breaking your heart until it opens," he said. As for Dylan, he was acutely aware of the pain and suffering of much of humanity from his very earliest days as a singer and a songwriter. He was extremely socially aware and had great empathy for ethnic minorities and the downtrodden and the poor. His feelings always ran deep and that is why he created such arresting music. He sang from the soul. He drew his lyrics from the deep wellspring of his heart and fell easily into the role of folk singer. He especially excelled at writing "protest" or "anti-war" songs and fighting for civil rights.

Dylan was just 20 when he wrote "Blowin' in the Wind" and just 22 years of age when Peter, Paul and Mary made a hit of the tune in 1963. To name just a few of the follow ups to that now iconic tune, we have "The Times They Are A-Changin'", "Masters of War", "The Lonesome Death of Hattie Carroll" and "A Hard Rain's A-Gonna Fall".

Sheer genius. (Even The Beatles at the absolute height of their global fame were infatuated with, and in awe of, Dylan. He was virtually the only musician the band members put above themselves.)

Robert Zimmerman was born the son of a Jewish couple

living in Hibbing, Minnesota. His father was an appliance salesman and his mother a stay-at-home mom. "Dylan", in stark contrast, was born of the Higher Self of Robert Zimmerman, which is why Dylan in his early years told tale after tale about where he was from and made-up countless stories about all that had happened to him in his travels on the road. All of it was pure fiction, but in the songs he sang, those road tales sprang to life and they were made real. Through his songs, Bob Dylan as a person became as true as the road itself. Such is the power of myth, for in effect, "Bob Dylan" is a myth and will always be a myth. He is a totally archetypal figure and a giant among humankind for that very reason. One of the things that he proved was that mythologizing one's own life is both liberating and illuminating, for the mythic dimension is rooted in the realm where the deepest patterns of psychic functioning reside. The archetypes are the root patterns of our instinctive behavior and are imbued with a collective level of consciousness. This serves us, essentially, in the guise of our "Higher Self".

We can't all have Dylan's talent, of course, and 99% of us certainly do not, but we can still mythologize our own lives and discover the archetypal powers that impel us toward the horizons to which we are driven. We are all the embodiments of soul, after all, but Dylan is overtly that. He is never anything less. Bono of U2, after visiting Dylan in his hotel room one time, said something to the effect that, "Yes, Dylan is great, but the trouble with him is that he just can't get over being Bob Dylan."

No, he cannot, and he does not apologize for that. He is a genius, and he knows it. He has every right to be proud and secure in that role. After all, he won an Academy Award for best original song in a film in 2001 ("Things Have Changed"); a "special citation" by the Pulitzer Prize Board in 2008 for his impact on popular music; the Presidential Medal of Freedom from Barack Obama in 2012 and the Nobel Prize for literature in 2016. He has won ten Grammys, a Golden Globe, been inducted into the Rock and Roll Hall of Fame and sold over 100 million records, which makes him one of the best-selling music artists of all-time.

Yes, he is the quintessential rolling stone with his "Never-ending tour" and, yes, he has blood on his tracks, but Dylan helps us all heal as we look back on our own tracks and see the blood that is there. And, yes, every drop has a story behind it and every story has a huge soulful mix of average, ordinary people living out their lives with one another. We are all in this life together, after all, and none of us is, in all reality, "just" an average, ordinary Joe Blow or Jane Doe of no high worth. Furthermore, none of those who think themselves so superior to others is quite as God-like as he or she might imagine.

Dylan lifts us up when we are down, and he is well able to rip us apart when we get uppity about ourselves. If we listen closely to Dylan's lyrics, we will be made to feel every emotion known to humanity. We will learn what matters in this world and, conversely, what counts for little or nothing at all. Dylan keeps us bonded to our past and to the actions of our ancestors, while pointing the way to a future that carries justice for all and equality under the law.

Dylan never wanted to be called the "spokesman of his generation", nor did he want to be the "conscience of America", which is what he was called when he received an honorary doctorate from Princeton University in 1970. Apparently, he winced and grimaced at the accolade. Nor, I suspect, does he want to be called what I dared to call him at the start of this essay, "the conscience of humanity". And yet Dylan knows why people say these things. He's just humble about it, I believe, while secretly knowing how true it is. In the end, he wants only to let his music speak for him and to be left in peace to pursue his art.

We should all be left in peace, likewise, to pursue the art of our own lives. To live with the integrity of Dylan we need to keep a close watch, as our lives unfold, on our own consciences.

So, yes, take me for a trip upon your magic swirling ship, forever and anon, Mr. Tambourine Man. I, too, am ready to go anywhere with you, so do cast your dancing spell my way. I promise to go under it.

# 10

# On Becoming the Spiritual "Superman" of Our Dreams

NEAR-DEATH RETURNEES almost invariably say that a number of things happen to a person when he or she dies. For starters, the mind essence of the person goes traveling at great speed through a long dark tunnel with full awareness of the flight. Eventually, however, the person sees a fantastically brilliant light ahead of them. When the disembodied consciousness of the person exits that tunnel into the light, he or she finds a beautiful paradise of sorts and is often met by previously deceased family members or friends who welcome them. After a sort of orientation phase, the person sometimes may meet a "Being of Light" who is full of love and great warmth and speaks to them in some telepathic way which proves extremely reassuring.

Quite often, what follows after that is that the person then experiences a life review. In that review the person not only sees and experiences virtually everything that happened to them over the course of their life, but they are also forced to experience how they made *others* feel – profoundly, deeply and fully.

This turns out to be massively important for the individual.

The pleasure we have given, the pain we have caused, comes back to us as a firsthand experience. It comes back to please us, or haunt us, during that life review and apparently that experience can be almost unbearably excruciating in scope when it actually occurs.

Imagine if you were a torturer, for example. Imagine if you were the *cruelest* of torturers... Imagine if you caused death to come slow and horrible to those who fell into your clutches with blood flying all over the place, with screams, tears and unspeakable suffering following on, as a direct result of your actions...

Now back it off a few degrees and imagine that you were just a little bit cruel, a little bit mean to someone. Or imagine that you were a tiny bit selfish, greedy or nasty, that you were a bit of a betrayer, a bit of a rat or a venomous viper who spit forth caustic rumors about those to whom you pretended to be a friend...

It actually hurts just to think about it, does it not?

It does me.

Which is why I try to stay vigilant of my every thought, word and deed. I try to do the right thing, the kind thing, the thing that helps and hopefully doesn't hurt. After all, what we do comes back to us. As we sow, we reap in this life and, apparently, this is true, too, in the next.

My personal favorite recounting of an NDE is by a man named Mellen-Thomas Benedict. His thoroughly intriguing account may be found on the internet under his name or, as happened for me, in a book entitled, *The Near-Death Experience, a reader*, by Lee W. Bailey and Jenny Yates. (Kenneth Ring also tells his story in his book *Lessons from the Light*.) Benedict's account is entitled, *Through the Light and Beyond*. It is one of the most positive, inspiring and fantastic narratives I have ever read and definitely beyond anything I ever imagined. He says that "It seemed as if all the creations in the Universe soared by me and vanished in a speck of light" during his time in the Great Beyond. He experienced the Christian Heaven, the Happy Hunting Ground of the Native Americans, the unspeakably majestic, magnificent Egyptian realm of transcendental bliss and many, many others. All are relative to a particular group mind, he reports, coupled with a collective belief system. He also says that the individual viewpoint that each person inexorably brings to that collective perspective has an effect on what is experienced. In "truth", we are all immortal beings, he insists, and that the "Ultimate

Godhead does not care" which religion we choose. He tells us that, "This body, that you are in, has been alive *forever*. It comes from an unending stream of life, going back to the Big Bang and beyond. This body gives life to the next life, in dense and subtle energy" and so on.

So it goes, in other words. We reincarnate again and again, going from dense, material realms into subtle, immaterial ones and back again. When we finally, fully understand this, he makes clear, the soul is set free. That is because one ceases to worry about anything because one knows the ultimate secret: we are immortal beings and no matter what occurs, we live on. He insists that he now loves every problem that humanity faces from climate change to nuclear war because these are simply spiritual challenges and, above all, because he is no longer afraid of death.

To my way of thinking, this is clearly a form of what is called "the Great Liberation" one hears about in religions such as Buddhism and Hinduism. It may also be what is known as "Salvation" in the West, though one would immediately need to qualify the term in a non-denominational sense, but surely those who live by this concept would doubtless agree that "true salvation" must bring one, at last, to spiritual immortality.

Benedict's account inspired me to think that like the "Ultimate Godhead" itself, we should all seek to reach a point in our lives where we do not care which religion anyone chooses. All religions are culturally relative institutions and each provides a platform for the *pursuit* of truth, but none *own* truth in some exclusive fashion.

In the end, Benedict states, all religious doctrines and dogmas must be transcended if one is to go beyond the relative to the genuinely universal. I have read this same message in numerous accounts by those who have made a similar journey of their own. The voluminous works of researchers such as doctors Raymond Moody, Elisabeth Kübler-Ross, Kenneth Ring and Ian Stevenson are full of such accounts. Also, well worth reading is what the neurosurgeon Dr Eben Alexander reports in his book, *Proof of Heaven*. An exceptionally concise overview of the phenomenon may be found in Professor David Fontana's book *Life Beyond Death*.

The truth that sets the soul free, then, is the one that comes with knowing, *really knowing*, that death is not the end of our existence. In that knowledge there is comfort and a level of certainty that allows one to overcome the biggest fear of all: that of dying and leaving behind the only world any of us have seemingly known.

However, as the proverbial saying goes, when one door closes, another opens. In this case, that door might well be a portal into another dimension. What that might mean for each of us is that there are an infinite number of experiences yet to come. What an exciting prospect! What a phenomenal measure of hope this concept brings to the open-minded souls among us.

Doing the right thing in this life, by the way, isn't just about what we can get out of the experience personally. We have to understand that our actions contribute to the physical, mental and emotional state of humanity as a whole. To do our part, to act in the interests of others, to lead by example where others, especially children, are concerned, contributes to the collective mindset of humanity. That, in turn, helps to make humanity a wiser and kinder species.

In the last analysis, I think that spirituality is more about compassion and love than it is about doing what some religious authority tells us to do. I personally do not subscribe to the idea of "defending" a faith or dying a martyr for certain suppositions and doctrines that have been handed down from a previous age. If something is true, then it is true whether any of us "believe" it or not. We should not have to fight over the veracity of a religious proclamation based on someone's subjective revelation from long ago. As Deepak Chopra once put it, "Religion is belief in someone else's experience. Spirituality is having your own experience."

In my opinion, taking hand-me-down beliefs as "indisputably true" is, unfortunately, a recipe for delusion.

The way out of delusion is by thinking things through for oneself, by making a moral or ethical judgment and then acting accordingly.

It is not difficult to figure out what the right thing to do is. One simply needs to follow the Golden Rule. "Do unto others as you would have them do to you."

In *The Tibetan Book of Living and Dying*, the lama Sogyal Rinpoche explains that those who wish to be enlightened like the Buddha should keep things in the right perspective. "Spiritual truth is not something elaborate and esoteric, it is in fact profound common sense. When you realize the nature of mind, layers of confusion peel away. You don't actually 'become' a Buddha," he writes, "you simply cease, slowly, to be deluded. And being a Buddha is not being some omnipotent spiritual superman but becoming at last a true human being."

Buddha himself, according to a talk I heard the Dalai Lama give once in San Francisco, was adamant that each of us should seek "individual liberation", or self-liberation, by our own hand, not through some organization. Each individual, he said, should create his or her own positive future. To do that, however, requires self-discipline and mindfulness of one's own impermanence. Death is the ultimate motivator in that regard.

This is wise advice. If we ignore our spirituality because we think it is something so beyond us that we can do little more than pay lip service to it once a week or so, then we need to realize that we are already in the throes of a delusion.

Becoming enlightened, saintly or wise is an impossibility for no one. After all, "The kingdom of God is within," as it says in the Bible (Luke 17:21). So is the "buddha nature." So, too, is the "Tao", the "Akasha", the "Pneuma", the "Great Spirit", the

"Cosmic Mind", the "Matrix" and the "Zero Point Field".

We have it all because we *are* it all. We are one with all that exists and to get in touch with one's spiritual essence is simpler than we suppose. Notice your breath, the beating of your heart, the clarity of your mind. None of us is consciously controlling these things. They are inherent to our very nature.

Thoughts, likewise, generally come to us unbidden, but we can control what thoughts we heed and to which we feed energy or ignore. We can also control what we say to others and what we do. To do the right thing, simply consult your own inner guru, your conscience.

To do these things well is to live and die in peace.

As the famous Tibetan sage Milarepa once stated: "My religion is to live – and die – without regret."

To do so means that one may enjoy one's life review with a clear conscience and, from a human perspective, that is a magnificent achievement, one clearly founded on a lifetime spent making wise decisions. It can be such an astounding and spectacular achievement, in fact, that it might even transform one into becoming a true "super" being.

And maybe, just maybe, by cultivating wisdom and dying without regret, one can become a "Being of Light" oneself in the next world!

Anything is possible.

To chance even the idea of it is already the beginning of wisdom.

# 11

# Bohemian Blasphemy

## *The Holy Goof's Haunt of Hipsters, Tricksters & Visionary Shapeshifters*

THE WRITINGS OF THE BEATS – Jack Kerouac, Allen Ginsberg, William S Burroughs, Neal Cassady, Gary Snyder, Gregory Corso, Lawrence Ferlinghetti, Michael McClure, et al – not to mention other certain highly influential visionary metaphysical literary rebels – came to me via a cool, tough cowboy free soul named Lauren Bowker. The year we met was 1973 and that meeting occurred in Las Vegas of all places. I had wound up in the city thanks to a friend of mine from Ohio who had temporarily dropped out of college with me for a semester to travel. I bought a van, made it habitable and then the two of us took off. We travelled to the Rockies and went roaming about for a time, then headed south to the Grand Canyon. We eventually pressed on to Los Angeles before following Highway 1 through Santa Barbara, Malibu, Big Sur and onward to San Francisco. After a short adventure at Lake Tahoe and in the Sierra Nevada mountains, we eventually ended up in Las Vegas purely because my companion had family there and wanted to visit with them.

Once there, however, my companion was almost immediately summoned to return to Ohio. His father needed his help with starting a new business venture. Fortunately for me, my friend's relations in Las Vegas were in a position to help with getting me into a construction workers' union so that I could begin earning money again as I was close to broke by that point. (As it happened, my friend's uncle was the entertainment director for a major Las Vegas hotel and, before my friend left, the kindly man treated the two of us to premium tickets for a performance by the King of Rock & Roll himself, Elvis Presley, who was still, I am pleased to say, in top notch form at the time. Quite amusingly, from my perspective anyway, Elvis was wearing his famous white jumpsuit with its big collar and studs, and that massive, decorated belt he can be seen wearing in so many photos at the time. The King at that point, by the way, was fairly fresh from barely missing out on a number 1 record on Billboard's Top 100 with his song *Burning Love,* which peaked at number 3. Ironically, the song that was at the top of the charts at that time was Chuck Berry's most juvenile and tasteless of tunes, *My Ding-a-Ling*.)

Once in the construction workers' union, like everyone else, I was told to report to the labor hall every morning to await an assignment. Eventually, I would be sent to work on the MGM Grand Hotel then under construction on the famous Strip, but before I received that assignment, I sat for many a morning awaiting my call.

It was on the very first morning, however, that I met Lauren. He had noticed that I was reading a book entitled *Wisdom of the Mystic Masters* by Joseph Weed and had grown intrigued. At once, he wanted to know if I read many books like that and went on to talk at length about his own literary interests. He quickly proved to be a passionate source of riveting information on many a topic, most especially the Beat writers. His personal hero was Neal Cassady who came to fame via Kerouac's most acclaimed work, *On the Road*. In that book, Cassady was called Dean Moriarty and he was also known as the "Holy Goof" on those pages. Lauren was so taken with the character and in such a fun way that I began calling him the "Holy Spoof". There is simply no way to convey the full extent of all that the two of us got up to in those years, but we eventually quit our jobs and journeyed northward through California, Oregon, Washington, British Columbia, the Yukon and into Alaska. We finally ended up on Kodiak Island where we worked on fishing boats and in a cannery specializing in the giant king crab industry for which Kodiak is best known. We tracked bear in the wilderness for fun and, at the end of the summer, we drove back down through Canada to Wyoming and spent time in Yellowstone National Park, as well as exploring the Snake River area and the unbelievably beautiful wilderness that surrounds the range of mountains that include the majestic Grand Teton peak before returning to Las Vegas.

We were free flying in those days and under the spell, not only of Kerouac, but of Ginsberg and Burroughs, as well, both of whom were exceptionally graphic as writers (to say the least) with their lurid, libertine amusements. Their pages were filled with tales of manic sexual activities, all night partying and drug-fueled epiphanies, which seemed to us to be exciting beyond measure. Like young people everywhere, we were hungry for thrills and sought to do whatever we liked without restraint, the same as the Bohemian outlaws we were reading about. The writings of these figures were made even more lurid by virtue of being connected to various and sundry underworld figures and to criminal narcotics cartels. Encountering Burroughs' notorious and hilarious book *Naked Lunch* had me in stitches from the beginning to the end and its surreal style was akin to pure literary anarchy in my mind. Rules be damned, it seemed; just say what you like any which way you want. Such an attitude had an incalculable influence on me as a budding writer. Here was freedom of expression as I had never before known it and, just to say, nothing stirs the imagination of a wild young buck more than the idea of forbidden knowledge and taboo curiosities.

Burroughs' motto was madly intriguing in that regard, for he happened to have a particular liking for a man named Hassan-i Sabbah, a Persian religious and political agitator from the eleventh century known as the Old Man of the Mountain.

Sabbah had founded the Ismaili state and its military group, the Order of the Assassins. Young men had been enticed to join his mercenary squad, legend has it, by being given copious amounts of hashish and the occasional secret liaison with a woman of the night. So pleasurable was life in the service of the Old Man, apparently, that these young recruits were easily transformed into heartless killers and did Sabbah's bidding without hesitation. (Quite interestingly, the word "assassin" is actually derived from a translation of the word "hashishim".) The reason Burroughs was so mesmerized by this crafty provocateur is that he had a saying that the writer absolutely loved and lived by. That motto was: "Nothing is true. Everything is permitted."

Could there possibly be a more liberating free pass to do whatever the hell one pleased? This attitude also went handily and perfectly with Aleister Crowley's notorious dictum that "Do what thou wilt shall be the whole of the law."

The Beats did just that. They flouted every convention that American society had locked in over the course of the first half of the 20th century. Two world wars alone were excuse enough to thumb their noses at those who claimed moral authority, while lining their own pockets and stealing an unfair share of the resources at their disposal.

My newfound friend, fortunately, wasn't simply into the Beats, however. He was also a big reader of what one might call "New Age" philosopher-metaphysicians, writers such as Alan Watts, Aldous Huxley and Timothy Leary, as well as the man we both considered to be the most important psychoanalyst of all time, Dr Carl Gustav Jung. Also of note at that time was an anthropologist named Carlos Castaneda whose alleged exploits with a "Yaqui sorcerer" named Don Juan Matus were mesmerizing tens of thousands of young people like ourselves with his "tales of power". Castaneda was not the only one to mesmerize us, however. We enthusiastically opened up to, not only "exotic" Eastern religions such as Yoga and Zen, but to the Dark Arts of the West with their occult magic and spooky, psychic mystery.

Both Castaneda and Leary were well-known purveyors at the time of psychedelic substances, most especially cannabis, hashish, LSD, mescaline, peyote and magic mushrooms. Such substances were said to be "entheogenic", for according to these writers these substances are able to engender mystical states of mind which can sometimes bring one directly into contact with "God", "cosmic consciousness" or entities existing in other dimensions entirely, some of which are good and some of which are decidedly indifferent or even inimical to humanity's presence or concerns.

Timothy Leary, to his credit, rather than trafficking in the occult, reimagined the *Tibetan Book of the Dead* in terms of the psychedelic, visionary insights he had personally experienced, and he promoted the use of these substances to become more spiritually illuminated. As many are no doubt aware, he was known as the High Priest of LSD in those days. The times being what they were, Lauren and I found ourselves curious. Much was learned; especially how such substances can indeed bring about a state of visionary ecstasy or can, if the circumstances turn out to be in any way less than ideal (and paranoia sets in), propel one down into one of the pernicious pits of hell. In the latter case, in other words, if one's "trip" happened to go askew, it could and did often get quite brutal.

In retrospect, I agree with any number of highly respected writers, philosophers and metaphysicians that entheogens are not for those who are not intellectually and emotionally mature enough to deal with the intense experiences which can result from indulging in them. That they can offer mind-blowing insights into the nature of consciousness and reality is genuine, however, but only instructive for those who have been seeking knowledge of a higher disposition in the first place and are well-versed in phenomena of a sublime nature.

Back in those years, however, there was a lot of talk going around that one could become enlightened simply by smoking or ingesting such substances. The two of us found that possibility nothing short of enthralling and, therefore, tempting.

While many use "drugs" for escapist purposes or a mere thrill, the one who partakes of entheogens as a sacramental pursuit does so for a very different purpose; not to escape, but to discover if the "divine" is for real and to enjoy a direct experience of it.

Another writer who was to have a great influence on us a few short years later was Robert Anton Wilson. His most famous work at that time was his and Robert Shea's *Illuminatus!* trilogy, which is a tale so huge and maddening that it includes every form of conspiracy the two men could include or concoct.

My personal all-time favorite book of Wilson's, however, was soon to make its way into my life. Titled *Cosmic Trigger*, this work proved to be a mindblower. It was flush with tales of the Illuminati, "the murder of Christ", the tortures of the Inquisition, the mysteries of the Masons, of Witchcraft, Sorcery and Magick. It had reams about Aleister Crowley, Uri Geller, puzzling messages from the dead, anecdotes of contact with Babylonian and Egyptian gods, multiple accounts of dazzling psychic weirdness, including interstellar ESP with an alleged entity from Sirius and, on top of all of that, something called "Operation Mindfuck".

That wasn't all. This tome stunned and shocked us with so many wild yarns that it proved difficult to keep track of them all. Only it wasn't just yarns that filled the book. Wilson was able to deeply explicate upon the rudiments of quantum physics, offer erudite insights into "reality tunnels" and "the prospect of immortality", dare to postulate a connection between "dope and divinity", not to mention speculate tirelessly on historical conspiracies and their continued existence today in the form of the Powers That Be.

In short, *Cosmic Trigger* messed with one's head in too many ways to count. It was the most mind-bending, enchanting and thoroughly riveting book I had ever read.

Little did I know in those years, nor even suspect, that Robert Anton Wilson would one day write an extensive introduction to my first novel, *The Dream Illuminati,* which was published by Falcon Press in 1988 and contribute another extensive introduction to my second novel, *The Illuminati of Immortality,* published in 1990.

To me, Leary and RAW, both Falcon Press authors, were entheogenic giants. They were brilliant writers whose ideas were radically daring, beautifully illuminating and fearlessly liberating. Both men slammed the notion that an individual should be a "good little conformist" and fall into line when "leaders" of a dubious character demand that one do so. I am referring, of course, to government officials who insist that one should do his or her "patriotic duty" and go off to fight and kill members of our own species in a country elsewhere on the planet and do so in the so-called name of "national security" and the "national interest".

This was precisely what was going on at that time and that particular "other country" happened to be Vietnam. In short, if one agreed, when told to do one's "duty" by those holding positions of "authority" one was considered a "patriot". If one lived through such a brutal adventure and actually survived the horrors there and subsequently came home from the war in relatively good shape, one was then expected to get a job, a mate and make a home like everyone else. This was considered the ultimate trajectory of the ideal citizen.

All of this was precisely what we rebelled against, if rebels we were in those years. We simply did not want to conform with this menacing and often deadly expectation just so we could pay taxes and let the elites do as they wished with the millions of dollars we gave them. Conformists are meant to say nothing, to make no waves, to live and die like worker ants and fill what RAW called the "hive economy"; that is, unless one happens to be clever enough to end up rich oneself and thus buy one's way into the stratosphere of the elites, by which I mean those who control the banks, the military and the intelligence agencies, the factories and the corporations of this world.

The counterculture of the day rebelled against all of that with a vengeance. As a result, we did as we pleased and we went rogue on the "Establishment". We did what Timothy Leary recommended. We "tuned in, turned on and dropped out." Above all, we went off traveling and, fortunately for many of us, we eventually learned that "The road of excess" does indeed lead "to the palace of wisdom," as the poet-mystic William Blake once stated in unequivocable terms. (It may take decades to arrive in that palace, but eventually one will if one eventually comes to understand that those who are "born to be wild" are also born to be wise.)

I did return to college to obtain my undergraduate Arts degree after a time and I fell into line to a great extent, for I am no anarchist and never have been. By then, though, the die was cast. I realized that I was a libertine rebel at heart and wanted nothing more than to be a free thinker and become a writer like my literary heroes. To remain at my healthiest, sometime in my thirties, I gave up smoking or ingesting any and all entheogenic substances, for by then I was an avid meditator and found meditation to be the best way to get in touch with "God", the "Divine" or the "Universal Mind" (whatever one wishes to call it). As Alan Watts once said of psychoactive substances, "Once you get the message, hang up the phone." That is what I did.

I was later to meet both Robert Anton Wilson and Timothy Leary in person. I even had the pleasure of spending a long weekend in the presence of Tim, who was a total legend by then. The year was 1988 and the venue was the Los Angeles Book Fair. By that point in his life, Tim was huge into computers and, as a result, he was especially mad about the work of William Gibson, who had just released his fourth book, *Mona Lisa Overdrive*. Gibson's most celebrated claim to fame, however, was his first novel, *Neuromancer*, from which came the notion of "cyberspace" and adventuring into "virtual realities".

I had assumed that once Gibson arrived at our booth, we would all be standing around talking megabytes and data, but Gibson had a young lady in tow with him at that particular moment and she easily stole all of the attention for herself with her purple hair, her brash charm and her outlandish commentaries on everything. Gibson, who was the hottest young writer on the planet at the time, said almost nothing while he was with us, but Tim, as ever, was his usual charismatic self and carried us all away with his boundless enthusiasm and wicked sense of humor.

That weekend, with the release of my first novel, *The Dream Illuminati,* stands today as one of the most exhilarating and fulfilling episodes of my life. I had much to learn yet, however, and to be blunt about it, I was not nearly as enlightened, nor as accomplished a writer as I thought I was. Still, that is the way of youth. Youth thinks itself invincible and perfect for the simple reason that that is how one *feels* when one is young and full of life. It is only after stumbling and making many a mistake that one finds out otherwise, which is good really, for it allows us to grow in wisdom and compassion.

Little did I know back then that I would still be making every effort to grow in wisdom and compassion almost half a century later, but such is life. Time may seem to be the enemy, but in truth it is a friend, for as Dietrich Bonhoeffer once wrote, "To *understand* reality is not the same as to know about outward events. It is to perceive the essential nature of things." One cannot become wise unless one sees into the essential nature of things with a clear mind, unless one gets well past all of the chaos and delusion that exists in this world. To quote another great line from *Crazy Wisdom*, by Wes "Scoop" Nisker: "Crazy wisdom sees that we live in a world of many illusions, that the Emperor has no clothes, and that much of human belief and behavior is ritualized nonsense."

Nonsense, indeed. The Holy Goof could not have said it better himself.

If nothing else, though, nonsense keeps us laughing and that is stupendously important too. Laughter is what keeps us young at heart and vibrant of mind. Laughter is what makes life worth living, even as we suffer the slings and arrows of the multitudinous vicissitudes of this world. In the wise words of the late Dr Christopher S Hyatt, founder of Falcon Press and prolific author in his own right, "We are all on the front lines of life and death. Take it very seriously... But don't forget to laugh, lest you miss the point."

Indeed, tune in, turn on, transcend.

# 12

# Altered Realities, Secret Spells & the Golden Dawn

KNEELING LIKE A KNIGHT before the Great Magus, my head humbly bowed, I could see – out the corner of my eye – the long silver ceremonial sword as it swept soundlessly upward, then came down with gleaming perfection to alight upon my shoulder.

As the initiation ceremony proceeded, I found myself listening quite intensely to the mighty master of all things *esoteric,* Doctor Christopher S Hyatt, as he chanted his ancient spells, his voice deep and grave, his powerful words entirely sincere, though fortuitously, summoned in the name of Liberation and Enlightenment, not in the name of any particular entity of darkness or evil.

No, indeed, it was no demon that Hyatt called upon that day to bless me upon my initiation into the Order, but his own Holy Guardian Angel, and I was thus dubbed an Honorary Magician of the Hermetic Order of the Golden Dawn.

This highly respected, but seriously mysterious, "magickal" order was founded in the 1800s and once counted among its more influential members the so-called "Wickedest Man in the World", Aleister Crowley. Also known as the Great Beast or the Beast 666, Crowley had come to the order with links to virtually every known occultist of the day, including Madame Blavatsky and her Theosophical Society, not to mention other secret groups such as the Order of the Oriental Templars and the Argenteum Astrum. Crowley was as controversial a figure as the world had, or has, ever known.

In fact, Crowley reveled in his notoriety and loved to shock people. Many called him a Satanist, but he always insisted that

that was quite impossible. Why? Because he did not believe that Satan actually existed, nor did he think that "God" as the Judeo-Christian tradition conceived "Him" was on the money either. In any case, he pursued extremes at every opportunity, usually making a great show of himself. "Do what thou wilt shall be the whole of the law," was his motto. In brief, Crowley was a man who lived large in every way. If people were put off by him, he didn't care in the least. He was of the opinion that shocking people woke them from their slumber. Most people, he believed, were sleepwalking through life (as did the legendary Gurdjieff) and that was unacceptable as far as he was concerned. The sleepwalkers were sheep following the herd and they were too frightened of standing out or appearing to be different for their own good.

This is what made Crowley the leader he was and his writings reflect his freestyle attitude. He was afraid of nothing. He was a libertine womanizer. He indulged as he wished in psychoactive substances and even narcotics. He called up "spirits" to assist him with gaining what he wanted and summoned "demons" to do his dirty work.

In short, Aleister Crowley was an eccentric with whom you messed at your peril.

This attitude appealed to some, those presumably of a similar nature, but turned off those who found him overbearing, overwhelming and downright scary and offensive. It is a notable fact, by the way, that The Beatles included Crowley on the cover of their album *Sergeant Pepper's Lonely Hearts Club Band* as one of their "heroes". David Bowie also paid homage to the man in his music as did Led Zeppelin's founder and lead guitarist, Jimmy Page, who was so obsessed with Crowley that he bought scores of the ceremonial magician's personal belongings and, eventually, even his former home, Boleskine House, located in Scotland (which was said to be haunted by ghosts and demons).

Personally, I never found Crowley's writings to be anything

other than arcane and cryptic. Hyatt, on the other hand, found the man to be a compelling iconoclast and loved his writings. In fact, the man and his work resonated so perfectly with Hyatt's own larger than life personality that Hyatt became one of Crowley's primary publishers.

Hyatt wasn't alone when it came to paying homage to Crowley. The same could be said of fellow Falcon Press authors Timothy Leary and Robert Anton Wilson, who were both fans of the great magician, or shall we say the man known to call himself the "Epopt of the Illuminati" – whatever that means.

As for Hyatt, I found him to be a highly intelligent and powerful figure. He, too, stopped at nothing and couldn't care less what the "sheep" thought of him. He did what he wanted and lived a free and exuberant lifestyle. In fact, so libertine, robust and wild was Hyatt in his youth, I was later to learn, that for most of his life he carried a bullet in his leg from an altercation of some kind and many a scar. All in all, however, his mind was ultra-sharp, and he was, quite simply, one of the smartest men I had ever met. In fact, he had three advanced degrees and did not suffer fools gladly, nor put up with bullshit. When he spoke, he did not mince his words.

I knew from Hyatt's books, which had titles like *Undoing Yourself with Energized Meditation*, *Secrets of Western Tantra*, *The Tree of Lies*, *The Enochian World of Aleister Crowley*, *Taboo: The Ecstasy of Evil*, *Pacts with the Devil* and *Urban Voodoo*, that he, too, was an iconoclast and that he, too, sometimes summoned demons to do his bidding. This concerned me, but Hyatt's sincerity and the deep spiritual insights he shared with me quelled any reservations I had in dealing with him. I was unsure about what I was getting into in those early contacts, but the good doctor assured me that his intentions were honorable. As a result, I agreed to the induction and can honestly say that never once in the aftermath of the ceremony did Hyatt insist on anything at all from me. As a free soul, I was my own man and

Hyatt respected that. In fact, it was *because* I was such a free soul that I was even invited into the Order. Hyatt had read my first novel and he had liked it. Under his auspices as owner of Falcon Press Publications, that book eventually came to be entitled *The Dream Illuminati*. This was the novel that catapulted me into the literary arena.

Compelled to plumb the depths of the esoteric and spiritual literature to be found at the time, Hyatt knew that I was pursuing "Truth" in my own way and discovering the meaning and purpose of life with fiery and determined resolve. That was more than sufficient for him and precisely what the mighty Magus respected. We talked at length in our time together and I certainly heard many remarkable tales. I also gained fantastic insights into, and about, subjects such as the "Illuminati", the "Secret Chiefs", the "Hidden Masters", "black magic", "Satanism" and so forth. I also heard about the activities and pursuits of fellow Falcon Press authors at the time: Robert Anton Wilson, Timothy Leary, Neal Freer and Antero Alli, among others.

In short, my initiation into the Hermetic Order came with no demands upon me and I was still very much my own man afterwards. I had been invited into the Order because my writings resonated with its essential teachings. Hyatt had explained that every individual has the right to his or her own opinion and to believe as he or she wishes. Whatever one did was fine by him so long as it did not abridge the rights of anyone else, nor cause harm of any nature.

What Hyatt and I did was to share information, insights, and ways of going about the pursuit of illumination, liberation and spiritual evolution. One of the most important lessons, he explained to me in detail, concerned the "Three Paths of Magick". (In case anyone is wondering, spelling the word "magic" with a "k" was instigated by Crowley to distinguish it from stage magic.)

Path 1 is called "White Magick" and what it involves is the ritualizing of intention with the summoning of beneficent powers or spirits in order to help oneself or others in a positive way.

Path 2 is called "Black Magick" and what it involves is the ritualizing of intention with the summoning of infernal powers or spirits for a self-serving purpose or for causing detriment to one's perceived enemies.

Path 3 is called "Red Magick" and what it involves is the ritualizing of intention by turning one's own passions fully inward in order to perceive or access higher dimensions or realities.

One should note here that all three paths turn or pivot on the word "intention". The desire to heal another, for example, is a positive intention, while the desire to seek revenge is a very negative intention. Both involve the planting of a karmic seed which will grow within the individual and return to him or her in some form. Positive intentions result in positive karma and negative intentions result in negative karma. "What goes around, comes around."

Hyatt, while clearly unafraid of any of the three paths was very much – in my view of him – a great magician of the White and Red paths. As for the Black Path, one may draw one's own conclusions about Hyatt and this path by reading his books for oneself.

Path 3, by the way, is a path that Hyatt contended was only for those of a more advanced level of knowledge and spiritual insight. In other words, it is only for those who are able to fully appreciate what the famous mystic William Blake meant when he wrote: "Those who enter the gates of heaven are not beings who have no passions or have curbed the passions, but those who have cultivated an understanding of them."

Hyatt once told me, "Look, you can spend your time struggling with your inner demons and you should, but not forever. Eventually, you have to get past them. You have to move on and tell the little bastards to go to hell if they won't leave you alone, because there are better ways of spending your time… Like, for example, by consorting with your inner Tantric goddess!" In other words, at some point, we have to let our inner demons die a natural death, purely by neglecting them, by *not* feeding energy to them. Otherwise, we suffer the consequences. The more we focus on them, the more magnified they become. Magick offers a way of getting past our inner demons and focusing, instead, on our Holy Guardian Angel or Higher Self.

What the Hermetic Order of the Golden Dawn gave me was the most comprehensive overview of all aspects of "magick" I had encountered. Their principal publication, *The Golden Dawn*, was written by the highly respected mage Israel Regardie and is a huge tome full of the most minute detail of an arcane nature imaginable. (Numerous insiders have described it as being the most important book on occultism in the 20th century.) Regardie had once been a close associate of Aleister Crowley but was of a far humbler and less aggressive constitution. Hyatt loved Regardie and told me many tales about his interactions with him, which I found deeply fascinating.

Despite my association with the Order, I did not seek to advance within it, for I was then – and I remain – a free spirit. As a result, I continued doing my own personal praxis, fine-tuning my insights and seeking the answers to the Great Mysteries of life according to my own "True Will".

Thanks to an avid interest in the latest cutting-edge science, such as quantum physics, I was among those relatively young ones at the time who were reading not only Wilson, Leary and Hyatt, but also books by men such as Fritjof Capra (*The Tao of Physics*) and Gary Zukav (*The Dancing Wu Li Masters*). I had already been to India, China and Japan by this time and had studied the Hindu myths in great detail, as well as the remarkable, enlightening teachings of Buddhism.

Once a Falcon Press author, I met and was also highly influenced by Antero Alli and his "Modern Shaman's Guide to Reality Selection", *Angel Tech*. As well, I had the pleasure of meeting Neil Freer, who was a true gentleman and an erudite scholar. We talked for hours on end. His book, *Breaking the Godspell*, offered a whole new paradigm for "The Politics of Our Evolution" (as that book is subtitled) and for human history in general.

Exciting new studies in the mathematics of chaos theory were emerging in those years, as well, and I was, more or less, among the second wave of writers who were welding the whole lot together in our private and public work, essentially weaving magick, occultism, quantum physics and chaos theory into great novelistic or cutting-edge tapestries. We even called ourselves Chaos Magicians. The most respected members of this emerging group were men like Robert F Williams, Jr., Phil Hine, Peter Carroll, Robert Brazil, Peter Conte and Ian Read.

Chaos magick certainly suited me at the time as my personal life had become mired in exactly that: chaos. I won't go into detail about it here as it is *too* personal, but suffice it to say that merely steeping oneself in the latest spiritual literature and trying with the best of intentions to sow only positive karmic seeds for the benefit of oneself (and the sake of all sentient beings) does *not* immediately result in heavenly relations with one's romantic partner, nor does it swiftly result in the full-blown blossoming of *Nirvana* in one's life.

Aleister Crowley defined magick as, "The Science and Art of causing Change to occur in conformity with the Will." He was famous for conjuring ancient gods and demons, essentially entities of all persuasions, via spells and chants (including the entity known as Aiwass whom he claimed dictated the notorious *Book of the Law* to him through his wife, Rose, in Egypt in 1904). My instincts, however, told me to steer clear of this type of praxis and for a very good reason: Who knows *what* might be unleashed into one's life by summoning such entities? At the very least, one needs to seriously ask if said entities are even the beings they claim to be. This is a major concern for would-be magicians and sorcerers. How does one really know for sure with whom one is consorting on the astral level? There is no way to prove anything one way or another. As far as I was concerned at the time, I did not want, nor need, any demonic assistance in my life and to risk even the chance of it was far too perilous in my estimation. The fact is that seeking power over others, as Crowley and many another magician seem to desire, was never an intention of mine, nor was I hoping for great quantities of money and material goods from my praxis. As any advanced student of spirituality knows, money and materialism are products of the profane world and to seek them with a passion only diverts one from the pursuit of the sacred.

I won't deny, however, that as a young man I wanted, not only freedom and endless bliss, but what the eastern yogis call *siddhis*: psychic powers; that is, the ability to utilize seemingly "supernatural" powers such as telepathy, clairvoyance, levitation and so forth, and to have out-of-body experiences at will.

In retrospect, I realize that much of this was innocent kid stuff really. Who doesn't want "magical powers" when one is young and full of high-flying notions? We all do. Physical reality, however, does have its limitations and things "supernatural" do not come easily. I have since learned that there is such things as psychic powers, telepathy, clairvoyance, psychokinesis, remote viewing and out-of-body experiences, but unless one is willing to sit in meditation for hours on end, day in and day out, for years really, one can, at best, only rarely access or experience these phenomena. Some people are born with certain of these abilities, it seems, but such persons are few and far between. One must, therefore, probe one's motives for desiring these talents and understand that to acquire them is a matter of investing one's time. If one doesn't put in the time, then one cannot expect to turn into a genuine psychic. Remember this, however: the pursuit of an advanced level of spirituality does not require the mastering of any of these talents. Spirituality is about compassion, empathy and treating others as you would have them treat you.

No one starts out knowing any of this, however. We hear or read countless stories about such phenomena and rightly grow entranced. We say, "Why not me? Why can't I have such powers?" When one is young, one feels invincible, and it is all too easy to believe that anything is possible. As with everything in life, therefore, a person makes attempts at various activities in order to gain knowledge of them. We try things and generally learn more from our failures than from our successes. Over time, however, we cannot but grow in knowledge and eventually discover what works and what doesn't, and from that determine our own true interests. I certainly did and what I learned was that I wanted to steer well clear of the "Dark Side"!

Nevertheless, I also had a burning desire to know the secrets that certain "secret societies" were said to harbor, which is why the "Illuminati" caught my attention and held it for such an extended period. What I learned was that there were two types of Illuminati: the romanticized notion of higher entities interacting with humanity in a clandestine manner and the profane model which centers around certain politicians and wealthy elites of a current or historic nature who operate clandestinely behind the scenes and virtually tell government officials what to do. This latter group was said to be operating behind closed doors within multiple organizations and are allegedly part of a colossal global secret society known as the Round Table. Its offshoots are said to include the Council on Foreign Relations, the Trilateral Commission, the Royal Institute of International Affairs, the Club of Rome, the

Bilderberg Group and so on.

I had no interest in the elites, however, for I realized at once that their manipulation of events in the world, whether true or false, are forever beyond me no matter what I do. In short, I knew I would never be among their ranks and that was that. After all, we are talking about the likes of the Rockefellers and the Rothschilds here. Nor could I ever get to the bottom of their secret intrigues, for they are too rich and too clandestine in their activities.

The idea of higher spiritual entities, however, is another story altogether. The thinking here is that with concentrated mental focus one might actually contact such beings. This is where the Golden Dawn offered hope, for its members believe that we humans enjoy a mental connection with a multitude of spiritual entities and virtually everyone is connected *directly* to a Holy Guardian Angel. Therefore, making contact with such beings can gain one a useful spiritual ally who just might, perhaps, help one discover the ultimate secrets of life.

Bear in mind that the "Hermetic" Order of the Golden Dawn takes its name from "Hermes Trismegistus", which is to say, "Hermes, the Thrice Greatest". The name Hermes is the Greek name for the Egyptian god Thoth, and Thoth was the god who gave humanity writing and magic, among other gifts.

And so I decided in my youth that reading and writing were road maps to magic and discovered that deeply pondering the right kinds of books, the ones offering insights and wisdom of a sublime or *otherworldly* persuasion, could be revelatory all on their own. In fact, they can reveal aspects of the Divine in surprising ways. What it takes is persistence and passion.

Let us remember what the wise Sufi poet Kabir once said: "When the Divine is being searched for, it is the intensity of the longing for the Divine that does all of the work."

That, then, is a key secret to success in the quest for the Divine. What one has to do, it seems, is just *search* and keep searching and the Divine will reciprocate that interest. It blesses us with knowledge of its presence and nothing on earth is more reassuring than that, for it allows us to know just how immortal we are.

# 13

# Radical Magical Thinking

## *The Quest to Liberate, Illuminate & Empower the Soul*

"MAGICAL THINKING" is a term with multiple meanings. For some, it is about giving one's fantasies free expression, most notably in order to keep the spirit buoyant in the wake of the death of a loved one or after some form of tragedy occurs in one's life. It may also provide a way to relieve stress, for engaging in "magical thinking" for many is about slipping off into fantasyland in order to escape the pressures of the "real" world, which is generally a harmless activity, unless one takes one's fantasies a step too far and does something violent or criminal based upon those fantasies.

For others, magical thinking is about the pursuit of salvation or enlightenment. It is about breaking from conventional thought and pondering the metaphysical or spiritual aspects of life, and the seeking of transcendental levels of experience. To believe in "magic" for such people is about taking action at a "higher" level, in the sphere of the "higher mind" or learning how to access what Jung called "the collective unconscious". Using deep states of meditation, a "magician" believes that he or she can influence events by bringing about synchronicities that will be of benefit to him or her in some way. Perhaps one might win the love of a certain person, bring a better job into one's life, a position of power or secure a large sum of money for oneself. Magical thinking, in this case, spans the full spectrum of activity between the physical and the mental, or metaphysical, realms.

The question, of course, is this: Is "magical thinking" for real in any way, shape or form, or is it a totally delusory undertaking by people who are essentially living on a "hope and a prayer" and a bit desperate for a better circumstance in their life?

The answer is far more elusive and uncertain than most diehard, pragmatic materialists would like or generally unfailingly contend. After all, hardcore materialists do not even believe that we humans have a "soul", let alone one that we can liberate, illuminate or empower.

It is a given, no doubt, that this topic is going to be of interest, almost exclusively, to those who already "believe" that a human being "has" or "is" a soul and that there is indeed a "spiritual" dimension to life as humanity knows it.

As an open-minded "free soul" and "syncretist" (one who studies the many religious traditions of the Earth, searching for whatever inspiration and wisdom that appeals, while generally purposely eschewing formal membership in any particular tradition), I can only offer up the insights I have gained over the decades and express my viewpoints in order to, hopefully, show how humanity is more united spiritually than many might believe.

My contention here is that, despite the apparent divisions that we see in the world – the many religious traditions and differing beliefs, dogmas, doctrines, and orthodoxies – most of those divisions stem from a purely cultural bias, not from any spiritual absolutes. For example, there is not a religion on this earth that does not extoll the virtues of kindness, charity, love, compassion, humility, gratitude and so on. Which, of course, begs the question: Why do we see so much conflict, persecution, ill will and outright violence, murder and even genocide in the world if such is the case?

The answer, I think, is down to the lack of clarity on the part of the individual, for every group of people can only be as wise as the persons which comprise the group. This is why working at an individual level is the best way to go about improving human unity.

That is not always easy, for life is often hard and unfair, and the vicissitudes of life can be extremely challenging. Sometimes those vicissitudes can even be life-threatening, but if we all work together to solve our problems, rather than working against each other and being greedy and cruel in the process, I think we really could all live together in peace and plenty.

That corruption is all too rampant, politically and socially at the top among the governing elite of this world, means that many, perhaps most, people are at a serious disadvantage from day one. Still, one can stand on certain principles and foster personal integrity for oneself while working at a grassroots level to be the change that is needed in this world. If we do work together, I believe, then, all aspects and challenges in life can actually enrich us spiritually if we are wise about it.

One must make the effort, however. That entails making a concerted effort to uncover the hidden gems of wisdom that lie in wait for us. Such gems are like chippings off the philosopher's stone of legend, but one need not be a philosopher in order to grasp the essential message that such gems are intended to convey, namely, that the vicissitudes of life are, crucially and decisively, the very forces that impel the spirit onward and ultimately compel the soul to evolve.

How? By exposing the individual to both positive and negative circumstances, to events that are exhilarating or tragic, to experiences which must be dealt with whether we want to deal with them or not, such as getting cancer or contracting a strain of coronavirus.

The vicissitudes of life will forever offer an upside and a downside. They will give us cause to celebrate or, conversely, a cause to mourn. If we humans did not experience the full range of mental, physical, and emotional happenstance that can, and does, occur in this world of ours, however, we would never be able to empathize with one another, nor would we ever come to deeply comprehend how complex, precious and amazing our lives are.

Life is miraculous no matter how it began. The odds of us existing at all were astronomically against us from the moment life sprang into being. That we do not have all of the answers as to how or why life began only adds a measure of mystery to the enigma. Many understand that, but millions in this world seem not to get it that even at its most mundane, this life of ours is phenomenal.

Unfortunately, when people miss this point, they tend to simply spin their wheels and go around in circles, instead of using whatever insights they happen to gain along the way for climbing upward on a rising spiral to a higher, more enlightened, perspective.

Needless to say, we all die, but say it we must, for otherwise we might pretend, not only that death doesn't happen, but that it will never happen to *us*. I remember thinking, while high on a pagoda in the ancient city of Kathmandu one day, how death *will* happen to me eventually and how my own death is a reality from which I cannot escape. That realization was like a dagger to my heart that day and the emotion I felt was so intense that it had me breaking out into a sweat. The same thing occurred when I found myself in India witnessing a cremation on the banks of the Ganges River in the sacred city of Varanasi. Staggered by the reality I was seeing, I made my way to where an old yogi sat dressed only in a loincloth, his face exotically painted and his long silver beard hanging to his bare chest. As I looked deep into his dark eyes, his holy presence spoke to me in a way that was light years beyond words. Here was a man, after all, who was giving over his entire life to the spiritual quest and there was no mistaking the radiant power of his sacred presence.

The fact that death does and *will* happen to all of us doesn't mean, however, that we are bound for oblivion as it appears on the surface of things here in this world; not if we take seriously the thousands of reports we have been given by the many mystics, sages, and yogis over the centuries, as well as the accounts of those who have returned from a near-death experience. Those mystics, sages, seers, yogis, and returnees from the Great Beyond come from all cultures and quarters of the globe and, as any unbiased reading of the literature from the many and various spiritual traditions of the Earth readily attests, these accounts are thoroughly illuminating and offer great hope.

Yes, there are those who will argue that there is no objective proof of what we call the "soul", nor proof of states of being such as "enlightenment", nor "salvation", and definitely no objective proof whatsoever that a human being lives on once he or she has physically passed from this planet. To such a person, the meaning of life and spirituality in general is a totally subjective phenomenon and no doubt a delusion.

The subjective nature of spirituality, however, does not automatically disqualify it from having validity. After all, even quantum physicists admit the vital role of the subjective observer. Consider what Gary Zukav wrote in his acclaimed work on quantum physics, *The Dancing Wu Li Masters*: "Our experience tells us that the physical world is solid, real and independent of us. Quantum mechanics says, simply, this is not so."

In other words, scientists admit nowadays that there is no such thing as a purely objective world. Max Planck, one of the founding fathers (along with Niels Bohr) of quantum physics, stated that, "All matter originates and exists only by virtue of a force… We must assume behind this force the existence of a conscious and intelligent Mind. This Mind is the matrix of all matter."

So, yes, spirituality has never availed itself of objective proof, but neither have quarks and gluons to date. Quarks and gluons are *inferred* to exist from the results of experimentation and inductive reasoning, not from direct evidence. Likewise, the *otherworld* of the mystics and the yogis, and that of the near-death returnees, is also inferred. The difference is that the mystic, the yogi and the returnee *knows* first-hand what actually occurred on another "plane" of existence and how "real" the experience was even if they cannot share the experience itself with anyone else *directly*.

What we *can* share with one another, however, are our own inferences… Our thoughts, our speculations, our sincerest and best guesses about the phenomenon of "spirituality", the meaning of life, the nature of reality, the verity of "magical thinking" and about the possibility of an afterlife. There is no need to be combative about those beliefs, though. One can make one's point and offer up insight on any topic under discussion purely to clarify one's own thinking on such matters and for getting feedback on those thoughts.

No one can claim to know anything *absolutely*, however, and this is a point which must be emphasized. After all, what one *believes* to be true on any subject is not the same as something *being* absolutely and indisputably true.

What we do know in concrete terms is that humanity is a single species sharing a particular planet in a universe so huge as to be unfathomable. We share the same biosphere, the same atoms, molecules and cells, and very similar sense impressions via our physicality.

At this juncture in history, unfortunately, people are badly divided in religious and political terms and if an individual can help turn the tide on that, I think it is a wonderful and positive thing. The hope here is that if as many of us as possible will take the time to look for what we have in common and appreciate the many aspects of unity that we do indeed share, then life on Planet Earth will get better.

Views can and do evolve over time. That is a good thing, despite the fact that politicians try to make it a virtue to hold fast to a single viewpoint forever. Viewpoints *should* change as better data emerges. There is something very right about views changing over time, for that is a sign of high intelligence. After all, an evolving and deepening viewpoint is precisely what can result in spiritual enrichment and such enrichment can and does come from both magical and mundane thinking.

It is wise, therefore, to occasionally look in detail at the underlying events of one's own life in a depersonalized manner. One should do this in order to discover the overriding myths out of which we, and the culture into which we were born, came to be. If we are persistent enough and dig deeply enough into our archetypal roots, we may indeed reap the great good fortune of liberating, illuminating and empowering the soul.

# 14

# Deep Space Dreams

## *From the Moon to Mars in the Rocket's Red Glare*

IN THE SUMMER OF 1969, I was seventeen years of age, free of high school for a few months, and working in construction. I had already purchased my first car by then – a Comet – and was driving myself to the job every morning at the crack of dawn. As part of a small crew of men building houses in my hometown in Ohio, I definitely had my work cut out for me, for this crew looked after every aspect of the undertaking. We jackhammered down through solid rock to put in the foundations for the homes, carpentered the walls and locked in the ceiling rafters. We put sheetrock on those walls and covered the roofs of the homes with asphalt shingles. We even jackhammered the holes for putting in the septic systems, spending days on end working our way ever deeper into the ground through solid rock until we were literally rattled to the bone.

It wasn't the famous "Summer of Love", 1969, but love was still in the air that year, despite the bombings and the carnage that was going on in Vietnam. The Beatles had a double-sided number 1 hit with "Something" and "Come Together", two songs from their *Abbey Road* album. They were still the top rock band on the planet at that point, while Elvis also enjoyed his last number 1 hit ever that year, a song called "Suspicious Minds".

Meanwhile, the festival at Woodstock in August showcased musical giants: Jimi Hendrix, Janis Joplin, Creedence Clearwater Revival, Crosby, Stills, Nash & Young, Jefferson Airplane, the Grateful Dead, Santana, Sly & the Family Stone, Ten Years After, Richie Havens, Country Joe and the Fish, The Who and numerous other acts.

It was definitely a summer that would go down in history.

The most historic event of all, however, was the Moon landing that occurred on the 20th of July. On that occasion a fellow Ohioan of mine, Neil Armstrong, became the first man to set foot on our ever-faithful orbiting lunar neighbor. Along with two colleagues – Buzz Aldrin and Michael Collins – he and the crew of Apollo 11 achieved a feat that will stand for all time.

There is only one future event that could possibly rank with it in importance and historical significance at this juncture in history: the first mission to Mars.

That is decades off yet, though, isn't it?

Only time will tell!

Nevertheless, let us remember that it was in 1961 that President John F. Kennedy announced to the world that the government of the United States was committing itself to putting a team of astronauts on the Moon by the "end of the decade and bringing them safely back home again".

A mere eight years later, in July of 1969, Apollo 11 fulfilled the assassinated president's great dream. Like millions of others at the time, I raced off from the job in my car to watch the proceedings on TV. Along the way, I heard the number 1 song of the week, "In the Year 2525" by Zager & Evans, and thought, *how flipping space age is this?*

Joining my workmates at the home of one of the men I labored alongside that summer, I remember staring at the screen transfixed as I watched the historic mission unfold live on television.

It certainly proved a riveting day in the life of millions of us, especially as we heard one of the most historical utterances of all time at that most memorable of moments: "That's one small step for man; one giant leap for mankind."

Now, all these years later, there is every reason for me to believe that I will still be alive to witness the first landing on Mars, which I find unspeakably exciting.

Mind you, when the first human steps forth onto the Red Planet, it will take fourteen minutes for the televised transmission to reach us here, but if all goes according to plan that is all we will have to wait. (Of course, some technologically superior communication device might well be in operation by then and the time delay significantly shorter!)

I have no doubt whatsoever that a Martian transmission, once it is under way, will be seen right around the globe and become the most watched, live, televised moment in world history. Billions of people will witness that stupendously profound event, for it will showcase the first ever interplanetary colony setting down its roots.

If we consider what an astonishing moment that is going to be for those of us who will be viewing the event, imagine what it will be like for those who will actually be there on Mars. Imagine what those on the crew will feel like as they follow their commander onto the Martian surface that day, their space boots sinking into the crimson dust of the Red Planet. Imagine how they will feel as they start forward in their spacesuits in the middle of a desert (in the middle of nowhere actually) and make their way toward the cargo vessels that will have arrived there ahead of them.

Hopefully those vessels will be close at hand or there will be trouble, for those ships will contain the bulk of the colonists' life-sustaining provisions onboard, including the components for building their first shelter and workstation.

Obviously, the landing and the initial foray onto the Martian surface will be critical moments, indeed. They will be life and death moments, in fact. They will be moments fraught with extreme danger and the ultimate challenge.

Nevertheless, our spacefarers must hit the ground running upon landing for that very reason or they will run the risk of not securing their own safety. Of course, no astronaut is going to *literally* hit the ground running on Mars as it is simply impossible to do that in clunky space boots and heavy spacesuits. Factor in the low level of gravity on the Red Planet and we add a dimension of no minor relevance to completing the work, which won't be easy, even under the best of circumstances.

Come to think about it, is there any aspect of this mission that is of minor relevance? I suspect not; not when you are part of a crew that has just traversed more than 35 million miles across space in order to arrive in one piece at your destination; not when you have set down on a freezing cold expanse of desert and must build your own safe haven there; not when you look around you and understand for real that there is no way out if things go wrong; that you are left totally to your own devices and resources to make a go of the situation or you will indeed pay the ultimate price: with your life.

How daunting: there you are, over 35 million miles away from everything you have ever known, and, suddenly, you must fight tooth and nail to survive.

Sounds like a challenge; like an *overwhelming* challenge?

Apparently not to the thousands of would-be astronauts who have volunteered their services for that first mission. According to those at the helm of enterprises like Mars One, SpaceX and other spacefaring groups around the world, their organizations are inundated with volunteers, with people who are willing to give up absolutely everything for a shot at this Great Adventure, no matter how difficult it may be.

I find this last fact pretty mind-blowing all by itself. How can such a staggering, life-altering, unbelievably dangerous and complex one-way ticket to Mars be so appealing to so many? And considering the magnitude of what is at stake in this competition, how cutthroat might this rivalry get in the near future?

This last question is precisely what plays into the plot of my novel *Crimson Firestorm Mars*. It could get bloody, indeed. Then, again, maybe that is just a novelist letting his fiction run away with him. Nevertheless, it is definitely one hell of a competition, and it is already under way. It is only going to get hotter as "Mars fever" grows ever more widespread across the globe and the rivalry heats up to a genuinely scalding degree.

Whether there will be real "firestorms" among these groups as in my novel, only time will tell.

In the meantime, there is plenty of time to ask ourselves this question: Space, the final frontier. What has it gotten us?

Permit me to name but a few of the wonders... The innovations of rocket science have gotten us a host of amazing devices that now save millions of lives, including MRI and CAT scans. They have gotten us medical devices employing LED technology which can relieve the pain of wounded soldiers, cancer patients and people with other diseases. They have gotten us solar cells, insulin pumps, artificial limbs, state of the art air purifiers and water filtration systems, compact workout machines for strength and muscle tone, shock absorbers for buildings, tires that are as tough as steel, top of the line firefighting equipment, as well as the first portable computer (called the Grid Compass) and the first "mouse". Rocket science has also gotten us scratch resistant lenses, invisible braces, freeze-dried foods and – the young will love these three – super cool running shoes that can take a pounding, wireless headsets and, yes, the very cameras which are used in cellphones and laptops today (so remember that when you take your next "selfie"!).

In short, there is plenty of fun to be had in our fiery imaginations as humanity pursues its greatest visionary dream yet: the dazzling dream of interplanetary travel.

# 15

# Is Reality Stranger Than We Think for a Reason?

GAZING ON STONEHENGE for the first time, my eyes sweeping across the prehistoric structure with its giant Sarsen standing stones weighing in at some 25 tons, topped by equally large lintel stones, I remember finding myself captivated by what I was looking on that day. There was a beauty in the symmetry of the structure, a graceful symmetry that had me in awe, especially as I contemplated how the ancient builders of the complex supposedly created it without the use of advanced forms of technology.

I also found myself ruminating with wonder on why such a huge complex of stones was necessary over 4,000 years ago, simply to know when the summer solstice had arrived. Clearly, there was more to it; a desire perhaps by the ancients to construct a temple that was worthy of the deep sense of numinosity they felt.

I remember thinking how here was another one of the world's great mysteries writ large.

In fact, I think now how this life seems, ever and always, to be one of strange anomalies and extreme improbabilities, but I believe that is a fortunate thing, for without a Stonehenge here or a Neolithic Bronze Age monument there (or indeed vast fields of grain such as those in Wiltshire and nearby regions of England that are punctuated with the occasional crop circle, symbol or complex glyph created by some truly bizarre, unknown agency), this world would be primarily about the very things that make for a mundane existence. London, which I had left prior to visiting Stonehenge, had been buzzing with people and traffic. There had been much to see, of course: Parliament and Big Ben,

Westminster Abbey, Piccadilly Circus and Trafalgar Square, to name but a few of the impressive edifices there. There had also been the River Thames flowing through the dense metropolitan cityscape, but even when sitting by those flowing waters for a good hour or two while looking at Tower Bridge, there had been no sense of numinosity.

In stark contrast, Stonehenge hummed with numinosity.

Numinosity swept across the giant, majestic megaliths of Stonehenge and the tall grasses as surely as the life-sustaining wind itself.

The word "numinosity" comes from the Latin *numen*, which refers to a presiding deity or spirit. Where there is numinosity there is a sense of the presence of divinity, of *transcendent otherness*, which charges one's spirit in a way that is indefinable. Such a feeling imbues the spirit with a sense of the sacred and transforms the mundane by raising it to a greater, more cosmic level.

Whoever built Stonehenge knew the truth of this assertion over four millennia ago and that tells us that, spiritually speaking, our ancestors were our equals or perhaps betters, so to speak. They were in touch with their sacred higher selves and that is the message, I believe. If we are likewise in touch with our higher selves, we can accomplish spectacular feats that will leave others in awe.

It was quiet on the Salisbury Plain that day and I remember well how I could finally catch my breath once there and how much I enjoyed the peace of the place. Since flying out of New York, my journey had unfolded at a hectic pace and while I was certainly looking forward to sojourning onward to many more European cities like London, cities full of the hustle and bustle of lives, I knew that the image of Stonehenge would stay with me. As in London I would be seeing cathedrals, museums, and stately parliaments as I went forward. There would be cafés, bistros, pubs, restaurants, and street vendors. All of that would be both inviting and exciting, I knew, but those cities would also be overrun with their own version of the rat race and the daily grind in general. What is it all for in the end, I wondered, when we ultimately lose it all upon our death?

Mad as it may seem, I have often told myself that I wouldn't trade this crazy world for any other. Why? Because I have come to believe that this world – exactly as it is – is more perfect than most of us generally imagine.

In that regard, I think how the late physicist JBS Haldane offered his colleagues – and all of us really – a very intriguing proposition to consider. "My own suspicion is that the universe is not only queerer than we suppose," he once purportedly stated, "but queerer than we *can* suppose."

That is a powerful supposition, indeed.

I might just mention before pressing ahead here that Haldane died in 1964, so if the line strikes anyone as inappropriate or odd in this day and age that explains it. The meaning intended, however, is easy enough to glean and I believe that the statement hits the proverbial nail on the head, for we humans do not know *anything* absolutely for certain. Stonehenge is just one among countless enigmas in our world.

What we do know is that some mysterious force, or source, gave rise to the stellar cosmos with its billions upon billions of hydrogen and helium-fueled stars, and that those stars, in turn, eventually gave birth to one or more planet upon which organic biological entities eventually came to flourish. This, of course, is the case with our own wonderland, the Earth. (I personally entertain a suspicion that there are billions of other flourishing entities in this universe of ours, but only time will tell in that regard.)

On this planet, at the very least, we see that there is an inherent power which animates every atom, every molecule and every cell in every living thing. Among those "things" is our own species, of course, with its seemingly unique sensibilities and its ability to consciously reflect on its own existence.

Some sages say that human consciousness might well be essentially a microcosmic unit of some Universal Intelligence or Cosmic Mind and that one may call this Intelligence or Mind, "God", or simply, "Nature".

What is the point of such a cosmos, however? One can hazard a guess, certainly (and we all do), but as Haldane suggests, we need to keep in mind the fact that we humans almost certainly have less than a full picture from which to draw our conclusions. After all, on the surface of this world it appears that we are but finite creatures – mortal, material beings – and that our perspectives are clearly, overwhelmingly, generated by the five senses, which means that we are subject to limitation by default.

What if consciousness itself, however, is not only stranger than we think, but *purposely* stranger than we think? What if paradox and contradiction have been deliberately built into the foundation of the human experience so that no single person can arrive at an *absolute* answer to life and thus render the quest for an ultimate answer *unnecessary* for others to discover in their own right? This is a good question, for without an absolute answer to the mystery of our existence, we are all made to pursue and search for the answers to life in our own way and in our own time, virtually throughout the whole of our mortal span on this planet.

Which is good. A deliberately elusive ultimate answer keeps each of us galloping off on endless Great Adventures, so that we inevitably and invariably grow, not only in consciousness and knowledge, but in life experience and, therefore, wisdom. This makes perfect sense as an ideal operative strategy for eternal beings who are in the throes of experiencing multiple lives or even beings who experience but one brief flash of existence. For experience is something that each of us must distil within our own minds and hearts. This distillation resides in memory to some extent, but mostly it is tucked away deep within our subconscious minds. To what end, though?

One possibility is that the Universal Field of Pure Consciousness is expanding and growing, in whole or in part, thanks to the trillions of sentient units within the field that are expanding and growing in each their own way by virtue of the life each individual experiences. In other words, perhaps, each of us, by uniquely experiencing this life, keeps uploading that essence into the Universal Field, thus contributing, however minutely, to the enrichment and expansion of the Field.

If this insight is correct, it might well offer a strategy by which one may come to accept life *exactly as it is,* despite the fact that there are such shockingly negative aspects to life as we know it. Without a sense of dissatisfaction with our personal situation due to adverse factors, for example, life as we know it might lead to stasis, to no one anywhere bothering to do much of anything. Perhaps if we did not see the world as being *imperfect,* then none of us would feel compelled to try and better things in this world. Perhaps, we might even end up doing little or nothing in terms of trying to overcome ignorant behaviors such as cruelty and evil, and thus never grow spiritually at all.

Because we tend to want things better and more satisfying in our lives, however, most of us venture forth into the world, kick up the dust and go for bust. We try this and that. We succeed in some instances and fail in others, but keep going for the gold, which is an incredibly productive thing to do, for *all* experience in distilled form may indeed be continually streaming inward via this ongoing process. By that I mean to include the good, the bad, the kindness and the cruelty, the pleasure and the pain, the heavenly joys we sometimes experience and the horrendous sorrows so many suffer. What may be happening, then, is that such experience may be continually being uploaded (or to coin a word: "inloaded") into the Cosmic Mind or Nature as a whole, for the specific intent of enriching the Source of All That Exists. If we see this process as enriching our own soulful self, as well, then it turns into a win-win no matter what happens along the way.

As a perspective or a paradigm, I believe, this is an extremely "enlightened" possibility, for the dualistic, paradoxical, contradictory mix of life experience – in all its unfathomable positive and negative nature – may be precisely what makes this life so precious and what makes the Great Adventure of life itself worth pursuing.

It is in retrospect, therefore, that much of what we experience during the course of our lives will finally make sense, strange as it may seem to us at any particular moment. To my way of thinking, such a speculative perspective can keep hope on the horizon, which in turn can keep us journeying adventurously onward with a numinous mind and a charged spirit.

# 16

# The Dream Illuminati

## *Are Flights in the Imaginal Realm More Than Merely Symbolic?*

THE ORBIT OF THE EARTH as it circles about the Sun on its yearly journey at 66,600 miles per hour traces out an ellipse, as well as a spiral. The spiral movement is the result of the entire solar system racing through space at a speed that truly staggers the imagination.

So huge is the Milky Way Galaxy that 225 million years are required for our solar system to make a single rotation about it and that is by traveling at 514,000 mph through space! This phenomenally extended voyage is known as a Galactic Year.

As the solar system and the Earth move against the backdrop of stars which surround it, another motion is traced out. It is a flight that takes roughly 25,800 – 25,920 years. This is a trip through what is called the ecliptic. This orbit is known as a Great, or Platonic, Year and, while traversing it, we Earthlings are cycling through what we call the twelve signs of the Zodiac.

Dividing the Platonic Year by twelve, we get an average of 2160 years, which is how long it takes for the Earth to roughly pass through any particular sign of the Zodiac. Most astrologers agree that at present we are transitioning from the Age of Pisces to the Age of Aquarius.

Mark Booth in *The Secret History of the World* says that in olden times, "The night sky was a living history, because the heavenly bodies were seen as the material bodies of spiritual beings or gods. The ancients believed that a wisdom master had the ability to communicate with these beings and could feel their influence."

Mercury, Venus, Mars, Saturn, Jupiter, Neptune, Uranus, these were *living* beings, not huge conglomerations of gases and matter. The Earth herself was known as Gaia. She was humanity's mother and was revered right around the globe by many names.

It was believed in the olden days that these celestial "gods" were unspeakably powerful and when one particular god reigned over the others, a period of tranquility or war could result, depending upon whether that god promoted harmony in the world or discord.

We humans are far more influenced by "cosmic forces" than we realize. The Moon exerts the most noticeable effect on our planet and its people. More powerful, by far, than either the Moon or the planets is the Sun. This is why the Sun-god was always the ultimate Supreme Being. Whether that god's name was Atum, Ra, Helios, Sol, Apollo, Ahura Mazda or some other name, this god was the central focus of humanity for very obvious reasons. The life-giving rays of the Sun were indispensable to the growth and sustenance of the animal and vegetable kingdoms. Even the soil itself comes from star bodies, like the Sun, to give us our vital minerals and elements.

Without the Sun, and without a cosmos filled with such suns, we humans would not exist. Without star power – the gods – there would be nothing. What this means is that all material bodies and forces are interconnected and, therefore, interdependent.

To fully comprehend the interconnectedness of all things and to fully fathom how each and every living thing has an effect on every other living thing in the whole of existence is crucial to gaining a higher perspective on the human condition. As the wisdom master Gungtang says, "If you understand interdependence, you understand ultimate reality. If not, then you don't."

Jung called the "gods" archetypal forces and wrote at length about how these forces shape the human psyche. He believed that the archetypes are inherent forces that drive human behavior and compel people to act in certain ways. While every person is "constellated" with these inherent forces, certain archetypes are clearly more dominant within each of us. To be an indomitable warrior, a formidable leader, a fantastic mother, a prodigious intellectual, a great healer or to have any other "natural born" talent is said to be down to these forces.

We humans, however, are not mere puppets. We have free will and even though we are driven to act in a certain way, our proclivities do not ultimately determine how the archetypes will play out for us. A warrior, for example, can act for good or evil. He or she can defend life or take life. A formidable leader, likewise, can persuade people to act for the greater good or whip up the masses into a frenzy of fear and hatred, and talk followers into marching off to war.

History is the legacy of how humanity has used its inherent proclivities in conjunction with free will for good or ill.

Highly driven people lead the way and others choose to follow or not follow.

Sometimes, of course, the freedom to choose has been denied the masses, but where true liberty exists, "freedom" refers to what we might call the "sovereignty of the soul".

Quite amazingly, the whole of human history, dating from the rise of the first high civilizations, is a scant five thousand years. That is but one-fourth of a single astrological age. Imagine what humanity will be like in another five thousand years! Imagine what humanity will be like when this Earth has cycled the full Platonic Year. Or try, if you dare, to imagine what humanity might be like when a full galactic voyage of 225 million years has passed!

Actually, humanity itself may be little different in a physical sense than it is now. According to paleontologists, the human body has been pretty much the same for tens of thousands, if not hundreds of thousands, of years, in fact. What will change is the technology and the architecture which surrounds humanity, the human lifestyle, and the way we perceive and fathom life.

What will we believe when we reach that future? Will we still be making war and murdering one another, or might we actually be more spiritually advanced than we are now?

In my first two novels, *The Dream Illuminati* and *The Illuminati of Immortality* (New Falcon Publications, 1988 and 1990), I wrote of a fictional band of savvy operators who were the first in history to have access to personal jetpacks. These people began using the devices as an evolutionary upgrade for themselves. They believed that humanity should evolve spiritually at least as much as it was evolving in the field of technology. The goal, then, was to utilize the new technology as a modern update on what the ancients called "sacred science".

In other words, there was a concerted effort to use the jetpacks as consciousness raising devices, instead of just for fun and thrills. As a result, the members of the organization began buying up old churches and cathedrals and holding elaborate flying rituals inside of them. They tied in these rituals to the innate archetypal drive of humanity to live its dreams of flying and to make its members aware of how every religion on Earth had offered symbols of flight as part and parcel of their essential spiritual message (wings being the most common symbol for obvious reasons).

Dreams of flying are down to a certain universal truth. Humanity inhabits two worlds at once: a physical and a metaphysical realm. We all know about the physical; how our bodies are sourced in the quantum and atomic domains and how they are sustained. What operates at a far more sublime level is the metaphysical body, which is energetic in nature and may be sourced in a subquantum realm that at present we are not able to even measure.

According to yogis, mystics and metaphysicians the "astral

body" or "soul" constitutes the real person we are, and it can exist independently of any physical structure, even the energy body itself which animates our physicality. Thus, we can have out-of-body experiences and can even sojourn into other dimensions and realms during states of deep meditation and dream, or while under the sway of psychoactive, shamanic substances and especially at death upon our exit from the body with its five senses.

Visionary flights are believed to be much more than merely symbolic. Yes, they "point" to a higher reality, which is what symbols do, but we should not simply leave it at that. The yogis, mystics and metaphysicians exhort us to act, to "take wing" while still inhabiting our physical bodies.

To do so it is possible, we are told, that one may experience a "sublime" light. That light is said to be so overwhelming and of such a fantastic magnitude that it may be taken by the percipient to be God, an angel of light or simply a highly evolved spiritual being, one who happened to radiate the purest love imaginable and could communicate profound truths about the nature of reality. To "see the light" in this way, by all accounts, is a life-changing experience.

After one has had such an experience, one is said to be "illuminated" or, as I poetically put it all those years ago, one has become one of the "true Illuminati".

The "true Illuminati", I argued, are not members of some wealthy, elitist group of individuals who, as rumor has it, covertly run the world from behind the scenes. Any elitist, power-mongering group of individuals that play one nation off against another, fomenting war, purely to sell armaments, while – at the same time – stealing the lion's share of the world's natural resources, cannot possibly be "truly" illuminated; not if they allow their fellow human beings to butcher one another, not if they knowingly and consciously permit poverty and mass starvation, not if they allow the Earth to become a polluted, depleted shadow of itself for their own selfish ends. These are, therefore, false "Illuminati".

Robert Anton Wilson, in his book *Cosmic Trigger*, writes: "The Order of the Illuminati has been traced back to the Knights Templar, to the Greek and Gnostic initiatory cults, to Egypt, even to Atlantis." He goes on to say that "...no two students of Illuminology have ever agreed totally about what the 'inner secret' or purpose of the Order actually was (or is)."

This may certainly be much too vague for those who like concrete rather than ambiguous answers to their most burning concerns, especially if haunted by the fear of losing what one has or loss of control over one's own autonomy. Such people reach, instead, for the controversial writings of David Icke or pour through a book like *The Illuminoids* by Neal Wilgus. Such souls are sure that there is one great, giant, global conspiracy operating surreptitiously behind the closed doors of mansions and international organizations, and they are a group that never lets the press through those doors. The most paranoid among them believe that these "elites" are secretly plotting more and better ways, ever and always, to force the governments of the world to do their bidding so that they can amass even more stupendous wealth, privilege and power. These people are the devious billionaires who demand that their lackeys spread disinformation in order to fool the masses and keep "lesser mortals" subjugated and weak.

Part of that disinformation campaign, numerous conspiracy theorists insist, is the way they cunningly, cleverly and devilishly call themselves the Illuminati – i.e. "illuminated" – when they are no such thing.

After all, those who are truly illuminated would surely always treat the welfare of others as of paramount concern, for they would clearly know how precious life is and couldn't care less what any particular person has in the way of possessions, nor what he or she may or may not have accomplished in this world.

What the truly illuminated soul does is dream big. He or she helps other people at every opportunity, no matter the person's social status, and always promotes peace, love, kindness, compassion and charity whenever and wherever they can.

In other words, the truly illuminated pursue spirituality day in and day out and understand that there are many dimensions to life and that the soul lives on even after it flies away from the earthly body it presently inhabits.

Above all, the truly illuminated know that "Time" is *not* running out.

What "Time" is doing is eternally flying away with us.

## 17

# Wild at Mind Like the Wild at Heart

SPECULATION IS A SWEET TEMPTATION, one rooted in the imagination of those – to coin a phrase – who are "wild at mind".

Just as the so-called "wild at heart" are willing to risk almost anything in order to indulge their reckless or romantic passions, the wild at mind delight in conjuring all manner of outlandish theories, however farfetched, simply for the fascination that it arouses and for the fun it can generate.

If a theory or idea happens to bring about a laugh for being "utterly ludicrous", then so be it and why not? Laughter lightens everything in this world.

At the very least, we should all be open to pondering the imponderable and willing to consider the impossible. There are scientists, after all, who have speculated that the laws of physics as we know them may not be as absolute as most of us like to think.

It does *seem,* of course, as if certain truths are absolute in our world, yet quantum physics – the most basic of all the sciences – is notoriously difficult to comprehend in conventional terms. Physicist Richard Feynman, for example, stated, "I think I can safely say that nobody understands quantum mechanics." Physicist Max Born said, "No language which lends itself to visualizability can describe quantum jumps." Physicist Niels Bohr insisted that, "Those who are not shocked when they first come across quantum theory cannot possibly have understood it."

The point being made here is that life in this world is not necessarily the cut and dry thing so many want or take it to be. "Truth" is simply not black and white in any absolute sense. As Shakespeare noted, "There is nothing that is either good or bad but thinking makes it so."

Most of us would prefer that it was otherwise. We would like "facts" to be absolute, but they are not. Nevertheless, to quote Richard Feynman again: "I'd rather have questions that can't be answered than answers that can't be questioned."

Therefore, wisdom dictates that we keep an open mind, especially perhaps when searching for a fresh approach to some problem, whether of a personal nature or one of a scientific or technological nature. The pursuit of a novel invention, of course, requires that a researcher ponder every possible angle, even ones that seem totally out of the realm of rational possibility at the outset.

Then there are the topics of spirituality and psychic phenomena to consider. Hearing about miraculous or impossible "powers" can be challenging, to say the least.

For example, religious leaders have long claimed that there are "angels" and "demons" existing in other dimensions, not to mention a place called Heaven and one called Hell. We now have thousands of reports of people who have had near-death experiences tell us that something very much like that is what they experienced while in their flat-lined state. There were "beings of light" and paradise-like pastures of plenty for most of these returnees, while a few did experience some very dark netherworlds. Most, however, were impressed with the notion that there are, indeed, other dimensions full of life and that we humans reap what we sow. In other words, "karma" is for real, and life does go on once the "essential self" departs the physical body.

In a similar vein, certain mystics, saints and yogis have insisted over the centuries that it is actually possible to levitate one's body in total defiance of gravity. (!!!)

There are also scientific, military personnel who have divulged in various publications that the human mind is capable of remote viewing – of "seeing" – a location somewhere far afield, a "target" elsewhere from where one is sitting, quite possibly on the other side of the planet or out in space even. They claim, as well, that anyone can be taught how to achieve such an end if only one cultivates his or her mind in a specific manner, putting in the requisite time and practice.

Then there are certain astronauts, astronomers, generals and high-ranking jet pilots in the air forces of the world who have informed us that there are ships of "nonhuman" origin that fly about in our skies. US Astronaut Gordon Cooper once said, "I believe UFOs, under intelligent control, have visited our planet for thousands of years." Likewise, Edgar Mitchell, Apollo 14 Lunar Module Pilot and sixth man to walk on the Moon stated, "We all know that UFOs are real: now the question is where they come from."

Should one believe such assertions?

I leave it to the reader... But, just to say, the truly "wild at mind" do not shy away from controversial topics, even ones that are mired in deep cultural taboos which can bring strong emotional responses from others in their wake.

The trick, I think, is to embrace an agnosticism about events in this world, a view that is steeped in the deepest compassion possible. We should all be free to think as we will as we go about discovering truth for ourselves, for this world is rife with enigmas and mysteries. Nor should we ever fear to ponder the imponderable, to think the unthinkable or to indulge our fascination with possibilities and potentialities.

Even at a mundane level, we need only remember that the Wright Brothers were told that it was impossible for heavier-than-air machines to take flight. Fortunately, the brothers simply ignored those who said such things and invented the airplane.

More recently, in 1984 to be exact, the brilliant author William Gibson, in his award-winning, futuristic novel *Neuromance*, had his antihero / protagonist "jacking in" to the Internet whenever he wanted to make an excursion into "cyberspace". At that point, the idea of "Wi-Fi" was still a concept beyond the scope of almost everyone, even the most forward thinking among us, but "jacking in" is quite obsolete now.

In my novel *The Dream Illuminati,* first published in 1988, I envisioned a time in the not-so-distant future when people would be flying about on personal jetpacks. It is gratifying for me to now see how various versions of single person flying machines have come into existence since then and can even be viewed in YouTube videos. No, we don't have rocket-packs as I envisioned them just yet, but we will.

I also wrote in that novel how our air laws would have to be rewritten to take such flying machines into account and already we are witnessing the havoc that drones can create around our airports and elsewhere. Clearly, action needs to be taken, and soon, on that front.

In short, I believe that we should stay wild at heart, wild at mind and especially brimming with wonder, for it is a very wild world we inhabit and anything might yet come to pass, which is exciting!

## 18

# The Merriest of Pranksters, the Son of the "Fastestmanalive" & the "Howl" of the Poet

DURING MY MANY YEARS OF LIVING in San Francisco and the Bay Area, I mixed on countless occasions with like-minded people who were similarly influenced by the Beats. That shared perspective that the Beat writers were a cultural phenomenon whose influence had spread far and wide in the Fifties and the Sixties, and eventually gave rise to both the "hippie" and the "punk" movements, bonded us in a way that served us as a form of social cohesion, whether we were attending a Bob Dylan, Grateful Dead or Jefferson Starship concert, a poetry reading by Allen Ginsberg or Gary Snyder, or simply hanging out at the City Lights Bookstore or in the Haight-Ashbury district of the city. It served us as we enjoyed the fleshly freedom of Baker Beach or strolled the vast, beautiful gardens of Golden Gate Park.

In literary terms, what unified the writings of the Beats was not style, but their libertine attitude to sex and drugs. Of the big three – Jack Kerouac, Allen Ginsberg and William S Burroughs – both Ginsberg and Burroughs were forced into court for their profuse use of profanity in their writings and their stark portrayal of sexual activities which were deemed pornographic.

While sex and drugs were the sensationalist aspects of their work, bringing worldwide notoriety to the movement, there was another aspect of great interest to many of us and that was their iconoclastic approach to spirituality. Both Kerouac and Ginsberg extolled the sacred and holy nature of the human heart and soul, and did so quite apart from the conformist, repressive dictates of organized religion. These men found both sex and cannabis to be pathways through to the Divine and did not mince their words in that regard. Needless to say, the religious authorities were outraged by this libertine approach to spirituality and railed against it at every opportunity.

Young readers in those more repressive times, however, loved all of that and thoroughly agreed with the attitude of these rebel writers. Most citizens, they believed, had been essentially turned into puppets by government and religious leaders who kowtowed to the Christian clerics (both Catholic and Protestant) and even more-so to the Military-Industrial Complex. We must remember that these writers came of age in the immediate aftermath of World War II and they were not impressed with what was going on across the planet.

Both *On the Road* and *The Dharma Bums,* by Jack Kerouac, proved sensational and highly influential bestsellers. I, like millions of others, was swept up in the libertine attitude which filled his books and found the attitude of the characters exhilarating. Daring to live so freely and exuberantly was vastly appealing.

I subsequently discovered even more amplified versions of this libertine, licentious behavior in Allen Ginsberg's notorious poem *Howl,* and in William S Burroughs's heroin-addled tales to be found in his thoroughly unorthodox novel *Naked Lunch*.

Ginsberg went on to become the quintessential hippie with his long hair and beard and his openly liberal lifestyle. He was all about "peace and love" and he influenced millions along the way. Ultimately, he would go on to become a fervent Buddhist, as did many other writers and poets of that generation.

As for Burroughs, there was just no containing his iconoclastic attitude. He was almost the exact opposite of Ginsberg and had a fondness, not only for heroin, but liked his guns, as well. The anarchic movement that came into prominence in the late Seventies (once the hippie factions were driven into disgrace by the likes of Charlie Manson and the diehard law and order types) would later hail Burroughs as the Godfather of Punk and many of the defiant young at that time, as a result, foolishly got into hard drugs themselves. (As is generally known, the punk movement had little or no interest in peace, love or spirituality, and basically got their "kicks" from violence and nihilistic pursuits of a very dark nature.)

As for Kerouac, he "tuned in, turned on and dropped out" as Timothy Leary advised, but not for long. Alcohol became his drug of choice and it soon had him hiding out in his home brooding. Not only did he *not* become a hippie, he went on to repudiate them and subsequently died a middle aged, redneck cynic.

Personally, I found the punk movement's attitude to life much too negative for my liking and stuck instead with what has since come to be known as classic rock. I also stuck with what I considered to be the higher ground by reading books of a New Age tenor and poetry. My favorite poet at the time was Gary Snyder, the man who had been cast as Japhy Ryder in Kerouac's *The Dharma Bums*. His work, steeped as it was in environmentalist concerns and Zen Buddhist themes, struck just the right note to my way of thinking. I met him and Peter Coyote once at one of Gary's poetry readings and found him to be very serious in manner and extremely conscientious about displaying any form of pride or ego. In fact, he was extremely reluctant to even allow me to photograph him, but eventually relented. Peter Coyote, in contrast, was much more cheerful and forthcoming in conversation, and showed a great deal more enthusiasm for my novel *The Dream Illuminati*, when I gave each of the men a copy.

As for Allen Ginsberg, I had been to several of his poetry readings over the years but finally had the pleasure of meeting him in September of 1992 while living in San Francisco. How that meeting came about was interesting in and of itself. It was through John Cassady, the son of Neal. As readers of Kerouac's most famous work, *On the Road*, generally know, Neal Cassady was the inspiration for that book's central character. Neal was notorious for his wild, licentious antics, which was precisely why he caught the attention of the deeply uptight Kerouac who could only really overcome his inhibitions when he was drunk. Something of a con artist, Cassady dazzled Kerouac with his uncensored stream of consciousness banter about sex and drugs. As a result, he was the libertine spirit that Kerouac longed to be and this was why Neal became the central character of the writer's dreams as the character Dean Moriarty.

Neal, who was known to love amphetamines – "speed" – was said to dash about with an energy level so manic that it left others in the dust. Apparently unbothered by much of a conscience in matters of the heart, Neal's womanizing became as legendary as his love of cars and joyriding. So hyper was Neal in temperament and lifestyle, in fact, that author Ken Kesey, famous for writing *One Flew Over the Cuckoo's Nest*, subsequently dubbed him the "Great Driver" and the "Fastestmanalive". He also enticed the Beat hero to join his band of "Merry Pranksters".

What Cassady was recruited to do was drive the Prankster's psychedelic bus (known as "Furthur") for them. The tempestuous, LSD-laced shenanigans which ensued were captured to perfection in Tom Wolfe's book *The Electric Kool-Aid Acid Test*.

I had read these books over the years and had been delighted, therefore, to go to the launch of Kesey's new tome, *The Further Inquiry*, in 1990. This made for a surprising encounter. Once in the building with my friend, Lauren Bowker, I took one look at Kesey and was instantly astonished. He appeared *luminous* to me. I mean this literally. I am not a man who sees auras, but Kesey definitely had a visible golden radiance about him that had me amazed.

After having a chat with Ken, buying a copy of his book and getting him to sign it, as well as chatting with some of the other

Merry Pranksters who were present that day, my friend and I made our way to the front of the building to have a look at a replica of the famous psychedelic bus, which the Pranksters had on display there. Coincidentally, the man we found in the driver's seat once occupied by Neal Cassady – the Great Driver – at that very moment was none other than Neal's son, John.

John had long blond hair at the time and he was passionately babbling on and on appropriately, it seemed, about music, much as his father had back in his day (Neal was notorious for his love of jazz and was depicted multiple times in *On the Road* in a swoon, sweating profusely, before a group of jazz artists who were blowing and wailing their horns like madmen on a stage somewhere as high on cannabis as he was.) John soon became fast friends with Lauren and me and, in the subsequent months afterwards, often partied with us. John filled those hours with tale after insider tale about his father, his mother, Caroline, Kerouac, Ginsberg and many other "Beat" personalities.

Then one day John told me that Allen Ginsberg was coming to San Francisco for a poetry reading and he offered to introduce me. By then, I had published my book *The Dream Illuminati* and John indicated that if I wished, I could give the famous poet a copy. When that day duly arrived, John did indeed introduce me to Allen, and I did indeed hand him an inscribed copy of the novel. What happened next proved a bit startling to me, however. The fiery-eyed poet scanned the cover, flipped the book over, read what was written on its backside and ever blunt, gave me a sour surprise. He said, flat-out, "I don't read books about machines."

I was shocked, to say the least, but decided at once to stand my ground and argue my corner. I explained to Allen that the jetpacks in the novel were quite simply a literary device. They were there so that the main characters could live out their amazing dreams of flying. "Dreams of flying are spiritual in nature," I said. "They are metaphorical, symbolic expressions of the human soul and may actually involve travel 'out-of-body' in the Astral realm." I was speaking at that moment about the energy body. I then went on to explain that, like William Gibson who had brought higher consciousness to the subject of computers and virtual reality, I had used the flying machines as a pretext to speak of the spiritual proclivity of human beings to soar in their dreams. "Dreams are connected to the higher dimensions," I explained, "and, anyway, in this day and age, we are always surrounded by machines, by technology. That's just the way it is," I went on. "What matters, though, is the soul. What matters is the ability of the energy body to travel to other realms or, at least, to perceive and understand that life exists on multiple levels. That is what expanded consciousness is all about, is it not? You, of all people, should agree with that!"

Ginsberg, in fairness, pondered the idea, then chortled in his devilish way. "So, dreams of flying are another way of getting high," he sniggered, grinning like the legendary hipster he was and finally offering me some friendly ground.

"Exactly," I said. "In an ultimate sense, dreams of flying are about transcendence and transcendence is what we all want at the deepest level of our being."

I told him how I believed that Jesus ascending into heaven symbolized that final flight we all pray for and to which we all aspire. When the mystics and yogis, likewise, speak of transcendence, I told him, this is what they are talking about.

At its crux, I believe, what *The Dream Illuminati* evokes is the split in Western culture between viewing Judeo-Christian orthodoxy in either literal or figurative terms. Are the stories we read in the Bible meant to be taken as historically "real" or are they intended to be understood primarily as spiritual parables?

My point is this: historians know that the earliest Western centers of learning were "Mystery Schools" and that a strong argument can be made that the stories which came out of those centers were meant to be teaching tools. What the wise elders did for the sake of their novices was to stage "passion plays". These dramatic plays were not intended to be taken literally. On the contrary, they were intended to move a spiritual aspirant *emotionally* in order that the sacred nature of life could be conveyed in a powerful way, one that could impact the spirit of the person. The equivalent in today's world are movies. Films have a far more powerful impact on viewers in our own time than does attending a ritualistic gathering in a church, temple or synagogue, even with the inclusion of a fiery speech or sermon.

Passion plays in their day were full of moral and ethical dramas and these resonated deeply with people when these stories were shared. We must remember here that these dramas preceded the written word and were the sole way in which profound information could be transmitted. The oral tradition, in other words, was everything in those days.

Another important point to consider regarding Christianity in particular is that the story of Jesus was not the first to describe a "savior-god" who died and subsequently rose from the dead in a miraculous resurrection. In fact, there were five such gods prior to Jesus in Egypt, the Middle East and Greece. These were Adonis, Attis, Dionysus, Mithra and Osiris. In fact, the highly respected academic J.M. Robertson, in his book *Pagan Christs*, published in the late 1800s offers the possibility that the entire saga of Jesus was a passion play that ended up being taken literally.

This is debatable, of course, and academics may never finally reach what can be considered an incontrovertible conclusion, so I will just make the following point: there is a genuine split in the way that religious tales are interpreted and that is as true today as it was in the olden times. The essence of the split is down to whether one chooses to consider them in literal or metaphorical terms. In the last analysis, the choice is up to each of us and, yes, we do stake our souls on that interpretation in a sense. By that I mean that what happens to us once we exit this

Earth and slip into some other dimension will be a moment of truth. The consciousness and life experience we bring to that moment will determine what happens next.

The good news is it would appear, by the multitude of reports we have from yogis, mystics and near-death returnees, that there is an almost infinite range of possibilities that await us once we become disembodied and leave this planet. Based on our personal spiritual depth of understanding, we will encounter that which our hearts and minds desire most.

To put it another way; once we depart the earth, we will experience the beings and environment that we deserve. If we have been loving and kind, then we will be enveloped by loving spirits and find ourselves in a paradise of breath-taking beauty. If we have been cruel and unloving, then look out! The demons of hell will come for us.

It is through making a forensic study of the roots of religion that opens one up to the greatest range of possibilities. I would ask anyone who is prepared to argue from a position of blind faith in any particular religion to consider putting their religion to the test by daring to study the entire range of religious beliefs which exist right around the globe. This strikes me as the best way to determine the authenticity of one's own faith. At the very least, it will provide a treasure trove of expanded knowledge that will serve one's personal spiritual evolution in profoundly liberating ways. As the wise Indian sage Meher Baba once said, "There is no difference in the realization of Truth either by a Muslim, Hindu, Zoroastrian, or a Christian. The difference is only in words and terms. Truth is not the monopoly of a particular race or religion."

How true.

As for Allen Ginsberg, I will never know if he read *The Dream Illuminati* or not, but I certainly hope that those who do will see my point and understand what a life-changer deeper knowledge can be. Symbolism is a powerful thing, after all, which is why I opened the book with a quote by Jung. As the great man wrote: "The most we can do is *to dream the myth onwards* and give it a modern dress."

That I did. The near future I envisioned in *The Dream Illuminati* embraced technology in exciting and novel ways. In fact, I see all of my books as modern versions of the passion plays of yore. I might even go so far as to say that we humans are quite possibly living out our days in a Mystery School of global proportions. We need only succeed in realizing it.

# 19

# Cairo Confidential

## *A Mad Dash for the Great Pyramid of Giza & A Magic Carpet Ride into the Great Beyond*

THE DAY I ARRIVED IN CAIRO, I hit the ground running... I had been traveling for months by that point and was full of the world. I felt as if the towering pagodas and stone temples of Kathmandu and the magnificent, soaring, snowy peaks of the Himalayas were coursing through my blood by then. So, too, the sacred temples and stupas of Varanasi, Rangoon, Mandalay, Bangkok, Hong Kong, Tokyo and Kyoto. My mind was boiling over with the imagery of those exotic cultures, especially the faces of the cheerful, polite people in their flowing robes, silken saris and beautiful longyis. I exulted in the delicious cuisine I had had the pleasure of enjoying and exulted even more so in the brief, but intriguing, interactions I had had with the yogis, rishis, swamis, priests and Zen masters of the East. I was in a state of perpetual ecstasy.

On top of being full of the world, however, cracks had appeared in the relationship I had once so enjoyed with my partner at the time and the two of us were in a questionable place as a result. Despite all of the amazing things we had experienced together, being on the road incessantly and out of our comfort zone had taken a toll on us. Eventually, the constant movement had become too much. Then, when the money began to run out, we asked each other one very important question: Which country is an absolute must-see for you before we return to the States?

My partner said, "China". I said, "Egypt".

Those words would prove to be another in a series of life-altering choices for both of us.

Nevertheless, after a final week together on the island of Koh Samui in Thailand, off I went on my own to Hong Kong and Japan. From there I flew to Egypt, my must-see destination.

With limited funds at my disposal, I had resolved to make short work of the country. After all, the Great Pyramid and Sphinx were the only things that I was mad to see at the time and, by all the gods and goddesses of that great land, I decided on Day One to make tracks straight for those legendary, celebrated Wonders of the Ancient World. I would not be deterred.

The camel traders, however, saw me as an easy mark. They saw dollar signs when they laid eyes on me, apparently, and were anxious for whatever funds I could throw their way. As a consequence, they hounded me from the second I entered their domain; one after the next and shouting loudly. In their best English, they would roar, "Yes, yes, you ride." It was not a request. It was a command. Their humped-backed beasts stood ready and the pressure on me was relentless. Soon the whole situation had me soured. I had come to the Giza Necropolis determined to experience some measure of mystic astonishment. The enigmatic wonders before me had me dazzled. I had read so much about how architecturally perfect and otherworldly the Great Pyramid was, for example. I was also in awe of the fact that even in the present day and age no crew of builders on earth could replicate the structure. I was acutely aware that this enormous edifice was comprised of over two and a half million blocks of stone; that the bulk of those blocks weighed in at over two tons each and that a few of those blocks within the structure weighed anywhere from 50 to 100 tons. That alone made for a staggering reality in my mind. Then there was the fact that the Great Pyramid was said to be a mathematical model of the northern hemisphere of the Earth at a certain scale and that its height in relation to its base perimeter was as the radius of a circle to its circumference. All of this was mind-blowing. On top of that some speculative writers had even insisted that the massive structure was over ten thousand years of age, and that the Sphinx might be older still.

So, yes, I wanted to look upon those magnificent constructs with the hushed awe they deserved, but instead I was badgered relentlessly on that first day by the swarthy camel boys in their big billowy jellabas and horribly assailed by their gruff manners.

Mood ruined, I joined a long queue and went inside of the Great Pyramid only to find that it was very dimly lit and totally unadorned. In fact, there was little to see. The Grand Gallery proved to be nothing more than a long, vaulted, ramp-like corridor of stone that led to the King's Chamber and, once inside of that particular room, I found nothing but bare walls and a stone sarcophagus of little intrigue.

Mingling in among the many tourists during that time frame, I certainly had no revelations and no electrifying mystical moments.

Disappointed, I crawled off, took an old, decrepit bus back into the heart of Cairo, found a hotel, checked in, ate my dinner and went to bed.

The next morning, there was another shock. I was awakened at the crack of dawn by a booming, amplified voice which literally echoed against the walls of my room at a volume that seemed ear-splitting. It was the Muslim call to prayer and, while I am a person who respects every religious tradition, I was left fitful by this intrusion on my sleep and, to be quite frank about it, I was less than enchanted by the sound of the loud, overbearing voice of the chanter.

There was nothing to be done about it, though, so I got up and got with it. Only what should I do, I asked myself. I had seen the Great Pyramid and Sphinx already. I had been impressed with the reality of their size certainly, but sitting and looking on them in the heat of a Sahara afternoon with the sand pelting me in the sultry breeze had not in the least been like looking on the gleaming golden spires and stupas of Rangoon or Bangkok, for example, nor had I enjoyed anything like sitting in meditative contemplation on one of the ghats on the Ganges River in the holy city of Varanasi amid yogis and holy ones in prayerful reverence, while mindfully soaring with cosmic exhilaration.

Then I thought about the Cairo Museum and decided to go there and see the many wonders I had read about, including the gleaming, golden stash of astonishing artifacts taken from the tomb of the pharaoh boy-king, Tutankhamun.

First, however, I decided to take a look around the city and give it another chance to impress me. I had little hope of that, however, as I strolled those dusty streets and, among other things, found myself passing fierce-faced men in turbans and long flowing robes with rifles thrown over their shoulders. The heat was already on the rise, as well, so I decided to escape it; I ducked into what turned out to be the largest bazaar in all of Egypt: Khan El Khalili.

Making my way through that huge, shaded marketplace proved plenty intriguing. There were countless food, drink and clothing stalls, statuary shops and rug sellers, jewelry and trinket hawkers, and everything else imaginable. It was such a fascinating, lively mix of people and things that I quickly found myself smiling and laughing with the locals, at last. I was finally back in the groove of enjoying myself.

Then I happened to discover the largest collection of hookahs I had ever seen. They were in a shop located well off the main corridors of the bazaar and I found myself alone there marveling at what I was seeing. There were hundreds of styles of hookahs, all made of brass and other metals, most lavishly adorned and huge in size.

The proprietor of the shop was very pleased by my wide-eyed wonder. "You like? Yes? You want to buy?"

I didn't exactly appreciate the pushiness, but still I laughed and gestured toward my backpack. "I don't think there's any room for a hookah in this little thing," I shot back.

The old, grizzled figure laughed, too. He eyed me up and down from beneath his turban, clearly noting the long hair, the white linen Indian shirt with its blue brocade and my yoga pants, then grinned in a curiously amused manner. "You do like the black magic, though, no?" His grin was a leering, lopsided thing now.

Puzzled by the words, I drew back. "You mean like voodoo?"

The man let laugh in a great booming voice. "The black magic!" he roared in a sardonic tone. "Don't be silly. I am talking about hashish, of course."

"Oh..."

The man laughed at my bemusement, the hairs on his chin quivering like a curvy patch of silver needles. "Oh, you do," he said in a playful, teasing tone. "I know all about you hippies."

I thought, *Look, old man, these are the Eighties now. The hippie movement is long dead and gone. I'm just a backpacking traveler.* Still, he wasn't too far off the mark, I knew, so I kept my humor about me and chortled along.

"Come," he said to me then. "You no buy hookah, no." There was firmness and finality in the tone. "I have something else for you. I have just the thing, in fact."

I thought, *Okay, here comes the hustle...*

Nevertheless, I played along. Why not, I figured. Tramping along behind the big man in his billowy jellaba, I was taken into his office at the rear of the shop. He made his way into a locked cupboard, then brought out a little box, which was also locked.

Admittedly curious, I waited with proverbial bated breath to see what was inside.

It proved to be a small, shapely sphinx. With his dark eyes gleaming, the old Egyptian handed it to me with a smug grin on his swarthy face, "Priceless. Perfect," he said. "Very old. Solid bronze."

The thing surprised me by its heaviness. Its weight was astonishing for its size.

Looking it over in more detail, I noted that this sphinx did not look like the Great Sphinx, but instead bore a human face looking sideways. The head was mounted on a graceful leonine body, which in turn was set upon a small pedestal. A pharaonic headpiece adorned the human face, and the small statue did, indeed, seem very old.

"Not a trinket for tourists," the old man scoffed. "This is the real thing. A work of art by a master of the craft," he added. "Hundreds of years old." Then he grabbed the sphinx from me and turned it over. "Look," he said, pointing at two incisions on the underside of the pedestal. "This is where the name of the museum and its serial number were cut away."

Suddenly, I was aghast. "You mean..."

"Yes, it was stolen," he retorted in a harsh tone, "but not by me. To be honest, I need to get it out of this shop... I need it out of here in case the police come checking. That is why I am willing to give it to you for a very good price."

"But it's stolen!" I objected.

"Yes, but not by me!" he bellowed. "And not by you. So... What we are looking at is a once in a lifetime opportunity for you. Do you understand? You would be a fool to pass this up, especially at the price I am about to propose."

I couldn't resist. It was, indeed, a once in a lifetime opportunity I realized and, wrong as it was, I cut a deal with the man and fled. I tore down the long winding corridors of the teeming bazaar, the sweat pouring from my face. Dying of thirst, all at once, I slipped into a small, enclosed restaurant with air conditioning, grabbed a chair at one of the empty tables and ordered a soda.

Once I had calmed down, I dared to draw my little prize from out my backpack and place it on the table. I then sat staring at it in awe, feeling like a true outlaw.

Only then I discovered that I wasn't the only one staring. A young man with a buzzcut was eyeing me up quite closely, I noticed, and especially my precious prize. He was wearing a white jellaba with blue stripes. To my horror, he suddenly stood up and came over to me. "May I see it," he said, gesturing with his cleanshaven chin, his dark eyes friendly and unthreatening.

Nervous, nevertheless, I hesitated.

"It's okay," he assured me in a warm voice as he swept into the chair across from me. He then took the sphinx in hand, straightaway turned it over and began nodding. "Be careful," he said. "This is the real thing; a genuine antique worth a lot of money."

I was thrilled with his words but felt very nervous about him holding the little sphinx.

"How much did you pay?"

When I told him, he just nodded in a knowing way. "Watch your back," he warned. "You did not pay anything close to the price that this statue is worth. The plan is probably to have some accomplice of the man who sold it to you attack you and take it back so that they can resell it to another unsuspecting westerner like yourself."

Shocked, I just sat staring at the young man.

"I'm Mo," he said then, thrusting out his hand. "Short for Mohammed, of course, and I look out for you." He asked all about where I came from and what I did for a living, then told me about his dream of going to America one day to make a fortune for himself. He had a lovely disposition and a very kind way of speaking. He then managed to shock me again. He said, "You come to my house now where it is safe. I live very near the Giza Necropolis. Have you been there yet?"

I said I had, and I expressed how disappointed I had been by the experience.

Mo laughed. "Yes, the camel men are very aggressive, but listen… I have hashish at my home. We smoke and then I show you the Sphinx and the Great Pyramid like you will never see them again. That is a promise."

When I appeared clearly taken aback by the offer, he noted the look of suspicion on my face and added, "I get you inside of the Great Pyramid by yourself…" His whole countenance was lit up now at the prospect of what he was offering. "You, alone, in the Great Pyramid… Think about it. Inside, all alone, high on hashish…" He then fairly mewled in a teasing tone, "My friend, this is a once in a lifetime opportunity."

I recoiled at the words. Here was the hustle again. Mo had just used the very same expression as the old man. He was surely enticing me into whatever scam he was running, I figured, so I said no. I said it all sounded very thrilling, but risky. I certainly did not want to end up in an Egyptian prison should I get caught with a stolen sphinx in my possession or busted by the police should they raid his home and discover hashish, which I assumed was illegal.

Mo was a charmer, however, and he proved so reassuring about everything and so good at painting a happy picture for me that I did indeed eventually come to believe that I was being offered a once in a lifetime opportunity. Then Mo reminded me that we had better get out of the bazaar and fast or I might be attacked. "You will have to watch your back now, my friend. Watch it very, very closely."

"Okay," I said. "Let's roll."

Roll we did… On a rickety old bus, the sweat pouring off me again, but Mo was true to his word and within half an hour or so I could see at the back of the row of houses where Mo said he lived the ancient towering golden sandstone head of the Great Sphinx. Suddenly, I was full of exhilaration.

"We get off here," he said.

We did. We got off the bus and stepped briskly along the sidewalk. "I live here," he said.

It proved to be a place where there was an old woman

dressed all in black from head to foot, sweeping the walkway. Mo told me to wait where I was, then proceeded to have strong words with the woman. Clearly, harsh words flew for tempers flared, but Mo was adamant that she go away and he eventually chased her off with flapping arms.

"Come," Mo then said. I felt guilty about the old woman, but into the house I went.

True to his word again, Mo quickly brought out a giant hookah and I watched in stunned silence as he rolled a massive ball of black hashish with the skill of an artisan.

Long story short, I was soon soaring along on the magic carpet ride of my life. I burst through the top of my skull, then up through the ceiling of the house and into the spacious blue Egyptian sky like a falcon in a whirlwind. I don't know where I went, but when I returned to the room, Mo was all smiles and we talked of many things, none of which I can remember.

None, except for one bemusing piece of conversation… Mo had talked about a sponsorship program he had heard about, and he wanted to know if I would help him with it; help him get into the USA so that he could make his fortune and live out his dream.

I was in no position nor condition for such talk, and I swiftly begged off. I then changed the subject altogether. I said, "Mo, my friend, my mind is racing! I can't be talking business at a time like this. Come, let us go see the Great Pyramid now. Please!" I was full of fiery resolve. "We can talk business later. This is a time for action. Come on, let's go!"

Mo's disappointment was unmistakable. It was writ large on his face and he clearly did not want to leave the house. "It is scorching hot out there," he warned. "You will not be up for it. Let us stay in here where it is cool and talk."

"No, no, no!" I shot back. "We must go. We must strike while the iron is hot. I'm in the perfect frame of mind for this, just as you promised I would be. Come. Let's go. Let's go now!"

Reluctantly, Mo led the way, and he was dead right about the heat. I nearly collapsed on the sidewalk it was so hot. I put on my sunglasses and took a big swill of water, then wobbled forth. Soon I was led up a hill, which I struggled to climb. When I got to the top, however, I encountered the sight of my life: the Great Pyramid and Sphinx in golden sandstone splendor, ancient and mighty, colossal, and stunningly picture perfect! It was as if I was suddenly in the throes of a staggering vision and was nearly knocked off my feet. In fact, I could not tell if I was still on some surreal magic carpet ride or on solid ground at that moment.

Mo was amused. "Come," he said. "I get you inside as promised."

Trailing along on legs made of rubber, I descended the far side of the hill with my newfound Egyptian buddy and went down onto the Giza Necropolis in a state of glee. My dream was finally being realized in the way I had always imagined it. Mo was proving not only to be my protector, but my champion. I was in ecstasy.

Approaching the Great Pyramid from the way we had come allowed us to avoid the camel hucksters with their hump-backed beasts and here, I thought, was another blessing. Mo then spoke quietly and furtively to the three young guards at the entrance of the edifice and within seconds a deal was struck. I was to give the guard a token payment once I was inside and he would keep everyone else, all tourists, out while I went off exploring.

All at once, a crowd of tourists came into view. They were exiting the Great Pyramid, which was fortuitous. Mo told me that one of the guards would hold up the next batch of tourists while I was inside. I shook Mo's hand and told him how much I appreciated what he was doing, and he just smiled. Quite frankly, I was in a state of disbelief at what a great dose of good luck I was having.

Then I was inside.

And, so, after paying off the guard, I proceeded along the long, ramp-like corridor of the Grand Gallery once more, creeping through the dimness on furtive feet. I kept thinking how amazing it was that I was inside of the most famous and, irrefutably, the most mysterious edifice on the face of the earth. Not only was I in the place; I was *alone* in it.

Pressing on, I made my way to the King's Chamber and went inside. I took one look at the so-called sarcophagus within it and resolved to clamber inside straightaway. My only hesitation came courtesy of that spooky, ancient rumor about a curse being put on anyone who dared to defile pharaoh's sacred resting place. *But to hell with that,* I thought. *I'm going in…*

I did. I climbed inside, sat back, and found myself feeling more ecstatic than ever. I rubbed my hands over the hard granite surface of the inside of the thing and fingered its impossibly perfect, right-angled corners. I thought about how certain speculative writers had claimed that this so-called sarcophagus was said to have been machine tooled by a massive drill bit. Yet, according to the history books, no such tools existed at the time the Great Pyramid was built, which was thousands and thousands of years ago. Indeed, the builders of the Great Pyramid were said to have used ramps and ropes and copper chisels. *Such bullshit,* I thought.

As I continued to finger the ridges of the corners in curious delight, I was struck all at once by a thought that put me right through the ceiling of the King's Chamber. *Aliens built this place!* I thought. *Aliens, for God's sake!* Or maybe the gods themselves had built it, I further thought in a state of wild delirium. The very idea of that had me sky high and off on another magic carpet ride. That old "black magic" was indeed living up to its legend and I was soon on Cloud Nine.

Then I was given the surprise of my life.

The lights in the room went out. Just like that… *Snap!* I was in the dark. I was in the darkest dark I had ever experienced. I was in the blackest of black voids imaginable.

Rather than panicking or even wondering what the hell was going on, I simply slumped back in the king's notorious sarcophagus and rocketed upward into the Egyptian sky. Words will never describe what happened at that point. All I can say is that history unfolded before my mind's eye at the speed of light, and I encountered so many faces and entities that I could not keep track of them. They flashed by at such a velocity that I could not even tell at times if they were people, animals, aliens, gods or what they were. One of the faces, however, was that of a white baboon. Maybe I just imagined it, but I had read once that Thoth, the Egyptian god of magic and writing – the two most all-consuming interests of my life – was sometimes depicted as a white baboon and now I was seeing him. I was face to face with him.

Astonishing.

Astonishing, mind-blowing, surreal...

Then I thought, *this isn't a crypt. This is a chrysalis! This is for getting out of the body and flying free as a bird!*

Exhilarated beyond all belief, I soared and spiraled for what seemed like an eternity. Only then another thought struck that was like a stab in the chest. In my bag was a priceless artifact that had been stolen from some museum and here was I, high on an illegal substance, in the Great Pyramid. All at once, paranoia hit with a vengeance and sent a boiling shot of adrenaline up my spine like a bolt of burning mercury.

I knew at once that I needed to get out of there. Some kind of intuitive flash took over within me and it was unmistakable. *Go! Get out!* I heard myself thinking. *Get out of here now!*

Simply getting up onto my feet, however, proved to be one hell of a struggle. Still, I fought my way up and, once I succeeded, I clambered back over the wall of the sarcophagus in the pitch-black room and made for the door purely on memory. I then staggered along the railing of the Grand Gallery and hobbled toward the door, which was outlined by a thin slit of light. *Go! Keep going,* I kept telling myself. *Get out of this place now!*

Within seconds I had made my way to the door and out into the bright, merciless Egyptian sun. The brightness of it was unspeakably overpowering. It was like coming face to face with Atum-Ra and having your eyeballs zapped by his golden molten magnificence. With my pupils dilated, I was completely momentarily blinded, but I staggered forward a few paces and managed to wrangle my sunglasses from my bag. With the glasses in place, I finally had a squinting look around.

What I saw was Mo and the three guards talking among themselves in the near distance. None of the four men was apparently aware of my presence.

Then I found myself staring with alarm at what I saw next. Two policemen were coming down the hill toward Mo and the other men. The officers were moving quickly and then they were clearly questioning the guards.

I knew this for certain because suddenly all eyes were on me! Shocked, I thought of the little stolen bronze sphinx I was carrying, panicked, and made a run for it. Racing off, I made my way on rubbery legs to the bus stop I had been at the day before and climbed on board as swiftly as I could. I slipped the driver a few coins and made my way to the back of the bus so that I could look out the window and hide if necessary. Sure enough, I could see the two policemen and they were definitely on the chase. They were waving their hands and shouting at the bus driver, but he either failed to notice or didn't give a damn, because he simply revved up his big engine, slipped the old vehicle into gear and rattled off. Continuing to wave and shout, the policemen soon realized that their efforts were in vain and finally gave up the chase.

As for Mo, I could see him following along behind the two officers at a slacker pace. He had a look of deep disappointment on his face, which made me feel quite awful, but under circumstances that bizarre, what could I do? In any case, the driver, either still oblivious of what had gone on or totally uncaring, pressed on and that was that. I let out an enormous sigh of relief. We were soon far away and then there was only one thing left to do: thank the gods or my lucky stars for what was surely the most amazing, mind-blowing experience of my life.

* * *

Postscript: Before leaving Egypt, I put the statue in a box and dropped it off anonymously with one of the curators of the Egyptian museum and promptly made my exit! I will never know just how old, how genuine or how valuable my little bronze sphinx actually was, but one thing is certain: it was indeed a gift of the gods for giving me that day as far as I was concerned, and I still hold it in my heart.

# 20

# The Divine, Sublime Connection on High

EINSTEIN ONCE SAID, "The intuitive mind is a sacred gift, and the rational mind is a faithful servant. We have created a society that honors the servant and has forgotten the gift."

While academic philosophers will quickly dismiss any argument which appeals to "authority" for its validity, we who live out our lives in the everyday world of endless decision making (whether deciding issues of a minor nature or those which become life-altering), tuning into and getting to grips with intuition is profoundly beneficial, which is why paying heed to the considered opinion of Albert Einstein is, therefore, something we should all do. After all, Einstein is not just the most famous of any of history's physicists, he is also regarded as being a renowned figure of sagely wisdom whose insights while alive extended far beyond the scope of his numerous scientific theories, many of which have altered the way virtually all of us view the universe. I might also note that Time magazine, in their December 31, 1999 edition, named Einstein the "Person of the Century". They did this because of his many scientific theories, of course, but also for the many wise insights the great man offered humanity and for how he was dead set against using atomic weaponry in the arena of war.

Time magazine's Walter Isaacson stated that the magazine's choice for Person of the Century was the individual who "for better or worse, personified our times and will be recorded as having the most lasting significance." Consider the competition: Gandhi, Churchill, Roosevelt, Truman and Hitler, among others. (Hitler? Yes, because for better *or worse* the individual had a major, lasting impact.)

Frederic Golden in the article following Isaacson's opening

remarks called Einstein "unfathomably profound – a genius among geniuses who discovered, merely by thinking about it, that the universe was not as it seemed." He also called him "relativity's rebel", a man who "combined rare genius with a deep moral sense and a total indifference to convention."

These attributes speak volumes as to why we should listen to the man and there are, of course, countless quotes which we could bring forward here, but the theme here is intuition, hence the quote at the outset: "The intuitive mind is a sacred gift, and the rational mind is a faithful servant. We have created a society that honors the servant and has forgotten the gift."

The great man does not call intuition simply a "gift", but a "sacred" gift. Why would a scientist do that? Isn't it only theologians who speak in such terms?

Let us look at that word *sacred.* It comes from the Latin *sacer sacri* meaning "holy". The word *holy,* in turn, comes into use in the English-speaking world via the Germanic *halig,* which is related to the word *whole* and is defined as something that is "morally and spiritually excellent or perfect, and to be revered", as well as "belonging to, devoted to, or empowered by God."

The question thus arises as to why Einstein would use the word "sacred" with intuition. Is it "Godly", "angelic" or is intuition quite simply the mysterious machinations of an unidentifiable "higher intelligence"? Or is it simply one's own "higher self" speaking to one's "lower", worldly self? (This latter notion suggests that the "self" exists in two dimensions at once, which is intriguing to say the least!)

As most artists know when they launch into any form of creative activity, whether writing a poem, a work of fiction, a new song or pondering an inspirational image to paint, the initial notion or idea for that work can simply spring into the mind, often with such power and force that one cannot but bring it into the world. Inventors also experience this phenomenon. In other words, an artist or inventor can be literally compelled to bring something new into the world.

Many an artist has publicly stated that some particular work arrived inexplicably into their mind "full-blown". Both John Lennon and Paul McCartney, for example, two of the greatest songwriters in modern times, have made comments to that effect (Lennon's "Across the Universe" and McCartney's "Yesterday" both arrived in such a fashion). Bob Dylan also once said that as a young man he was almost afraid to go to sleep at night for fear of missing out on yet another incredible song coming through from somewhere somehow, even he couldn't say. Bach, Beethoven and Mozart in their day all enjoyed the fruits of their musical intuitions with works that simply poured out of them. Countless poets, of course, have spoken of the "muse" whispering into their inner ear as they sat with pen in hand. Likewise, writers as diverse as Charles Dickens and William S Burroughs have indicated that their most inspired works came to them in such a rush that it was as if they were doing little more than taking dictation.

Dictation? From whom?

That is the question…

The answer is: Nobody knows for sure. Yet, thanks to intuition, works of art and scientific breakthroughs do come surging forth into fruition from time to time to secure a particular person's place in history and it has sometimes even been known to save a life.

Equally important for the majority of us, intuition can give us the kind of guidance that can carry our lives in a whole new and significant direction.

Indeed, guidance is a hugely mysterious aspect of human experience that occurs to all of us whether we are an artist, a scientist, a butcher, a baker or a bricklayer. This guidance can save us from getting involved with people who will do us no favors and all kinds of troublesome situations. What we may sense when intuition speaks can be surprisingly simple:

the impression that "Yes," we should do this, or "No", we should definitely not do this! Such a statement generally does not come to us in the form of words, but as a feeling – a so-called "gut feeling". My understanding is that if we sense a palpable rise in our mid-section over any particular decision we are contemplating, that is a yes. If the gut turns palpably downward, that is a no.

So pay attention. When intuition speaks… *Listen* to it. If your gut tells you yes or no, go with that guidance and show it the respect it deserves for looking after you.

In other words, be humbled before this superior source of knowledge and wisdom, for it is your very own personal divine, sublime connection on high. It is your greatest ally.

# 21

# Magic Cadillac Flashback

GROWING UP IN POST-WORLD WAR II America was like no other era in global history. Even those of us who were living in modest circumstances were treated to an impressive phenomenon in the form of exotic technological marvels. These left our minds awestruck, for novelty abounded in those days and those marvels came in all sizes, shapes and colors. The gamut ran from state-of-the-art, battery powered toys to jumbo jets; from flashy bicycles with gleaming chrome handlebars to Harley Davidsons roaring down the highways of the country; and from transistor radios in every conceivable variant of cool to space age ornamental architecture on broad city streets.

Then there were the cars... The long, wondrous, often gas-guzzling Chevrolets, Fords, Lincoln Continentals, Chryslers, Pontiacs, Plymouths, Buicks and those phenomenal Cadillacs, which only the rich could seemingly afford.

Truly, the phrase "Thunder Road" was no mere metaphor in those years.

In fact, in Post-World War II America, almost anyone could afford a Cadillac if they made that particular car their priority over having virtually anything else of quality.

I still remember to this day seeing a crimson Cadillac convertible pull into the driveway of our modest family home, its long slender body like a horizontal rocket ship, its elegant fins flying high and proud. I was left utterly thunderstruck by the beauty and majesty of the car. To my young eyes, this was an exotic technological marvel beyond any. It was a spectacular work of art and it looked to me as if it had been flown in from Mars, not from some factory in Detroit or wherever. It truly dazzled the eye to see it.

The owner of the Caddy was a friend of my father's. The man worked with my father at what was then called Sears Roebuck. My father was in charge of the automotive department in those days and his pal was a mechanic. Over the years I learned a few things about that kindly man.

For starters, his home was a shoebox sized shack and probably not worth half the value of the 1959 Cadillac that the old boy parked in its driveway. He had a wife and two daughters, and on one occasion our family attended the wedding of one of those daughters. I can still see in my mind's eye her handsome groom in his black tux dancing the "Twist" and looking an awful lot like the King of Rock 'N' Roll, Elvis Presley.

Elvis, of course, was himself known for having many a fine Cadillac in those days, but he was a millionaire rock star with more Number 1 hits than any other singer in history at the time and my father's friend was a reed of a man with pale skin who generally wore a dingy gray hat atop a narrow head with thinning wisps of silvery hair. His shirts and pants were invariably stained with motor oil.

Beside the old man's little box of a home, almost directly across the street, stood the water tower of the small city of Fostoria, Ohio. It was a cylindrical structure that looked like a giant grain silo, aquamarine in color with a domed roof, and it stood at least twenty times higher than the old man's home, or any home on that ramshackle street, in fact. In retrospect the tower looked as if it could have housed a rocket ship or served, perhaps, as a missile silo in disguise. It has since been torn down and disposed of by city officials who built a huge reservoir on the other side of the city.

In those days, there was a lot of talk about missiles. After all, the Soviets, like the U.S., had hundreds of them and they were equipped at their tips with atomic bombs. An atomic bomb could blow an entire city to Kingdom Come, we were informed, and the so-called "nasty pinko Commies" over in Russia might choose to do exactly that to one of our fine American cities if they were riled up enough by whatever the hell we were up to as a country in those days. In fact, at school, our principal and his staff would occasionally initiate bomb drills designed to prepare us for just such an all-out atomic attack by the Soviet Union, a country which quite bizarrely had formerly been America's ally in the fight against Hitler and his killer Nazis.

I actually saw my first picture of an exploding atomic bomb at the old man's home, for he and his wife loved buying the various and sundry tabloids that were on offer in those days, as well as the National Geographic magazine. It was in the latter that I first laid eyes on a photo that showed American scientists blowing the Bikini Atoll to proverbial smithereens.

The tabloids, however, were mind-blowing for another reason, for they were loaded with the scandalous shenanigans of Hollywood celebrities and featured many a photo of a racy female siren. I did not yet get it about humanity's proclivity for titillation, but what struck me in a way that I found inexplicable, yet riveting, were the pictures of people with strange diseases and bizarre malformations of the body. These were a shock to my young system as I was a true innocent at that point and those photos invariably set my pulse racing. I simply had no idea that anyone could be like that, and my heart broke for the afflicted souls I saw on those pages, a few of which I have never forgotten.

To humanity's eternal disgrace, some of the unfortunates depicted in those tabloids were known as "freaks" in those days and, on the rare occasion, such a soul would appear live and in person whenever a carnival happened to come to town. For example, I once saw a man who stood but two feet tall or so and I paid a few coins to go into his tent and have a look at him. I found him sitting on a little chair on top of a table in a bright golden spotlight. He held a microphone with his doll-sized fingers and spoke about his life as a midget. It was a deeply troubling visual image for me at that age and, afterwards, I had nightmares for weeks. Again, the problem was quite simply that I had never encountered such a sight before and, looking back on it, the fact that a person thus afflicted could be put on show and exploited as a "freak" spoke volumes about the state of society's thinking at the time.

I also remember seeing a child in one of those tabloids that – as the saying goes – "freaked me out" even worse. The little girl had a disease that had ravaged her tiny body so severely that it had her looking as if she were as old and wrinkled as a ninety-year-old. How could the world be like this? I wondered. How could it be so bizarre? Indeed, how could people survive with such afflictions and misfortunes of this magnitude? It all seemed unfathomable to me and left me reeling for days and months. (This was well before I came to realize that it is deformations of the personality that constitute the real tragedy in this world.)

"Come on," the old man would say, though. "Let's get out of here and go for a drive in the Caddy."

It was a welcome relief to say the least. And so, we would all pile into his magic convertible, my father, my two brothers and myself, and once the old man had his pipe lit and had the radio turned on, off we'd go, sailing down the street like a boatload of intoxicated sailors lost in a very pleasant dream with the smoke and the music wafting.

Years later, in the late Sixties, I would own my own crimson car, but it was definitely not a Cadillac. It was a Comet. It was like something out of the space age, too, though, only shorter and with fins far less extravagant and impressive. I would crank up the tunes once in it, nevertheless, and this was where I had it over the old man: my music was rock 'n' roll, and I would have it blasting out at a sonic level that sometimes had me levitating in my seat.

Off I'd go with my buddies, then, usually to buy beer and smoke a bit of reefer. By then, the Cuban Missile Crisis had come and gone. Kennedy had been assassinated and his brother, too, as well as Martin Luther King. Meanwhile, Elvis, the "King of Rock 'N' Roll", was also fairly out of the picture by then, for The Beatles were riding high in the charts and had stolen the King's crown. In short, life went on for most of us, but not for all of us. This was because the war in Vietnam was raging away and there were few families in my hometown that did not know some young man who had been killed and sent back home in a box.

Worse, in my estimation, were the ones who came home with missing limbs. I can still see one such man in my mind, someone I had gone to school with and, when I went to pay him a visit once he had come home again, I found him on his couch with just a pair of pants on. His bare torso made me blanch, for not only was his left arm missing, but a small bit of muscle had been saved and it looked very much like what it was: raw meat. The muscle was somehow attached atop his shoulder for a reason I was way too in shock to ask about, but it was there presumably so that a prosthetic limb could one day be attached.

The crazy world was getting crazier, I thought, despite the rock and pop stars of the day warbling on and on about how the "Age of Aquarius" was dawning and the world was heading, by the grace of the gods, into paradise. *Maybe so, maybe not…* I cautiously told myself, for by the time I sold my crimson Comet I was on the verge of having to go to Vietnam myself. Not a very pleasant prospect for a young man.

As a consequence, I marched against the war in those days and saw many a young man burn his draft card. None of us wanted to go off to Southeast Asia to fight the Commies. In fact, it was the last thing that any of us wanted to do. Our lives weren't being directly threatened, we figured, so why *should* we? It seemed a pointless sacrifice of one's life by our reckoning and to hell with that. We wanted to spend virtually all of our time being high and happy, and dancing at rock festivals.

We wanted to groove to the music and free our souls, not go thrashing our way through the jungles and swamps of Vietnam with guns and grenades, watching American warplanes drop bombs on the "peasants" and spray their lush tropical foliage with Agent Orange.

What the American troops were made to do there was obscene and inhumane in our estimation. In our young minds, heartless and horrible atrocities were being committed there in the name of "freedom" and "democracy" and we wanted no part.

When, I wondered, would humanity evolve to its highest potential and achieve the "Aquarian" dream with its space age utopian perfection? It certainly couldn't be by spraying Napalm across the far-flung lands beyond our shores, I reasoned.

Fortunately, hope springs eternal and eventually, thanks to taxpayer funds, NASA was able to put two astronauts on the Moon. A species with the ability to manufacture exotic space technology, I told myself, and with the ability to conjure crimson Cadillacs, could do better and *should* do better. We could go to Mars one day, we could fly away to the stars and become *galactic* in our thinking.

What I simply could not understand was why there was such resistance among the generations in whose footsteps we were following to our message of peace and love. Why were the leaders so determined to foment further bloodshed and why did they so despise the Flower Children who were sticking daisies into their rifle barrels at demonstrations against the war in Vietnam?

None of that made sense to me. Why was the world so fabulous on the one hand and so crazy on the other?

Fortunately, as I came of age in the Sixties and continued to have such an obsession with The Beatles, I was introduced to the teachings of the sages of the Far East. This occurred after the Fab Four journeyed to India in 1968 to sit at the feet of the Maharishi Mahesh Yogi. While I never became a follower of the bearded, ever mischievous, grinning guru myself, seeds concerning the nature of reality and the "truth" about the human past were planted in my mind that would later bear fruit in a way that I could never have predicted, for I eventually learned that thousands of years ago the "gods" of India were flying around in magic Cadillacs of their own, only those machines were called Vimanas. And, in a really bizarre twist of fate and to my lifelong astonishment, I also came to realize that the flying disk that had flown over our family home in the summer of 1963 was perhaps a version of just such a vehicle. (Much more about this on the pages that follow!)

# 22

# Metaphors That Mirror the Mysteries of the Mind

TO SAY THAT THE HUMAN MIND moves in mysterious ways is scarcely an overstatement. One need only peruse the historic record, pick up a newspaper or scroll a few minutes on various websites on the Internet to find ample evidence of a myriad of beliefs, views, theories, claims, doctrines, dogmas, statistical data and more. There are highly literary and scientific writings, deeply moving personal testimonies, stories of love, loss, illumination, comedic tales, useful everyday commentary, pure gibberish, as well as seemingly extremely disturbing irrational forms of thinking which have the potential to incite all manner of troubling responses in the more vulnerable among us.

In other words, the gamut runs from the level of human genius to the very depths of human madness and depravity.

While neuroscientists still admittedly do not know how consciousness arises from the electromagnetic and biochemical processes in the brain, it is common enough these days to compare the workings of the brain to the processing capabilities of a computer. The tendency, however, is generally to use ordinary computers in the analogy, but that may not be the best choice, for ordinary computers use binary code: ones and zeros, which is rather exact. A switch is either "on" or it is "off".

The human mind, however, is anything but exact.

A truer model for the human mind – if we wish to employ such an analogy – is the quantum computer, which operates with "qubits" rather than a binary processing system. These computers function with a system that works like an ordinary computer with zeros and ones ("bits"), but also include an additional informational state.

That additional informational state is where the zero and the one exist simultaneously.

In other words, qubits can take on the value of zero or one, or both at the same time.

The analogy that is generally used to clarify the way a quantum computer works is one where a coin is flipped and while the coin is in the air, the head and the tail are equally present. At that moment, the two are in a state of potential, rather than in a definitive state.

Crucially, in the quantum realm, the field which underlies everything in this cosmos of ours, *potential* is its actual base state.

The key to quantum computing is the system's ability to operate on the basis of a circuit not only being "on" or "off" but occupying a state that is both "on" and "off" at the same time. This is in accordance with the laws of quantum mechanics, which allow very small particles to exist in multiple states until they are observed or disturbed. When a particle is in such a state it is known as being in a "superposition".

In a similar way, a coin spun in the air cannot be said to occupy a "heads" or "tails" state until it lands and a definitive result is revealed.

When we humans make a decision to go one way or another on an issue, it is usually only after turning the problem over and over in our minds until, at last, we make a decision and say, "Okay, this is it. This is what I am going to do." Arriving at that decision often takes a great deal of time and, even after the decision is struck, we might well be left wondering if we actually made the right choice.

If we are lucky, hindsight will prove that decision to be correct. If we are unlucky, we can get a very unpleasant surprise and end up sorely disappointed.

That is how it goes in life.

Physicists tell us that nothing is definitive in the quantum realm until there is a "collapsing of the wave function". They tell us that an observing mind is required to achieve that end.

The human mind is ideal for doing just that, of course. Since we humans are constructs of the cosmos, this might well be our primary evolutionary function. In other words, perhaps nature has created us so that we can continually collapse the wave function by observing phenomena and perceiving our universe in a certain way for an evolutionary end.

At the level of sheer functioning, we humans are all equally able to collapse the wave function and perceive events in a similar manner. This is what gives us a consensus view of reality. In this reality, all perceptions are equally efficacious at achieving the necessary result.

After we become acculturated, however, and acquire a specific mindset, our views invariably diverge, and we each take on a diversified interpretation of what is perceived.

The bottom line is this: until a wave is collapsed, it resides in a state of potential and is neither real nor unreal. Or one might say, it is both real and unreal simultaneously.

Of course, we humans are generally not overly comfortable with being in an indeterminate state of mind. Like the coin, flipping over and over, round and round, it makes us feel "up in the air" and we don't like that. We like definitive states. We like yes, no; this way or that way; one or the other. "A choice must be made," we say and then we take action.

To our eternal frustration, however, right and wrong are rarely clear-cut issues even after we *do* take a position. Arguments continue over what is good or bad, what is positive or negative about a situation, what the value of an event is, what it means and so forth.

This is why people end up saying things like, "Each to their own" or "Beauty is in the mind of the beholder."

That is because *everything* is in the mind of the beholder in terms of both perception and interpretation. That, too, is our reality. Each of us processes the raw data and stimuli of the quantum field of which we are an intricate and interdependent part and offer up our view of what it means and what it is worth, which itself runs the gamut from the utterly mundane to the fantastically miraculous.

Welcome to Qubit City.

Welcome to the world *as it is* rather than how we think it should be or wish it was.

## 23

# The Paranormal Pipedream

THE CARTOON OCCULT is a curious phenomenon. It all began in the last century when a character named "Superman" flew into comic book fame. It then continued on in that idiom with any number of amazing figures following in Superman's wake, each bearing superhuman powers of some dimension, whether due to a freak accident of nature or by science gone wildly awry, such as someone accidentally swallowing a potent untested chemical concoction or getting haplessly caught up in a burst of atomic radiation.

The cartoon occult subsequently worked its way into numerous television shows and, ultimately, into the Hollywood film industry. In fact, thanks to the wizardry of special effects technology the cartoon occult has transmogrified over the decades into flesh and blood characters and the resultant pantheon seem to actually dominate action films these days. If our hero or antihero hasn't a slew of paranormal powers, after all, then he or she cannot possibly overcome such a mundane menace as a blazing pistol, a burst of machinegun fire or a searing flamethrower. A superhero *must* have superpowers.

Tales of the paranormal actually go back much, much further than the first half of the twentieth century, however. They go back to the foundational myths of virtually every religion on the face of the planet.

Whether these miraculous foundational "myths" are "true" is a matter beyond all of us, but that doesn't mean that the mere exposure to them doesn't exert a powerful influence on our thinking. The fact is we wrap ourselves in these stories when we are young and for good reason. Blow by blow, we are all made to learn the hard truths of life and they can be devastating and brutal. A fist fight, a broken limb, a car crash, a disease, a fire, a bankruptcy, a divorce, a hurricane, a murder… The list of possible tragedies, large and small, is virtually endless. Indeed, any number of upheavals can come along in a young life and virtually alter every aspect of that life. If nothing of note happens in one's childhood, it will likely come later in some form, for no one seems to escape the myriad of vicissitudes which life throws forth, not even the privileged and the wealthy among us.

So, yes, we take great comfort in thinking that there are supernatural beings who will rectify everything somehow and protect us from having to suffer further tragedies.

We also dream of becoming "superbeings" ourselves in one form or another and quite happily envision ourselves possessing paranormal powers such as telepathy, clairvoyance, the ability to move objects with our minds or to influence others at a distance. We might even imagine ourselves gaining the psychic prowess to revel in revenge when slighted and put our "enemies" and "nemeses" in their proper place, by damn.

This latter desire to show one's detractors just exactly who is the true superior between oneself and anyone who happens to disrespect us, use us, abuse us, harm us or otherwise do us wrong in some way is where superpowers begin to veer swiftly and dangerously down into the risky realm of evil. Sorcery, black magic, dark witchery and voodoo spring from indulging in the desire to enact revenge. Through the ages, that effort has often been intensified by the use of psychotropic substances by those who seek to boost their powers to superhuman levels.

In fairness, it must be said that the use of such substances is, and has been, primarily tied into the healing arts associated with shamanism, Wicca and other ritualistic practices down through the centuries, most of a positive nature. What I am looking at here, however, is what pop culture has made of the paranormal. In the name of an enthralling plot, comic books,

TV action shows and blockbuster films have invariably raised up some version of a villain intent on exploiting "good folk" or destroying them completely. Usually, this wicked figure is out to take over the world and will stop at nothing to achieve his dastardly aim. Of course, a hero eventually emerges to put a halt to the malicious figure's ruthlessness and save the day, but let's face it, there would be no thrill at all for viewers if this malevolent joker hadn't stepped forward with a plan so evil and destructive that the boring, daily grind, i.e. mundane reality, was all we were left with to look at on our screens.

Just as a hero needs to overcome a villain, so good must overcome evil, if not at a worldly level, then at a cosmic one. This paradigm has been the basis of religion at least since the days of Zoroastrianism, hundreds of years BCE. Since then, the world has seen various forms of conquering divinities come along, all lording their supernatural powers over the devilish mutants who have fallen into malevolent disrepute at various times around the globe and, while it is always a horrible struggle, good does always win out in the end, if not in this life, then in the world to come.

Why have scenarios such as these arisen, again and again, over the centuries and millenniums?

There are countless volumes offering insight into this phenomenon, but the fact is no one knows anything absolutely, which is why virtually everyone will have his or her own answer to this question.

I would contend, however, that this is quite possibly exactly as it should be.

Why? Because I suspect that each and every one of us is endowed with much greater powers than we generally realize, but these powers lie dormant within us until we have evolved sufficiently in terms of our spirituality for these powers to be used properly. Imagine, for example, if we could see into the future so clearly that we could never be challenged by a random event that would otherwise force us to deeply consider our moral or ethical values. Imagine if we could zap our perceived enemies with a lightning bolt of displeasure at every slight. Imagine if we could kill entire populations and play God with impunity! Would anyone still be alive?

The point is this: humanity, as a whole, has shown itself – and continues to show itself – as being profoundly unenlightened.

If we are not some level of a primitive species, why then is there still so much racism, bigotry and violent forms of nationalism in the world? Why is there murder, war and any number of other afflictions of an abusive, aggressive, or deeply vile character taking place virtually on a daily basis right around the globe?

An enlightened viewpoint is one in which kindness and compassion reign; in which people are seen as being equals in this world enjoying the same rights as everyone else no matter who they happen to be or where they reside. An enlightened viewpoint says that we should all be able to live in peace and pursue our own notion of what constitutes happiness and fulfilment so long as that pursuit does not abridge the rights of others nor cause harm to virtually anyone else.

That humanity is still shamefully far from this ideal and so rancorously divided in terms of race, religion and nationalist affiliation is a point too obvious to belabor these days. Sadly, there seems to be no sign of it changing anytime soon.

Can it change? Will it change? If so, when?

The answer to such questions in a single, blunt and succinct sentence: It will change when each and every one of us can finally wish our "rivals", our "enemies", our "nemeses" and perceived "detractors" *enlightened*, rather than dead.

# 24

# A Close Encounter with Jim Marrs & the Alien Agenda

IT WAS IN THE LATE NINETIES, shortly after the author Jim Marrs released his phenomenal, meticulously documented, study of the whole UFO issue in a book entitled *Alien Agenda* that I had the privilege of meeting him – quite appropriately – in Aurora, Texas where an "airship" had once reportedly crashed. Indeed, this particular incident was actually cited in the *Dallas Times Herald* in 1897, so it is a tale that is more than mere hearsay. In fact, one of the occupants of that craft was said to be buried in the local cemetery in Aurora and Jim had included a photo of the headstone of the "pilot" of the craft in his book. The marker, unfortunately, was stolen (or ominously removed) sometime in the 1970s.

In any case, Jim (who was the very picture of sagely wisdom with his long white beard) and I had a deep and lively conversation that afternoon in one of the diners there and he had many a tale and insight for me. In turn, I told him of my own experiences, the most astonishing of which concerned a round, silver flying disk which flew just barely over the roof of our family home in the summer of 1963 in broad daylight with not a cloud in the sky. Jim found that fascinating but owing to his long years of research into the "Phenomenon", he was not in the least surprised by this or any of my other revelations. After all, *Alien Agenda* is subtitled: "Investigating the Extraterrestrial Presence Among us."

That subtitle is a rather staggering statement all on its own.

*Alien Agenda*, by the way, has – according to *Publishers Weekly* – gone on to become the top selling book on UFOs in the world. (See Wikipedia for the complete details on Jim's amazing career.)

He appeared numerous times on TV, had multiple radio and video credits, and a host of other achievements. What's more, Jim was such a powerful and credible figure in the often murky domain of this particular phenomenon that he was brought into the highly successful television series called *Ancient Aliens* in its opening episode. In that episode, the crashed airship mystery is explored in detail and includes some pretty astounding puzzlements, especially in regard to the subsequent health of the owner of the ranch where the craft was said to have crashed.

Jim's book, *Alien Agenda,* was and continues to be a best-seller for one very important reason in my opinion: it goes beyond all other books in a certain area of the subject in quite a unique way. It not only relates all of the best-known UFO mysteries, from the most ancient of times to the present, that have dazzled the general public for decades, but also includes a lengthy section on what is known as Remote Viewing.

Remote Viewing began as a military experiment in response to tales coming out of the USSR that the Soviet military was using "psychic spies" to covertly uncover many of the technological secrets of the West and to determine what the US and European leaders were up to logistically in a military sense and where exactly the Cold War was going. With atomic and hydrogen bombs mounted on huge numbers of ballistic missiles, this was no small deal. The fate of the world was very much in the balance.

As a result, the Western powers set to work on their own psychic programs, one of which came to be known as Remote Viewing. This is said to be the learned ability to transcend space-time in order to view people, places or objects at a great distance. To view in this way in military terms primarily serves as a way of perceiving enemy targets.

To make a long story short regarding remote viewing, this ability was assessed to be both valid and efficacious, but the strangest aspect of it was how virtually all of the remote viewers eventually perceived alien craft and entities in abundance. The details of those perceptions are expounded and expanded upon in startling elaborations in *Alien Agenda*. This, as mentioned earlier, is what sets Jim's book apart from most others. It would appear that, as Jacques Vallee, another man of impeccable credentials in the field of UFO research, famously pointed out, these beings, who are apparently not of this earth, seem to be interdimensional in nature and inhabit a spectrum of reality which we humans can neither see nor measure with our current scientific instrumentation. In other words, these entities are said to reside within a parallel dimension to our material plane in what is known as an "overtone" and have the ability to make their presence visible or invisible in the proverbial blinking of an eye.

The human mind, however, can and does – on occasion – perceive these beings and their vehicles (which may or may not be material in nature) and this is precisely what ties us into a relational situation with these beings. It appears that we are all a part of a greater reality united by consciousness itself. In brief, this sphere of cognizant awareness contains a myriad of layers, each separated by the speed of the energy at play in any particular one of the layers.

This concept is nothing new. It goes back to the very dawn of civilization, one may discover, and there is every reason to believe even predates it. One might even validly ask at this juncture if the renowned yogis of the East were, in fact, the first remote viewers, for they most assuredly perceived other worlds and other beings as the sacred literature of the East amply testifies. The Vedic literature of India, in particular, has huge portions of testimony regarding flying machines known as Vimanas and many detailed reports about the "gods" who piloted them. (For as complete a version as one can find in the West on details of this testimony, a book entitled *Alien Identities*, by Richard L Thompson, Ph.D., is highly recommended. This book is cited in Jim's book and is also a must-read for all serious researchers into the phenomenon.)

By the way, it is not just accounts about remote viewing that takes readers of *Alien Agenda* deeper into the phenomenon, but also the reports by respected psychics and trance channelers whose expositions very much seem to corroborate what has been revealed about these beings and their interests. What is particularly impressive is the consensus that there seems to be three main groups of extradimensional entities that are most connected to humanity. 1.) Humanoids 2.) Grays and 3.) Transcendentals.

The Humanoids are the ones who are said to be "Nordic" in appearance, transit our skies in exotic technological craft and easily interact with humanity directly due to the fact that they are almost indistinguishable from us. I have personally seen two of these beings on the silver flying disk as mentioned above.

The Grays (or Greys) are those diminutive entities with the huge black wraparound eyes that have, over time, frightened so many of the those who have encountered them. Their presence has been most notably expounded upon by Whitley Strieber in his many books, beginning with his most famous, *Communion*.

As for the Transcendentals, they are "energy beings", according to Marrs, who are "shapeless" and "phantomlike", but may "pop" into our dimension and manifest in any shape they choose. He adds that, "For all intents and purposes, the descriptions, activities, nature, and capabilities of these beings matched the characteristics that Church fathers have attributed to 'angels'." The Transcendentals, in short, care for us and look out for us, and are interested in our evolutionary progress in spiritual terms, but by and large do not directly involve themselves in our day to day lives. After all, evolutionary learning is a slow process and must be rooted in what we humans actually experience or we cannot grow in any genuine nor meaningful way.

The good news is that there is definitely a very positive reassurance in *Alien Agenda* that if these various "extradimensional" beings had wanted to eradicate us or turn us into slaves they could and would have done so long ago.

The Transcendentals, according to those consulted, are very much a part of that reassurance and it is heartening to remember that these beings over the centuries have been known as "angels".

Is there a genuine connection between the spiritual entities we have heard about over the centuries and the beings some have encountered in UFOs? According to Whitley Strieber the answer is yes. In his book *A New World* he tells us that during one of his earliest abductions when he was taken aboard a spacecraft against his will, he saw among the entities on that craft a dead friend he had known. He had been so bewildered by the presence of this person that he had initially purposely left him out of his account in the book *Communion*. How could that dead friend possibly be riding along on a spacecraft like that? It made no sense to Strieber and so he chose to keep that piece of information to himself. As he discovered more and more about the peculiar nature of what he calls the "visitors" and their vehicles, however, he says he came to realize the significance of this person on the craft during the course of that event. The realm of the dead is not as we have imagined it to be over the centuries, he insists. This otherworld which exists in some parallel dimension to our own is much more complex than we thought.

As for me, what my brother, Bob, and I saw in the summer of 1963 was a round, silver craft with two humanoids aboard at close range on a bright sunny day with not a cloud in the sky. We waved at the handsome couple as they calmly flew by. They smiled and waved back at us. We then ran into the house as it cruised on and called our mother to come and see. Rushing from the house, she too witnessed the exotic, futuristic craft, which was still visible in the distance. There was no mistaking what the three of us saw. I subsequently had another close encounter with a friend of mine a few years later, this time at night, with a most mysterious, and indeed peculiar, flying object which exhibited some very bizarre and jolting behavior.

I remember how Jim just smiled with sublime equanimity at my tales. After all, he was way ahead of me on every level at that point having written *Alien Agenda*. What's more, he was already an award-winning journalist and author of the New York Times bestseller *Crossfire: the Plot That Killed Kennedy* (which went on to become the basis of the Oliver Stone film *JFK*).

Jim subsequently went on to write *Rule by Secrecy* and *Above Top Secret*, among other books. All his works are testaments to the man's dogged determination to uncover truth of the deepest nature, however taboo or controversial, and clearly, what he gained along the way was great wisdom and knowledge.

For me, Jim (who died in 2017) was the perfect model for the archetypal Wise Old Man and the exchange that day proved both reassuring and rewarding. What he gave me was wonderful encouragement to continue with my literary pursuits and my own quest for truth no matter how strange and impenetrable that search might become.

"Above all," he told me, "trust your own instincts, keep a sharp eye out for synchronicities and never give up. I know only too well how elusive truth is. In fact, the truth of a situation can often make no sense whatsoever, especially at those times when you wonder day and night if a thing is for real or not, but with perseverance you can gain a perspective that will carry you far beyond where you are now and maybe even farther than you ever thought you would get in this life. If you do, quite frankly, the view can prove pretty damn stunning."

Jim then went on to tell me about some of the amazing synchronicities that had occurred in his life and he was greatly amused when I told him how just as my second book, *The*

*Illuminati of Immortality*, was in its final stage ahead of being printed, the Berlin Wall came down. This was significant because in the novel I had my "flying mystics" (as Robert Anton Wilson called them) streaking out over the Berlin Wall and wreaking havoc with the military men there who were notorious for making every effort to kill anyone who dared to try and escape from the east side of the city. Fortunately, I was able to call Hyatt at Falcon Press when the Wall fell and shout, "Stop the presses!" Had I not enjoyed that stroke of luck in timing my book would have been obsolete upon arrival.

"It was more than a stroke of luck, though," Jim countered. "That kind of timing is a gift of the gods, my friend, or you could say it was your higher angel, or self, looking out for you. Synchronicity is an amazing phenomenon and plays heavily into our lives. We think of it as dumb luck, but it is that and so much more. Knowing this is one of the truths that helps to set the soul free. After all, it's not just luck that we meet a certain person at a certain time. Events happen in their own way and in their own time, and they happen for a purpose, one that has to do with our personal spiritual evolution. This is why we have to stay super aware at all times."

Several decades after that fascinating meeting I know exactly what the man meant by all that he said. To that end, what follows here is my own synthesis of the UFO phenomenon and my carefully considered perspective on the subject of "otherworld mysteries" that so haunt our enchanted planet. The extract is from my novel *Crimson Firestorm Mars*. Just to be clear, what the fictional character "Simon" says in the extract is based on the above-mentioned personal experiences which have so impacted me over the years.

# 25

# Otherworld Mysteries

### *An extract from the novel Crimson Firestorm Mars*

AS SIMON SAT ON A MARBLE STEP in the Roman Forum with son Shane beside him, he was in a calm, but lively, state of mind. The two were quietly speaking. Then the cameraman was ready to roll, and the director of the documentary asked Simon to begin speaking about a certain few events in his childhood. The man had heard the stories before and he liked them. He now wanted to capture Simon telling those tales to his son on film.

After introducing himself, Shane asked his father what had originally sparked his interest in astronomical themes and in matters of the spirit. "What are your earliest memories concerning these topics?"

Simon had a ready answer to that question. "I grew up in the country and one advantage that those who grow up in the country have over their city counterparts is that they get to spend a lot of time outdoors under the stars. This is especially true in the summertime and there is nothing quite like a dark, balmy summer night under the stars with the fireflies flickering their greenish-yellow luminescence as they flutter about the meadows and groves. In my mind, no image can better evoke Shakespeare's *Midsummer Night's Dream*. The world at night is alive with all kinds of life, especially the crickets in the grass and the cicadas in the trees chattering with each other at full volume.

"The most incredible thing of all, of course, is the light-spangled grandeur of the mighty Milky Way.

"My love of the stars began then, but there were also other

influences that had a huge effect on me in those early years. All through my childhood, I often had dreams of flying, sometimes zipping about freely like a bird or, as on a few occasions, riding a great golden lion. The golden lion is a very alchemical image, though I had no idea about that at the time. Still, growing up with a magical character like Superman on TV, perhaps such dreams could almost be expected of a young impressionable mind."

Shane smiled. "It sounds like Superman for you was like Batman was to me in my childhood. There were a series of movies that I followed all through my adolescence and into my teen years. I was totally entranced by them."

"Yes, I know. I took you to see quite a few of those movies, as I recall. Anyway, I can't remember how taken with Superman I was in those years, but I do know that I sometimes looked up at the sky when playing outdoors as if almost *expecting* the man to come streaking over the house, out of the blue, at any moment. To my innocent, fledgling mind, Superman was as much a part of the 'real' world as anything else. After all, I was learning from the adults in my life – parents, teachers and priests – that our 'savior', Jesus Christ, had been crucified and died, but had subsequently risen from the dead after three days. He then, according to those same adults, had ascended into heaven in the flesh. Angels, too, were said to have wings and to fly, and Santa Claus, a Christian saint, was said to fly about on a sleigh pulled by a team of magical reindeer on Christmas Eve. What could be more spectacular than any of that?

"The Superman of TV fame never did fly over my childhood home, of course, but one summer afternoon in the bright Ohio sunshine, when I was eleven years of age *something* inexplicable *did* fly over the family home and it was to have an enormous influence on me. In truth, that *something* still baffles me to this very day, and I do not know exactly what it was, for it was a UFO in the most common sense meaning of that phrase – an

'Unidentified Flying Object' – and it remained exactly that: unidentified. It *may have been* a craft belonging to so-called 'aliens' or it may have been an earthly craft that had originated in some secret military installation somewhere, in a place like Area 51 in Nevada, perhaps. Both are possibilities, I am well aware, but until I know for certain, I can never make a final call."

"Can you recreate the moment for us?" Shane asked.

"I can. It was a sunny, summer day. I was playing games outdoors with my siblings, enjoying the radiant sunshine and the green grass, just having fun with my brothers and sisters, and the family dog. Then, at one point, my brother and I began tossing a ball back and forth in the front yard, as we often did.

"The sky was cloudless and pristine, the air perfectly still. The day was essentially one like any other, but then it became one like *no* other, for without any advance warning whatsoever a round, low-flying object came cruising at a very modest speed over the roof of our home and it passed directly between my brother and me."

"What did the craft look like?" Shane asked.

"To describe the vehicle is easy. The craft was a small, round, silver disk. We saw this disk in extreme close-up, for the craft was very low in the sky. In fact, this disk was only barely above the rooftop of our home, and it caught our attention no differently than any airplane might have stolen our attention that day, but in retrospect I now know that this was clearly an object of exotic technology.

"I should point out, perhaps, that so-called 'newfangled' machines in America in the early Sixties were increasingly common. We were well aware of them. Helicopters were being seen on the rare occasion, for example, and many different types of planes often cruised over, their shapes ever more aerodynamic and exciting. To see any such flying object at the time would have delighted us and we were, indeed, quite pleased with the little round disk that caught our attention that day. Neither of us was shocked by it, nor even too surprised by what we were seeing. Here was simply the latest, most amazing, craft yet, we figured.

"The thing we realized in retrospect, however, was that this craft was entirely unlike any other craft at the time, and, *to this very day*, I have never seen such a craft again, not even a *photo* of such a craft."

"So, we're talking a flying saucer, then, are we?"

"No, believe it or not, I am *not* here describing the stereotypical flying saucer, although I will hasten to add that it *may have been* some form of 'alien' disk, but one that, if so, would have had to have come from a larger craft, a so-called mother ship. I ended up calling it a little *daytripper UFO*, for it appeared to be nothing more than a shuttlecraft for moving people from one place to another. I say that because there were two very human-looking people on board, a man and a woman. There was nothing else to be seen, however, no provisions or cargo of any kind. The two people were simply standing together at the rear of the vehicle against a waist-high railing, gazing calmly back at the sights all around them. They were certainly *not* watching where they were going, nor could we see anyone piloting the disk, although someone may have been piloting the craft in a small cabin at the front. I just don't know. The possibility that the craft was being flown on autopilot has also occurred to me.

"In any case, my brother and I, of course, were astonished at its abrupt entry into our lives, but we both waved up at the exceptionally attractive couple we saw above us. They were attired in mocha brown outfits like something out of Star Trek and they, in turn, waved right back at us with big smiles on their faces as they cruised along, their pace quite unhurried."

"So, they were perfectly fine with you seeing them? They were friendly, in other words."

"Oh, they were. They were calm and happy, and apparently

just making their way across the sunny Ohio countryside for somewhere. Who knows where?"

"And there was nothing strange about the vehicle?"

"No, there wasn't and I had no idea at the time that I would never again see such a craft. The vehicle was totally silent and had no visible means of propulsion. The couple on board seemed to be protected by some invisible force field that shielded them from the wind, for neither person's hair nor clothing was being blown around.

"I must say, the sight of the flying disk with the friendly people onboard was wondrous. Indeed, the attractive couple were almost like *gods* to us that day as we waved up at them; but then we probably would have perceived Elvis likewise should he have come streaking by on the highway in one of his massive, shark-finned Cadillac convertibles," Simon laughed. "In truth, though, we didn't really think of the sky people as gods that day, just two very lucky human beings in a very cool flying vehicle, getting a ride on the latest, most mind-blowing, technological marvel yet to grace the brilliant blue sky."

Shane nodded, then pursed his lips as he pondered the image. "Sounds fascinating, all right."

"It was. Enormously excited, my brother and I both raced into the house and shouted for our mother to come and look. By the time she had rushed out the door, the exotic little flying disk was fairly far in the distance, but still clearly visible, so she saw it too. Then it was gone."

"And life went on as it does?"

"Yes. Eventually our excitement just died down and the flying disk became a distant memory. However, many decades later, I did happen to see a sketch of a similar vehicle in a book. The sighting of that similar craft took place at Boianai, New Guinea, and was witnessed by some 38 people in all, among which was a very highly respected missionary by the name of William Booth Gill, a man also known as Father Gill. In the New Guinea case, the UFO hovered above the village at dusk and there were four humanlike 'beings' on the craft. The big difference between the two vehicles was that the New Guinea vehicle had two levels to it, not just a single flat disk shape.

"I remember another strange event, too, one that occurred to me during my early teen years and it still baffles me."

"What happened this time?"

"One night, I was with a neighbor, a close friend of mine, and was walking with him to his home. It was a cloudless, moonless summer night. The stars were bright and the air was sultry with crickets, chirping as ever in their loud and persistent way. I was maybe thirteen or fourteen years of age at the time, but my friend was some three years older than me. As the two of us set out, we happened to notice a bright light in the sky. I would describe it as a luminous oval light, one very low in altitude and the craft itself was soundless. It was most assuredly no airplane, nor helicopter, and it was way too low in the sky to be a jet.

"We had no idea what it was as we pressed on across the field which separated my family's property from his, but it dawned on us that this object was not only moving at an *extremely* slow pace, it was barely moving at all. Stopping to look, we were mystified by what we were seeing. As we kept staring, we talked back and forth between ourselves, speculating about the nature of the object, and being thoroughly entranced by it. 'What is that thing?' I remember asking.

"Before either one of us had a chance to offer an opinion, however, the object, quite abruptly, shifted direction. Instead of cutting across our path as it had been doing, it seemed to draw itself directly in line with the trajectory that we were ourselves traversing. Jolted by the sudden turn of the thing and startled by the realization that the flying object had somehow *seemingly* become aware of us, we were both rendered speechless and we froze in our tracks. With mouths hanging open, we looked at each other and then instinctively bolted in fear. The impression that the object was aware of us was both overwhelming and extremely spooky. As a result, we ran as fast as we could. It had us thoroughly frightened.

"The object then further surprised us, however. It suddenly burst into flames! It simply grew all fiery there in the sky above us and was so close to the ground that we could even hear the flames crackling quite loudly as the object flew forward."

"The object was flying along on fire?"

"Yes, and it just pushed on leaving a long, sizzling trail of smoke. We assumed, of course, that the vehicle was in distress, only then the flames simply went out as if somehow smothered instantaneously, leaving a mere silhouette of a craft silently floating along in the starry sky."

"So, the object was completely dark at that point, but it had smoke trailing from it?"

"It did. The fire was out and the bright oval luminance was gone, but the smoke continued. Then the craft simply flew out of view and disappeared into the night."

"So what did you make of it in your mind? It sounds pretty weird."

"I didn't know what to make of it and I still don't. It was an event that definitely sounds absurd on the face of it, but that is not all that unusual, it seems, when it comes to UFOs. I sometimes wonder if there is a concerted effort by some species of being to keep us mystified for an ulterior motive. An event like that one certainly achieves that end. Young people, of course, imagine all kinds of things, but the object had definitely been for real and it had certainly startled us by *seemingly* becoming aware of us, which by the way, is really not that unusual either. People who report seeing UFOs often mention how the occupants of the UFO were somehow inexplicably aware of them."

Shane sat frowning. "So, again then, you were left with a true UFO, another Unidentified Flying Object, an anomaly of the night. It came, it went, and you can only speculate."

"That's correct. At best, sometimes, all one can do is say, 'Here is an anomaly,' and leave it at that. We can speculate what an object like that *might* be, but until an object is identified definitively then one simply cannot say what it *actually* is. As the late, great Doctor Isaac Asimov once wrote, 'It's not what you see that is suspect, but how you interpret what you see.' An anomaly lasting a mere three or four minutes isn't worth much perhaps, but then again… A luminous, glowing object was seen, it burst into flames, it did not crash. On the contrary, it flew away. No mention of it was ever made in the local newspaper, nor did I ever hear anything about it on the radio. Our parents were given our personal report, of course, but they had no idea what the object was and so the episode simply faded from our young lives."

"Did you ever see anything else over the years?"

Simon took a deep breath, then slowly exhaled. "There was a particular experience I had one time while living in a place in California called Wildcat Canyon that is far too complex to get into in a casual discussion like this, but I can tell you that it proved quite challenging on multiple levels and may have included an interdimensional or multidimensional aspect. I will, therefore, just say that on two occasions I saw very bright lights circling high up in the heavens amid the stars and hovering there.

"The incidents I earlier recounted, however, involved objects that were very low in the sky and were pretty straight forward. There are scores of books to read on this topic, of course. All through recorded history, people have seen strange things in the sky and have encountered non-human entities, from the fairies and 'little people' of yore to 'Men in Black,' to the menacing alien 'Grays'. We also hear about beings from Sirius, Orion, the Pleiades and other regions of the galaxy. In the Middle East, there are ancient tales of the magical 'Jinn' – from which we get the word 'genie' – and, in the sacred literature of the Far East, one can read serious scriptural accounts of beings known as 'Dakinis', 'Asuras' and 'Nagas'. The last of these are described as reptilian-looking beings. Even the Bible, in Genesis, has 'men of renown' known as the 'Sons of God' from the heavens. Apparently, these 'Sons of God' saw that the daughters of men were attractive and took a number of them to be their wives. These were the Nephilim.

"It would seem, then, that beings from elsewhere have always been with us. Sometimes they streak about on flying craft and at other times, they just step into our lives without warning, appearing before us in a way that can only be called 'high strangeness'. These beings can appear and disappear at will, as can their craft. On the rare occasion, some of these vehicles have been photographed or captured on video cameras, and radar operators around the globe have locked onto these craft thousands of times. In many cases, the fastest jets that humanity possesses have given chase to these vehicles, but they easily outpace our jets and either disappear without a trace or streak off at speeds far beyond human technical capabilities, oftentimes making turns that absolutely defy the known laws of physics.

"A review of the data forces us to consider that UFOs may not be extraterrestrial. They *could* be, but then again, perhaps a more *likely* possibility is that they are beings from a supraluminal plane capable of interdimensional activity. We just don't know. What we do know is that some of these craft can operate in hyperspatial geometries and achieve hypersonic velocities without a sonic boom. They often have no flight surfaces to be seen and, when some of our own craft have gotten involved with them over the years, these UFOs have shot off at speeds that we cannot comprehend. Some very experienced military pilots, for example, estimate that these craft can achieve speeds of seven to eight thousand miles per hour in a mere instant, for example going from stationary to Mach 10 in mere seconds. One craft being tracked on radar by England's Royal Air Force reportedly covered 250 miles in two seconds. That is patently impossible. As well, these vehicles can make right angle turns which human pilots could not physically endure given the level of g-forces that such turns generate. That means that the occupants must be very different from us in a biological sense or those vehicles are unmanned, remotely controlled or they are projections of some nature.

"I remember one account of a UFO being chased by a military jet when, in the blink of an eye, the object was *behind* the jet all at once and following it. The pilot learned of this 'impossible' occurrence from a radar operator who was tracking both vehicles. In conventional terms, there is no explanation for this.

"According to the career intelligence officer, Luis Elizondo, who resigned some years back from his position as head of the Advanced Aviation Threat Identification Program, the reality of UFOs is indisputable. That particular program is housed in the Pentagon and funded by the US government with 'black ops' money, which the Congress of the United States admits *does* exist. Elizondo cites gun camera footage from an FA-18 fighter jet near San Diego. The man flying that jet was Commander David Fravor and the commander afterwards stated, for the record, that the rotund object had no wings, was about forty feet long and quote, 'was not of this Earth.'

"Elizondo called Commander Fravor a 'national hero' for speaking out and said that there are many credible witnesses who have shared their experiences with members of the program. He also said that the prime 'geographical hotspots' for UFOs are nuclear missile facilities. One of the most famous reports in that regard occurred in and around Rendlesham Forest near Ipswich in Britain. That forest is situated between two top level military bases. Many high-ranking, elite officers there have sworn to the reality of what happened with UFOs in and around their facility over numerous nights. One officer, Staff Sergeant Jim Penniston, actually touched a pyramid shaped UFO that had landed. He is quoted as saying afterwards, 'What I once believed is no more and what I've witnessed defies all that I have ever imagined.'

"That is a very powerful and moving statement. We should remember that the modern UFO era began almost immediately after atomic bombs exploded at Hiroshima and Nagasaki in Japan during the final stages of World War II.

"Elizondo resigned his position out of frustration. He said it was because the US government is not willing to stop being so secretive about UFOs. 'In my opinion,' he said, 'if this was a court of law, we have reached the point of "beyond reasonable doubt"'. He added, 'I hate to use the term UFO, but that's what we're looking at.'

"US Army Colonel John B. Alexander also made an incredible statement in his book *UFOs: Myths, Conspiracies and Realities*. He wrote, 'Acknowledgement that craft of nonhuman origin exist, appear to be under intelligent control, and transit our atmosphere from time to time has already happened.' In other words, many of our highest military authorities around the globe have *already* admitted the reality of UFOs. Certain governments, notably France, Britain, Belgium, Russia and Brazil, have publicly acknowledged the validity of the reports made by their military authorities. Most people, of course, don't believe that and they are still awaiting an 'official' announcement when it has *already been given*. Most recently, it was the US Navy which has admitted the reality of UFOs.

"Anyway, it's not for me to convince anyone of anything and I can certainly sympathize with military leaders who are reluctant to admit to anyone, either foreign or domestic, that they are not in total control of the skies above their own respective nations. Knowledge of this fact really could cause panic among the people whom military leaders are sworn to protect, but I think the general population may finally be ready for honesty on this topic.

"In that spirit, I might note here that at least two astronauts have made very strong statements about UFOs. Gordon Cooper, the commander of the Gemini 5 mission, personally claimed to have seen UFOs on two occasions. He is quoted as saying, 'I believe UFOs, under intelligent control, have visited our planet for thousands of years.' Likewise, Edgar Mitchell, the Apollo 14 Lunar Module Pilot, has publicly stated that, 'We all know that UFOs are real; now the question is where they come from.' Doctor Mitchell was the sixth man to walk on the Moon and he later created the Institute of Noetic Sciences and the Foundation for Research into Extraterrestrial and Extraordinary Experiences, or FREE. He, too, believes that the possibility exists that the UFO phenomenon may actually be interdimensional in nature, as does the highly renowned and impeccably credentialed Doctor Jacques Vallée, who may have been the first to offer this viewpoint as a valid possibility in his book *Passport to Magonia*. By the way, Vallee theorizes that what these mysterious beings are doing is strategically drawing us, via what he calls 'cosmic seduction', into adopting a more complex and profound paradigm of reality. They are doing that in order to expand us as psychospiritual beings and to help us to go beyond our isolated, lonely, solar-centric existence to become members of the galactic community at large."

"So, who are these beings?" Shane asked.

"Who they are remains a great mystery and there may, in fact, be numerous species of nonhuman entities involved in this situation. Certainly, descriptions vary. The alternative is that these beings are fantastic shapeshifters and can appear in whatever form they choose.

"Whatever the truth of the matter, most of these beings do seem to be benevolent and sympathetic to us, while a few apparently aren't. Personally, I am partial to Jung's theory that there is a third order to the reality we inhabit, which he called the Psychoid Realm. This dimension is "betwixt and between" as folklorists put it in the past. This dimension is a plane that exists in the borderland between the purely mental and purely physical realms. The beings which inhabit this dimension can appear and disappear at will and, as paraphysical entities, are obviously much more powerful than we are. They may even be the gods, angels, demons, elves, fairies, satyrs, fauns, elementals and other beings that humanity has encountered over the millenniums and written about in the world's oldest literature. Perhaps, it is only because humanity at present is so science oriented and dominated by technology that we interpret these beings as 'aliens' from other planets.

"Then again, maybe these beings quite simply possess a technology that is so far in advance of anything that we humans can even fathom at present that they enter our world in a way we cannot understand. Or maybe they are indeed interdimensional beings of some nature with powers that we simply do not have or have yet to mentally cultivate and master. Perhaps they are so highly evolved that both possibilities are true at the same time. In other words, perhaps, they have engineered nuts and bolts machines which are capable of feats and maneuvers far beyond what we humans have created to date *and* they are themselves constituted in such a way that they can appear and disappear on our Earth as they wish. Who knows? What we do know is that they can manipulate space and time, and that they can materialize or dematerialize objects at will, including their own bodies. This does add a metaphysical component to the phenomenon, which is precisely why a metaphysician like me finds such endless intrigue in it.

"The simple fact is there is no obvious evidence of any advanced civilizations in our solar system, so all we can do is put forth speculative possibilities grounded in observational and deductive data. I will say that if the occupants of these UFOs share the same material reality as us, but are from another star system, then we have to remind ourselves that the nearest of these in our own galaxy is Proxima Centauri. Its distance from us is roughly 4.2 light-years, which is about twenty-five million million miles away. Yes, you heard me correctly; that is a *million* million. Light alone coming from that star takes more than four years to reach us."

"That kind of distance is mind-boggling," Shane remarked.

"It is. And consider this: we know that light moves at 186,000 miles per second. A spacecraft by definition must possess mass, so it will only be able to fly at a fraction of that speed. To offer something with which to contrast this we might recall here that the rockets that went to the Moon flew at about 25,000 miles an hour. With our space probes, we achieved a speed of 100,000 miles an hour, which is what any vehicle needs in order to escape the gravitational pull of the Sun. So even at a speed of 100,000 miles per hour a spacecraft coming here from Proxima Centauri would take thirty thousand years. Obviously, any craft originating from further away would take even longer."

Simon was silent for a moment, then said, "So that's the problem when we consider the prospect of interstellar craft visiting us here on Earth. Would spacefarers arriving here from so far away play cat and mouse games with us once they did get here? I seriously doubt it, unless they view us as so essentially primitive in comparison to their own state of being that it becomes a risky proposition for them to come straight out and present their true faces. If they do consider us primitive in a relative way, we could easily be viewed by them as being a danger. After all, we know perfectly well how most humans react when confronted with a threatening situation. We break out whatever weaponry is available to us and let blast. We call out the defense forces and go straight in with the bullets, bombs and missiles.

"Maybe playing cat and mouse games with us, then, is just a gentle way of bringing us around slowly to the notion that there is other life in this galaxy of ours. If the intruders into our airspace are an advanced species, the last thing they would want is to incite mass panic and that might well occur if millions of people suddenly had their worldviews overturned in a single instant. It isn't difficult in the least to imagine what the reaction would be if a spaceship did land on the White House lawn and confront humanity in the full glare of prime-time media coverage. There *would be* panic. It would be unavoidable.

"In contrast, random spectacle by advanced beings on their own terms is the equivalent of stage magic, of sleight of hand, 'Now you see it, now you don't' trickery, and it leaves everyone unsure what to think. That leads to exactly what we now have; those who believe and those who laugh at the notion. Throw in all of the nefarious activities that surround the field of ufology by operatives who answer only to their own interests and who really knows what to think? Add to that the fact that daimons or psychoid beings are known to be trickster figures and you really are left wondering who will get the last laugh here.

"In any case, it's not like we have any choice in the matter. These beings have the upper hand in every way; and they are obviously setting the agenda. Throw in high-level government and military personnel manipulating people and events, as well as disseminating disinformation, and no one finally knows what the truth of the situation is.

"In the meantime, in my humble opinion, we humans have witnessed many and varied forms of craft over the millenniums, not to mention actual entities, and we still see them on occasion far more than most people realize. Many, of course, don't want to believe a statement like that. They fear the 'big picture' and are only comfortable with the idea that we humans are alone in this vast universe of ours. I know what I personally saw, however, and if a person cannot believe his or her own eyes, then what hope does one have of making sense of this reality in which we find ourselves?"

Shane laughed with nervous bemusement at those words.

"Well, all I know is that I'm even more in the dark than you are," he confessed.

Simon smiled and was quiet for a moment, then simply shook his head. "So, there you have it. Should anyone care to know what originally piqued my interest in the stars and space, and space travel in general, here is the answer. My experiences are unique to me, of course, but tens of thousands of people have had experiences of their own and the time is ripe for them to speak out, especially as we now sit poised on the brink of going interplanetary."

Simon let that last word hang in the air a moment. "It's not science fiction. It's science fact. We are going to Mars. We might well be there within a decade. One day, I predict, UFOs will have a basis in fact, as well, but until that day comes, we can only speculate and report what we happen to witness. Thousands of credible observers, however, would already agree with the physicist Eric Davis who said, 'UFOs are real phenomena. They are artificial objects under intelligent control. They're definitely craft of a supremely advanced technology.' These objects have been tracked by reconnaissance satellites, electronic sensors and on radar. They have been photographed and there is video footage in various private, military and government archives. The book that best elucidates this phenomenon, I think, is one by the investigative journalist Leslie Kean. Her work is entitled *UFOs: Generals, Pilots, and Government Officials Go on the Record.*

"Despite the fact that millions of people believe that there isn't any form of confirmation on this topic, there actually is. Such people don't want to hear that, however, for once it proves an indisputable reality it will complicate every aspect of human history almost beyond comprehension. Ancient worldviews will be utterly shattered.

"The truth of the matter is, nevertheless, that some people have experienced genuine phenomena and that makes these phenomena part of our reality, whether we want to believe that or not. And, yes, there are those who staunchly prefer to believe that we are alone in this immense cosmos of ours. Ridiculing those of us who have had encounters of a mysterious nature is not only disrespectful, however, it smacks of the tactics we now associate with bullying, intimidation and oppression. It also smacks of a cover-up, which plays right into the hands of the conspiracy theorists.

"Surely, we are a more enlightened species than that in this day and age. Surely, we can study this particular phenomenon with as much scientific objectivity as we bring to any other, more conventional, topic of interest. Remember what the physicist, Niels Bohr, said one time. 'If quantum mechanics hasn't profoundly shocked you, you haven't understood it yet.' He is speaking about the most basic level of reality of all. So, this world of ours is a very mysterious place. How it came into existence, whether it exists for a reason or not and so on, these questions are enigmas at the moment, but only the dullard mind will take this life for granted and see something mundane, instead of something spectacularly fascinating and, yes, spiritually compelling.

"The important point is we are indeed going interplanetary now and that means that we need to fully grasp the scope and magnitude of how that will play out in the near future. I don't wish to sound a dark note, but there have been several suspicious losses of space probes that various countries have sent to Mars in the past and these losses cannot be glibly dismissed. We need to understand that we are opening ourselves to a broader reality with any mission to Mars. Once we humans land and establish a colony there, we will not just be earthbound creatures anymore.

"So, events are unfolding. We have already landed astronauts on the Moon. Soon we will land a human mission on Mars. Space cities will follow in short order. This is going to happen. Once we *do* go interplanetary, a new era will definitely be underway," Simon concluded, his smile huge now. "I predict that it will prove to be one of the most fantastically surprising epochs ever and how could it not be?

"We must brace ourselves, then, and keep an open mind, I say. We must step wisely into the future with intelligence and compassion, with a bold and fearless spirit, ready to accept all that life has to offer in its full phenomenal magnificence. In a word, the ride is going to be absolutely *amazing*."

# 26

# Trickster's Twisted Matrix

## *What Anomalous Phenomena & Paranormal Events Tell Us*

IN THE EPILOGUE of his well-documented, highly researched book, *UFOs – Myths, Conspiracies, and Realities*, Colonel John B. Alexander offers us "*Alexander's Law of Appropriate Complexity*" which states: "Every time someone believes that he or she fully comprehends their situation in life an entire new order of complexity is encountered. This holds true for every person and for every situation. Just as you have it nailed, something else comes along and changes the game."

The Colonel goes on to say, "With UFOs, every time we think we have an answer, new observations make the problem more complex. Evaluation of the characteristics of UFOs and related phenomena suggests that the extraterrestrial hypothesis is too narrow, and once again the paradigm shift eludes us. In the end it is clear that the universe is far more complex than we ever imagined."

Indeed. When all is said and done, what do we really know for sure? Even our most highly acclaimed physicists agree that reality manages to defy almost every aspect, facet and shred of common-sense humanity has.

The Buddhist lama I studied under for several years once said that learning to live with ambiguity is, above all, what we humans need to get to grips with and accept.

Should you choose to smoke DMT, drink ayahuasca or ingest psilocybin and trip off down into some rabbit hole, what may happen is that you will find yourself confronting beings who can speak to you in your native tongue and address virtually any question you would like to have answered. Strange, but true. Be forewarned, however. Finding yourself face to face with nonhuman entities is not for the faint of heart.

So-called nonhuman "extraterrestrials" tell us things too. Some of what they say seems deep and profound, while other bits prove preposterous. Why do these entities mess with our heads the way they do? It makes one wonder at times if the Planet Earth is for real or if it might be an illusory object flying about, not just in space, but in some cosmic trickster's matrix?

What I am wondering here is this: Are these advanced intelligences, or astral entities, in the realms beyond as equally real as ourselves? If so, might we, therefore, call them "Astralites"? Or would the name "Overjokers" be more appropriate since they seem to be cosmic provocateurs of some type who only communicate with us on the rarest of occasions as they go about fulfilling their own lives in a way that is in keeping with their separate intellectual, emotional, and spiritual natures?

Then again, might it be that a new order of complexity simply keeps playing out as we humans evolve, as we keep expanding both our minds and our horizons? Could this be what Ralph Waldo Emerson called the "Oversoul" acting out its caretaker function on our behalf, but only offering a direct hand in our affairs when it is deemed necessary? Is it an imperative among those who enjoy a higher perspective that our free will choices should unfold without interference?

When singer-songwriter Bob Welch was with the band Fleetwood Mac, he wrote a beautiful and compelling song called "Hypnotized". In it, he sang about how it's a meaningless question to ask if the stories we hear about aliens or extraterrestrials having come to our planet long ago are right or for real. Instead, what matters is the feeling we get from hearing those stories, for they are not just enchanting, they are spellbinding. They make us feel positively hypnotized. In fact, that enchantment is so realistic and so compelling that few ever see through it, nor come to understand that the narrative they cling to in their lives is a fiction that has been collectively conjured by humanity over the course of untold millenniums.

It's a mad world. It's a lovely world. It is the world of our dreams, it seems.

The question, then, is this: How does it make you *feel* to fully realize that not all in this world is as it appears to be and that we may very well be living in an enchanted land of dreams?

In his book *Reality Denied*, Colonel Alexander tells us how he was one of the few people in charge of programs designed to study the possibility that the mind could be used to affect matter in ways that defied the laws of physics. This particular ability is known as psychokinesis. Why would the Army be interested in such a thing? For one reason, it was because at that time computers were only coming to the fore and being relied upon more and more. What if the enemy, through psychokinesis and the manipulation of electrons, could make your computer data unreliable? That could put the military's defenses in jeopardy. We have to understand that the term "cyber-warfare" was only beginning to be discussed in serious ways at that time and today, certainly, we know how destructive cyberattacks can be. (Just ask those who have been the victims of a ransomware hacker!) So, here was indeed a matter that required research and Colonel Alexander was the officer put in charge of looking into it, which he did, especially after hearing about the spoon-bending exploits of Uri Geller.

In attendance at one of the spoon-bending sessions the Colonel sponsored was his superior, Major General Albert N "Bert" Stubblebine, the commander of US Intelligence and Security Command. At least one CIA operative was also in attendance and, yes, a fork in the hand of another attendee simply flopped over at ninety degrees at one point and the whole room fell into awestruck silence. The "impossible" had just happened before everyone's very eyes.

The colonel's book *Reality Denied* is full of such stories, which is why the book is subtitled: "Firsthand Experiences with Things that Can't Happen – But Did." The insights offered on remote viewing and telepathic communication are among the many incredible offerings in this remarkable tome (not to mention the many spooky tales about what is going on at the notorious Skinwalker Ranch!). When things that can't happen do, it can prove mind-bending.

This sort of thing frightens many people, however. It can feel much too scary for comfort to them. In their joint book *The Super Natural*, Whitley Strieber and Professor Jeffrey J Kripal go deep into this extradimensional matrix and do their best to come to terms with the very weird and terrifying experiences that Strieber has had over the years. For those familiar with Strieber's controversial book, *Communion*, with its graphic depiction of an alien on its cover, you will know well how this sort of thing can leave you shuddering in the dark at night, wondering if aliens might float in through a closed window and steal you away for a ride on a flying disk. In Chapter One of the book, Kripal kicks things off in a way that no other book has ever done, I believe. He says, straight out, "I am afraid of this book." That is a shocking statement, but somehow one immediately understands why he would say such a thing, especially as one sits in hushed silence, too, with one's pulse pounding away in one's chest. Kripal then goes on to say, "There is something about it, something explosive and new. It is not a neutral book. It is an apocalypse of thought waiting for you, the reader, to actualize." He soon also tells us, however, that the possibility exists that the actualization has, in fact, already occurred, that a "new world" has "already arrived" and he then does his best to help us make sense of it. Both men, in fact, go to great lengths to help us understand the phenomena that has so taken over Strieber's life, and they do so with a rigorous level of insight and intelligence that is commendable. Along the way, they speak with genuine heartfelt concern for the future of humanity.

In Strieber's book *A New World,* Kripal kicks things off again by stating forthright and outright that "This book is contact." If so, there is clearly nothing airy-fairy about that contact and one can scarcely envy the mind-blowing and genuinely shocking experiences that Whitley Strieber has had to endure.

How does it make us *feel* to know that there are indeed alien entities who are not of this earth, but are already here with us somehow? How does it make us feel to know that unidentified aerial phenomena are a reality in our world and admitted to be so by many military authorities around the globe now?

Perhaps, *vulnerable* is the most appropriate word.

Nevertheless, I welcome the day that we make irrefutable contact.

On that day, however, none of us has any idea *exactly* how such contact will make us feel, but we had better prepare ourselves because it is coming.

In the meantime, how does it make us feel to know that consciousness can exit the body and fly freely about, looking down on that same body from a vantage point near the ceiling or else speed off across a cityscape or landscape, or even rocket off into space? How does it make us feel to know that people who have been clinically pronounced dead can be revived and, upon recovery, tell extraordinary stories about time spent in another realm, one full of meadows, trees, and rivers? How does it make us feel to hear that a returnee met deceased loved ones while there or encountered a "being of light" who was like an angel to them, one full of love and able to converse with them telepathically?

How does it make us feel to know that there are psychics in the world who can remote view objects on the other side of the planet or even in outer space? How does it make us feel to know that mediums can converse with the dead? How does it make us feel to know that there are practitioners of shamanism who can pass into other dimensions and converse with "spirits" there and decipher what ails a sick individual or discover how to heal that person?

How does it make us feel to know that some people are able to walk on scorching hot coals or play with fire all over their bodies and not get burnt or affected in any way? How does it make us feel to know that there are people who can move objects with their minds or levitate before our very eyes?

For my part, I find such phenomena daunting. They make me feel as if I am but a wide-eyed novice who has barely stepped across the threshold at one of the Mystery Schools of yore. At the same time, however, it makes me feel optimistic. I have always suspected that there is more to this life than meets the eye and that the arrogant, know-it-all types with their authoritarian snideness are in for some shocking surprises one day. It makes me feel as if such phenomena may be part of our natural birthright, our innate potential, and that we humans are only starting to get our wings.

In the last analysis, however, I think it makes me feel as if we humans are unbounded souls, infinite in constitution, who are being made to live through a human experience as part of our growth as souls. As a human being, we are given the opportunity to start from provincial origins and, through earthly challenges, become worldly. Once worldly, we are challenged to become greater again, galaxial in scope and, ultimately, cosmic in magnitude. Once cosmic, we will understand that the universe and every dimension within it is a natural part of our own wholeness. It will prove to us that we are immortal for real and that there is no limit to what we may subsequently choose to experience.

Keith Thompson's fascinating book *Angels and Aliens: UFOs and the Mythic Imagination* offers us a very simple question with enormous ramifications. "Are UFOs from outer space or from the ongoing mythology of humankind?" he asks. "The answer," he says, "could be: both." In other words, the reality of UFOs may not be a case of either/or. "Even if UFOs are actual extraterrestrial spacecraft," he goes on to say, "they have succeeded in slipping into traditional mythology, next to other gods and goddesses. In that sense – if only in that sense – UFOs have indeed *landed* and may be here to stay."

Oh, indeed, they may be here to stay and, in all likelihood, *are* here to stay. And, yes, the occupants of UFOs are *like* gods in our eyes, but they are *not* gods, they are quasi-gods at best who inhabit an intermediate realm between mind and matter. Any which way we look at it, nevertheless, they are way ahead of us on so many fronts that we can only be in awe of them.

How, then, do we feel about that?

Personally, I think that what one must do is stay open-minded about these interdimensional activities. Author Patrick Harpur calls this interdimensionalism, "Daimonic reality", and notes how such occurrences have been going on since time immemorial. Plato, we must remember, gave us the first account of what a near-death returnee had to say about the afterlife. Since then, tens of thousands of accounts have come down to us through the ages of all types of strange daimonic encounters, including ghost and monster tales among so many others.

Perhaps what these occurrences do is keep human evolution progressing and expanding through events of an inexplicable nature in the form of pure novelty. Perhaps "Trickster's twisted Matrix" is all about bending minds for a higher purpose. Perhaps, though, we have interdimensional overseers who are our spiritual allies and, yes, who operate in a beneficent, but clandestine manner, for our own good. The reason for this may be because we, ourselves, are simply not sufficiently evolved to handle their existence in any other way, which they know. As a result, they look on us kindly and have a sense of humor about it. After all, millions of people in this world are indeed like children or adolescents at best, or to put it more harshly, like primitive savages. Consider, for example, how millions of people cannot rise to the noble level of treating others not of their own race as equals when clearly, scientifically, all of the races on this earth are genetically a part of the same human species. Consider, too, how millions of people are ready and willing to kill those who are not a part of their tribe or nation merely at the command of some leader who has chosen to brand a group of fellow human beings as the "enemy" and is skilled at firing up a form of mob mentality.

Alexander's Law keeps us evolving. We start out knowing nothing at birth, but work our way through elementary knowledge, then move on into high school levels of math, chemistry, biology, physics and so on. Some of us then move on again, this time to college level courses and our understandings grow even more complex. After that, again (for some only), it is on to a master's program and a doctoral level of complexity. Then, finally, the few are ready for the complexity of the real thing in a highly specialized field, such as astrophysics or quantum mechanics, which contain facets of cosmic activity that utterly defy everyone's very grounding in knowledge and comprehension.

One thing is sure about those trickster-like occupants of UFOs: they clearly could have wiped humanity off the face of the earth many times over if that had ever been their intention. Instead, their legacy has given us a very strange blend of beneficence and detriment: some of it has been healing, some of it hilarious, some of it horrendous. In short, we have gotten a roiling mix of the weird, the wonderful and the shockingly awful.

In the last analysis, perhaps, all of this is simply food for thought and maybe that, in and of itself, may be something much greater than we generally realize. Perhaps, even, such metaphorical food is the *real* ambrosia of the gods!

# 27

# Rock the Chakra

## *The Radical Magical Power of Dream Yoga*

I WAS MORE FEARLESS in my younger days than I am now. I took chances and engaged regularly in what I called "shamanic pursuits", as well as yogic ones. As an avowed metaphysician, I considered these rituals vital to my quest for insight into life's great mysteries and worked tirelessly on these intrigues both day and night via Hermetic, Taoist, Tantric and, primarily, Dream Yoga practices. (The great thing about being a syncretist is that you can use spiritual practices from virtually any tradition in any way you choose. Truth, to a syncretist, is where you find it.)

Some inexplicable things certainly happened during those years, some of which I will keep to myself, but overall, I experienced many episodes which I found encouraging. Once, for example, during the early Nineties while I was living alone in Wildcat Canyon near San Francisco, I was amazed by a certain happenstance while performing my usual Friday night shamanic ritual. (Some people go to the bar to unwind at the end of their work week. At that time, I went into the darkness, solo, for exploratory purposes.)

What happened was this: after meditating for a time and consciously opening my "chakras" – the energy centers in the body which yogis have charted over the centuries – I managed to charge up my energy field to a very intense level. I was then able to channel that focused energy into a single blast toward the sensor on the cable box of my television set. That blast caused the set to turn on. In other words, I was able to energize my being in such a way as to transform a blast of mental energy into a powerful radio wave and project it straight ahead toward the TV control box, thus forcing it to respond. I did not do this consciously, I hasten to add. It was just something that happened, and it surprised the hell out of me! In any case, I subsequently turned the set off and, in a surreal turn, a further surprise awaited me. That surprise came in the form of a knock on the door. I was certainly not expecting any visitors, so I quite cautiously opened the door and peered out. What I encountered was a Man in Black. Or perhaps to put it a little less dramatically: a Man in Black-looking figure – presumably a mortician – who wanted to know if there was a "dead body" in the house! *Not to my knowledge,* I thought! *And how flipping weird!* The encounter certainly put a bizarre twist to my night.

As it happened, many nights during that particular phase of my life while living alone and meditating extremely deeply, I experienced astounding bursts of light and many an incredible, hyperlucid dream in the night; dreams of a yogic nature which connected me directly to a higher consciousness. Profound teachings came through as a result and helped me to consolidate and expand my perceptual insights. In this way, I gained reams of fresh metaphysical writings, filling notebook after notebook.

A few times during that phase of things I even found myself in dreams so lucid and real that it seemed as if I were in some other dimension entirely. In one such situation, I found myself with a woman who seemed as real as any flesh and blood woman and very powerful emotions passed between us as we looked deeply into each other's eyes in a face-to-face encounter. That same night, I dreamed that a UFO passed over my house and that all of the lights in the valley went out as it passed over.

Quite ominously, just after I had that dream, to my great surprise the television set came on. It came on in the living room in the middle of the night all by itself and the sudden onset of people talking woke me and sent a shiver up my spine. Asleep in the bedroom, I was startled to say the least, but I cautiously made my way, feeling very spooked, to the living room, went to the TV set and switched it off. I then found myself looking about the house with a suspicious eye. It was 3 o'clock in the morning, after all, and there was a heavy feel to the air. It was as if I could vaguely sense some vast pervasive force-field of some kind and it struck me as almost oppressive.

However, since there was clearly no intruder to be found, I soon went back to the bedroom. Before attempting to go to sleep again, though, I decided to take a quick peek out the window, just to have a reassuring look out into the night. When I raised up my blind, however, I received quite a shock. I could see the streetlights of El Sobrante shimmering in the distance. There were also houselights to be seen right across the valley, but just then, *at that very moment*, all of the lights I could see winked off one by one down the hillside until the whole valley was in absolute darkness.

Staggered by the event, I sat back on my bed wide-eyed with astonishment. I had just dreamed that all of the lights in the valley had gone out and suddenly they had! My dream had been precognitive and I was seriously astonished. In fact, I could only sit there in barking mad amazement wondering if an alien craft had actually just flown over my home as I had also dreamed.

Another time during this phase of things, I had the most profound experience of my entire life. During this episode, I entered into a stunningly lucid dream, wherein I found myself in telepathic contact, not with some angelic nor alien entity, but with a vast field of high intelligence which essentially told me how and why life had come into existence!

Upon awakening, I lay in stunned silence in my bed, literally overcome with awe, my mind soaring and my body thrumming with energized elation. I kept thinking in the moment how simple it all is really – the reality of our world – as a feeling of bliss continued to absolutely blaze away and suffuse my entire being in the most rapturous way possible.

Eventually, however, I fell asleep again and, in the morning when I awoke, I thought to write this information down. To my enormous surprise, however, I realized with a start that I could not remember even a single word of what I had learned. Had the teaching, therefore, not been in a language of this Earth, I wondered, or is telepathic knowledge simply not amenable to a linear mode of cognizance, the way in which we humans generally think?

Despite this "cloud of unknowing" I was under, the bliss was persisting and, though I had no words for explicating the deeply profound knowledge I had been given, it kept me steeped in ecstasy for hours on end. The inability to recall any details, however, was frustrating. Nevertheless, I knew that the information I had been given had been genuine and knowing that much alone – that there was indeed an answer, an explanation, to the mysteries of life – proved a great comfort that has continued to this day.

Subsequently, I read how advanced teachings are *always beyond* conceptual thought, beyond language altogether. That is apparently why one cannot put such teachings into words post-facto. This is an *extremely* important point to realize as one pursues the path of enlightenment. People ask what the "great secret" is which explains this life of ours and when no one can tell them, they assume that *there is no answer*. Many will even ridicule those who think otherwise because whatever explanation is given generally seems either glib or a mere platitude or cliché. This is a major mistake. It is fine and even important to be a skeptic when it comes to these matters, but to dismiss the quest in its entirety simply because the intellectualized explanations fail to satisfy or enlighten on the spot is foolish. As the Buddha himself essentially said, words can point, but they do not, cannot and will never deliver up the "thing" itself. Philosopher/metaphysician Alan Watts tells us not to mistake the menu for the meal nor the map for the terrain itself.

In any case, the event that night, for me, was clearly something of a *satori*, a genuine insight into the ultimate significance of life and into my own true self, including the knowledge of how life came into being and how it continues to persist. Having experienced it, I was convinced that spiritual revelations are not only "real", but they are absolutely authentic in the most profound manner imaginable.

This *satori* could as easily be called a moment of *gnosis*. For the meaning of the word "gnosis" means "to know". According to the Hermetic sages of yore, a Gnostic is simply one who *knows*, who has had a direct spiritual epiphany of the Divine. The Zen Buddhist word "satori", likewise, comes from a word that means "to know".

"Knowing", however, does not make one straightaway into either a saint or a sage. Months and years are subsequently necessary for assimilating one's revelations and realizations. As time goes by, however, one ceases slowly, but surely, to be less deluded and more directly insightful. To be blunt about it, one finally comes to recognize what is bullshit and what isn't with an immediacy that reassures.

The real trick here, then, is to realize that an initial dose of gnosis is merely a beginning on the path to higher knowledge. Most of us think quite the opposite, of course: that we have deciphered the truth of life and know it well once we get a great flash of insight. Many highly intelligent people are downright arrogant on this point and even hubristic about it, which is a grave error. The "truth" is this: we are born with very limited physical sensory input and indoctrinated into a particular culture. We, therefore, see the world as we sense it, are taught to see it and come to understand it. This is not brainwashing, as such, but it is a situation with clear limitations which causes us to lose the purity of perception that every child enjoys in its earliest years. Our task, therefore, is very biblical: each of us must become again as a child. When we do, we are able to feel and know something quite astounding, beautiful and beyond words: the proverbial peace that surpasses understanding.

# 28

# A Visionary Voyager, a Buddhist Lama & the Call of the Bodhisattva

NIRVANA WAS THE TOP BAND in the world at the time and their album, *Nevermind*, was being called a cultural phenomenon. This was the early Nineties when electronic dance music was also something of a phenomenon and it had the young people of San Francisco flocking to "raves" in various venues around the city and going wild in the night. For my part, I was a bit beyond such scenes by then, but did attend a rave that featured an evening of performance art by Terence McKenna who was famous in those days for "rapping" in his own way about the state of the world in general and about many a controversial topic such as shamanism, entheogenic substances, UFOs, the "rebirth of the goddess", virtual reality and especially his obsession with the idea that the end of history was imminent. Behind him (and his wild head of hair, bushy beard and brilliant eyes) was a giant screen filled with the protean imagery having to do with such topics. That imagery was certainly larger than life and, as electronic music blared loudly through the hall, absolutely every bizarre aspect of our world seemed to flash across the screen in staccato bursts of color as he spoke, as did countless surreal, mythical and *otherworldly* marvels. It was nothing short of captivating for viewers and we were all left enthralled and wide-eyed as we listened to the man.

It was definitely impressive stuff. By then, I had read McKenna's book *The Archaic Revival* more than once. In fact, I was truly fascinated with his visionary perceptions and his elegant use of language. A prose poet magician of the highest magnitude, McKenna had me mesmerized with his speculative notions about the "elf clowns" of inner space and his profound ruminations on all things esoteric and enigmatic. At the time, there was great interest in his "Timewave Zero" computer program, as well, which he claimed synched in exactly with the Mayan calendar set to end in December of 2012. (An event that, alas, as I suspected, came to nothing; life simply went on as usual once we reached that date, for eras and epochs operate in a cyclical manner the same as any form of calendric time. Quite interestingly, I happened also at that time to have a very direct link to Jose Arguelles, the man who had fired up all the global talk about the Mayan calendar in the first place, although I never had the pleasure of meeting the man.)

Declaring that, contrary to popular scientific opinion, the world was not made of atoms nor subatomic particles, but of *words*, McKenna had locked into a very Hermetic / Buddhist way of viewing the world in which *thought* actually "creates" the "reality" of the perceiver by locking in labels and concepts, and thus ascribing a certain understanding of things and events. In short, a "thing" becomes what we *think* a thing is. That perception, however, is but one among many versions or interpretations that may be imparted. (This relates, as well, to what physicists call the "collapsing the wave function", which has to do with the boundless potential of the quantum field and how it essentially generates a specific paradigm in direct relation to an observer.)

I, too, at the time was closing in on the idea that words and labels were the prime determinants of perception, but the discussion I had with McKenna after his show did nothing to help me understand this complex notion. He was quite cryptic with his responses as it transpired, but his mischievous eyes sparked out with a charismatic vitality that was reassuring to behold. You could almost see his manic mind boiling over with volcanic intrigue at life's rich bounty. In any case, he had way too many fans vying for his attention for me to get into any depth on the subject, but it was hardly the venue for a deep discussion on such a topic anyway. The place was a bit of a full-blown circus, in fact.

I didn't mind. I had moved well away from the pursuit of entheogenic adventures, by then anyway, not to mention the more exotic amusements of the maddening crowds, for living in San Francisco was expensive, which meant that I needed to keep my shoulder to the wheel, my nose to the grindstone and my mind on the business at hand. A lot had happened as the Eighties had unfolded. I had become the manager of a personnel agency in San Francisco for five years, had moved to Dallas for a few years while opening my own personnel agency under the auspices of the same company and then had returned to California to take up the position of Chief Administrator for the corporation. What this meant was that by the Nineties I was overseeing 17 offices located all across the state and was basically working from sunup to sundown five days a week. In brief, my carefree days were over.

Fortunately, I was able to take advantage of the many extraordinary cultural wonders of San Francisco on the weekends. There were museums and art galleries galore to visit, great bookstores, music shops, every form of restaurant, diner, deli, bistro and bar imaginable, and a myriad of fantastic, neon-lit night clubs to enjoy when the urge struck. Whether I was Downtown or in Chinatown, in North Beach, the Marina, Fisherman's Wharf, Haight-Ashbury or Golden Gate Park, there were endless things to see and do. Coit Tower was an especially spectacular place to go for a panoramic view of the city as were the views from across the bay on the far side of the Golden Gate Bridge. I met scores of incredible people over the years, saw countless bands, did a lot of drinking and dancing, played guitar with a group of my own just for fun, went hiking, spent time at the beach, wrote songs, poetry and bits of novels that never got finished, but I didn't care, I was streaking along at the speed of light and loving every minute of it. As far as I was concerned, I was living the dream and never mind that the years were simply flying by.

Eventually, however, I had the great good fortune of meeting just the right person at just the right time. She happened to be a lovely, charming, highly intelligent young Irish lady named Karen Naughton who had come to the city to work for a summer. We took it slow and easy with our first few years together, going back and forth over whether or not to commit ourselves to the relationship, but at last found ourselves inseparable. In time, we would marry in Rome and have two bright, amazing children together, but in the interim the two of us spent most of our time working hard together at our mutual business concerns, then moved to Texas and opened four more personnel agencies between us, which in addition to my original Dallas office gave us a total of five. Once we had managers fully trained and in place in all our offices, we moved to Galway, Ireland and made a new life for ourselves.

Living on the Emerald Isle, I was to discover, made for a very different lifestyle, but one I quickly came to love. The beauty of the land, the quaint buildings, the friendliness of the people, pub culture, the lively music, the "craic", all of it was a pleasure and a privilege and I settled in with a fiddler's ease. Over the course of our first six years, we had two children, Ciarán and Aisling, ran our business from a distance and made the most of the social scene when we could.

At the same time, I continued with my meditations and my writing, but my forward momentum with both had stalled due to the necessity of looking after a family and a sizeable business. Then one day my wife happened to read in the local paper that a three-day Buddhist seminar would be occurring in the city and she signed us on. This event would prove highly significant for me. Fresh to the western world after some twenty years of study in a Tibetan Buddhist monastery in India and from earning the degree of "Geshe" (basically the equivalent of a Doctor of Divinity), the primary speaker at the course was an American-born lama by the name of Michael Roach. After setting up a Buddhist center in New York City, Geshe Michael had begun touring and lecturing and had come to Galway with a small entourage. The teachings proved to be not only incisive, but positively life-changing for me. Indefatigably patient as he went about explaining the ancient concept of *shunyata,* what the Buddhists call "emptiness" (or sometimes "luminous emptiness"), Geshe Michael delivered the equivalent of a direct transmission of the *Dharma* to me, for in the snap of a finger or the blink of an eye at one point, I simply "got it", fully and completely. We humans project our interpretation of the world on what is essentially a blank screen and take it to be objectively real. This projection is all down to karma and karma is down to what we think, say and do. This sudden understanding really surprised me, for I had been reading Buddhist literature for well over twenty years by then but had not been able to quite figure out what this concept of "emptiness" was really all about. The definition according to the *Encyclopedia of Buddhism* by John Powers is: "The notion that all phenomena lack an essence or self, are dependent upon causes and conditions, and so lack inherent existence." Buddha Mind, for example, is self-existent because it is not dependent on causes or conditions, while almost all the things of this world are dependent on other phenomena for their existence. We humans, for example, must have sunshine, a planetary body to live on, a conducive biosphere, water, food and so on. The one great exception is the mind itself, which like Buddha Mind is a self-existent phenomenon, dependent on nothing, most especially the human brain as materialist science insists. (This is why consciousness can persist even with the demise of the body.)

In retrospect, this direct transmission was one of the most significant events of my life. I quickly came to realize that there was no insight more important to get to grips with and truly comprehend than this particular concept.

So taken was I by the sessions with Geshe Michael, a truly gifted teacher, that I volunteered to start a study group and a large number of others quickly joined in, one exceptionally kind gentleman offering his home as a meeting place for us. We began taking lessons from the Asian Classics Institute, the enterprise Geshe Michael had founded in New York City. These lessons came to us thanks to members of the institute translating and uploading the sacred literature of the Tibetan Buddhists onto the Internet for all the world to gain access. We kept the study group going for quite a number of years and, eventually, I even took the Bodhisattva Vow which, in brief, is to help all sentient beings become enlightened. (These writings are a part of that or at least an effort in that direction!)

So, McKenna, in his way, was right. The world one perceives is indeed made up of words, or to be more precise: words don't "create reality" in its ultimate sense, but they do create our *perception* of reality. Words label everything from subatomic particles to the atoms and molecules in the biosphere, to the cells that make up our flesh, to the heavenly bodies which ceaselessly fly across the vastness of the cosmos. Without such labels, phenomena in the form of raw data would still appear, but a percipient would not, and could not, differentiate that which was manifest before his or her eyes, nor ascribe any meaning to such data. All that any of us can know, even the most highly enlightened individuals among us, is simply what is: a primordial whole with forms coming and going in an ever-changing dance of energy. Its meaning is simply what we choose to make it and that choice is generally based on what we are culturally exposed to during the course of our childhood and what meaning our caregivers, teachers and religious leaders ascribe to the various phenomena we encounter.

This pivotal, fundamental revelation truly is vital beyond

measure for those of us who are questing diligently to attain liberation and enlightenment. It is the *key* concept for unlocking and opening the door to higher levels of knowledge and wisdom and must be profoundly understood if progress is really to be made. Yes, we have to *use* words in order to go *beyond* words, but once beyond words, one arrives at a place where one understands that every thought, word and deed plays into creating the karma which comes back to us and gives us the world as we take it to be.

If we fail to comprehend how emptiness works, we go about our lives lost in the fictions which we tell ourselves. Since every cause has a karmic effect, the result is generally a distorted mix of verity and delusion, for to sow unconsciously is to reap chaotically and that in turn can give rise to suffering. This is why freeing ourselves from delusive thinking is so important.

In effect, one's worldview is generally a direct result of living in a state of obliviousness; that is, we are oblivious of how the reality we encounter occurs. What is the cause of this obliviousness?

The answer to that question is: Not understanding about *emptiness* and karma.

Reality, the Buddhists tell us, is *luminous emptiness* itself. It is that invisible Zero Point Field or blank slate of pure energy out of which the quantum realm arises and in which each and every sentient being sows the karmic seeds of its own future.

Buddha, as usual, put the essence of the matter best when he said, "What you are is what you have been. What you will be is what you do now." The revered Tibetan wisdom master, Padmasambhava, put it this way: "If you want to know your past life, look into your present condition; if you want to know your future life, look at your present actions."

The present – now – is all there is.

This *now*, this very instant, is the only chance we have to sow wisely and, if we do sow wisely, we may one day reap the ultimate karmic reward: Nirvana, a state of being beyond all suffering, and what could be better than that?

# 29

# The Firewheel of Wonder

WHEN THE CARNIVAL comes around, people flock to it for a bit of respite from the daily grind. They ride the loop-the-loops, the tilt-a-whirls, the merry-go-rounds, the roller coasters and the Ferris Wheels. They wander through the haunted houses, make their way across the challenging obstacle courses and roar with laughter at their own images in the Fun House mirrors.

It is pure escapism – for a little while – and then it is back to school, back to the job, back to having one's shoulder to the wheel.

It is back to the box.

Thinking outside of the box is an inside job, however, and people forget that. If we are creative and clever with our thinking, we can come up with some pretty amazing ways of turning that box into a magic lantern of sorts and seeing things that we had never before imagined while going about our daily lives.

Inventors and entrepreneurs are especially good at thinking outside of the box and coming up with clever and novel ways of making money that are certainly intriguing. Making money, however, should not be the sole criterion for expanding one's horizons and conjuring things of interest. This is where the old slogan, "Do what you love and the money will follow" comes into play.

The marketplace isn't the only game in town, though.

The spiritual arena, too, offers novelty beyond measure if one is intrigued enough to go off chasing chimeras of the mind. One can, of course, travel to other countries to study what is on offer in the spiritual traditions in those countries or just do some serious reading on the various traditions and let the uniqueness of those traditions play through the mind as the days go along.

The Hindu tradition, for example, has thousands of gods and goddesses. Among them, there is an elephant god, a monkey god and a god with a hundred arms. Why? There are also giant flying bird-beings called Garudas and the sacred Vedic literature speaks of a race of half human, half reptilian entities known as the Asuras. Are these "beings" for real?

When we look at the Greek and Roman myths from the Pagan tradition, we get every type of being imaginable, including one that is half bull and half human: the minotaur. We also get one that is half goat and half human: the satyr. Then there is the griffin, which has the head and wings of an eagle, the body of a lion and the tail of a giant snake. One of the most famous of all the Pagan gods is Pan, who was naked from the waist up, had hairy haunches and legs, and cloven hoofs for feet.

The Egyptians were famous for their gods, as well. Their deities had the attributes of both humans and animals. Thoth, for example, had the head of an ibis on a human-looking body. Horus was hawk-headed, and Hathor had horns on her head like that of a cow.

The Chinese, needless to say, had their flying dragons, of which everyone is well aware, but what about the Tibetans with their "Wrathful Deities", some of which had the snarling faces of beasts along with colossal bodies and some other pretty savage properties.

What is going on with all of this? Is this just crazy or hallucinatory fabrications on the part of the ancients? Why did these cultures go so far as to enshrine this lunacy – if that is what it was – in their "sacred" writings? Were the animal aspects meant to be purely symbolic of qualities or strengths?

These are good questions.

Here's another good question: What about the Bible? In Isaiah 13:21, "satyrs" are mentioned. In 13:22, the "Good Book" – which is so often interpreted as being the "literal" Word of

God – talks about "dragons in their pleasant palaces."

That's not all. Isaiah 30:6 mentions "dragons" along with "flying serpents". Isaiah 34:13 reads, "And thorns shall come up in her palaces, nettles and brambles in the fortresses thereof: and it shall be an habitation of dragons, and a court of owls." 34:14 states that, "The wild beasts of the desert shall also meet with the wild beasts of the island, and the satyr shall cry to his fellow…" In Isaiah 43:20 we get "dragons" once more.

And, no, we're not finished just yet. Isaiah 34:7 mentions "unicorns" believe it or not!

Of course, the Revelation of St John talks about God laying "hold on the dragon, old serpent, which is the Devil, and Satan," and bounding him in a bottomless pit for a thousand years.

As for Ezekiel, he talks about seeing "living creatures" each of whom was standing beside a wheel. "In appearance their form was like a man but each of them had four faces and four wings." Famously, the creatures with their wheels flew up into the sky, which led to a few writers speculating as to whether or not Ezekiel had been looking on extraterrestrials with a spaceship. Ezekiel, however, insisted that his were "visions of God". In other words, they were God-given visions and not physically real.

Be that as it may… What is going on here? How did these reports end up in humanity's most prestigious religious writings, in its most esteemed and revered of books?

Quite interestingly, the oldest paintings on the face of the Earth are to be found in caves and they too carry scores of images of beings that are half animal and half human in nature. These "creatures" are called therianthropes by paleontologists and are affiliated with shamanism, the earliest of all humanity's spiritual traditions.

The tribal shaman was said to be a healer of physical ailments, as well as a healer of metaphysical afflictions. In other words, he or she was a healer of anything which caused distress. The shaman often used plants as an aid in his or her work. Some of those plants were for helping the patient's body to heal and some were ingested by the shaman him or herself as an aid for accessing the spirit world. Once there, the shaman would work for the patient's benefit on the metaphysical plane in order to put an end to whatever was causing the affliction. The cause of the distress was often believed to be that of a malevolent entity of some kind, one of an ethereal nature: deceased humans, ghosts, elementals, demons.

The question is: Are any of these creatures real in a physical sense as, for example, we believe that dinosaurs once existed based on the fossil record, or were they purely beings to be met on the metaphysical plane? Were they simply figures rooted in the hallucinatory realm brought on by the use of psychotropic plants or schizophrenic minds?

Generally, Westerners have no trouble believing that the Hindu tradition is rife with drug-fueled hallucinations (thanks to the acclaimed "soma" of the gods) and that the Greek and Roman "myths" were pure fantasy tales with no basis in reality (though full of life lessons).

What about Isaiah and Ezekiel, and St John who wrote Revelations? What were these guys smoking? What might they have ingested to have been given such visions or were they "really" revelations from God?

The Judeo-Christian tradition blanches at any suggestion other than the last of these possibilities. The prophets of the Bible, we are assured, were not people who indulged in any "shamanic" activity. They were ordinary, but holy, personages to whom God "bestowed" visions, we are told, or in some instances, an "angel of the Lord" granted the sacred vision. Why?

So that the full scope of God's glory might be shared with humankind?

Satyrs and dragons, though? Flying serpents, half human-half animal beings? Unicorns?

Maybe what it was really all about was dreams. After all, dreams are explicitly mentioned in the world's sacred books as being a direct channel to, or from, God or the gods.

There is an excellent argument to be made that it is the "third eye" – the pineal gland – that allows we humans to see what appears to us, unbidden, in the night.

Thinking about the pineal gland, I am reminded of a band called Third Eye Blind, a name I find exceptionally clever. It's a name that strikes a humorous, ironic tone in my mind, and always gives me pause to think. That thought is this: *Am I also third eye blind?*

It's a good question to ask oneself, for I suspect that there are millions upon millions of us to whom this situation applies. I don't mean that in any unkind way, but we all have pineal glands, we all dream, so why turn a blind eye to the third eye, so to speak, and simply ignore it? In my opinion, it is foolish to close one's mind to the visionary potential of this organ.

Millions do that, I suspect, because they are simply oblivious of it. Or, perhaps, they fear to think outside of convention, outside of the cultural box that so surrounds them, not with walls, but with invisible mental boundaries beyond which there may be creatures that might frighten the life out of them or cause their carefully crafted worldview to be blown to smithereens.

What *is* "out there" beyond those invisible boundaries? What is beyond the comfort zone so many of us so enjoy? What is beyond the average, ordinary mindset?

Like the maps of old, do we subconsciously fear that, "There be dragons" in the uncharted waters or lands beyond? And why did those highly respected, ancient mapmakers put that phrase, "There be dragons" in the uncharted waters or lands beyond? Why? Why? Why?

It makes one wonder.

It can make one wonder *a lot*, maybe even enough to consider that a carnival or a fun fair is not nearly as entrancing as the metaphorical "firewheel of spiritual wonder" to coin a phrase.

To my way of thinking, the ordinary, conventional, mundane viewpoint is the lesser wonder when pitted against the curious possibilities of life's visionary phenomena and what might possibly be experienced in other dimensions, whether in this life or potentially in some "afterlife".

Either way, in my mind, wonder itself is the greatest of all the God-given gifts.

# 30

# Survival of the Deadest

THOSE GIVEN TO DARK HUMOR and tales of a mordant nature will hopefully appreciate the title of this essay, which is a play on that universally famous line given to Darwin's theory; namely that what his thesis essentially boils down to is the "Survival of the fittest".

While it is commonly understood that this well-known encapsulation is essentially apt, I intend to offer commentary on a subject which no hardcore evolutionist would give credence to in any way, shape or form: that human consciousness survives once we pass from this earth.

I recently read a most remarkable volume on the topic by the investigative journalist Leslie Kean. Her book is entitled *Surviving Death*. It begins with the fascinating account of James Leininger who from the age of two had an obsessive interest in airplanes and eventually began insisting that he had died in one. For several years, he had nightmares about crashing and burning during an air battle. Without revisiting the numerous details of this incredible story with its wealth of accurate memories from James's previous life as a pilot (all of which proved true once the historic record had been pursued), I will just note here that researchers have by now documented hundreds of cases of children who have been plagued by past life memories. I say "plagued" because most of these cases involved a tragic death that left the person in a kind of limbo with their life unresolved, which is why they were – or are – so haunted by those memories.

Past life memories that can be corroborated, of course, greatly bolster the claim that we humans live many lives as those who espouse reincarnation have long insisted.

As appropriate, Leslie Kean also goes into great detail on

the anecdotal reports of those who have had what is known as a "near-death experience". A near-death experience is where a person suffers some acute trauma and, by every marker at medical science's disposal, is declared dead. There is no detectable brain activity in these instances, nor any evidence of respiration nor heartbeat. Despite all of that, these persons insist that they retained a form of consciousness while in that dire condition and witnessed many events which they should not have been able to witness. Many of these people report floating above their body, for example, and looking down on it, as well as observing the medical professionals attending them. They hear what is said by these medical personnel and witness certain procedures which they could not possibly have seen with their eyes closed and having virtually no brain activity. Yet, their subsequent reports, upon resuscitation, prove accurate.

Many near-death returnees also subsequently report going to what is essentially another dimension where they meet deceased loved ones and sometimes angelic beings of light or other spiritual figures. Almost invariably, these "souls" are told that it is not yet time for them to leave their earthly life and so they go back to their body and eventually return to conscious awareness.

Intriguingly, most of those who experience this phenomenon are never again afraid of death and say that life on the "other side" is actually *even more real* than life in this world.

There are, of course, scores of books on this particular topic and many are to be recommended, but I wish to concentrate solely on Leslie Kean's book for a reason, for the journalist carries her investigation into the generally murky realm of psychic readings and what is known as "mediumship", actually daring to pursue the possibility that some people are genuinely able to communicate with the dead. She describes in detail how she attended numerous sittings in order to witness this phenomenon first-hand and does so with what seems to be credible objectivity.

While many a reader might immediately dismiss this entire category of activity, Leslie Kean investigates this phenomenon in a very persuasive manner. She deals exclusively with persons who come off as being both sincere and believable. Above all, she discovers that there is historic evidence that those with whom the mediums speak were once human beings like ourselves who lived at a specific time and place, and the facts bear out their contentions. These beings on the "other side", it seems, have a powerful desire to assure those of us alive on this earth at this time that consciousness does, indeed, persist after the body ceases to function. They want that especially for their loved ones. What is most reassuring for attendees are little details that only the person who has passed and the bereaved could possibly know.

Here is the really good news: Not only do we live on, according to this fascinating volume, we live on with our personality whole and intact. In other words, we are the same person on the "other side" as we are here, which I believe is a wondrous thing.

Yes, even the "deadest" among us live on! By that I am playfully referring to scientific materialists and hardcore evolutionists who believe that oblivion is what awaits us upon our passing from this world. Talk about a dead end! Quite amusingly, Leslie Kean visits with two different mediums for the express purpose of communicating with a particular close friend of hers who has died. He was a man who had insisted all through his many conversations with the journalist prior to his passing that there was no afterlife. In short, he absolutely refused to believe that consciousness can survive the death of the body, but apparently found out otherwise and said so via both mediums. This man was Budd Hopkins, a man famous (or notorious?) while alive in our world for investigating so-called "alien abductions". Thus, upon being contacted, Hopkins reportedly blurted out that Kean was correct, that we humans do survive bodily death. This along with many other details convinced the journalist that we do, indeed, live on elsewhere once we pass from this earth, and we do so with our personalities and memories fully intact.

There is a wealth of corroborating details in all of the above cases that were merely touched upon here, and it is well worth one's time to study those details in order to satisfy one's curiosity on this crucially important subject.

Death, of course, is a matter which affects us all in a decisive way. What we *believe* about the possibility of continuing on also affects us, for we will live our lives one way if we think that it is but oblivion that awaits us once we die and quite another way if we believe that we are eternal beings who live life after life.

The latter case carries the corollary that there are consequences to our actions beyond our mortal life span, either in a karmic sense or in the dispensing of divine justice.

Believing that one will go on, however, does bring welcome peace of mind, not only for oneself, but in relation to one's loved ones. How reassuring to know that we can be together again with our loved ones, for they, too, do, or will, live on!

To gain such reassurance about our loved ones and ourselves is quite possibly the most life affirming insight one can ever enjoy.

Above all, it can transform every life into a positive force in the world, one that brings hope to all those who follow.

# 31

# Killer Tales of Daring, Peril & Power

WHEN THE QUAKE STRUCK, there was no mistaking it. The walls of the office building I was in violently rattled, as did my desk, and then the floor noticeably began to buckle beneath me. Clearly the entire building was under threat. In fact, it was shaking so hard that, in my alarm, I did exactly what Californians are told not to do: I leapt up from my chair and ran for the door.

Once on the sidewalk, what I saw was astounding. The street at the front of the building was rolling with waves of upheaval. It was as if the street itself had become as liquified as an ocean and giant undulating currents of surf were cresting toward me in the form of asphalt and concrete.

I was staggered by the sight.

The powerful momentum of the rolling waves did not last for long, however. Nevertheless, sometimes seconds can seem like an eternity.

At the end of it all, there seemed to be no visible damage anywhere that I could see, so eventually I thought, *Okay, that was interesting, but not so bad really*. The building I worked in hadn't collapsed, after all. No streetlights or power lines had come down. Surely everything was fine, so I returned to my desk and my colleagues, and we all shared our amazement at the strength of the quake. Soon, however, we simply shrugged it off and decided that we had better get back to work.

Then someone turned on the radio.

Not only had many buildings in San Francisco collapsed, we discovered, something far more pernicious and deadly had occurred. The San Francisco-Oakland Bay Bridge had had a 50-foot span of roadway drop down into the sea. Cars had plunged into the water and the fate of the occupants of those vehicles was unknown. Then we learned that on the Oakland side of the bay a freeway overpass had collapsed and smashed down on top of many an unlucky motorist who happened to be driving beneath it, killing them in their cars. Meanwhile, a section of San Francisco, the Marina, had been set ablaze and all hell was apparently breaking loose there.

The quake had been massive, as it transpired, and it had been lethal.

When all was said and done the 1989 Loma Prieta earthquake had struck at a magnitude of 6.9. There were 63 deaths in total and 3,757 injuries.

When I arrived at my home in Wildcat Canyon, I found precious statues I had brought back from the Orient broken on the floor, potted plants upended and my furniture in a state of surreal disarray.

Perhaps that was no surprise really, however, as I knew when I had taken the place that the house was situated right on top of the San Andreas Fault, so what else could be expected? *What the hell was I thinking?*

The lesson I took away from that stunning episode in its immediate aftermath is that at any given moment in time, I am, in all reality, mere seconds from death. That is certainly true in many parts of California.

Prior to moving to San Francisco, I lived for a time in Boulder, Colorado and one day while out hiking in the Rockies with some friends, I had learned this same lesson, only this time it was a killer rockslide that almost got me.

We were high up on the side of a mountain when we heard the first cracking of stone near the peak. Then a proper rockslide kicked in. Suddenly giant stones were hurtling down the mountain and what seemed like a ton of rocks came whizzing by our heads at an astonishing speed. We had leapt for our lives by then; some of us leaping behind trees and some of us diving for shelter behind the largest boulders we could get to.

Again, the seconds ticked by, but seemed to take forever to do so.

In the aftermath of this admittedly exhilarating episode, as we came cautiously out from our myriad hiding places, we could only look at each other and wonder if that was that, or if more deadly stones might suddenly come hurtling down the mountainside again and similarly without warning.

Fortunately, not.

Nevertheless, for days afterwards I found myself hearing that haunting, deadly sound of rock striking rock and the mighty snap of runaway boulders shattering tree limbs, which had been the case as that rockslide had come crashing through, smashing against everything in its path. I thought, too, about the fact that it had almost nailed us, as well.

Life can be harrowing, it can be dangerous as we all know, but danger can also be a game-changer in the sense that it can be a powerful reminder if we really stop to think about it of just how vulnerable and tenuous our lives are. We humans like to think how tough we are and many of us live our lives as if we are invincible, but that clearly is not the case. News shows are full of catastrophes and killer tragedies day after day. To be absolutely blunt about it, somewhere in this world someone is always coming into the hour of their death.

Yes, we know that. We sometimes are even willing to risk quite a lot for the exhilaration that danger can bring to our lives and for any number of reasons. Perhaps it is because at times we feel as if there is no excitement in our lives or maybe we have been living our life too timidly. Perhaps we are simply feeling unfulfilled but cannot say why. We, therefore, seek to spice things up. We want more fun, more electrifying sensuality, many more fantastic death-defying adventures and we are willing to chance quite a lot for those things. Sometimes we are willing to put everything on the line for a fleeting thrill.

Witness those who go screeching across the sky at supersonic speeds or leaping from airplanes with a parachute. Witness those who thunder up mountains on a motorcycle, go drag racing down city streets, drink themselves stupid and play chicken on the roads of our world. How many go willingly and daringly down into the proverbial Valley of Death via narcotics or powerful pharmaceuticals which can make their way into our bloodstreams and carry us to some alternative reality of spectacular pleasure with hyper-sensual intensity?

Do we do that for the sheer buzz of it? Do we humans routinely play with fire, seeking out the more dangerous exploits to be had, the ones that thrill in the extreme, just to feel more fully alive?

In many cases, that is almost certainly true, but most of us know that we don't have to risk life and limb to feel more fully alive. To feel more fully alive, we need only be more aware of our every thought, word and deed; to be more attuned to our emotional state and our own physicality.

A high-octane life is about energy and drive, but it can also be about charging forth in a smart way or a dangerously foolish way.

The wise will choose the former over the latter.

Smart living begins with consuming the kind of food and drink that enhances physical wellbeing and boosts energy. It begins with mentally firing ourselves up, motivating ourselves to be focused, as well as disciplined in whatever activity we choose to undertake.

Fortunately, in this day and age, there are literally thousands of books to read on the subject of motivation, health and fitness. There are countless gurus to consult. We humans now have a huge arsenal of knowledge at our disposal online where we can get every form of advice on what we can do, or not do, in order to enjoy maximum health and achieve any number of goals.

Discipline, as it transpires, is the real game-changer in this world and while it may sound as if being disciplined makes for the exact opposite of the allure of risky thrills, it leads to longevity and fewer wounds. It leads, at last, to wisdom, for it is from life experience and lessons learned that wisdom proceeds.

As for mental equilibrium, nothing is more effective for cultivating neurocognitive balance than meditation and mindfulness. If one is seeking a game-changer of a positive nature, these are the ones that serve us best.

Meditation serves us by facilitating downtime on a regular basis in our lives so that we can rest and recuperate and have some respite from the daily grind. It allows us to enjoy a bit of vital and well-deserved tranquility. It also sharpens mental acuity and helps us to notice with keen awareness any diminishment in our energy levels, emotional wellbeing, or general physicality.

Mindfulness serves us likewise by sharpening mental acuity while we are out in the world and in the rush of things. A higher state of awareness at every moment can mean the difference between getting caught up, or not caught up, in other people's dramas, most of which are fomented by unconscious behaviors; the ones that trigger anger, disdain, irritation, resentment, jealousy, envy or any number of other sentiments or passions which can drain a person of his or her wellbeing.

Mindfulness is like radar. It helps us to pick up the subtle signs of trouble in advance, so that we can steer clear of problems and not get involved with those who unconsciously generate distress and violence. It allows us to sense potential trouble within, as well, most of which starts with a subtle hint of anxiety, with the sense that something just doesn't feel quite right. When we feel a sense of unease like that, we need to take action at once and make every effort to mentally make our way to the source of that anxiety. Intelligent reflection and disciplined insight can generally root out the problem and bring it to the fore so that the problem can be solved before it spins out of control.

In short, to feel more fully alive, we don't need to seek out a game-changer that carries mental, emotional, or physical risks to us. We need only amp up our awareness, focus our minds on positive goals and take full conscious control of what we think, say and do.

There is a popular saying: "In my discipline lies my success."

That prescription may not sound overly exciting or electrifying, nor as powerful as a mind-blowing charge like some visionary revelation, but for millenniums discipline has been shown to be a crucially effective strategy for delivering up a fulfilling and enlightening result.

Such a prescription may just be the ultimate game-changer.

# 32

# Evolutionary Spiritual Alchemy

## *An extract from the novel Dragonfire Dreams*

IN MY NOVEL *DRAGONFIRE DREAMS*, the plot revolves, in part, around a cross-country road trip from San Francisco to New York City. The driver of the car, a sleek little vintage Thunderbird convertible, is a character named Peter Skyler. What sends Skyler on his great road adventure is a series of events that begin when a gunman lets loose with a pistol in a nightclub just as Skyler and his band are about to play the biggest gig of their career.

The gunman, it transpires, is fleeing the police for a crime he has just committed and, as a diversionary tactic, he takes out the mirrorball which hangs above the dance floor in the club.

It is Skyler's girlfriend, Shannon Youngblood, who is caught beneath the exploding mirrorball and is almost killed when the bullets go flying.

As so often happens in today's world that violent episode in the story is captured on the spot by someone wielding a smart phone. Almost immediately, an anonymous man somewhere – a self-styled "shock artist" – does the unspeakable after seeing the clip on the news. Captivated by the beautiful Shannon, he edits the piece, sets it to music and gives it an overtly erotic twist. The video soon goes viral over the Internet, becoming a YouTube sensation and an utter nightmare for the striking young woman who, traumatized by events, severs her relationship with Skyler.

What happens next stuns everyone even further. A man in New York City – a recluse with severe facial injuries – jumps in on the act and begins copycatting the violent episode in the club. Along the way, he inadvertently kills two people and goes on the run. This sparks a police manhunt of epic proportions. Eluding his pursuers, the unrepentant figure brashly reinvents himself as a self-styled "shock artist" too and begins perpetrating, "stunt punk gun fun", calling himself "Vlad the Imp" – a play on the name of the medieval prince, Vlad the Impaler, of Transylvania, the very man who has gone down in history as the inspiration for Dracula.

Eventually, "Vlad" takes out a crystal chandelier in a swank hotel above a stunning red-haired woman and, later, he takes out a giant screen TV in Times Square when he happens to see Shannon Youngblood in a news flash there, for he has fallen madly in love with her and is frustrated that he cannot have her for real in his life.

Such exploits bring the police manhunt to an absolutely feverish pitch.

Finally, with the whole world hanging on his every move, the increasingly psychotic felon perpetrates a series of devious exploits meant to ensure his criminal notoriety forever. That includes a bloody, blasphemous sacrilegious act intended to insult the God he feels has abandoned him.

To that end, he succeeds. He also succeeds in cleverly outfoxing the police and making off with Shannon, now the woman of his dreams, for a sizzling night of passion to which she must submit or else...

Skyler, meanwhile, believing that Shannon has finished with him for good, can only tune into the evolving madness surrounding her with horror, even as he tries his best to get a fresh start in life for himself. To that end, he rips out across the country in his T-Bird paying homage to his literary hero, Jack Kerouac, author of the legendary "Beat" novel *On the Road*.

There are many ups and downs to the journey, including several affairs, as well as many a party and many a profound moment.

One of those moments of insight occurs when Skyler is

passing through Northwest Ohio and hears a man on the radio speaking about the region, saying that in prehistoric times this particular area was known as the Great Black Swamp. At once, Skyler muses on how the image of the Great Black Swamp is one that he can easily connect to his study of the ancient art of Alchemy. As he cruises along, he recalls a discussion he once had with a man named Killian McLaughlin (whom he and his friends call "McQuark" due to the man's interest in quantum physics).

Below is an extract from the novel:

"In spiritual terms," McQuark had explained, "the first phase, known as the *nigredo* or the blackening phase, correlates to that time in our life when we are stuck in the mud or when we feel as if we are sinking down into a quagmire that is threatening to engulf us completely. It corresponds, in short, to a time when almost everything seems to go far more wrong than right in one's life, when there is very little light in sight. Yet, if one does keep slogging through the black muck, staying patient and trusting of the process, keeping utterly faithful and devoted to the higher ideals – even as one battles with his or her own darkest impulses and lowliest of desires – then, and only then, can the purification process begin."

Purification was said to be the second stage of the Great Work and Skyler had learned that it involved overcoming lower emotions such as greed, envy, selfishness and so on. As one purged oneself of such base level sentiments, the *albedo*, the whitening phase of alchemy, could begin in earnest. If the aspirant single-mindedly pursued the higher ideals of compassion, forgiveness and understanding during this phase, the *nigredo* could be left far behind. After that, one could grow in wisdom until the reddening phase, the *rubedo*, of true spiritual passion seized one completely.

This was how one arrived at last at the culmination of the Great Work to claim the spiritual gold of myth and legend. "But never forget," McQuark had insisted, "without that beginning in the dark and terrible phase in the black muck, amid the fetid putrefaction of one's own fear, stupidity and ignorance, there can be no purification, no growth in knowledge, no fathoming of the vast contrasts of this world, and no choosing of the higher ideals over the lower, animal and reptilian, instincts. Without experiencing the *nigredo*, there is no impetus to rise up."

McQuark had smiled broadly after saying that. "Every life is actually an alchemical adventure whether one is aware of it or not," he said. "Unfortunately, some never get beyond the swamplands, but that's why they keep coming back into this world... To learn, to grow, to seek the gold again and again, until finally realizing what life is all about and then seizing that which is precious beyond measure, once and for all."

Skyler wondered now, as he cruised along, if he had yet shaken off the black muck that had him trapped for so long or if he was still in the midst of it. He hoped that it was no mere coincidence that he was hearing the radio program about the Great Black Swamp as he was passing through.

"Reality mirrors what is going on within us..." McQuark had said.

According to the man on the radio, the region was a "veritable breadbasket" now, which pleased Skyler. That particular fact tied in well with how spiritual alchemy had been summed up for him.

"Putrefaction leads to enrichment and enrichment gives way to fecundity," McQuark had explained. "This is more than metaphor for a very simple reason. That which seems to be the refuse and rot in our lives is actually something of value, for every experience whether good or bad goes back into the mix of who we are, and it invariably enriches the ground of our being. Without it, a person would never deepen nor grow, never become better nor more spiritual in nature. People would simply stay at the same base level of existence if there was no struggle.

They would never even think to reach for anything higher, for any transcendental level of being, for the *real* alchemical gold!"

The name of the novel, with its use of the word "Dragonfire" in its title, was intended as a metaphor for the passion that is within each of us and the aspirations that come of that passion. Such passion is spectacularly incendiary, potent and irresistible. It is what ceaselessly impels us to risk life, limb and reputation to satisfy our deepest desires and it is what incessantly inspires one to cast off on a great adventure of his or her own in order to reach true fulfilment.

The ultimate point of the novel is simple enough: We all have our "dragonfire dreams" and we are all in the grip of those dreams.

Which is, perhaps, precisely what makes life so exciting.

There is another aspect to consider, as well, however. Anthropologist Jeremy Narby makes the point best when he says in his highly acclaimed book *The Cosmic Serpent*, "There, I thought, is the source of knowledge: DNA living in water and emitting photons, like an aquatic dragon."

In the last analysis, we humans are forever under the sway of our DNA, of our genetics, of our cultural backgrounds, the depth of our personal knowledge and, especially, our deepest impulses, passions and aspirations. How these all play out together determines what we do with our lives, what chances we take and what finally becomes of us.

In short, human destiny and fate are entwined within us exactly like the double helix of DNA and like the twin serpents on the medical profession's symbolic Staff of Life, the Caduceus.

To use yet another metaphor: We are dealt a hand. That is fate. How we play those cards is where free will comes into the equation and it is free will that ultimately drives us onward toward our destiny and, therefore, *determines* our destiny.

## 33

# In the Shadow of the Birj Khalifa & the Tower of Babel

WHILE IN DUBAI ONE DAY, standing near a wide blue wading pool with scores of fountains gushing upward like fabulous geysers, making a spectacular waterworks display near the Birj Khalifa, currently the world's tallest building, I began remembering a dream that I had had once about the Sufis, a mystical sect that was said to have originated in very ancient times. "A Sufi always listens to his inner voice," a dark-eyed man had whispered in my dream, "but he dances without babble..."

Looking on the Birj Khalifa, I could not but think about the biblical Tower of Babel and wonder about the meaning of my dream. For in that dream, I had also seen a group of old Arab men around a huge hookah, and they were smoking and laughing together. I hadn't thought about the men possibly being Sufis at the time, but suddenly I thought perhaps they might have been.

The Sufis, I had learned, had originally been Gnostics like some of the early Christians. Then I discovered, via a reputed expert in the field, that the Indo-Tibetan Buddhists also had Gnostic origins. And where had Gnosticism itself originated? In Egypt most experts agree, though some point to Babylon and Sumer before it.

Sumer, of course, is regarded by most historians as being the first 'high' civilization on the face of the earth. It was located in what is now Iraq. Sumer, in time, grew into the Mesopotamian Empire and the Mesopotamian Empire, in turn, evolved into the Kingdom of Babylon. Essentially, all of the various facets of high culture originated in Sumer and were a gift of the gods according to the Sumerian clay tablets which certain linguistic experts have thus-far managed to decipher.

Generally, Gnosticism is associated with the Egyptian god Thoth. However, certain archaeologists have insisted that Thoth was the Egyptian name for the Sumerian god Enki. Again, according to the Sumerian clay tablets, the original name of the highest god of all in those days was Anu. Anu had two sons. One was named Enki and the other Enlil. This father-son motif is reminiscent of Adam and his two sons, for in the clay tablets there is a lengthy tale of lethal rivalry between the brothers and in the case of Enki and Enlil, all-out war.

Among the gifts that Thoth was said to have given to humanity was the first written language, the first architecture, arts and mathematics, and religion itself. He was said to have divulged the deepest secrets of life to those humans who were advanced enough to understand them and to have given the world 'alchemy', the very foundation of what has subsequently come to be known as chemical science.

Later, Thoth was identified as Hermes in the Greek literature and it was with Hermes Trismegistus, the 'thrice-greatest', that alchemy ultimately came to be associated. The original tracts on alchemy were revealed on (what are now known as) the 'Emerald Tablets'. These famous tablets are said to be the original source of Gnostic knowledge and wisdom.

The word 'Gnostic' has its roots in the Greek word 'gnosis' which means 'to know'. A Gnostic, then, is a *Knower.* A Gnostic is one who has had a *direct perception of God*. A Gnostic is not a Gnostic until he, or she, has had a direct spiritual epiphany of the Supreme Source of All That Exists. Without such a revelatory insight, one has only an intellectual understanding of the way life works, a *conceptual idea* about who we humans are, and why we exist. An intellectual understanding on its own, however, is not sufficient according to the Gnostic sages. A direct perception of reality is the only 'true knowing'.

This accords precisely with the tenets of Indo-Tibetan Buddhism as I understand them. So, at last, the final piece of the puzzle fell into place for me. All of the world's great religions are derived from a single source and their mystical schools have all extolled the same ultimate message. Buddhism, Hinduism, Christianity, Islam and the Jewish religion are all rooted in a form of *knowing* which transcends language. The Gnostics were the original Christians. Sufiism is the mystical branch of Islam now, but it preceded Islam. In ancient Israel, the Kabbalists were the original Jewish mystics, the learned men who wrote the Talmud.

All is one finally.

And yet it certainly doesn't feel that way when one ponders the staggering degree of diversity that exists in this world. The number of nations, sects and languages is massive. As a result, when people choose to look at differences, rather than commonalities, the idea of all being one seems essentially ludicrous. In fact, it can seem as if, once upon another millennium, there really was a Tower of Babel and that humanity had been and still is living beneath a terrible curse for centuries on end, a curse which has all of us gazing upon each other with suspicious eyes, seeing only how different we are from one another, not how alike we are in our desires, wants and needs.

What the Birj Khalifa represents, I believe, as magnificent as it is, is the competitiveness that seems to have millions of people deeply spellbound. It represents worldly ambition of the highest degree. It states in concrete, steel and glass the irresistible human desire to be Number 1, to be greater than all others. Our religions seem to reflect this attitude, as well, and the historic record of religious violence due to that is a chronicle of disgrace to say the least. Competition has given us wonder upon wonder in this world, but also a species that is at war with itself.

While perusing the Internet one day, I came across a rather

pithy statement. It read as follows: "A religious person will do what he is told… No matter what is right… Whereas a spiritual person will do what is right… No matter what he is told." These are wise words. They are words to live by. And the Birj Khalifa may stand out as the world's tallest building at this time, but what is far greater in my mind is a human being with principles and integrity, a person who sees every living thing as sacred and does the right thing without fail, which is to say, dances without babble and does right by others at every opportunity.

## 34

# Einstein's Pipeline: Flying the Light Sublime

AT THE SPEED OF LIGHT, physicists tell us, time freezes. This implies to metaphysicians that if one actually attained the speed of light and arrived at a state in which time had stopped moving, or ceased to exist altogether, then one might well have burst through into what we commonly call "eternity".

Eternity is said to be "beyond time". It is said to be the spiritual home of all that exists and, therefore, the source of the human soul.

It goes without saying that a human being could never reach the speed of light in embodied form, but how about in a disembodied state? What if the "soul" or "energy body" or the "mind" itself *could* actually reach such a speed in some way? What if it did so by taking consciousness down to a subquantum level purely by will alone, or by exiting the body and flying off in some direction unimpeded by gravity?

People who have undergone near-death experiences tell us that they often arrive in the "Great Beyond" by first shooting off across the universe or by traveling through a kind of tunnel or pipeline at a staggering speed. Once they are in that place on the "other side", they are sometimes able to move about there at astonishing speeds. Many have told us that just by desiring to be elsewhere, they essentially arrived in their chosen location instantaneously.

Some near-death returnees have reported being disembodied during these episodes, while others have stated that they had an ethereal form of some nature. All of this goes on while the gross physical body of the person remains on earth without any vital signs whatsoever.

The anthropologist Jeremy Narby, in his remarkable book *The Cosmic Serpent*, speculates that a tribal Amazonian shaman might well be taking his consciousness down to a molecular level when he drinks a psychoactive brew such as *ayahuasca* and subsequently flies off into some "otherworld" in an effort to find a way to heal a patient or to gain valuable knowledge on some matter by conversing with the beneficent entities which exist there.

Einstein, of course, is famous for the thought experiments that led him to conceive his General and Special theories of Relativity. In these, he imagined himself riding a light wave. So vivid and sublime were these imaginings that they preceded his efforts to describe his insights in mathematical terms. Years later, Einstein stated how he believed that one's "imagination is more important than knowledge", which was no small declaration for a man of his genius to make.

Since Einstein's day, countless people have imagined themselves flying down through his pipeline, seeking to experience what such a journey would be like for oneself.

The short answer is: It makes for a transcendental experience.

That is because the mind is capable of sensing a range of vibrational frequencies which *transcend* the energetic frequencies found in the material world. This is why it is totally acceptable, in both scientific and spiritual terms, to identify these frequencies as *transcendental* in nature.

As we know, atomic systems are constantly in motion at all times and in all places in the universe. It is the speed of those vibrations that generates the solidity we experience in the material world. The atoms in our fingers, for example, are moving much too fast to pass through the vibrating objects that they touch.

At transcendental speeds, however, the vibrating forms are less dense and, just as X-rays can pass through other X-rays, there is no impeding of one form in relation to another.

If the speed of vibration in a transcendental realm is such that it might in fact be the base domain of consciousness itself, then the ultimate creative ordering essence which pervades virtually all of the universe might well constitute what we could rightly call, "Supreme Being".

Phrased in this way, "Supreme Being" is different from the ancient manner of alluding to "God" as "the" Supreme Being.

"Supreme Being" *can* be synonymous with "God", however, if we postulate that this "Supreme Being" is never separate from creation, but permeates, penetrates, suffuses and sustains it.

Like "beingness" itself, energy is ever in perpetual motion. We who are in this world are simply "being" ourselves as we go about our lives. We like to think that we are a permanent fixture in this world, but nothing is permanent in the cosmos. All is transient and fleeting. All things are *being* what they are for a finite time span. This is why the ancient sages insisted that change is the only constant.

One might speculate, therefore, that "Supreme Being" is simply all beings together in totality. "All in one and one in all," in other words, in some sublime holographic manner as opposed to viewing this totality as a "God" who is apart from creation.

In a similar way, it is truer perhaps to say that each human being "is" a soul or energy body, not that each of us "has" a soul or energy body. This is because the soul or energy body is primary and the physical body secondary.

If this energy body "is" the psychospiritual complex, pure consciousness in essence, then it makes sense that one would feel like the same person at fifty years of age as one felt at five – which most of us do – and that this psychospiritual complex will go on once it exits the physical body.

It's a comforting thought certainly.

In the above paradigm, we humans can rightly see ourselves as a unit of the greater Cosmic Mind, a holographic unit of

"Supreme Being", for all rays and waves in the whole of the universe are, after all, irrefutably intertwined and span a range, or spectrum, of vibrational frequencies which goes right off the measurable chart.

The rays and waves that can be perceived by our human senses are limited, as we know, but we cannot speak with the same certainty about the sensing capabilities of the human mind when it is detached from the five physical senses.

Yogic masters often speak of their ability to achieve transcendental states of being and do claim that they can go so deeply "down" into meditative states that they are able to perceive forms of life existing there. At least one of these planes is called the "astral" plane and the "beings" there are said to be embodied, just not grossly so. The Vedic masters of India and other mystics around the globe have even gone so far as to describe these beings in quite precise terms. In the West, the ancients simply called them gods and angels.

Since the mind is capable of experiencing such beings, we might describe these entities as being a part of the same mental continuum that we inhabit. Perhaps, such beings could be described as superluminal in nature. Anything superluminal is said to be composed of photonic essences which can exceed the speed of light as we experience it in this world.

Both yogis and returnees from the dead tell us that to think a thing in the Great Beyond is to immediately experience it. Perhaps all happenstance there occurs instantaneously. If so, one could never be wanting in such a "world" since instant fulfilment would be the norm. Such a realm would be, in a word, paradise.

If these superluminal entities exist in an eternal state that is not subject to time, which is to say in a much different way than we humans normally experience life here on our planet, then these beings could well live for thousands of our Earth years, just as legend has it. From a certain perspective, perhaps, such a transcendental paradise might well be what we westerners have long called Heaven. Once in it, perhaps, we could live for thousands of years ourselves, or simply exist in a timeless state, which is a comforting thought, if yet another great mystery.

Mystery is not such a bad thing, though, for as Einstein put it, "The most beautiful thing we can experience is the mystery." We are all free, of course, to at least attempt to find out how true all of this is by becoming yogis, mystics, shamanic psychonauts or Einsteinian pipeliners ourselves.

There's a saying: The proof is in the proverbial pudding. For the brave and determined among us, this *particular* proof is in the pipeline.

## 35

# The Crucible of Mystery

WHEN ONE EXPLORES what is known about the dawn of human history, one discovers that there is far more mystery to it than certainty, but one also discovers a colossal touchstone for the imagination.

Recorded history is one thing, of course, and those epochs *prior* to recorded history another.

The possibility exists that what separates recorded history from the unchronicled millenniums which preceded it may be down to a world-wide apocalyptic deluge that wiped out, or significantly diminished, the civilizations that were already extant on the earth in those days.

While the current historical epoch places civilization's roots in Sumer and a myriad of noteworthy cultures that followed on from Sumer, such as Babylon, Mesopotamia, Egypt, Russia, India, China and so on, what is generally not accepted in orthodox circles is that any collective peoples who lived anywhere in the world prior to the rise of Sumer were anything other than primitive tribal groups or wandering nomads. Such primitives were said to be lucky if they could build any form of shelter for themselves, never mind edifices which could house governing hierarchies and structured public organizations for an entire society.

That is certainly what conventional archaeologists would have us believe. So, too, virtually every academic institute around the globe. Those who are not beholden to the "Establishment" for their funding and salaried positions, however, are free to openly dig much deeper into the cryptic archaeological record and follow the evidence wherever it happens to lead.

What has been postulated by researchers such as Graham

Hancock, Robert Bauval and Robert Schoch is that prior to the Great Deluge, believed to have occurred in or around 10,000 BCE, there were indeed some significantly advanced civilizations on this Earth. Maverick geologists and archaeologists point to the Great Pyramid as being much older than orthodoxy would have it. Schoch is especially famous for insisting that the rainwater erosion marks around the base of the Sphinx could only have come about prior to the Sahara becoming a desert.

Researchers also point to the phenomenal temple, Nabta Playa, in Egypt as a pre-Sumer site that incorporates astounding astronomical knowledge in its layout. So, too, Baalbek in Lebanon with its mysterious Trilithon blocks, each of which weighs in excess of a thousand tons. Who had the technology or wherewithal to move blocks of stone that size thousands of years ago? Who had the ability to inscribe hieroglyphics into hard stone and carve the precision statues we see in Luxor, Egypt's Karnak Temple Complex?

More recently, there is Gobekli Tepe in Turkey, a temple complex which is indisputably at least 10,000 years of age.

South America, too, has sites of interest such as Cusco, Machu Picchu, Ollantaytambo, Puma Punku, the Kalasasaya Temple complex and the massive, phenomenal, gigantic "jigsaw puzzle" walls in Sacsayhuaman. Again, who could lift blocks of stone that size, cut them to perfection and place them in situ? How did the ancients do that?

As for those giant heads on Easter Island, they just leave one scratching one's own head.

The amazing thing about all of this is that these ancient sites embody astronomical and mathematical knowledge which positively defies notions of the primitivism to which the establishment forever relegates them. The fabled Golden Age, establishment figures say, is pure fantasy. They say forget about the Sumerian clay tablets and all of the carved symbols, the hieroglyphics and the petroglyphs in stone around the globe which attempt to convey important explanatory knowledge about who built these places and why. Forget about the "tales" that have survived the ravages of time in one form or another, stories about "gods" from the sky. Such stories are pure myth. They are all balderdash.

In fairness, no one can say for sure that specific civilizations such as Atlantis, Lemuria or Mu actually existed prior to the Great Deluge, nor that any particular group such as the Anunnaki (the Nephilim or "Sons of God" written about in the first book of the Bible) existed for certain. The Anunnaki allegedly came here from the "heavens" according to the Sumerian Clay Tablets and directly gave rise to that culture.

As for Egyptian culture, it left a staggering legacy in hieroglyphics on its great stone temples. Those hieroglyphics speak of "gods" imparting knowledge to them. Indian culture, too, offers a wealth of information about "gods" in its most sacred literature, the Vedas.

That humanity today still cannot replicate the phenomenal temples and pyramids that were built in those most ancient of days stands as proof positive to many that some form of advanced civilization had to have existed prior to the founding of those cultures which appear in the historical record. The establishment, however, will have none of that and dismisses this notion with a wave of an arrogant academic hand.

Nevertheless, there are researchers, such as those mentioned above, with exceptionally open minds and a passion for solving the great mysteries of this world. They bravely tell their alternative histories. What emerges is a surprising progression in the narrative. These researchers claim that the "gods" spoken about all around the globe were "advanced beings" of some nature, whose technology was so far beyond the primitive tribal nomads who roamed about the Earth in those days that the native inhabitants could *only* regard them as "gods". After all, what did the natives know for themselves? They knew that survival was difficult, that nature could be catastrophic, that shelter was tenuous at best. They knew that food sources were sometimes scarce, that fellow members of their tribe often fell sick, or worse, fell over dead and that there was nothing that could be done about any of that. Such was life.

All of that changed, though, when a mysterious race of Advanced Beings came on the scene and began working with the native inhabitants. Those Advanced Beings lived significantly longer lives than the primitive tribal peoples and thus, perhaps, the concept of the gods being "immortal" emerged. And, of course, the gods could construct edifices that took one's breath away. They could build entire cities, in fact, and were said to have flying machines that could take them anywhere they wished to go, including into the heavens above.

Some of these "stories" may indeed be simply tall tales, but certainly not all of them. When stones weighing in excess of a thousand tons are cut and lifted up from out of a quarry, then carried up a hill to be placed in clear astronomical alignment with the geometries of the Earth and the heavens above, there is no way that one may dismiss such evidence out of hand.

Theories abound, of course, and many try very hard to keep as down-to-earth as possible with their theories, which is prudent, but still there is a great deal of mystery about it all.

It's great fun, nevertheless, to conjecture and speculate, and imagine scenarios that are not so down-to-earth or mundane. After all, where would we be today if Einstein hadn't imagined himself riding a beam of light and streaking out across the universe like the greatest surfer of all time? What if the Wright Brothers or others like them hadn't believed it possible for heavier-than-air objects to fly?

Our world is unfathomably rich in terms of the sheer mystery which underlies the origins of virtually every culture. To believe that this world is but a humdrum, mundane, profane affair is to rob the human imagination of all that is fantastic in my opinion.

What those structures tell is a mighty tall tale, indeed, but not one that is but "mere fiction" as the establishment would have us believe. There is too much that is still unexplained by the orthodox, academic community. There are still too many possible alternative histories to consider, which is why there is great gain to be made by the more imaginative among us.

Immersing oneself in the crucible of mystery and stretching one's horizons without apology is an indulgence, but one rooted in intellectual freedom and the right of the so-called "average, ordinary person" to speculate to his or her heart's content. After all, great things can come of it; namely, inspiration of a sacred and soaring magnitude that is uplifting and, above all, fantastically heartening.

## 36

# On Finding an Aboriginal Power Stone

### *A True Tale of a Dreamtime Close Encounter*

THE DREAMTIME. What is it? Is it for real? Why do the Australian Aborigines believe in it so fervently?

I must tell a story, a *true* story, one of the most amazing, unique and astounding experiences of my life. What happened was this: I had been traveling with my partner at the time in Australia. We had crossed untold kilometers driving from Melbourne to Perth on the shores of Western Australia and, as time passed, we eventually started back again. Along the way, while on the open road in South Australia, we decided to take a break from the rigors of our travels and spend the afternoon on the beach. As we drove along the coast road, we could see endless expanses of golden sands from which to choose. One place was as good as another, it seemed, that part didn't matter, so we simply stopped at random finally. We pulled off the coast highway and made our way down a small road to the blue waters of the Southern Ocean and found a place to park. Pitching our tent, we set up camp and then relaxed into the afternoon.

At one point, feeling a little restless, I went off exploring on my own and came to a rugged outcrop of rock which tapered down into the water from a coastal hill. The stony outcrop had been heavily battered by the sea and there were small cliffs with broken boulders lying about in the sand. I picked my way over the rocks as brilliant sunlight poured down, the roar of the waves rushing in and receding time and again at my feet.

Then I noticed a cave. It had a very low entrance and I hesitated going into it at first for fear of getting caught inside it should a massive wave suddenly rise up and inundate the cavity. As I bent over to peer into it, however, I discovered that I could see light inside it! Curious, I crawled in on my hands and knees. Once fully inside, the cave proved to be quite spacious and exceptionally lovely with a large circle of golden sunlight pouring in through an opening in its ceiling. I realized at that point that at high tide, the cavern doubtless turned into a blowhole.

Then I noticed an amazing stone in the midst of the bright patch of sunlight. It was a long stone, almost as long as my forearm. There were crisscrossing ridges at various places around its length and the whole of it had been worn smooth from the briny oceanic waves which had been washing over it, no doubt, for hundreds or perhaps even thousands of years.

As a collector of stones, I was fascinated. I picked up the oblong stone and turned it round in my hands. It was heavy and had an interesting feel to it. Quite curiously, its shape reminded me of Ayer's Rock, or Uluru as the Aborigines called it, which is also oblong and rather flat, unlike the saw-toothed peaks of the Rockies or the Alps that I had seen. My partner and I had climbed Uluru the previous year and I will never forget the phenomenal beauty of it, especially at sunrise in the golden rays of the dawn. I assumed while holding the stone in the cave that it was simply one of those wondrous natural objects that one sometimes finds. In fact, I felt doubly lucky at that moment, for I had already found another stone a little earlier that had really gotten me excited. Made of gleaming white quartz crystal, the other stone was smaller and rather egg shaped, though much larger than an ordinary egg, and it had fit nicely into the palm of my hand. It, too, had a great feel about it and I had instantly dubbed it my "philosopher's stone". It was like an alchemical egg of absolute purity in my mind.

This other, newfound one, though, had a very powerful, astonishing feel to it. It was almost mesmerizing the way it felt in the hands. I didn't think twice about taking it with me when

I left the cave. Never once did I consider that it might be an Aboriginal power stone or that a being of the Dreamtime might actually be residing within it.

* * *

That night, back in our home in a suburb of Melbourne, I emptied the car of our suitcases and the various other things we had picked up along the way on our month-long travels. Tired, but exhilarated from the journey, I laid a fair few of the objects – stones, pebbles and shells – on the floor of the bedroom and settled back into city life. A meal was taken and then my partner sat back to read the newspaper in the sitting room, and I wandered off into the bedroom to read as well. I remember taking off my shoes, propping myself up against some pillows on the bed, turning on the bedside lamp and taking up Gary Snyder's Pulitzer Prize winning collection of poetry entitled *Turtle Island*.

In time, the doorbell rang, and a friend and colleague of my partner came in and the two women went to the sitting room to chat. Since there was business to discuss, I shouted out a hello, but did not join them. I stayed where I was. I was enjoying my book.

As I grew steadily more absorbed in the poetry I was reading, however, I happened to look up at one point for no real reason that I can remember and was met with a bit of a surprise to say the least. For the upper half of the room was suddenly filled with mist. It was especially evident around the green Chinese lantern shade which hung on the bedroom light suspended from the ceiling in the center of the room.

For a moment, I just sat looking at the mist, wondering how it had gotten there. Then it occurred to me that perhaps it wasn't mist at all, but smoke. There was no odor, however. Still, if it was smoke, that could well be a problem.

Then I noticed something else, something that seriously astonished me. Over by the bedroom fireplace, there was something *moving* in the mist. It took only seconds to realize that it was a spiraling form of some nature about as large as the upper part of my body. The room, suffused in a *very* thick mist by then, was the medium by which I could see this form. The form itself was invisible. It was completely transparent, but because it was whirling around in the mist, I could see it quite plainly.

Baffled, I called out quietly to my partner, inquiring if perchance she had a fire going in the sitting room and I wondered if smoke was somehow wafting about the house because of it. She told me no.

"Are you smoking then?" I asked, knowing that this was highly unlikely. "No," she said.

Still puzzled, I tried to pinpoint one more option. "Do you have incense burning then?"

"No! Why?"

Why indeed. "Would you mind coming to the bedroom a minute?" I asked. When my partner appeared at the door, I stopped her. "Is this bedroom full of mist or am I just imagining it?"

My partner gazed about and then said, yes, that she did see it. It was clearly visible to her as she stood at the door looking in.

"Do you see a large spiral hovering over there by the fireplace?" I then asked.

Surprised by the question, my partner gazed and gazed, but said, no, she couldn't see anything there.

"Maybe it's the angle," I said. "But I see a large spiral shape turning in the mist by the fireplace. It's really quite amazing."

Realizing that something highly unusual was happening, my partner politely took her leave. "Something special is going on for you," she said. "I won't interfere. I'll be in the sitting room if you need me."

Some ten minutes or so had transpired by this point and neither the mist nor the spinning, churning spiral were showing any signs of disappearing. Impressed at the situation, I was nevertheless determined *not* to let myself be fooled into thinking that some extraordinary event was going on if it wasn't. What I did at this point, then, was begin playing with the lighting. First, I turned my bedside lamp off and looked. The mist and spiral were still there, so I turned the light back on. Next, I very slowly slid off the bed and made my way to the bedroom light switch and switched it off. Even without the overhead bulb blazing, the mist and spiral were both still very much visible to me.

Switching the overhead light back on, I sat on the side of the bed at that point and just began speaking in a soft voice to the spiral, which I was now taking, intuitively, to be an entity of some sort. As if in response to my inquiries as to who or what it was, the spiraling entity slowly floated across the room and then it entered me.

For a minute or two the entity whirled and churned away inside of me as if "checking me out". I could clearly feel its energy, its subtle vibratory being and the hair on the nape of my neck began standing quite erect. As I sat feeling the buzz of the spiraling entity during those moments, I grew more astonished than ever.

I had to wonder, though, what might happen next. For a second, I even wondered if the "thing" was going to stay within me. Yet, no panic came of it. I sensed an intelligence there and the entity, or force, certainly had a powerful, but tranquil vibe. There was nothing to fear I decided. In fact, a short time later, the entity simply floated back out of me and returned to where it had been hovering beside the black painted mantel of the old Victorian fireplace.

There was a clock beside the bed and, after that, for close to an hour I just sat gazing at the spiraling form, totally absorbed in its curious presence. *What was it? Why was it here? What did it want? What exactly was going on?*

Then I could hear my partner and her girlfriend coming up the hallway and my partner told me that she was taking the woman home. Saying their goodbyes, the women passed by the bedroom door and went straight out of the house. Momentarily, I could hear the engine of the car and that's when things took a sudden and dramatic turn.

All at once there was a crackling sound, a very distinct, fiery electrical sound and it was as if an electrical discharge were occurring by the fireplace. Sizzling with increased intensity as it shot upward through the mist, the spiraling entity abruptly exited the room at what I can only call light speed. Barely visible puffs of black smoke accompanied the flight upward and then, in the proverbial blinking of an eye, the entity went right up through the ceiling and was gone.

That wasn't all that vanished. The mist itself cleared out in a flash too. One second it was there, saturating the entire room and then, *snap* – just like that – it was gone. The room was crystal clear.

Staggered by the sudden turn of events, I just sat there on the bed and gazed wide-eyed at the green Chinese lantern shade over the bedroom light. There wasn't a trace of mist in the room now! It had cleared out in a split second, but only after the spiraling entity had exited first.

* * *

I didn't immediately make the connection of the spiraling entity with the stone that I had brought home. For days I remained amazed and astonished by the experience, but life went on and our routine of work at the University of Melbourne returned. It was a week or so before an Australian couple happened to come to visit one evening and the stones and shells were shown to them. I was tipped off at that point that the long oblong stone that I had brought home from the cave was perhaps something more than a cool and interesting piece of ocean-worn sandstone. "I'd say that that's quite possibly an Aboriginal artifact," one of the two told me.

Wandering about a few days later in an area of the city that we had never been to before, we came across a shop which specialized in Aboriginal arts and crafts. There were boomerangs galore, wooden drums, didgeridoos, spears and spear-throwers, as well as all manner of fantastic visionary art, intricate carvings on bark and paintings on natural objects of every kind such as are found in the Outback.

Speaking with the Aboriginal woman working there, a woman who was extremely nice and happy to converse with us, I raised the issue of the stone. "I found this really interesting stone in a cave in South Australia," I explained, "and the more I look at it the more I wonder if it's not quite the natural object that I had at first taken it to be. I'm starting to wonder now if maybe it was *carved* rather than simply looking the way it does because of Mother Nature..."

The woman gazed ponderously at me. "Are you thinking that it's perhaps an Aboriginal artifact?"

I said I wasn't sure, but *perhaps* that could be the case. Describing it to her, she advised me to have it looked at by a professor friend she knew at the university who specialized in such objects. "He's part Aborigine," she said, "and really knows his stuff. He'll tell you if it's an Aboriginal artifact or not."

Curious, I brought the stone around to the woman within the week and that would prove to be the very last time that I would ever see it. For when I phoned the woman at her shop a few weeks later, she said that her professor friend had indeed determined that it was, not only an Aboriginal artifact, but a *sacred* one. "The Professor told me that it's a *churinga*," she said. "It's a sacred power stone."

"Really!"

"Yes, and it was actually illegal of you to remove it from where you found it," she added. "There's a law against doing that, but he did give the stone back to me."

Instantly on the defensive, I pleaded ignorance. Fortunately, the woman was sympathetic. "Yes, I know, and that's what I told the Professor. You see, he called the Aborigine Society of South Australia and, once they were informed about the stone, they immediately sent a tribal shaman and his assistant to retrieve it. The two men were actually *flown* here. When they arrived, they came to me and demanded that I give them your name. They wanted to have you prosecuted, but I told them that you hadn't realized what you were doing. Nevertheless, the shaman was angry. He said that I was to hand the stone over to him. I explained that it wasn't mine to give, but he didn't care. There was more than a veiled hint from the man that if I didn't give him the stone that he was going to 'point the bone' at me."

Shocked to the core of my being, I was speechless. "But I didn't know! I just thought that it was a natural made object that had been rolled in the surf for centuries on end and that was why it looked like it did."

"Yes, yes, I'm sure you didn't realize," the woman said in a quiet voice. "That's why I wouldn't give the men your name or give them your phone number. But it's okay now. I gave the shaman the stone and the men have flown back to South Australia with it. He is going to put it back where it belongs, he said. So don't worry. It's all over now."

Indeed, it was. Hanging up the phone I was in shock. *A churinga! A sacred stone! A power stone!* For days I agonized over whether I should call the woman back and tell her about the spiraling entity that had apparently emerged from the stone in the bedroom and then had flown off. I wondered, as well, how on earth the shaman was going to put the stone back in the cave in which I found it since I hadn't given the woman any details about the cave's location. As for whether or not the men had been serious about "pointing the bone", or even capable of such a reputedly dangerous form of Aboriginal "voodoo", I will never know.

In any case, there were two good reasons for not making that phone call. One, I had committed an illegal act by taking the Aboriginal artifact in the first place and, two, if the shaman had indeed made that threat about "pointing the bone" was I willing to chance his wrath? I had read about that. If a tribal shaman pointed the bone at someone, they died. Plain and simple. Maybe only an aborigine would die, since they were the ones that believed in that kind of shamanic power and would, therefore, be the ones who were susceptible to it in a psychosomatic way. Then again was I *really* willing to take that chance, I kept asking myself, thinking that I was immune simply because I thought that kind of "primitive magic" was mere superstition and nothing more?

No, that wouldn't be too smart, I decided. I was safely out of it at that point and I was positive that I should just *stay* out of it. I would be a fool to weigh back in!

Exploring the connection in my mind between the power stone and the incident with the spiraling entity in the bedroom really got my imagination working overtime, however. The totality of the experience hit me full force to say the least and my mind raced! *Of course, that is what had happened!* I had taken the *churinga* from its sacred cave and the "Dreamtime" entity residing within it knew it! That was why it had emerged the way it had. Imagine, though, I thought, if I had let that shaman know that I had seen a spiraling entity emerge from the stone and that it had simply vanished up through my ceiling after an hour or so and then had flown away, up into the sky over the city of Melbourne! He would have been furious. Where had the entity gone and where was it now? That was the question. Where on earth was it now?

That night I had awful nightmares. It seemed as if I could actually *feel* the sizzling psychic anger of the tribal shaman stalking me in the astral realm, looking for me in order to avenge the illegal removal of the sacred churinga, but I also felt the loss of the thing itself. It seemed now as if something precious had been taken from me. I could not get over the fact that I would never again hold that stone, nor feel its numinous energy and its great power. The whole of the night through I could see aboriginal warriors coming for me and causing me terrible anguish. I awoke in the morning exhausted.

In the days that followed, I did a great deal of research into the published writings that I could find on the Dreamtime in general and about power stones in particular. I discovered that the Dreamtime was said to be the real home of the Aboriginals, that the Aboriginal ancestors had been residing there for all of eternity and that this was where the dead went once they left this world. There were also gods, as well as ancestors, in the Dreamtime and I could only wonder if I had encountered an ancestor, or indeed a god, that night when the spiraling entity had emerged from the stone and had hovered in my bedroom near the Victorian fireplace! With the hair on the nape of my neck standing erect once more, I remembered how that spiraling form had entered me and lingered for a time. Was that a good thing or a bad thing?

Whichever and whatever it was, it was a *real being*, I decided. There could be no doubt about that in my mind. It was real and it had acted with intelligence, otherwise it could not have come toward me, entered me, then backed away to where it had been before. This amazing, spiraling entity, I decided, had been able to manifest mist in order to make its presence known. Clearly, this invisible being was one of enormous power, for it was regarded as being *sacred* by the Aboriginal peoples. As such, it could only be an entity of tremendous importance in the greater scheme of things, and I could only wonder how powerful it really was.

Perhaps I had been shown a bit of mercy when it had entered into me that evening and "checked me out". Perhaps, I considered, it might have "pointed the bone" all on its own if it had chosen to, but it hadn't, so that settled the matter for me. I thought, no, a *sacred being* would not be a killer as such, nor evil in any way. Sacred beings are compassionate souls. There was nothing to worry about. It would be okay.

For some forty thousand years, I later learned, the Aborigines of Australia had been carving and pecking spirals into rock all over the country. These "petroglyphs" were said to be depictions of the spirits of the Dreamtime. Such spirits, absolutely real in every way say the people, reportedly reside to this very day in sacred stones throughout the land. Such spirits have supernatural powers. They promote the growth of crops, increase fertility in both humans and animals, they cure wounds and heal disease. These spirits are the ancestors and the gods of the Aboriginal peoples.

The Aborigines further say that the very source of everything in this world is the "Rainbow Serpent". It is the ultimate Great Spirit. Life has its origins in this cosmic being and all knowledge comes from it as well.

Quite interestingly, the Rainbow Serpent is said to follow a spiral path as it weaves the universe into existence. Thus, we have the spiraling galaxies, the stars and the planets. We have the Earth itself from out of the Dreamtime, which is eternal in nature and ever fecund.

"As above, so below," the ancient Alchemists said.

Likewise, the Gnostic Christians rephrased this same truism as, "On Earth as it is in Heaven…" And so, I wondered… Had I simply encountered the primordial microcosm as a living, spiraling holographic reflection of the macrocosm itself?

The more likely answer, I believe, is that when one dies, no matter the culture to which one is attached, one enters an astral realm in which one will reside for a time in order to clarify thoughts, reflect on deeds, learn deep spiritual lessons and evolve. The Greeks, for example, called this plane of existence Hades. Other cultures have had other names for it, but here is where a soul goes upon exiting the physical dimension. In the minds of the Greek wisdom masters, those who had entered Hades were known as "shades", for Hades is a murky realm. Such a place is a reflection of a semi-conscious mind that has entered it. One sees it as murky because one's mind is lacking in spiritual clarity.

Ancient seers and visionaries have always insisted that Hades, or a similar realm, is but one of seven planes inhabited by the dead and that as one progresses on the spiritual path, one grows in clarity and, as a result, one's surroundings also grow more clear and more beautiful. The higher realms are, therefore, perceived as being paradise-like. They are also described as being "magical" in the sense that with a mere thought one may construct a fantastic personal habitat for oneself or burst forward at light speed and arrive instantaneously anywhere one wishes to go. The Buddhists say that what the great beings of these realms do with their time is conjure spectacular celebratory parades and essentially express their joy at the wonderment of life in the most stunning and astonishing fashion they can imagine.

So perhaps the Dreamtime is essentially the Aboriginal Land of the Dead and among those dead are many great souls and many who are struggling still to expiate their misdeeds or distorted understandings, the same as in any conceptually similar realm. Great souls are apparently able to pass down into the lower planes where the less evolved are working out their past transgressions and errors of judgment. They do so in order to help those souls who are ready to take to heart any information that will assist them in their efforts to escape their wanderings in such a dull and dreary plane and advance into the higher realms.

Metaphysicians and psychics have always noted that there are "earthbound" spirits who do not understand that they have passed from the physical body or beings who simply refuse to believe they are now deceased. These are the ghosts of legend, and it appears that these are souls who either died tragically and suddenly, or who have unfinished business which keeps them attached to their former existence on earth. It is easy enough to understand that anyone who dies tragically and suddenly is bound to be bewildered by the instantaneous shift in their existence and would, therefore, naturally be unable to make sense of it for a time. Such a death could be from any type of accidental situation, be it a car wreck or a heart attack or anything else, including from being murdered or dying in war.

Perhaps, the being, then, who came forth from out the sacred stone that evening was such a soul; that is, an earthbound entity inhabiting the rock and, therefore, living its life as a ghost.

That the stone was considered "sacred", however, seems to put a different spin on such a notion. Yes, it could be the Aboriginal people's way of looking after an earthbound soul or it could be that the entity residing there was, indeed, a "great soul", one who had chosen to remain close to a particular tribe in order to be of assistance to the peoples of the tribe.

While I can only speculate in this way, I do think it important to note that there are petroglyphs of spirals right around the globe. In Ireland, for example, the most famous megalithic structure in the land is known as Newgrange. This monumental construct is said to be over 5,000 years old and, at both its entrance and within the heart of the edifice, within its innermost sanctum sanctorum, there are numerous spirals (including the breath-taking "triple spiral" that the Celts came to revere most especially).

I might also mention that in my home state of Ohio, there is a huge effigy figure on the ground that very much resembles the image of the Rainbow Serpent. That is the Great Serpent Mound in Adams County, and it is the largest serpent effigy figure in the world. Why this mound was built and by whom is unknown, for there has never been found within it any buried bodies, nor even artifacts of any kind. Archaeologists have speculated that the mound might have been built as early as a few hundred years BCE, but without any items from inside it with which to work no one knows for sure.

A final speculation, then... Could it be that upon passing from the earth plane, the soul or spirit of each of us might well assume a spiral or serpentine shape as we continue on in what we think of as a disembodied state? Could this be why the phrase "slipping the mortal *coil*" came into being? Perhaps, like DNA itself, such a living, energetic form may actually be the primal structure of each and every one of us at this very moment, even now.

# 37

# The Dark Lord of Song

## *The Night Nick Cave Pulled a Fast One on Me*

THE MYSTERIOUS TWISTS AND TURNS of life can move a person in many a strange and fascinating direction. This point is occasionally driven home to me in spades when I happen to see a new record by Nick Cave, the so-called "Dark Lord of Song"; a man who has also been called a "genius". After all, as if being famous for his music wasn't enough, he also writes novels and participates in movies, whether as a scriptwriter or as a soundtrack composer, or both.

The reason for my interest is down to one simple fact: I attended Nick's 21st birthday party in 1978 at his family home while I was living in Australia for a few years in the late 70s. I had barely heard of the man at that stage and that happened to be only through a member of his own family; namely his brother, Tim. Over the decades, however, Nick went on to become something of a phenomenon and his musical styles as listed on Wikipedia now include post-punk, alternative rock, gothic rock, art rock, experimental rock and garage rock.

The invitation to the party had not come from Nick himself, but from his brother's wife who was a professional colleague of my partner at the time.

I had not met Nick before the big night, but I do remember going along thinking that this would simply be a social occasion like all the others we had been attending in and around Melbourne in those years. This was held in Nick's backyard with thirty or forty people (That's just a guess in retrospect) and, yes, the beers did flow.

Then it was announced that Nick and his band would play

for us.

Nick's brother, Tim, whose company I had enjoyed on quite a number of occasions by that point, had told me about Nick prior to that night certainly and he had even raved about him. I hadn't given the man much thought really, however, since he was said to be a "punk" rocker and I was definitely not a fan of the genre.

When Nick stepped up to the microphone with his bandmates, I was not in the least impressed. Here was a tall, lanky kid with jet-black hair and a very disheveled appearance. He laughed a lot and cut up with the lads in his band, but the songs were indeed pure punk (or proto-goth as some were describing his style that night), which, to be honest, didn't impress me either. His opening song, if one can believe this, was a ripping send-up of a tune by an English pop singer named Lulu. The song was, "To Sir with Love". He played it twice that night and, after hearing it for the first time, I was already asking, "Why?" But, of course, that was precisely the point probably: to devilishly confound the expectations of older musicians like myself (I was 26 at the time) who took ourselves and our music so seriously. Perhaps this was proof that he didn't give a damn; that he could do whatever the hell he pleased.

Punk, as a musical movement, was still in its infancy at that time. I had grown up with The Beatles, The Rolling Stones, Jimi Hendrix and Bob Dylan. As a guitar player myself, I had been playing their songs for years along with "newer" stuff (at the time) by the likes of the Eagles, the Doobie Brothers, Crosby, Stills, Nash & Young, Creedence Clearwater Revival, America, Cat Stevens, James Taylor, Leonard Cohen, Eric Clapton, Bruce Springsteen and so on. The top band in the world at that moment was Fleetwood Mac.

In retrospect, of startling and humorous interest, I think, is this: this was not only the era in which punk was in its infancy, but the very days when disco was actually in full flower. A true fact: The Sex Pistols released their ground-breaking, controversial album *Never Mind the Bollocks* on the same day that the Bee Gees released their massive, world-wide, super hit "Stayin' Alive".

Could any two styles of music be further apart?

Obviously, Nick was tuned more into the Sex Pistols than the Bee Gees.

For my part, as an aspiring songwriter myself, I had left the party that night thinking that Nick and his band would never amount to much, nor get too far in the world; not with a set list like I had heard and not with a style of music that doubtless had stray cats in the home neighborhood scampering for their lives.

A year or two later, though, I heard about a punk band in London called The Birthday Party (this name would later strike me as amusingly ironic) and, as far as I could tell, they were just a bunch of hard druggies whose members would doubtless end up dead well before their time. I had no idea that Nick Cave was among them.

Years later again, much to my surprise this time, I heard about a singer with a band known as the Bad Seeds whose name was Nick Cave.

Could it really be? I wondered. Could this really be the same Nick Cave who had brutalized "To Sir with Love" with such gleeful, devilish malice?

Yes, indeed, it was one and the same, and his star was on the rise I learned. He had apparently cheated death on quite a number of occasions thanks to heroin and other drugs but had emerged a wiser man. And *not* just a wiser man, but a more spiritual person, it seemed. His lyrics were said to contain depth and no small amount of references to biblical sin, degradation and debauchery. He was apparently playing Dylan at his game and giving the style a thrashing.

Nevertheless, I did not run straight out to buy any of Nick's albums, since I knew the genre from which it had been spawned and that genre had still not grown on me. Punk performers were much too violent for my taste and its practitioners were boisterously opposed to the overblown "Machine", i.e. the Record Industry, with its "superstar" bands like the ones I personally loved. To the punks, the "peace and love" of the hippie generation was a notion to be spat upon. Literally. I found that reprehensible.

Eventually, though, I discovered that Nick Cave wasn't just a punk figure of minor significance. He was his own man with his own brand of music, and he was being hailed as a great artist. He had obviously *evolved,* I realized.

The first of his albums I bought was *The Boatman's Call*. The opening song on the album is called "Into My Arms". It is a song that contains some profound lyrics about Nick's belief that God is not an "interventionist" deity. I found that intriguing and very different for a love song.

Then, someone gave me *Murder Ballads,* which contained a real shocker: "Stagger Lee". (Do not play this song for your parents or your children!) It also contains two exceptionally beautiful ballads, one with Kylie Minogue called "Where the Wild Roses Grow" and one with PJ Harvey called "Henry Lee". After hearing the last two tunes, I was hooked on Nick's haunting way with a song.

Then Nick published a book called *And the Ass Saw the Angel*.

Now, from way back when, certainly by the time I had attended Nick's 21st birthday party, I had aspirations to be a novelist. It took me some ten years after that night to finally achieve my goal, but eventually *The Dream Illuminati* was published in 1988 and *The Illuminati of Immortality* in 1990. I thought, therefore, that I had at least some measure of success to put up against the famous Nick from all those years ago, but no, Nick got the upper hand here as well. His book was a hardback and acclaimed far and wide. Never mind that Robert Anton Wilson had contributed extensive introductions to both of my novels, they were paperback books, and, in short, very non-mainstream, which meant that sales were not in Nick's league at all.

With the release of *And the Ass Saw the Angel*, I realized that Nick had pulled a fast one on me the night of his twenty-first birthday party. I had had him pegged that evening as being a mere punk joker whose music would never appeal to a very large audience and I had never once suspected that he would morph into a "genius" and rocket out ahead of me so far that, even now, I can barely see him in the distance.

The arc of Nick's trajectory and evolution as a songwriter and musician I think is one in which any young, upcoming artist can find much inspiration. An artist must expand, must grow, must evolve. Nick did just that and he is now a singer, a songwriter, a performer, a novelist, a scriptwriter and a film soundtrack composer. He is, in a word, a "superstar", but still a rebel, still a "dark lord of song", still an artist who refuses to "sell out". He has stayed true to himself, it seems, which is what we should all strive to do, whether we are artists or not.

Being true to oneself means speaking one's mind no matter the topic. For example, Nick is quoted on Wikipedia as saying, "I'm critical of what religions are becoming, the more destructive they're becoming. But I think as an artist, particularly, it's a necessary part of what I do, that there is some divine element going on within my songs." He is also quoted as saying, "I believe in God in spite of religion, not because of it."

I am in full agreement with these insights, and I congratulate Nick on his success, his astounding artistic output, his amazing number of awards in the music industry, his honorary doctorates, his novels, everything. He has scaled the Olympian heights and good for him. Blake's "road of excess" definitely led to the "palace of wisdom".

In a similar way, we can all stay true ourselves if we try and, no matter the life we have led (however decadent and self-indulgent) and we can still find spiritual fulfilment in our own way, too.

Along the way, we need to remember this, though: the young guy or girl we happen across in the street or in some minor venue exhibiting their raw talent, giving their art an honest lash, may have more potential in them than we might think in the moment. There can be a quantum leap lurking in their spirit that might well catapult them far above the average man or woman eventually.

More to the point is this: there is a quantum leap lurking in the spirit of each of us. How our dreams will, or won't, manifest only time can reveal, but the many mysterious twists and turns of life can offer many a fascinating and life-altering surprise.

For me, Nick Cave is the proof.

## 38

# Chasing Quasars

### *The Soul-Quest as a Multidimensional Journey in Evolutionary Novelty*

THERE ARE FAIRY TALES buried in all our souls and not just the ones we hear as children. We are also influenced by the ones born of our cultural influences: the people with whom we interacted during our formative years, the architectural environment that surrounded us, the stories we heard, the books we read, the television shows we happened to see, the movies that inspired us to seek adventure and to reach for Olympian heights in our lives.

Ours is a world full of stimulants. As Robert Anton Wilson writes in his book *Cosmic Trigger*: "Out of the hundred million buzzing, bright, busy signals received every minute, the human brain ignores most and organizes the rest in conformity with whatever belief system it currently holds."

Clearly, when we are in our formative years that belief system is malleable, mutable, and subject to major forms of influence. We see, we hear, we leap to youthful conclusions at every turn. We give every event, every encounter, every piece of information a personal twist or spin in our minds in such a way that, in retrospect, every aspect of those events and encounters attains a certain mythical quality that turns them eventually into storybook tales.

The same holds true when we become adults. We continue to mythologize our lives via the narratives we share with our friends and families, which is to say that what we make of what happens to us is down to what we choose to remember. At times, we embellish; at times, we choose to forget.

It seems evident to many of us that we do not come into this world as blank slates. Rather, we seem to be hardwired from the beginning to be driven by unconscious predilections, instincts and impulses, and to be gifted with a certain level of intelligence, intuitive insight and talent.

Where, we must ask, do we get these inherent drives and qualities? If these derive purely from our genetic inheritance alone, then we should all pretty much think and act as our mothers and fathers have thought and acted. In other words, there should be as much congruity in terms of our personalities as there is in the way most people physically resemble their parents.

Yet, almost invariably, children prove to be very different from their parents in terms of their predilections, drives and desires. A very feasible explanation may be that we humans really do reincarnate and come into this world having already experienced multiple lives. Of course, experience does hone behavior. What serves us well, we seek again. What has caused us problems in the past is doubtless what we consciously strive to avoid.

In any case, our current life is an opportunity to pursue experience as we will. Whether we have lived before or not, we naturally gravitate toward certain types of people and whatever activities happen to appeal to us. Our circumstances play a huge role in what choices can be made, of course, but what most of us get is a mix of the fortuitous and the disenchanting, which strangely enough is ideal, for if we simply had a free ride, one full of pleasures only, we would end up self-centered and lacking in empathy for others. Conversely, too tough or horrific a life does little but drive us into the depths of despair, which is the antithesis of an evolutionary imperative that places surviving and thriving as its chief directive.

The natural world favors balance, fortunately.

Even more fortuitously, reality itself manifests as a union

of subjective and objective rudiments. "Self" and "other" arise together as a unity in a polarized continuum of potential and it is within this spectrum that we are compelled to live out our lives.

From the objective viewpoint, the world is a *given* reality which we must subjectively confront day in and day out. From a subjective perspective, however, reality is not a given. It is more like a magic mirror. That mirror reflects the evolution of our perceptions and the sense we make of those perceptions. This translates into insights and understanding, and hopefully wisdom.

Life can, therefore, be perceived as a miraculous adventure, a banal grind or an absolute horror.

Whether life seems an amazement, a commonplace circumstance or a nightmare to us, however, is ever and always based on our predilections, our intelligence and our emotional constitution. How we react to an event, to other people and to the circumstances of our life determines what we make of things.

In brief, perception is the most vital component of our essential being. It energizes our inner drive to take action and boosts the desire we generate in order to transcend the conditional environment in which we find ourselves. These inherent promptings are doubtless as natural to us as the burgeoning of a seed in relation to the subsequent growth of a plant.

The key to creating positive growth is through understanding that reality is indeed like a magic mirror and that we can actively and consciously put forward into it our best face at all times.

This, it seems, is the way to make *real* magic.

Real magic is not the fairy tale variety that children so love, nor is it the kind that results in fireworks that dazzle the eye and boost the superficial self.

We don't need to be great sorcerers or wizards.

What real magic results in is a form of experiential wisdom which dazzles the inner spirit and inspires a person to become capable of conjuring a wondrous life of transcendental magnificence. The whole cosmos awaits us if only we are open enough and expansive enough to chase all of the wonders on offer, not literally, of course, but metaphorically. Those distant mysterious giant balls of energy known as quasars are flying off in every direction and can take us with them if we are daring enough to take wing along with them. After all, the imagination is boundless.

If we carefully read the work of most wisdom masters, we discover their belief that a higher power exerts a tremendous influence on us during the entire course of our lives. These higher powers can be viewed by us as impersonal autonomous forces such as the archetypes of the collective unconscious, as Jung posits, or as personal entities to which we are connected; to wit: angels, daimons or Transcendentals of some nature. Whatever way we choose to characterize such enigmatic powers, these personal or impersonal forces or entities might be properly considered to be the allies of each of us. They are psychoid allies of the highest order.

In other words, no matter how alone we may feel at times, we are ever and always connected to a higher power, one that stimulates and exerts an influence on us, but we are also possessed of free will, which means that we can make of life what we want.

Crucially, however, what we make of what we see in any given fleeting moment factors into, and ultimately determines, both our destiny and our fate.

39

# The New World Order of Social Media

CONSPIRACY THEORISTS the world over for decades have written and spoken about something called, "the New World Order". This is generally characterized as a global government consisting of all the nations of the planet pulling together for the express purpose of achieving total domination and control over all the peoples of the earth.

Recently, I was speaking with a man who stated that he had overheard a group of radio presenters speaking about the challenges that people face today and apparently one of those persons spoke of the "New World Order of social media". Whether this particular person (whom I have no way of identifying) originated this term or heard it elsewhere herself I may never know, but that in itself is a reflection of the way social media information spreads. In other words, it is part and parcel of the medium that information, whether in the form of labels or phrases, gets buffeted about like leaves in the wind. To track down the origin of any particular aspect of a commentary or news story takes far more detective work than most of us are capable of initiating or, indeed, have any interest in pursuing.

Yet, there is a great deal of truth to the notion that there is a New World Order and that it is indeed associated with social media, for social media has billions of us caught up in its ubiquitous network of platforms and outlets.

As a result, social media nowadays can actually make or break a person with relative ease. A major endorsement of someone, or something of a positive nature going viral about a person, can put that person in an instant position of influence, which they did not previously enjoy. It can sell books or films or any number of products or have people tuning into vlogs or blogs or other social media outlets in the tens of millions.

Should the opposite happen, however, and a negative story goes viral, whether true or false, this can harm or ruin a reputation overnight. An event of this nature whether of a significant or minor magnitude can send a person spiraling down into a very dark place full of anger, bitterness and resentment, especially if the information is unfair, incomplete or skewed in some way.

Unfortunately, it seems that a first report almost always carries far more weight than any subsequent denials or efforts to set the record straight afterwards. This is what makes the New World Order of Social Media so dangerous.

Still, we must not imagine that this New World Order is anything like what George Orwell famously depicted in his novel *1984*. In that book, the inhabitants under the control of "Big Brother" are not even free to do as they like in their own homes. There are cameras virtually everywhere and every movement is spied upon.

In one of the book's more notorious warnings, Orwell wrote, "Who controls the past, controls the future. Who controls the present, controls the past." Look at any nation's history books, and one can immediately spot the authenticity of this insight. Whichever person or party that happens to be in power will dictate the way the past is presented and, as the citizenry echo this viewpoint, it has a direct influence on the direction of the country and, therefore, the future.

Nowadays, of course, we do have closed circuit TV in virtually every public place, but it is touted as being for the public's safety. When an event occurs which involves violence of any nature such as a street brawl, a murder, a theft, a rape and so on, the movements of the suspect, or suspects, are carefully tracked so that the guilt or innocence of those involved can be properly ascertained.

This is actually good and does benefit those who are not engaging in antisocial or criminal behavior. If such is the case, there is presumably little to worry about as street and shop cameras track our movements. A society must have laws governing it, after all, and we are doubtless better off with a way to backup any particular alibi or testimony than to go on mere hearsay. Add in DNA testing today and law enforcement officials can generally construct conclusive evidence where a crime or a private dispute has occurred. This is far better than what has happened in the past where bias and prejudice have landed many an innocent person in prison or gotten them killed.

Social media, of course, is something which we can voluntarily participate in or not. There is a risk if we do, of course, but generally not one of great or grave consequence. Thank goodness!

Still, there are those who find it amusing to take pot-shots at others or, worse, to become a troll and continually snipe away at someone with an unjustifiable vengeance.

Then there is the whole disinformation and "deepfake" phenomenon that is coming evermore to the fore in our world. These two unfair corruptors of truth have directly given us the "post-truth era" and are wreaking havoc on our politics and our democratic institutions. This is lamentable, for these falsehoods are creating polarization within the societies of the Free World in ways that serve only the interests of a particular authoritarian person, organization or industry, and not the citizenry in general. An example of this is the climate change debate which has the world reeling over what is true or not true about the phenomenon. A second example is the political polarization in relation to the extreme left and extreme right viewpoints and their unwillingness to compromise on issues of the day.

The above two examples alone are creating an unprecedented amount of turmoil and turbulence in the social and cultural orders of our world nowadays, which means that it is up to those of us who have a sense of fairness, compassion and civility to act as big brothers and big sisters to each other to the best of our ability. Our attitude should ideally be, "I'll have your back if you have mine" if we are to raise up a New World Order that is a credit, rather than a detriment, to the human species.

As an optimist, I keep hoping for the best.

## 40

# Stark Truth & the Dark Web

WHAT WE SECRETLY BELIEVE, or profess to believe, whether to ourselves alone or to others in private, or again to others in a public setting, says so much about who we really are. This is especially true when it comes to conspiracy theories, which are currently proliferating as never before thanks to social media.

There is no mystery about this latter point, of course. Social media, as we all know by now, is a total free-for-all. Anyone can say anything he or she wishes and with as much passion, fervency or vitriol as desired, although there is now a movement afoot in government circles to rein in, not just hate speech, but posts intended to incite violence with legislation that still allows for freedom of speech up to a point.

The question thus arises: which of us is the more gullible? The one who goes searching for "truth" on platforms that thrive on conspiracy or the one who simply takes what the "authorities" publicly pronounce as being the "true" story?

It is best, no doubt, to listen to both sides, keep an open mind and patiently wait for more details to emerge, which is not always easy considering how fast information moves on the World Wide Web

Thanks to the Internet, we can also pursue our darkest interests and unleash the beast within us if we want. If it is horror that makes our blood boil, if it is violence that triggers a rush to the head like a blast of heroin to the veins, then there are ways to go for that, as well, if gravitating to the land of dark horrors happens to excite.

The wise Lord Macauley once said that "The measure of a man's real character is what he would do if he thought he would never be found out."

Sobering words.

The general anonymity of the Internet has offered us lessons on that front in spades. What it has unleashed is certainly a horde of bullies and countless men and women of all ages who are perfectly willing to be rude, crude, cruel, vindictive and spectacularly juvenile in what they will write or post there.

Fortunately, these horribly mannered, thoughtless brutes constitute but a small percentage of all internet users, but they have managed to hurt millions of people's feelings over the years and have even driven many a delicate, vulnerable soul to take his or her own life.

Which is unforgivable.

In the post-truth era, however, such a level of interaction among us is simply the tip of the iceberg.

I read an article once about the so-called "Deep Web". It was a jolt to the system to say the least.

The most horrendous thing mentioned was that some people are actually willing to pay in bitcoin or some form of crypto to watch an anonymous heartless savage torture a fellow human being to death.

As unspeakably heart-wrenching as that is to contemplate, some few will be enticed by such a notion and actually take the steps required to open up that revolting peephole. In brief, to see such a show, one must first work his or her way deep down into that shadowy world of nightmares.

To do that one has to obtain a TOR browser the article indicated.

At first, I thought that "TOR" must be short for "Torture", but soon learned that it is an acronym for what is called "The Onion Router". What this router does is give a person "Tor anonymity". It does this by dropping the stealthy, determined internet "surfer" down through a series of layers via encrypted access points that progressively strip away any and every possible means of being identified by any member of the cyber-police or any intelligence agency operative.

What Tor anonymity does is allow one to search through all kinds of websites that are off the official map, so to speak, and down in the gutter of modern culture.

Mainly, the desire for access stems from a yearning to buy drugs. Crystal meth, opioids, crack cocaine, heroin, you name it. It's all there. It's a true drugs bazaar apparently and the supply and variety of substances is vast, running the gamut from naturally occurring psychoactive enticements such as marijuana, magic mushrooms, peyote and mescaline to hard narcotics and super potent pharmaceuticals. The choices appear to be pretty much infinite.

Then there is the Dark Web where one can purchase guns, counterfeit currency, stolen credit card details, forged documents, cyber-weaponry (that cursed malware crap) and child pornography among them.

An interesting point that was made was to distinguish between what is known as the "Deep Web" versus the "Dark Web". For clarity's sake I went into Wikipedia and found the following definition: "The dark web is the World Wide Web content that exists on darknets, overlay networks that use the internet, but require specific software, configurations or authorization to access. The dark web forms a small part of the deep web, the part of the Web not indexed by web search engines, although sometimes the term deep web is mistakenly used to refer specifically to the dark web."

So, the dark web is just an adjunct or basement room in the deep web and the deep web is simply any website that is not indexed by web search engines. The deep web, by the way, was originally created by one of the US Intelligence services for the purpose of sending encrypted communications.

Today, its use includes all of those aspects mentioned above, plus gambling, forbidden books, directories and blogs, multiple forms of violent porn, hacking services, whistleblower links, fraud services and crypto sites, not to mention every form of marketable item one can imagine, including hitmen for hire.

Actually, the Wikipedia article stated that the "hitmen for hire" thing proved to be a hoax and I am hoping that the same can be said in relation to the aforementioned reference to violent voyeurs paying to watch forms of torture, with or without a sexual component, as well as other forms of violent extremism, which I prefer not to imagine at all.

A word of warning though… The author of the article I read specifically noted that some of the people he personally knew who had subscribed to Tor anonymity and had gone down into the heart of that rotten Onion ended up, not just shocked by what they saw there, but fundamentally changed in some very significant way. He said that he couldn't say exactly how, but those persons were never the same again afterwards.

My guess is that they were gutted. That's my word, not his, but if you have any form of a conscience, I'm guessing that there are things to be seen there that would surely sear the soul of any person of integrity to the core. Seeing what should never be seen or done is doubtless soul destroying, in fact.

If you do, though, you would do well to remember Lord Macauley's insightful words. What you look up, what you access, what you pay for, what you subscribe to, all add up to the measure of who you "really" are as a human being, as well as who you are as a spiritual being.

For example, if you find tales of true crime a thrill, that says something about you. If you gravitate toward slasher movies, violent video games or videos depicting beheadings or people being stoned to death that definitely says something very disturbing about you. If you seek out details of the most brutal persuasion that is telling.

If, on the other hand, hearing such details appalls you, gives you sleepless nights and the kind of inner turmoil and anguish it takes days or weeks to get past that is a sign of spiritual sensitivity of the highest order.

Once, for example, while reading a magazine article, I quite unwittingly came across details of some of the "experiments" the demented, malicious, so-called "Angel of Death" Dr Josef Mengele performed during World War II on behalf of the Nazis and it left me in a deep funk for days. (That appellation, by the way, was totally ironic. If anything, the man should have been called the "Devil of Death".) In any case, I could only wonder how any human being could listen to another scream in pain for hours on end, pain you yourself inflicted, and not feel guilt, remorse or anguish yourself, but apparently the thoroughly wicked Mengele was fine with it. A huge bulk of his sick, psychopathic experiments, by the way, involved children, no less, and without anesthesia. No different than the lunatic Hitler himself (the all-time most evil, depraved, heartless soul ever to set foot upon the earth), one can only wonder how this unspeakably vile, monstrous, subhuman brute could possibly have lived with himself. I was gutted by the story and could barely sleep for a night or two.

Whether we ultimately answer to any version of "God" or "advanced spiritual beings" or simply to our own "higher self" at last, or just wish to die without regret on our deathbed, answer we must and answer we will for our actions in this life. We will also gravitate toward those souls in the Hereafter with whom we most resonate at the deepest core of our being, just as we did in life. In short, the loving and kind soul will gravitate to a tranquil, fulfilling paradise, while those who enjoy inflicting pain and suffering on others will find themselves winning a very real ticket to the hell realm of their dreams for a long, torturous stint.

Beware, therefore… Tor anonymity will not hide nor shield anyone who exits this earth with a mind full of the darkest dreams and desires imaginable should there prove to be an afterlife and not the oblivion which so many believe means that nothing ultimately matters.

The fact is whatever we do is *not* fine. Actions do have consequences and if you believe otherwise, I say: "Want to bet?"

# 41

# Cybergeddon It

## *Fear, the Deepfake Firebomb & That Dread Orwellian Mirror of Conspiracy*

THE ASSASSINATION OF PRESIDENT John F Kennedy was an event that affected millions of people in America and all around the globe. It certainly gave me my first real brush with death and was a murder that haunted me for many years afterwards. Shot through the head in broad daylight on a street in Dallas, Texas, there was simply no way JFK could have survived that horrid, high-powered assault on his life. I will never forget seeing his black Lincoln Continental convertible flying through the streets of Dallas at breakneck speed and hearing the words of the news anchors on television with their voices cracking, full of shock. They were soon to make the formal, tragic announcement of the president's demise.

That assassination proved to be a killing that unleashed more conspiracy theories about who did it and why than any other such intrigue in history. To this day, we are still unsure. Was it the Mob? Communists? White supremacists who were unhappy about the civil rights issues that Kennedy seemed to be championing? Or was it a stealthy member of the "Deep State" who feared that the president was about to reveal who was really running things in Washington, blow the cover of the true Powers That Be and steal away all of their clandestine control?

These are questions that are still being asked.

I lived in Dallas for a time and happened to meet a woman there at a business function one time who eventually revealed to me that she had once been a dancer – or to put it more bluntly, a stripper – at one of Jack Ruby's clubs back in the day. Jack Ruby was the man who daringly shot and killed Lee Harvey Oswald live on television a few days after the murder of the president. He subsequently claimed upon his arrest that he was simply an outraged citizen who was livid about what Oswald had done.

Most of us believed his story for the simple reason that we were equally outraged by the killing, and it seemed only right that the assassin should lose his life, as well.

The authorities saw things differently, of course, and were doubtless furious that they suddenly had no suspect to interrogate so that they could ascertain if the gunman had acted alone or as part of a conspiracy. As for me, everything about the assassination and its aftermath boggled my mind, for I was a mere eleven years of age at the time, and I was fairly shaken by seeing a man murdered live on TV. Over three decades later when I moved to Dallas, I was still baffled and curious about it all and I told the lady that. I explained about why I had come to Dallas and mentioned how I had always wanted to walk the street where Kennedy had been shot. This is what led the lady, after some initial hesitation, to tell me her story. She revealed that she had been an "entertainer" at Ruby's club and that she had, since those dark days, become a "born-again" Christian and now thoroughly repented her licentious past. She said that this was why she didn't mind talking about her past and I could see that by confessing these things, she sincerely believed that she was in some way cleansing her soul and helping herself to move on with her life. As a result, I did not hesitate to ask questions and to probe.

What I subsequently heard was quite stunning. The lady told me that her husband, who had also worked for Ruby, had fled Dallas on the day of the assassination. She said that after that day of infamy, November 22, 1963, she never again saw her husband. This was a shocker. In a quiet, sad voice, she told me that in all the intervening years she had never once even heard from him and had no idea if he was alive or dead.

She then claimed that she had been grilled by FBI agents in the aftermath of the shooting, but she had never shown her interrogators a particular notebook with some damning evidence relating to her husband in it, since she had believed at the time that it would compromise him. She said that he had never spoken a word to her about any plot to kill Kennedy. Yet, her husband's notebook had a simple notation in it that was incriminatory. It read: "Oswald. $10,000.00."

My mouth fell open. "And you didn't show this to the FBI?"

"No," she admitted. "I figured that my husband would come back to me one day and I wanted to be able to say to him that I hadn't betrayed him."

I was silent for a time and stood shaking my head. "But that means that he was in cahoots with Ruby…" I finally stammered in a hushed voice.

The lady simply raised an ambiguous eyebrow. "Maybe so," she agreed. "But all of that is long ago now. It's history. And once I realized that my husband wasn't coming back, I started using an alias and I've been using one ever since."

I was wide-eyed at the implication. I suddenly had no idea with whom I was actually speaking. Then I took a daring leap. "I'd love to see the notebook sometime," I said. "If you wouldn't mind. This is blowing me away."

The lady mulled over my request a moment, then said that she knew of another business function that was coming up in the near future and asked me if I was planning to attend. When I said that I certainly would if she was implying what I thought she was implying, she nodded in a furtive manner, her dark eyes flashing and dancing about with no small measure of mischief.

She kept her word. I saw the notebook with its little scribbled notation with my own two eyes.

However, I never again saw the woman after that.

What I subsequently made of the whole affair after meeting

her was that indeed there must have been a conspiracy to kill Kennedy, as so many have speculated over the years, and apparently it did have to do with the Mob, for Ruby was clearly a gangster through and through. Nevertheless, the full story of the Kennedy assassination will forever elude me, just as it will elude virtually everyone, even those who are insiders in the government and the FBI, for there are so many angles to the tangled web of lies surrounding it and so many possible links to the "truth" behind the murder that no one can be one hundred percent certain of anything about it ever, I suspect.

Life can be that way. It can be totally crazy as well. Another woman I met once while living in Dallas showed up at the home of a person that I had likewise only met once. The man was having a small party and I had gone along to it as the new kid in town, so to speak, just to check it out and get to know people in general. At some point during the course of the evening, however, I saw the woman go out into the backyard of the house in order to smoke a cigarette. She later came racing back in, full throttle, alarmingly agitated. When someone asked what was wrong, the lady claimed that she had just seen the ghost of Kennedy in the man's backyard.

I later learned that this same woman could not go anywhere near downtown Dallas because she would get hysterical if she ventured too close to the street where Kennedy had been slain.

Murder, death, conspiracy… They can drive people insane.

Or to be gracious about it, maybe just a bit unhinged…

I know that when I first heard about the Illuminati through the writings of Robert Anton Wilson my intrigue was piqued in a huge way. In fact, I was soon spellbound by the notion and began reading everything I could find on the notoriously enigmatic group which had operated for centuries, according to reports, ever and only behind the scenes. They were said to wield colossal power and could make governments do their bidding. The Illuminati were said to control everything from war and peace to economic prosperity or poverty for the masses. With the rise of banking and the hording of financial supply chains, they were said to give loans at their whim and will or, conversely, could bankrupt entire nations with an ironclad demand for immediate repayment of whatever monies they had been loaned.

Millions seem similarly spellbound these days by the idea of secret societies and clandestine operatives who are still pulling the wool over the eyes of the general public about what is really going on in this world. Indeed, if current news cycles have been dominated by any one ideological perspective, it is by those who most believe conspiracy theories of this nature: namely, right-wing extremists. From the violence perpetrated by fundamentalist religious zealots to that of the numerous vicious uprisings of armed political authoritarian sympathizers, guns have blazed and bombs have blown. As a result, our screens have grown inundated by rampages and outrages in ever greater numbers.

What we have been witnessing is religious and political theater at its most dramatic, most captivating and its menacingly best.

One must immediately qualify that last word, however, for the word "best" is misleading. Such theater may be mesmerizing in a cinematic manner, and it surely is enthralling, but at root it is activity that is deeply, spiritually unconscionable and too often downright deadly in nature. It shows humanity at its worst, not its finest.

To be fair here, one must hasten to add that in the previous century, especially in the Sixties and the Seventies, the dominance of violent, left-wing extremism was likewise rife and equally disturbing. Those protests, however, at least had a modicum of noble intentions about them, for they were against an unjust war in which innocent people on both sides were dying by the thousands. At the time, it even came to light that

US government and military leaders were clearly lying to the general public about many aspects of the war as the "Pentagon Papers" proved and so I, too, took part in protest marches at the university I was attending.

I especially remember my own outrage after a certain event that had all of America in shock. It was the killing of four students at Kent State University by National Guardsmen during the course of a protest march in my home state of Ohio. I happened to be working part-time in a store which sold electronic appliances when the story broke, and I vividly recall how riveted I was as I stood before a virtual bank of blazing television sets when the story first aired. Beside me was a potential customer, a middle-aged man who was considering the purchase of one of those sets. The two of us froze as the details emerged and I remember well how we stared in disbelief at the scenes we were seeing on those screens. I could only wonder if I was hearing things right. Guardsmen had brutally gunned down four university students for simply protesting against the war? The man beside me, however (to my eternal horror), actually screamed out in the aftermath of the report, words that I will never forget. "I wish to hell they had killed the whole goddamn lot of them!" he roared.

I couldn't believe my ears and just stood there in stunned silence at hearing those words. The man was like a snarling beast, his face pinched tight with anger and hatred. This was how divided America was at the time and, in many ways, sadly, it seems equally divided now. It appears that there are those who genuinely wish to subjugate anyone who does not subscribe to their worldview and who apparently desire authoritarian fascism over democracy.

In any case, whether it is right or left-wing extremism, both are unwelcome intrusions on our social civility. Violence is, quite simply, never justified and "truth" either way remains as elusive as ever.

The problem is the same for all of us. *There is, quite simply, no means by which to determine what is absolutely true or false.* Even the "laws" of physics are only "true" until such a time that the latest scientific evidence happens to alter the validity of those laws.

As Robert Anton Wilson once wrote, "Some minds cling to certitude, not because it can be clearly justified, but evidently because such minds have an emotional need for certitude."

An *emotional need*... Here is the crux of everything in this era in which we find ourselves precisely as in the past. We are living in a realm of relativity in which our emotions reign over so many of us. Many a great mind has understood this over the centuries, most especially the more persuasive of political and religious leaders. These leaders have used it to their advantage time and again. In brief, there are facts and then there is the interpretation of those facts. There is the unvarnished truth and there is truth distorted by emotion.

What we see in today's world is that every ragtag, tinhorn group of disaffected individuals has access to internet platforms which can easily spread the ideological views of extremists like runaway wildfire. Such groups also have access to the kinds of technology and weaponry that special effects movie teams in the past would have envied beyond all measure and so they are able to get their message across with an impact far beyond what these malicious purveyors deserve.

Personally, I had entertained the great hope that the New Millennium would surprise us by taking a massive quantum leap beyond the crazy antics of the previous millennium and that humanity's half-baked stabs at post-modernism would finally come to fruition properly.

No such luck. As Horace of Rome once put it: "Power without wisdom collapses under its own weight."

Those words are ringing truer than ever now. In fact, considering all that is going on today, it can seem as if humanity has its collective head inside of a giant bell, one upon which Thor, the ancient god of thunder, has just brought his colossal hammer smashing down against with a merciless vengeance.

After all, not only are we presently in a "post-truth era" where telling lies outright in order to charge up a political base and hold onto positions of power at any cost is apparently the new norm. Now there is the "digital soldier" and the "Deepfake" firebomb with which we must contend.

What is a Deepfake? It is a video which has been manipulated in such a way that a person's mouth can seem to be uttering whatever words a master cyber-provocateur desires.

One does not need to be a cynic to know that such a person will not use the medium to proffer platitudes of wisdom. On the contrary, the false message which is sure to be put into the mouths of any number of hapless victims will be words meant to destroy that particular person's reputation or foment a violent backlash against the position which he or she represents. Indeed, I have heard news hosts say that such fakes are so convincing nowadays that even forensic experts may not be able to tell what is real or unreal anymore.

This is an extremely disturbing new reality, and it bodes very ill for all of us, especially given the touchy partisan, polarized state of world politics these days. There is just no glossing over this unhappy state of affairs.

It may sound like a cliché to ask it, but the question for each of us now is this: Are we going to be part of the problem or are we going to be part of the solution? Will we help to heal the rift between people or hold hard and fast to our divisive position of choice come what may? In other words, will we choose to help the cyber-provocateur's message of deceit go viral and assist in sending it hurtling through the cybersphere, knowing that it will cause genuine harm? Or, if we have doubt as to the validity of the message, will we instead choose restraint?

As always, the choice is ours to make.

One thing is certain: We will never arrive in a Brave New World worthy of the phrase unless we unite.

Only is that going to happen? For centuries and millenniums now, humanity has battled back and forth over issues of a moral and ethical nature. We have skirmished over political, religious and scientific matters. We have fought wars of such destruction that millions have been left dead in their wake and countless cities and villages reduced to rubble and ruin.

Is this really the best we can do?

I think not. I contend that there are enough people of conscience in the world to push back against the primitive foolishness of the few and believe this is precisely what we *must* do. We must push back at every chance against Deepfakes, for like so many other Orwellian terrors, they are here to stay.

It can be said, of course, that the arrival of Deepfake technology on the global scene was inevitable, given the state of our technological proficiency nowadays and that at least some of the time it will be used in harmless and amusing ways. This is no doubt true, but will that be the primary thrust?

One would do well to seriously doubt it.

So let's think smart. Let's pursue a better world by getting to grips with Deepfakes early on. They will be used as tools of provocation and deception, and if we are not careful, they will have us all spiraling down into what has been called "Cybergeddon" or, worse, into a very real, physical "Armageddon" at which point – tragically – all will be lost for humanity.

We must remember: the mirror of conspiracy reflects every face which stares into it and the eyes in those faces tend mostly to be full of suspicion and fear. Fear is soul destroying. So don't go there. Stay well away. Keep with a positive attitude and have faith in the inherent goodness of people. This is the best way to remain faithful to *our own* inherent goodness.

# 42

# Lives That Matter Equally

## *Apocalyptic Politics, the Rising Tide of Gun Violence & Sovereignty of the Soul*

IN HIS CLASSIC WORK *ECSTATIC RELIGION*, author I.M. Lewis wrote that, "Out of the agony of affliction and the dark night of the soul comes literally the ecstasy of spiritual victory."

Humanity is collectively in such a dark night of the soul at this very moment. There is both conflict and affliction; there is pain and suffering.

This is, of course, a moral concern and, therefore, a spiritual issue of great consequence. How we react to the many issues now confronting us, whether it is apocalyptic politics, rampant nationalism, malicious fundamentalist ideologies, racism, the blatant disregard for truth, climate change, vaccine hesitancy, modern day slavery, human trafficking, the obsession that so many seem to have with lethal forms of weaponry or any of a thousand other subjects of concern, we are all being affected by the turmoil that is to be seen in every quarter of the world.

How we react to these tumultuous worldly issues tells us exactly who we are as people. Our reactions tell us how spiritually evolved we are in the starkest terms imaginable.

In effect, the degree of empathy we show others determines our humanity. If we couldn't care less that some people are politically enslaved or that they are subject to dire forms of disease and malnutrition, then that speaks volumes about who we are as spiritual beings. If we cheer only for those who think like us and collude with us, then we prove ourselves to be narrow minded and deeply prejudiced. If we would like to "blow away" those who are different from us with the blast of an assault rifle, then we are in the grip of a very dark soul indeed.

Not all is lost for such people, however, for we must remember that what the heart illumines, the darkness has nurtured. Somewhere deep inside of each of us is a spark of divinity that will eventually flare up with such brightness that one's delusional thinking will be seen for what it is.

In the meantime, however, delusion is where the action is. It is what excites us and incites us to live fast and grasp for whatever we can get our hands on.

It all begins with the pursuit of pleasure.

The pursuit of pleasure is pretty much what human existence for most people is all about. People like nice homes, classy cars, fine food and drink. They like interesting travels, beautiful landscapes and, especially (seemingly), endless diversionary, mindless entertainment of one kind or another.

At a deeper level, however, life is really more about discovering *why* we exist and attempting to find a way to deal with, or get around, that great stalker, the Grim Reaper.

Here is a weird notion to consider, however: Maybe death becomes us.

On the surface of life, it certainly appears that way. Many of the most popular books, films and video games that so entrance us in this day and age have a certain common denominator; namely, that they revolve around violence and death. Check out all of the murder mysteries on the bookstore racks, all of the many thrillers there, not to mention the killer/slasher movies at the cinema or available online. Check out all of the mad murderous rampages that go on with the countless interactive video games that people – including *very young* people – can buy and play.

It boggles the mind.

That's not all, of course. One can also listen to "death metal" music and to violent rapper tunes that give us "blood on the tracks" in a way that even Dylan never imagined. Then there is the "skull and cross bones" motifs to be seen on T-shirts, jackets and designer jewelry, and as tattoos: permanent etchings of the image on the skin.

Why does the skull and cross bones image so entrance us? Why do so many of us find it so compelling?

Could it be that death really does become us?

We live in a time when the world can seem totally topsy-turvy. "Bad" can be good. "Wicked" can be cool. "Killer" can be *beyond* cool.

More often than not these days, our heroes are drawn from the ranks of the antiheroes. They include not only the badass rock 'n' rollers and rap artists, but also the sports stars who get up to all kinds of mischief off the field of play, not to mention over-the-top figures such as cage fighters and professional wrestlers, who seemingly wouldn't wince at delivering up a death blow in the course of their careers. Add to this list the volunteer warrior-soldiers who populate the intelligence agencies, the military and the paramilitary forces of the planet and the number of "badasses" among us goes shockingly astronomical.

Then there are the vigilante crusaders who murder in the name of religion and the radical extremists who wage "holy war", not only on those not of their faith, but sometimes on those who are not of their particular sect, as well.

Back in the ancient times, people were sacrificed in an effort to appease the gods. The Romans were known to stage public spectacles that included gladiators fighting each other to the death or hapless victims getting mauled to death by vicious beasts. Why the Romans did this seems to have been for purposes of both entertainment and for giving its citizenry an extremely clear picture of what might happen to them if they chose to defy the reigning Caesar and his henchmen.

Multiple cultures throughout history have publicly stoned people to death or staged public beheadings for alleged transgressions and some still do. Why? To keep the masses in line.

Death becomes us.

Death fascinates and mesmerizes us. It captivates us so thoroughly that millions upon millions of people voluntarily participate in the wars and battles which spring up from one end of the globe to the other. Along the way, many of those warriors and soldiers, willingly and mercilessly, torture the perceived enemy, happily administering the most excruciatingly horrendous and painful executions that they can dream up.

Likewise, tens of thousands of highly intelligent mechanical engineers will, and do, spend their days on the job dreaming up ever more lethal weaponry, including forms of super deadly hypersonic technology, and proudly selling it on to any ragtag band of guerrilla fighters with barely enough brains to learn how to use that weaponry.

Why? Because death becomes us.

Is this psycho? Insane? Has the Devil gotten into us?

No, the Devil has not gotten into us. We have only ourselves to blame for this state of affairs, not Satan and his imaginary circus. For so many, unfortunately, the thinking is that so long as death happens to others and not to oneself, then it is of little consequence.

The mass shooter takes this form of heartless, distorted thinking to its ultimate end: he wants to punish others for his own suffering and so sets out to kill as many people as possible. That he will no doubt die in the process seems not to matter. He has become Death Incarnate. He has become the Grim Reaper himself; a sad, tragic, deluded figure who fully intends to cut everyone down to size for daring to see him as a nobody. It is not anyone else's fault, though. The mass murderer is the one who has let his inner demons fly away with him and he proves it by exploding before our very eyes.

Devil, devil, dark and dreadful…

While we have every reason to fear such a person, the fact is such an individual can never possess us beyond the way we think and feel about them, for each of us is a sovereign soul with an impregnable psychic shield to protect us from all others, whether those others are from this world or any other; by which I mean that, yes, there are desperate entities which populate a myriad of dimensions beyond this world who would take others over and possess them if they could. Fortunately, they cannot.

Nevertheless, one must be on one's guard and stay vigilant. After all, the deluded will do deluded things. So it goes.

The only way out of such a terrible situation is to offer enlightened, loving kindness where we can, because pleading for every individual to think twice and do the enlightened thing won't solve the problem, even though there is nothing tricky about doing the enlightened thing. It simply refers to doing the respectful thing and to offering up a genuine act of compassion when we can.

Death can only become us if we choose to let it become us. It can only get into our minds if we are enthralled with some version of the dark arts, if we are mesmerized by macho warriors who love violence and rage against those who dare to challenge them. It can only dominate our souls if we are besotted with those corporate hotshots who score the big deal, no matter who is financially destroyed in the process, and with the cunning politicians who set out to win every debate regardless of how crude, rude or denigrating the effort is to others.

Death becomes us maybe because we humans are foolishly full of fantasies that have no basis in reality. Witness how many couples in the flush of a romantic liaison swear eternal love to one another, only to call off their relationship at the first hint of emotional friction. Witness how many singers of love songs warble on and on about how they would climb any mountain or cross any ocean for their beloved. The reality is that many of the most passionate of lovers quite often end up calling each other every name in the book and threatening to knock each other's lights out! It's madness. (If you want to see a real flying saucer get yourself caught up in the middle of a love spat in some couple's kitchen! You'll see that and a few glasses shattering off the walls, as well.)

The long and the short of the story is that we humans are full of ideals we cannot realistically live up to and, on top of that, we crave excitement. We get bored with the ho-hum, mundane, workaday routine and with being around the same people all the time. (The saying that familiarity breeds contempt is often all too true.) As a result, we seem to need the screeching of cars and the blasting of bullets to take our minds elsewhere. We need the scent of blood and the smell of the fallen corpse just to get the whiff of a thrill and a bit of a shock. We need the thunder of the warplanes and the bombs bursting in the air, the gangland shakedown and the daring swagger of the unscrupulous drug lord.

Pleasure comes in many forms. The darker the thrill, the deeper the pleasure maybe?

Let us remember this, however: one person's nectar is another person's poison, and the day always comes when one must pay the piper.

When all is said and done, therefore, to whom will we humans ultimately answer if not to ourselves? In the meantime, let us hope that I.M. Lewis is right that "Out of the agony of affliction and the dark night of the soul comes literally the ecstasy of spiritual victory." It is definitely what we all need.

## 43

# The Pop God Conspiracy

LONG BEFORE RAPPERS, Rock stars, chart topping singers and social media personalities were turned into pop gods, there was a war of words for centuries and millenniums over the reality of the ancient gods as worshipped in places like Sumer, Babylon, Mesopotamia, Egypt, Greece, Rome, India and China, and what those gods actually looked like.

This last fact was especially true regarding the appearance of Yahweh, the Almighty God of the Hebrews. While the mystics of the faith knew better, Yahweh was depicted for the "masses" as a patriarchal, father figure and that image carried over into the Christian era with "God the Father", a Being who reputedly has the appearance of an old man with a long white beard, wears the robe of a monarch and sits on a throne.

So deeply engrained is this latter image that even the more enlightened Jewish and Christian peoples have trouble getting past it, which is why patriarchal behaviors persist and why women are still having to fight so hard for equal treatment on every front around the world.

The Muslims, to their credit, never attempted to "flesh out" the appearance of their Supreme Deity. Allah was said to be beyond any image his followers could conjure or even fathom. In fact, it has always been expressly forbidden in the Islamic faith to create *any* likeness of Allah. Nevertheless, history has clearly shown Allah to be masculine in behavior and the suppression of women in Islamic countries continues unabated. In truth, such suppression is a violation of basic human rights.

The point is that people all over the globe have given a name and attributes to their Supreme Deity over the centuries and have often fought to the death to proclaim their "God" as the one and only Creator of the Universe, even though those vanquished were supposedly created by the same God. Bizarrely, rather than seeing this One Universal Supreme Being as a transcendental entity whom others on the Earth would naturally describe in their own native tongues, thus generating an obvious disparity of one description from another, many peoples, instead, have chosen to go to war over these differences.

We must ask, therefore, has that discrepancy merely been an ulterior motive or a pretext for the desire to pillage and steal whatever one could forcibly take from one's neighboring peoples?

The idea that one's maker is "the one and only true" Supreme Entity is a concept that has always been narrow-minded in the extreme. It is prejudicial and dangerous, as history has shown, time and again.

To label non-believers as "heretics", "infidels" or other such names – basically, as *enemies* – is Step One toward the persecution of those persons. Step Two is to actively conspire against them by whipping up mob frenzy. It is to incite crusades, jihads, pogroms and so forth in order to eradicate that "enemy".

This cannot possibly have anything to do with any God of Love.

Over the centuries and millenniums almost every culture on the face of the Earth has come up with a name for their Supreme Being. Besides Yahweh and Allah, as mentioned above, there was Anu of the Sumerians, Osiris of the Egyptians, Baal of the Canaanites, Marduk of the Babylonians, Brahman of the Hindus, Mithra of the Persians, Ahura Mazda of the Zoroastrians, Zeus of the Greeks, Jupiter of the Romans and so on.

All conspiracy is fear based. Why, though, should one fear what another believes if that belief poses no real threat? The answer is that it is fear which compels us to force people to convert to our religion. It is fear that sends armies to conquer or eradicate people who look and think differently from us. Such fear is rooted in bigotry and xenophobia.

Surely in this day and age, we are global enough in our perceptions to understand that every culture has its own way of looking at life and explaining it. If we can accept that there are other races, lifestyles and languages besides our own, it is no distance at all to accepting that a Supreme Being will have a name and certain basic descriptive attributes that are culturally derived.

In truth, it is not difficult to comprehend that "might" does not make right, nor that the greater the number of adherents to a particular religion does not make it "truer" than any other. In fact, how can the "popularity" of a particular Supreme Being be *proof* of anything? Surely, the quasi-religious Nazi movement alone back in World War II tells us everything we need to know about the topic of numbers and belief.

At the moment, Christianity has roughly 2.2 billion adherents, Islam 1.6 billion, Hinduism 1 billion, Buddhism half a billion, the Jewish faith 15 million and so on... Yes, there is safety in numbers and comfort in knowing that so many others profess to believe as we believe, but any Supreme Being who is, by definition, universal, infinite, transcendental and, therefore, beyond the limited mental powers of we mortals, is surely not a "Being" who would harbor favoritism. All people and creatures would be precious in such a God's heart, especially if that God is indeed a God of unconditional love.

So let us ask ourselves what we believe in our own hearts to be true.

If the answer is what I suspect it is, we might well want to leave off with the pop god conspiracies and emulate the One Supreme Being, the Source of All That Exists, and understand that we are a single species with a singular origin. We are all brothers and sisters on this planet, and we always will be.

Even if there is no God and life on Planet Earth arose owing totally to naturally occurring forces, this point still holds true.

Regardless of our race or religious (or atheistic) predilections, the Earth is our mutual home. We should, therefore, be working together, not conspiring against each other, to protect our home and the precious life within it.

Scientific materialism, which contends that there is no creator God, has not shown itself to be innocent of such conspiring either. Nevertheless, the physicist Steven Weinberg once said, "With or without religion good people can behave well and bad people can do evil; but for good people to do evil – that takes religion."

When we look around us and see the zealotry and violence that does, indeed, often go with religion, it is not too difficult to nod one's head in agreement to such a statement. The carnage is utterly obvious and shockingly atrocious. Then again, if one wishes to be objective about the rather difficult situation with which we humans are currently wrestling, we see that many of the great minds of science have put their knowledge and skill to work for a sinister end also: the designing and manufacturing of armaments.

The 20th century, in particular, raised the deadly craft of weaponry production to an industrial level never before seen in the annals of history.

As World War II ground on, for example, it was the Manhattan Project that drew in the most advanced minds in the world to work feverishly toward a single end: to build the most lethal and destructive bomb ever built. Quite alarmingly, when that bomb was first detonated, J Robert Oppenheimer and his colleagues were far from certain that if they did succeed in splitting the atom that it would not have a knock-on effect and set off a chain reaction with all of the other atoms that make up our world and split them, as well.

In other words, these highly esteemed scientists chose to run the risk that blowing that first atomic bomb might actually end up destroying every man, woman and child on the planet, not to mention all of the other species of life here, whether insect, reptile, fish, fowl or mammal.

The deed was done, of course, and we all survived it, save for the unfortunate inhabitants of Hiroshima and Nagasaki.

The outright killing of people with such a bomb was only part of the problem, however. In their haste to succeed, these brilliant thinkers also chose to test the efficacy of atomic weapons over and again with only minimal regard for where, upon its release, the deadly radiation went. These men acted in full knowledge of the fact that radiation would rise into the airstreams which surround our planet and that there would also be an enormous amount of deadly waste generated in the refining of the uranium and plutonium needed to produce the bombs. Where and how does one safely dispose of such lethal waste?

Even after the war ended, testing continued. In all, there were 543 atmospheric tests conducted around the world before global leaders grew wise enough to finally sign up to a Test Ban Treaty in 1963 that forbade the spewing of radiation into the air we all breathe. That radiation, of course, was *known* to take thousands upon thousands of years to dissipate from its unspeakably lethal state.

What happened after that? The treaty sent our brilliant intelligentsia underground where another 1,876 atomic, hydrogen and neutron bombs were blown to devastating effect up through 1998, according to a French government official, Jean-Jacques Velasco, and there have been many more tests since that time. Those bombs were blown – again with full knowledge that these detonations have a highly destabilizing effect on the planet, but scientists willingly continue to chance those consequences. Who can stop them is the question, for such scientists have become pop gods in their own right who answer to no one, save their peers.

After seeing such numbers, do we dare crow about how wise

our scientists are? Do we reframe Weinberg's statement to say, "With or without religion good people can behave well and bad people can do evil; but for good people to do monumental, catastrophic damage to the planet – that takes science." (I leave it to the reader to draw his or her own conclusions about whether or not the building and testing of atomic bombs is "evil".)

Where, I ask, was the wisdom back in those days and where is the wisdom now?

The problem of climate change is presently haunting us even worse than the crimes of the radical fundamentalist religious right. Clearly, climate change is more the result of science than spiritual zealots rising up in arms and storming the citadels of their religious rivals. Unfortunately, it is not just carbon emissions that fill our upper atmosphere. There are windblown layers of radiation there, the deadly particles dancing about like atomic demons.

So, no, it is not just religion that incites good people to do destructive things, though destructive things have been, and are indeed done, by some very deeply misguided souls who believe themselves to be advocates of the "real" or "only" God: their own.

As it stands, there is blood on the hands of many on both sides of the great divide between religion and science, but what needs to happen now is for all of us to come together for the one common cause that concerns us: the survival of our species and Planet Earth itself.

If we do work together, while there is yet time, we can transform the terrible, catastrophic past into the most perfect and fantastic future imaginable. It is, quite simply, up to us.

# 44

# The 44,000-Year-Old Roots of Religion

THAT SPIRITUALITY IS A NATURAL, instinctive impulse of humanity is by now one of history's clearest truisms. This was made strikingly obvious recently when archaeologists discovered the earliest-ever cave art paintings on a small Indonesian island. These graphics date back almost 44,000 years. In the paintings, there are human beings shown hunting large mammals.

As well – and this is the really revealing part – there are also figures which are part-human and part-animal, the same as in many of the cave art paintings discovered all around Europe in the past decades. These part-human, part-animal figures are known as "therianthropes". According to the article in the newspaper, archaeologists believe these figures represent humanity's proclivity for "imagining the existence of supernatural beings". Note the word "imagining" there. Such a description is based on a penchant by scientific materialists to render all so-called "supernatural" entities as unreal.

Indeed, if "supernatural beings" are *only* imaginary, then we must conclude that untold numbers of people throughout history have been given to illusory musings on a profoundly persistent basis and that *this* is part of our nature.

If, however, as scientific materialists maintain, virtually every action of a human being is down to an evolutionary impetus to survive, then that means that there must be some measure of reality to these instinctually persistent scenarios where otherworldly entities, including therianthropes, are experienced.

Be that as it may if therianthropes are depicted alongside human beings engaged in hunting activity, that ties them into the most fundamental of all human needs: the necessity of acquiring food for survival.

Some scientific materialists will say these therianthropes only happen to be part of ancient cave art because particular personages ingested psychotropic substances back in the day. In other words, the encounters with therianthropes were strictly a hallucinatory phenomenon and, therefore, again, unreal. In effect, the event or experience was essentially all in the mind of the person.

Today such a visionary is called a "shaman", which is a Tungus word meaning "between the worlds". This is an interesting definition in itself, for it does distinctly admit that the phenomenon is not to be regarded in a strictly materialist sense.

The question then becomes this: What do we mean by "all in the mind"?

Many cutting-edge researchers today do not take that to mean that the experience was, or is, merely hallucinatory in nature. That is because the "mind" being referred to here by these cutting-edge researchers is not down to being solely the conscious awareness conventionally attributed to the brain of a human being. On the contrary, the mind to which these researchers are referring is what many call "Universal Mind", which is a higher level of collective consciousness and said to be multidimensional in magnitude and scope.

William Buhlman in his many fascinating accounts of out-of-body exploration in books such as *Adventures Beyond the Body* and *The Secret of the Soul* states that on multiple occasions he has encountered part-human, part-animal beings while on one of his adventures. One thing he makes quite clear in his books is that he is able to pursue these adventures, not through the ingestion of a psychotropic substance, but purely through a method of deep meditation he has perfected for himself.

Yogis of the East make precisely the same claim and the

abundance of literature on their perspectives is rich indeed. The Vedas, for example, are thousands of years old and among the most revered sacred texts in all of Asia.

The Egyptians, of course, preceded all modern-day western explorers in the area of out-of-body adventures. In fact, it's probably fair to say that the Egyptians were one of the most advanced practitioners of adventures into otherworldly dimensions *ever,* as their hieroglyphics so famously show. The depiction of their gods as half-human and half-animal is ubiquitous within their culture and the iconic Sphinx is just one colossal example of this persistent perspective on the so-called "supernatural".

Scientific materialists are correct, of course, to note that no bones of any half-human, half-animal entity have ever been uncovered by archaeologists, but this fact only bolsters the claim that such beings are not "strictly physical". At the same time, however, this fact does not "prove" that such entities are unreal and do not exist, for there are energetic levels within the multidimensional universe which are simply too subtle for our current technologies to capture. One need only read how physicists are trying their best to prove the existence of "dark energy" and "dark matter" in order to understand how true this statement actually is. (An exception to the above argument may be in the realm of digital photography, which does appear nowadays to be able to capture very fine intelligent, energetic, spheroid entities known as "orbs". This is something that has occurred to me in a few of my own photographs, so I do find it quite intriguing.)

At least one passage in the Bible is surprisingly relevant to this discussion, as well. Isaiah 34:14 states that, "The wild beasts of the desert shall also meet with the wild beasts of the island, and the satyr shall cry to his fellow..." I would remind the reader that "satyrs" are indeed half-human, half-animal creatures.

As for Ezekiel, he talks about seeing "living creatures" each of whom was standing beside a wheel. "In appearance their form was like a man but each of them had four faces and four wings," which only birds have so far as we know!

Of course, the Greek and Roman "myths" powerfully present the notion that we humans have been encountering "gods", "goddesses", "dragons", "satyrs" and so on for millenniums ahead of the Common Era. "Pan", to cite just one example, was considered to be a nature deity of the highest level and he was clearly half-human, half-animal looking in appearance.

In light of all of this, I believe it is irresponsible of scientific materialists to dismiss one of humanity's most persistent of beliefs: that there are nonphysical entities with which we humans sometimes interact. That they are not purely physical in nature does not mean that they are unreal, only that they are not *solely* physical, but they apparently *can* and sometimes *do* manifest as physical entities on the rare occasion. People instinctively know this, which is why religion is so meaningful to them and has been for millenniums on end. Indeed, 44,000 years is one amazingly long time span!

On a positive note, one may speculate, I think, based on the existence of these ancient cave paintings that these "supernatural" entities are, by and large, spiritual allies of the human species. We certainly perceive "angels", "gods", "devas", "dakinis" and "spiritual guides" in such a light, and for good reason. They sometimes aid us in what appear to be miraculous ways and sometimes save lives in the process.

So it may have been with the all-important, life-sustaining hunt in more primitive times. This may seem far-fetched to many, but cave art is real, and humanity did survive and thrive! This is an inarguable fact. Therefore, if nothing else, here is a colossal banquet of food for thought.

# 45

# The Ghost of God Almighty

## *The Madness of the Dark Ages & the Deadly Legacy That Is Still with Us Today*

THE ROOT CAUSE OF ALMOST ALL conspiracy theories in the West these days, many historians contend, goes back at least as far as the split between the Pagan, Hebrew, Christian and Muslim faiths in earlier epochs. As historians have pointed out, once the Christians splintered away from their Hebrew origins, animosity quickly developed, while the Romans, who had the greatest army in the world at the time and worshipped their own pagan gods, came to dominate both of these religious groups and in quite violent terms. It was not until the 600s that the Muslim faith entered powerfully into the shifting religious and political spectrum with further violence and upheaval.

If we take the entry of Jesus onto the scene as our starting point, we have three major faiths coming into conflict with each other. We know that the Hebrew leaders were not pleased with Jesus and the dissent he brought about in the political and social arena of the day. The Romans crucified him for his outspoken political activism, which was antithetical to the State, and the Hebrew Pharisees did not object, which speaks volumes.

Then, in the year 325, Emperor Constantine altered history forever by becoming a Christian himself, while remaining, it should be noted, *Sol Invictus*, the Invincible Sun-god of the pagan faith. Roman Christianity subsequently grew by way of an authoritarian campaign by the use of force and by the sword. In time, as the historic record amply testifies, the Roman Empire floundered. As a result, it cleverly recreated itself in another form of colossal might: the Roman Catholic Church. The Pope, in effect, became the new emperor.

And rule he did... Not always lovingly. In fact, there were popes that sometimes ruled quite abysmally. Witness the violence of the Crusades. In 1208, for example, Pope Innocent III ordered a Crusade against the Cathars in France. The Cathars, who were also known as the Albigensians, had apparently been outraged by the corruption they saw in the Church and had vowed to keep to themselves well away from the evil they saw within the hierarchy of Christendom. They did so for the sake of their own purity. These were people who did not eat meat and whose central vow was to observe strict chastity at all times, even between married couples. They were a gentle people, it seems, and posed no threat to the Catholic Church really, but the pope thought them heretics for their insolence and was upset that he could not control them, nor force them to do as he commanded. As a consequence, he sent an army of Crusaders to wipe them out and essentially fomented the first genocide in European history.

The greatest outrage of the campaign came when 500 or so Cathars were mixed in with the citizenry of the city of Béziers. When the Crusaders demanded that the Cathars be handed over, the townspeople refused. They knew what good people the Cathars were and that whatever ill treatment the Crusaders had in mind for them, it would not be deserved.

The Crusaders were therefore left in a quandary. Not knowing what to do or how to proceed they sent one of their soldiers to ask the papal legate, Arnaud-Amaury, how they might distinguish the Cathars from the other citizenry. The man made a statement so cruel that it has haunted humanity ever since and has echoed down through history with the kind of nightmarish pall only satanic evil can evoke. He said, "Kill them all, God will find his own."

Only Hitler himself, or one of his cold-blooded, murderous Nazi cronies, could have uttered such heartless words.

Sadly, the Crusaders did not cease with their campaign even after slaughtering virtually every man, woman and child in the city of Béziers. As Mark Booth writes in his book *The Secret History of the World,* "At Bram they stopped off to take a hundred hostages. They cut off their noses and upper lips, then blinded all except one who led a procession to the castle. At Lavaur they captured ninety knights, hanged them, then stabbed them when they took too long to die. An entire army of prisoners were burned alive at Minerve."

Ten years later, a new pope, Gregory IX, was still not pleased with the Albigensian situation and decided that it needed a further investigation. William Bramley in his book *The Gods of Eden* writes that Gregory, "gave the Dominican Order full legal power to name and condemn all surviving heretics. Out of this campaign grew the full inhuman machinery of the Catholic Inquisition which sought to stamp out heresy of every type. The Inquisition generated a fearful climate of intellectual and spiritual oppression in Europe for the next six hundred years."

Known for its tortures, the medieval Inquisition was one of the most cruel, irrational and oppressive institutions ever conceived by human beings, Bramley tells us, and the fact that it was convened by a religious organization that claimed to be acting in the name of a loving God is a hypocrisy so colossal and revolting as to beggar belief. Clearly the Church only survived by virtue of the sword and not the kind words of Jesus, who ceaselessly extolled the virtues of peace and begged everyone to simply love one another.

In short, the Inquisition was a product of distorted thinking so warped, so twisted and so inhumane as to defy reason completely.

Unfortunately, such popes were never tried in a court of law for being the war criminals they were, and their priests continued all through the Middle Ages to preach hellfire, brimstone and eternal damnation to their hapless congregations.

Many evangelists today, quite tragically, carry this same tradition forward and manage to scare the bejesus out of their sheepish flocks. (I dare not even get into the whole scandalous malevolence of clerical sex abuse or the fates of the children of unwed mothers as uncovered in recent times or this book would simply become much too voluminous.)

Perhaps the problem is that in the Western world we have been haunted by the ghost of the biblical God Almighty, Yahweh. After all, this is a God who reputedly stated "I am the Lord, and there is none else, there is no God beside me: I form the light, and create darkness: I make peace, and create evil: I the Lord do all these things." (Isaiah 45: 5 – 7). If true, if indeed God does create evil, and if indeed God is omnipotent and omniscient, and if indeed God subsequently damns those who have committed acts of evil, how can such damnation be justified? It would seem that the God-damned dead are set up, thrown to the proverbial wolves, so to speak, and abandoned. This is not divine justice, this is a disgrace of apocalyptic proportions as all evil is apparently God's own *by choice*. Do we really wish to believe this? Do we really wish to believe that a "Supreme Being" would "smite" any peoples who did not pass muster with him? Or believe that all of the horrors as found in, for example, Jeremiah 19:9, Deuteronomy 22:28 – 29 and 28:53 or Hosea 13:16 are reflections of a fair and compassionate God? Where is the unconditional love in all of this? How do we not say that this is indefensible behavior? For actions do indeed speak louder than words. Meanwhile, the people of one religion continue to kill those of another as in the Dark Ages of yore. How can God condone this? Personally, I can neither accept nor understand how people who believe they were created by a loving God – a God who created all the peoples of the earth – can attack and kill those who happen to worship this same God, only by another name?

I know these are strong and unwelcome words, no doubt, to

the righteously faithful, but all of this is not just hypocritical in my mind, it is genuinely pathologically insane. When Islamic fundamentalist extremists crashed two jumbo jets into the Twin Towers of the World Trade Center in New York City in 2001, it was viewed by most people in the West as an act of war. It was also widely viewed as an act of insanity and why wouldn't it be? In a similar vein, when an Islamic fundamentalist extremist exploded a homemade bomb laden with shrapnel on a huge crowd of young people attending a pop concert in Manchester, England, in recent times that too was seen as insane. Other examples could be cited, but the point is made, I believe, and would anyone today say that Hitler and his Nazi warmongering cronies were *not* insane? Of course, they were. They perpetrated the most colossal mass murder campaign in human history. Millions died and not just those of the Jewish faith, but Catholics and Protestants, too, as the war progressed.

The witch hunts of the Middle Ages were also among humanity's most shameful stretches of insanity. During those extended horrors, over 40,000 women, according to historical estimates, were burned at the stake or suffered other unspeakable outrages on the flimsiest of charges. These were Christian people killing their own kind! Witness the ever-bellicose threat of eternal suffering in Hell issued by bullying Catholic priests and Protestant clerics to this day. This is unacceptable. The Dark Ages are over. And this is not to say that Christianity does not offer billions of people some very beautiful spiritual teachings. It does, but threatening people with eternal damnation is not in the least a loving thing to do, for Hell is a complete fabrication or, at the very least, a misunderstood insight into what happens in the Afterlife.

When will we ever learn? When will we humans stop perpetrating hate crimes against one another?

What many historians see as quite possibly the ultimate catalyst of conspiracy in the modern era was the rise of an alleged Jewish cabal which was plotting to take over Europe and, therefore, needed to be eliminated. What came to light in 1903 was a document which purportedly detailed in shocking depth how this cabal was going to do the deed; that is, take over Western civilization and rule forever and anon. Entitled the "Protocols of the Learned Elders of Zion", this document was a fabrication cobbled together by a group of unknown conspiracists and it set the Christian world abuzz. In fact, it ramped up resentment toward the Jews like nothing before it.

One might well wonder if this was the very source material which so alarmed Hitler in the 1930s and catalyzed his determination to wipe out the Jewish presence in Germany as he rose ever higher into power. Of course, speculate is all we can do, but this possibility is neither a small, nor an insignificant, one. It could very well be what set Hitler's brain ablaze.

In his well-researched book *Rule by Secrecy*, author Jim Marrs writes that the Protocols presented a "list of procedures for world domination." He went on to say, "This document may have wreaked more havoc than almost any other piece of literature in recent history."

It is an established fact that Hitler viewed his "mission" as one, not just of political importance, but even more-so of religious significance. Marrs writes, "This Nazi cult grew from a variety of organizations, theologies and beliefs present in Germany at the end of World War I – all stemming from the mysteries of older groups such as the Bavarian Illuminati, *Germanenorden*, Freemasonry and the Teutonic Knights."

Hitler himself once stated that, "Anyone who interprets National Socialism merely as a political movement knows almost nothing about it. It is more than religious; it is the determination to create a new man." This "new man" in Hitler's view would enjoy "occult" powers, as well as unprecedented political clout, which is why the occult so enthralled him.

We know, of course, what subsequently transpired: World

War II. It cost humanity something in the order of 75 million lives lost, as well as immeasurable damage and destruction to countless cities, villages and rural lands all across the continent of Europe and in the Far East. Hitler and his Nazis, along with Mussolini and Imperial Japanese government officials in Japan, perpetrated carnage on an industrial scale such as was never before seen on this earth of ours and let us hope that we never experience the likes of it again.

We must, therefore, take care to steer well clear of persons and subversive groups which have a propensity for violence and a philosophy of self-righteousness stemming from the belief that there is a "mission" which must be mounted against certain perceived "enemies". These persons and groups are "mad" in more ways than one. Sadly, their lives are consumed by the darkest of energies, including hatred, prejudice, jealousy, envy and bigotry, as well as some terribly distorted notions of supremacy over all other peoples.

Such dangerous forms of thinking are founded on the lowest of emotional realities and are the root cause of endless strife, not only against others, but for the very people who choose to indulge their minds in these dark qualities. A fleeting experience is one thing, of course, but growing obsessed with such thinking is quite another. Ultimately, one must be careful not to become so intoxicated or narcotized by the adrenal and dopamine rushes that go with political extremism, whether of the left or the right, that one is unable to form an objective viewpoint any longer.

In fact, conspiratorial thinking does little but bring about anger within those who grow increasingly convinced that others are out to destroy them. This is, in a word, paranoia. To indulge oneself in one's worst nightmares is to plant the darkest of karmic seeds imaginable and those seeds can ruin a life, for such thinking hardens the heart and causes one to cease seeing the good in the world any longer. This is why treading the broad, middle way is best for everyone. It keeps the peace and provides the greatest good for the greatest number. Above all, it allows for compromise and compromise is really the only fair way to go in this world. As for divine justice, if it is genuine and real, it must be founded on love and equality for one and all and, personally, I believe it is. My great hope is that all of humanity will one day believe it, as well, and with unmitigated conviction.

# 46

# Spiritual Liberation & the Chrysalis of Christ

ROME, THE ETERNAL CITY, a metropolis like no other on Earth. Once the seat of power in the Pagan Empire, subsequently the seat of power in the Christian Empire. To walk her streets is to time travel, to go back centuries and millenniums in time. Whether strolling the gleaming marble floors of St Peter's Basilica, the stones of Via Sacra, Rome's "Sacred Way" or sitting in the ruins of the Roman Forum, one cannot but be awestruck by the colossal grandeur and the historic majesty of the place.

Meeting the pope, as I once did, certainly adds a further layer of historic intrigue to the experience. By a strange twist of fate, full of irony from my perspective, I met the charismatic John Paul II in 1997 at the Vatican (or as the institutional hierarchy would have it, at the Apostolic Palace of the Supreme Pontiff), St Peter's Square. This particular pope has since been elevated to full sainthood. Such a status only occurs once miraculous cures or events are directly attributed to such a figure by more than one person. I must admit that I had very mixed feelings as I stood before the man and shall just note in passing here that the event certainly proved to be ritualized religious theatre at its pompous best. Nevertheless, to view the fantastically ornate interior of the basilica and the artworks there, such as Michelangelo's sculpture, the Pieta, as well as his paintings in the Sistine Chapel, turns any visit to St Peter's into a truly moving and divine experience.

I remember thinking once as I slipped past the three remaining arches of the *Basilica di Constantino,* the church named in honor of the Emperor Constantine, how this singular figure altered the course of Western history perhaps more than any other person in all of antiquity. It had been Constantine's decision, after all, to adopt the Hellenic version of Christianity as the official religion of the Roman Empire. That adoption is precisely what changed everything in terms of the history of Western civilization. The Hellenic version was essentially an adaptation of Egyptian Hermeticism, Persian Zoroastrianism, Christian Gnosticism and Pagan Neoplatonist thought as found in the Mystery Schools of Alexandria at the time. Known as "*Sol Invictus*", Constantine was the "Invincible Sun-god" to his minions and during the course of his reign, he convened the single most decisive group think tank ever in 325: The Council of Nicaea. This collection of men virtually created Catholicism out of whole cloth, so to speak, building on Christianity in general and more specifically on the revelations of the man now known as Saint Paul who had been well versed in the teachings of the Mystery Schools. At that assembly, those men set forth most of the doctrines and dogmas that still reign over the Church to this very day, including the Nicene Creed which sets out the full majesty of the divinity of Jesus as the One and Only Son of God.

Why did Constantine do what he did? He did it because Roman culture was breaking down. People were evolving. They were hungry for new ideas and alternative perspectives. They were doing what people always do: seek better answers to the vicissitudes of life, which is only natural, especially given how much suffering and pain events often generate. One of the problems with Paganism was its vast number of gods. There were so many of them that the religion had become too complicated for people. Constantine sensed that and so he sought a fresh, new way of uniting the people under his rule and he saw a way to do that through Jesus. It was the Greek version of Christianity he used with its link to the monotheism of the Hebrews, who worshipped a deity named Yahweh, and the Persian Zoroastrians who worshipped a deity named Ahura Mazda (as well as an angelic divinity named Mithra, whose attributes and life story were later welded to the life of Jesus). Constantine surmised that monotheism was much easier for people to relate to than a complex pantheon of gods, all with different powers and diverse domains. This consolidation and synthesis of doctrinal attributes of a monotheistic deity proved as perfectly effective as he had hoped.

One day, so the story goes, Constantine had a kind of waking dream or vision in which he saw a cross in the heavens as he was preparing to go into battle against a particular enemy. What he discerned from the vision was that if he went into battle under this particular symbol that he would be victorious and, when that proved to be the happy result, it sealed the matter for him.

The Council of Nicaea preceded their collection of writings on the ministry of Jesus with the Hebrew writings about the coming of a messiah. This preface added a massive magnitude of gravitas to the proceedings, legitimizing the divinity of Jesus in the eyes of potential converts who believed in the idea that a prophet could foresee the future. After all, the ancients were said to possess wisdom of the highest standard, living as they did in a mythical Golden Age where peace and prosperity reigned supreme.

People nowadays ask why the Ten Commandments of the Hebrews begins with the injunction, "I am the Lord thy God and thou shalt have no other gods before me." The answer to that is quite simple. The pagan world had literally hundreds of gods during the course of that era and so Yahweh's deal with the Hebrew people was this: if they would worship him exclusively, in return he would look after them as his "Chosen People".

Constantine we now know was a master at entrenching his council's doctrines and dogmas. He simply did what today's Islamic fundamentalist jihadists are trying to do: force everyone to convert and believe or else. Constantine achieved his ends primarily by turning the profoundly mystical, metaphorical teachings which surrounded Jesus into a *literal* historical event, just as some (but not all) of the earliest Christians had done and by subsequently enforcing that belief under the threat of death. Yes, people were run through with a sword if they resisted. This is what happens when people are put under the sway of an absolutist agenda.

Again, what many do not understand is that the sacred teachings of the Mystery Schools were couched in dramatic tales full of potent symbolism. These tales were never meant to be taken literally. They were meant to summon emotional, soulful responses to the various enigmas and vicissitudes of life. That is why Jesus generally spoke in parables. Stating so-called "facts" does not impact on the average person like an emotionally charged tale full of heroes, villains, kings, queens, warriors, saints, sages and a slew of ordinary folk who get caught up in extraordinary circumstances.

Was Jesus a historical character, then, or not?

The answer is yes, he *was* a historical character, but his ministry was so brief that it was only noted in a few of the historical writings of the era. How, though, did Jesus become God incarnate? According to one of the most renowned and eminent of Bible scholars, Bart D. Ehrman, this is a crucial question to ask, and he does so in his book *How Jesus Became God*. "How", he asks, "did a crucified peasant come to be thought of as the Lord who created all things?" After all, "Jesus was a lower-class Jewish preacher from the backwaters of Galilee who was condemned for illegal activities and crucified for crimes against the state." It requires a full tome to answer this question, but Ehrman meticulously works his way through the facts with the precision of a forensic detective and what he eventually concluded was that Jesus was an apocalyptic prophet who believed that God was soon to intervene in the affairs of the world and bring about a situation where there was no longer any evil. This new world would be full of goodness. It would be a wondrous world where there would be no more pain or suffering. Apparently, Jesus thought this intervention was imminent and would happen in his, and his disciples', lifetime, but as we now know that did not happen. It is interesting to note here that Ehrman began his quest for truth as a "born-again" evangelical, a true believer in the divinity of Jesus, but admits that he is no longer a believer. As an expert in the many relevant ancient languages from which the original writings of the Bible were derived, his quest for answers led him to discover thousands of mistranslations and so many alterations to the texts of the Bible that there was simply no way he could continue to cling to the myth of Jesus through blind faith. His eyes had been opened much too wide for that. He has noted, for example, that in the earliest Gospels, those of Matthew, Mark and Luke, Jesus makes no explicit claims of divinity for himself. Such rhetoric only came with the later Gospel of John and the visionary influence of the Apostle Paul who set out his belief in the "Risen Christ" in letters sent to various churches over a great number of years.

It was the followers of Jesus, of course, who kept his teachings alive, but Jesus did not create his teachings out of thin air. Many scholars believe that he might well have been an Essene. The Essenes were a very mystical Hebrew group who were extremely well versed in the core teachings of the Mystery Schools of their day. The Essenes put no importance on worldly things, which is why Jesus always told his followers that his kingdom was not of this world and why he taught that, "the kingdom of God is within." The phrase, "the kingdom of God," is a metaphor. This is an extremely crucial point to understand. The teachings of the Mystery Schools revealed great spiritual truths, but in a subtle, emotionally moving way for the simple reason that psychic reality operates very differently from physical reality. The fact that there actually *is* a psychic, or spiritual, reality is why the apostles were able to experience Jesus as a transcendent being.

A master like Jesus was no doubt in command of his energy body and could appear to his followers as a divine emanation, just as a few other highly revered meditation masters, yogis and sages have likewise done over the centuries. In fact, it is vitally important to emphasize here that millions of people over the centuries have seen loved ones who have died. (I personally know two people to whom this happened. Both said that a deceased friend or family member appeared to them after their death and that the person seemed as real to them in the moment as the very room they were in at the time. Colonel John Alexander's mentor, the medical doctor Elisabeth Kübler-Ross, once made the extraordinary claim that at a crucial moment in her life when she felt like giving up her investigative work on death and dying, a former student of hers who had died ten months prior appeared to her and begged her not to give up her efforts as a pioneering figure in the field. Quite astonishingly, once the psychiatrist promised not to give up, the woman agreed to sign her name to a document and date it. The handwriting was later proven to be authentic.)

In the eyes and minds of the followers of Jesus, seeing him as they did after his passing *proved* to them that if they took his teachings to heart that they, too, could enjoy eternal life. To believe in his message and emulate his way of living, Jesus knew, was what could save those who chose to follow him. That is as true today as it was back then and why Jesus is still relevant as a teacher.

Jesus basically explained that what counts in life is living from the heart. The word "heart" in this sense is a very simple and easy metaphor to understand. Everyone knows that when we speak about "having heart" we are not talking about the physical organ of the body. We are talking about feelings, insights and intuitive understandings of life at a very deep and very soulful level. We're talking about values and virtues, about things like compassion and emotional intelligence. To *know* this is a form of transcendent knowledge. The word *gnosis* itself simply means *to know*. If one understands this, then one is a Gnostic, a *Knower*, and Jesus was most assuredly a "Knower". He had had a direct experience of that higher dimension from which we all come. Most religions call that source *God*. Jesus certainly did. He also referred to that source as the Father. He was a genuine holy master, one capable of performing miracles and worthy of being revered, but it was Saint Paul and, subsequently, Constantine and his cohorts who created Roman Catholicism, the version of Christianity that has since become historically entrenched.

Only those who had experienced God directly, by the way, were considered true initiates by the sages who ran the Mystery Schools and if a person *did* experience God directly, then he or she *knew* that they were one with the metaphorical Father. They understood that *all people* are one with the Source of All That Exists, even those who have yet to fully realize it for themselves.

Unfortunately, most of humanity has never been taught how to go about achieving such an experience. In fact, most Christians have been essentially forced into believing that this was and is an impossibility. The result has been a form of indoctrination that has kept the esoteric teachings of the mystics out of the hands of the average, ordinary person and made members of the Christian faith puppets of the popes and priests, and now also the preachers and the evangelicals. A literal history was imposed and, eventually, blind faith in the biblical teachings came to reign across every quarter of the globe.

In his various books Ehrman's research revealed that the first *written* scriptures came many decades after Jesus lived and that Church fathers doctored those scriptures over time to suit their own self-interests and views of the teachings. Given that fact and how oral teachings when passed around, person to person, for decades can easily and innocently get altered or embellished no doubt explains why the Gospels of Matthew, Mark, Luke and John have conflicting descriptions of many of the events surrounding Jesus' life and death and offer substantially different versions in various instances.

Despite all of this, the beauty of the teachings of Jesus is that, by and large, Jesus speaks of loving one's neighbor as oneself and even one's enemies. This is spiritual gold. I say, "by and large" for a reason, however. See Matthew 10:34-35, for example. Here Jesus is quoted as saying, "Think not that I am come to send peace on earth: I came not to send peace, but a sword. For I am come to set a man at variance against his father, and the daughter against her mother," and so on. There is more such talk in certain recovered documents such as the Dead Sea Scrolls and the Nag Hammadi's "Gospel According to Thomas".

Despite these troubling, contradictory and mystifying statements, most people think of Jesus as a peacemaker and the greatest exponent of cosmic love in world history. That is well and good without a doubt, for if the primary message is to love one's enemy and one's neighbor as oneself, then that is to everyone's benefit. What this form of thinking can do is wrap one in a veil of compassion and empathy and serve as a metaphorical chrysalis for spiritual metamorphosis if one is wise enough to take the teachings to heart rather than accepting them on blind faith and promulgating the erroneous view that there is only one "true" religion and that all other spiritual traditions are inferior, outright wrong or under the sway of Satan. To indulge in fearmongering by preaching sermons of hellfire and brimstone is especially pernicious and destructive to the welfare of the innocent among us.

When one does take the teachings as metaphorical parables of wisdom, one may eventually grow liberated in one's own right. Clinging to literalism, unfortunately, is antithetical to setting the soul free. We might remember here the wise words of St John of the Cross: "The soul that is attached to anything, however much good there may be in it, will not arrive at the liberty of the divine."

What this means is that one must accept full responsibility for one's own salvation by living the teachings of Jesus day in and day out, rather than paying attention to the notion of salvation once a week or so and expecting Jesus to forgive us our erroneous ways, believing that we can do whatever we want so long as we believe that Jesus is the one and only Son of God and that he will eventually save us and spare us the tortures of hell, when in truth we must save ourselves.

To do that we must cultivate and actualize humanity's higher ideals of love, charity, kindness and compassion, rather than arrogantly creating divisions among people and thinking ourselves righteously superior to those of other faiths.

In *The Gnostic Gospel According to Thomas,* Jesus is quoted as saying, "The Kingdom of the Father is spread out upon the earth, but people do not see it."

In a similar vein, the Buddha once said, "Intrinsically all living beings are Buddhas, endowed with wisdom and virtue, but because men's minds have become inverted through delusive thinking, they fail to perceive this." Nirvana is a state of mind, not a place.

Spiritual fulfilment, in other words, is a matter of *perception* as both Jesus and Buddha made very clear to us many millenniums ago.

The chrysalis of Christ, therefore, may be seen as a beautiful thing, but only if we eventually come to understand that indoctrination into the faith is like wrapping oneself in a veil of spiritual bromides and taking comfort in the notion that a higher power will look after our salvation for us. In such a larval state, we are like children in thrall to God the Father. Once we realize, however, that we must become the catalyst of our own transformation, we slowly begin to gain greater sensitivity. If we are persistent, if we are strong enough in our self-belief to break free of these veils and learn to wing our way forward in the world under our own auspices, we become a fully realized being.

The ultimate result is that by having the courage of our convictions and the integrity to openly live them, we may become advanced spiritual beings in our own right.

# 47

# The Karma Harvest in All Its Glory or Horror

IN THE MOVIE, *LIMITLESS,* Bradley Cooper plays a writer named Eddie, who – thanks to a bad dose of writer's block – has become down and out. He has become someone who is going nowhere fast. His girlfriend has left him, and he is at wit's end. In fact, he has no idea how he can turn things around in his life given the fallen state in which he finds himself.

Only, then, by pure accident, he happens to meet someone from his past out on the street and he is given a drug that utterly transforms everything for him. This illegal pharmaceutical, he is told, will give him access to ALL of his mind rather than to the measly 5 to 10% with which most of us average, ordinary souls are forced to make do.

Think of it this way: most of us are consciously aware of roughly 50 bits of information as we go about our business every day. This is out of the 11,000,000 signals that are processed by the body every single second!

In any case, once the little innocuous pill hits, Eddie immediately sets about cleaning his apartment and putting his house in order. When he finishes, he sits back on his couch amazed and amused. In narration he wonders, "What was this drug? I couldn't stay messy on it. I hadn't had a cigarette in six hours, hadn't eaten… So abstemious and tidy. What was this? A drug for people who wanted to be more anal-retentive?" He laughs as befits the sardonic comment and then – his mind sharp as a pin – says, "I wasn't high, I wasn't wired, just clear. I knew what I needed to do and how to do it."

Indeed. With access to the whole of his mind, Eddie wowed his publisher with a full manuscript in four days and then moved on to the stock market, where he was soon wealthy beyond his wildest dreams. He also won back the woman who had given up on him in the past, joined the jet set and flew off to where the rich luxuriate and entertain themselves as only the wealthy can.

Inevitably, trouble set in, and all hell broke loose.

Of course, all hell broke loose. It's a movie! Wouldn't it be something, though, if we humans *did* have access to more of our brain? Even 20%! Or imagine 50%! One hundred percent would be so utterly fantastic and dynamic that it would probably blow our minds completely!

We would then feel limitless, too.

The good news is that at death we may, quite possibly, be gifted with this very thing by the grace of God or by the natural colossal, collective field of consciousness itself.

Buddhist meditators and Vedic yogis say that when we pass from this world, we automatically gain a sevenfold increase in intelligence. That is a remarkable magnification of conscious awareness, one which apparently allows us to review our life and understand events at a whole higher level so that we may learn life lessons with unmistakable comprehension.

Likewise, near-death returnees tell us that the clarity that can be experienced at our moment of passing is nothing short of astonishing. The mind penetrates every aspect and facet of our former life, and one feels every infinitesimal exhilarating twinge or excruciating cringe of emotion that has informed that life. Apparently, we not only feel that emotion from our own perspective, but also from the perspective of those with whom we came into contact. In other words, in the immediate aftermath of leaving our physical bodies, the range and depth of feeling and emotion to which we have access expands exponentially. Our minds literally explode outward in all directions to encompass all those around us and, in that moment, the way we made others feel is revealed to us in inescapably agonizing and almost unbearable detail.

In short, one's life review is the ultimate trial by fire, and we will all go through it whether we want to or not.

Perhaps, the life review, then, is where we *really* reap the seeds we have sown. Perhaps, this is where karma reaches its decisive turning point and rebounds back on us with such power and consequence that we will finally, fully understand with profound clarity just how interdependent and at one we are with our fellow human beings.

Imagine if you were cruel and abusive to others on a regular basis, how painful this will prove for you. Imagine if you tortured people or chose to murder someone for supposedly doing you wrong. Imagine if you chose to become a mass murderer and took the lives of others in a senseless act of violence that you thought would make you notorious in the annals of crime or ignorantly believed that going on a mass murder rampage would see you leaving this world in a delusional blaze of glory.

Imagine, conversely, if you were resolutely kind and compassionate to others how this magnification of virtue will rebound upon you and fill your heart with such illumination and love that the life review itself will become a transcendent and heavenly event too wondrous for words.

Perhaps, if we have indeed shown love and compassion to one and all, the angels, the buddhas and the saints will all sing your praises, and wouldn't that be nice?

By the way, what near-death returnees universally insist is that such an experience is not dependent in the least upon which religion you subscribed to in life. You may have been Christian, Muslim, Jewish, Hindu, Jain, Buddhist or subscribed to no religion at all and this same magnification will occur. One's mind simply becomes lit up; so they tell us. It is lit up in multiple magnitudes and the scope of one's insight expands beyond all boundaries. In fact, in that moment, we are absolutely limitless in our ability to comprehend our actions and are able to grasp information at a level that transcends whatever level of understanding we happened to enjoy in this earthly life of ours. Perhaps this is how karma plays out in an ultimate sense and so the moment of truth arrives: what we have done to others comes back to us in such force that there is no mistaking it. We fully reap what was sown and there is no hiding from the harvest.

This is why we all need to follow our inner compass of compassion to ensure that the harvest will be full of beauty and abundance and not the terrible opposite.

# 48

# Gone with the Zen

THE WIND BLOWS through, the clouds quiver, the rain drizzles down and then, finally, the sun bursts through once more, radiant and magnificent.

Life goes on.

*We* go on... All of us. Separately and together.

Physically, we quiver like clouds ourselves, our bodies composed of fiery atoms, airy molecules and watery cells, every part of us in endless motion. Every animate and inanimate thing in the world is likewise vibrating.

We are vibrant beings in a vibrant world.

I remember feeling this vibrancy with powerful intensity as I sat cross-legged in Ryoan-ji, the beautiful, tranquil Zen garden in Kyoto. With its stones positioned in perfect artistic harmony to one another and its raked sand mesmerizing to the eye and mind. It proved an enchanting place to sit in contemplative meditation and just "be", by which I mean *be nothing*, be everything. It was glorious.

Physicists talk about vibrational rates in relation to light and point out that the gross elements of the material world are built on vibration.

Dr Wayne W. Dyer in his book, *Manifest Your Destiny,* tells us that, "Sounds are a powerful energy. Every sound is a vibration made of waves oscillating at a particular frequency. The frequency range of the human ear is approximately sixteen thousand vibrations, up to roughly forty thousand vibrations, per second. Higher up on the scale, with increasingly faster vibrations, is electricity, at about one thousand million vibrations per second. At two hundred billion vibrations per second, we find heat. Light and color are at five hundred billion vibrations per second, and an X-ray manifests at two trillion vibrations per second. It is theorized that thoughts and the unknown etheric and spiritual dimensions are in the realm of increased vibrations beyond anything that is calculable at this point in time. Vibrational frequencies are very clearly the very nature of our material universe."

How does one even begin to conceive of energy – however microscopic – oscillating at five hundred billion vibrations per second, let alone two trillion? How can one begin to get one's mind around the idea that anything can, and does, oscillate that incredibly fast?

The answer is, I suspect, "We can't." Nevertheless, all entities, whether human, animal or otherwise, whether here or elsewhere, do vibrate and each does so in a unique manner. That energetic vibration is as individual as our physical bodies and that uniqueness is known as a "signature". We humans don't "have" a signature, we "are" one. (This is rather like how each of us signs our name in a unique fashion and can be identified by our signature in a court of law in such an absolute way.)

So, to "be" is to have a singular, energetic signature and we humans experience this phenomenon with other human beings virtually all the time, whether those people are family, friends or complete strangers. It is because of this energetic signature that people either make us feel comfortable or uncomfortable. It also generally determines whether we like, love or are repelled by any particular personality.

Simply put, where resonances are closely aligned, the more in tune with each other any two people feel. In many cases, the resonance is a more neutral thing, but where there is a sense of dissonance, a very dark feeling can prevail. One might even interpret that dissonance as being hostile, unfriendly, unloving or even demonic in extreme cases.

Near-death returnees, freshly back from that mysterious "otherworld" of which they speak, also tell of experiencing people or entities while there that either attracted or repelled them. The most compelling of these entities have come to be known as "Beings of Light". Invariably, these beings have a unique vibratory nature that radiates out from an energetic core and fairly overwhelms those who are temporarily in their presence. This radiance can come across as exuding an enormous sense of love or some other positive quality like compassion or pure understanding. Many people, it seems, leap to a conclusion about who such a being might be when encountering one. They assume, based usually on the religion into which they were born, that such a being is either "God", "Jesus", an "angel", "Krishna" or "Buddha" or whatever other holy figure they have been moved by in the past, but that is most likely a guess based on expectation, for these beings do not say who they are.

We ourselves might simply say, therefore, that such beings are "highly evolved souls", but all such labels are *impressions,* and no one can say with absolute certainty, in real terms, exactly who these beings are. The reason for this, quite possibly, is that names are meaningless in the higher dimensions. The energetic signature is sufficient for identification purposes, after all, and, in any case, the worldly self is ever and always but one among many identities we humans temporarily assume during the course of any particular incarnation on earth.

Once, after hearing of the murder of a young woman with whom I had been deeply infatuated while in high school, I spent many days in a deeply disturbed state. The young woman, I learned, had been killed by her husband after he had come home from a nearby military base where he worked and had discovered her with another man. Apparently, the enraged husband shot, not only his wife in the back as she attempted to flee, but he also gunned down the woman's lover (who coincidentally had the same first name as me). The husband then fled the scene and hid out in a nearby woods, but when the police closed in on him, he took his own life. I remember being so horrified by this terrible tragedy that I could not stop thinking about the woman for days on end and lamenting her death even though it had been five years since I had last seen her.

Then, one night while lying in bed reading a book, I dozed off into a kind of twilight state and what happened next was startling. The woman burst into my mind so vividly and in such a lively way that I was taken profoundly by surprise. At first, I had no idea what was happening. I just knew that there was a woman's face in my mind's eye and that she was quite radiant. There was something *familiar* about the energetic presence of the woman, however. Then, it dawned on me, without a word being spoken, that this was she. This was the murdered young woman whom I had once been so infatuated with and I realized in that moment that she had come to me in my grief. When I opened my eyes in surprise, I saw a ghostly form floating off and disappearing down the hallway. In the aftermath of this strange encounter, I was left with the distinct impression that the woman was alive and well in some other dimension, despite her tragic demise. She had appeared so beautifully radiant, however, when she had burst in on my mind that I was forever after satisfied that she was okay. More could not be done, I realized, so I let her go from my mind and heart and moved on with my own life. Nevertheless, that experience gave me an insight into the reality of how each of us has a unique vibratory, energetic essence that endures. It strikes me now that this is precisely how we will know each other in the Afterlife when we are in a disembodied state.

According to returnees, the beings of light encountered in the Hereafter interacted with them via a telepathic form of communication, offering whole thoughts or powerful visual images, and many even offered explanations about how life came into existence and how it manifests in the way we experience it. Many returnees say that virtually every question one has may be answered while in the presence of such an advanced soul.

I found out how true that possibility is once in a very profound, hyperlucid dream state when I realized, to my astonishment, that I was in another dimension entirely. I have no recollection of meeting a Being of Light there but did encounter what might be described as a primordial power; or, to put it in more supernal terms, a superluminal matrix of metaphysical sensate intelligence.

In any case, no matter what words one uses, that incredible, intelligent power seemed to give me all of the answers to life in one fell telepathic swoop, so to speak. After I came to in the middle of the night, I found myself in an incredible state of bliss. My entire body was buzzing. "So that's how it all came to be," I sighed quietly to myself. It seemed so simple. I even murmured that very thought aloud. "It's so simple…"

How it was simple and how it all came to be, though, turned out to be beyond my ability to put into words. In retrospect, the only thing "simple" about it was how *simply ineffable* it turned out to be.

Which I found incredibly frustrating.

Nevertheless, I knew what I had experienced. That part was solid, so to speak. From that experience I gained the consoling affirmation that there *was* an answer to the Great Mysteries of life and that the spiritual dimension is preeminent. I learned, too, that life goes on for us, even if we are in a disembodied state.

Near-death returnees and mystics to this day say something very similar in their attempts to explicate what they experienced while on the "other side". Words can approximate the knowledge that was imparted, they say, but the proverbial simile about the menu not being the meal perfectly describes how very different words are from the actual experience.

Zen masters know this truth better than most and tell their monks to meditate without dependence on words. They give their students what are called "koans", which can be totally nonsensical questions or questions without actual answers, such as "What is the sound of one hand clapping?" or "What is your original face before your mother and father were born?" The idea is to raise the intensity of the pursuit to the breaking point. When the intellectual mind finally quits trying to answer what is ever and always ineffable in nature that is when the great breakthrough can come.

To experience the "ineffable" directly is the ultimate goal of Zen and to experience it is to have a "satori". This word is derived from the Japanese word *satoru* meaning "to know". In Zen, this refers to the direct, non-conceptual apprehension of the true nature of reality. Satori is a transcendent experience which goes beyond words and concepts, and perfectly corresponds to the notion in the Western Hermetic tradition of "gnosis" which also means "to know", though in the case of Hermeticism this word refers to one having a direct epiphany or experience of "God".

The Gnostics would, of course, say that God *is* the true reality. For example, Hermes Trismegistus in *The Hermetica* says that "Atum" (God) is "Oneness, the Whole, the Primal Mind, the Supreme Source of All That Is". He also says that "To define him is impossible."

To reach a state of gnosis or satori, however, does not mean that one is automatically ready to expound upon the origin and meaning of life. It means only that one has glimpsed ultimate truth and experienced one's own essence. That essence is about being directly aware of consciousness itself. This is how one may actually perceive one's "original face".

Even afterwards, answers will continue to elude. Where consciousness originates, how it began, whether there is a God or not, these will still prove impossible to say. Thus, the answer to such questions remains ineffable.

The enlightened one is then left to sit in wonder, staggered by reality, intoxicated by its sublime and transcendent nature.

This is a beginning, not an end.

So I discovered when I awakened that night from my stupendous realization. All that I could do was sit in silence, awestruck, thinking how life is its own answer and that what I had been looking for was precisely what had been doing the looking (and still was!).

This is doubtless why the Zen master, Rinzai, stated, "If you know that fundamentally there is nothing to seek, you have settled your affairs." In other words, we already have what we are seeking: it is awareness itself and life would be nothing without it.

As to how the universe, and life as we know it, originated... Why it came to be and to what end...

What beautiful, sublime wonderments. What ceaselessly fascinating koans!

# 49

# The Martian Odyssey as Magic Theater

TRAVELING ABOUT THE EARTH, daring the unknown, climbing the highest mountains, exploring the oceanic depths takes bravery; it takes determination, fearlessness and, at times, a near reckless attitude to one's own precious mortality.

Still, those who are given to great adventure, who love novelty and are willing to risk life and limb in an effort to explore the countless possibilities of this world are precisely those people who end up living the most exciting lives.

This particular truth, I believe, goes a hundredfold for those who are presently considering the possibility of exploring *another* world.

I am speaking about Mars, of course, for just as many a climate change activist now carries a sign reading: "There is no Planet B", Mars it seems is the sole "other world" in the whole of our solar system which we humans can reasonably hope to colonize.

The very idea of that, I believe, is a genuine enchantment on more fronts than one.

While most of us would not for a second entertain the notion of going to the Red Planet, thousands have already volunteered to boldly go forth with the many organizations that are currently competing to launch the first mission to Mars. Each volunteer, no doubt, has his or her own sense of what requirements, stresses and dangers such a pioneering excursion would entail, but above and beyond that they undoubtedly each have a sense of what personal fulfilment they believe might come of it.

For starters, it would be an incomparable experience, one that only a handful of people out of the billions and billions on this planet will ever get to know. In terms of sheer novelty and unparalleled excitement, there is surely nothing else like it at present.

Then there is the historic first that this initial mission will create and, let's face it, going down in the history books appeals to all of us. Who wants to bite the proverbial dust, after all, and have that dust simply blow away into nothingness? We all imagine ourselves as mattering in this world, as being "somebody", as being a person of value.

We should remember here, however, that history has as many villains as it has heroes and to simply "go down in history" may be of questionable value in certain respects. Far better, the sages and wisdom masters of the world say, to find your worth within, as a spiritual being, rather than in the realm of gross materiality.

Scientific materialists, of course, insist that there is no such thing as spirituality. They insist that what cannot be measured, seen, touched nor sensed in any form is unreal. These, we must remember, are the masters of rocket science, the science that will one day carry humanity to Mars, so who are we to argue with them, right?

The answer to that is that millions of us would argue with them and for good reason: ignoring one's inherent spirituality puts one at peril. Why? Because our essential humanity hinges on intuitive sensitivity at every level of life, most especially in the way we interact with each other and ultimately view our worth. We are not mere animals nor automatons, after all. Humans have a sublime side, and it is ineffably important.

This is a major point that is made in my novel *Crimson Firestorm Mars* and why I propose here once more that the entire notion of a Martian odyssey can be seen as an ideal meditative form of contemplation or, if you will, as "magic theater".

Why? Because those who will one day blast off for Mars will never, ever, return to this Earth. At present, the journey is one-way. In other words, the technology does not exist at present to allow our initial colonizers to blast off from the Martian surface once they land, which means, quite simply, that they are there for good.

And that is the end of it until further advances are made in our various technologies.

Leaving the Earth forever is what happens when we die, of course. With the demise of our physical bodies, we exit this planet never to return. (Never to return *in precisely the same form*, I might add, though the possibility does seem to exist that we may indeed reincarnate and come back in another form!)

The point is this: contemplating one's mortality is a profoundly effective way to focus the mind. It virtually forces us to consider what is or isn't important in life. With months and years of meditative contemplation a person can arrive at insights into life that would otherwise elude. By concentrating on our spiritual natures, we become more empathetic and compassionate. We come to realize that all people are equal no matter their race, religion or nationality. We understand that to harm another is to harm ourselves (which holds true for the planet, as well. To harm it is to harm ourselves).

Above all, with meditation we can discover that each and every one of us has an essential self and that that essential self is a psychospiritual entity which inhabits a physical body for the express purpose of navigating its way about on a planetary surface. When that physical body ceases to function, the essential self does not. The essential self simply moves on and continues to spiritually evolve elsewhere in ever more subtle dimensions.

To believe or not believe the above is a choice, but meditation is an activity which anyone can pursue at no cost, save for a bit of one's time in some form of regular basis. Just as one cannot become a rocket scientist by not attending a university for a great number of years, so one cannot become a proficient meditator without making a similar effort and putting in the time.

The idea of going to Mars on a one-way journey is very much

like what Buddhists call a "death meditation". In brief, a death meditation concerns itself with leaving the Earth forever when we "pass away". It is not a notion that one can take lightly, for the question is where do we go if we survive and what happens once we arrive there?

This is something to which one must give tremendous levels of thought if an answer is genuinely sought, for it is only by ruminating deeply on what is to be gained and what will be lost upon one's death that we can discover what is really of value in life.

The exact same thing is true for those who want to go to Mars, for it is only by giving these issues deep levels of contemplation that one can possibly become a qualified candidate for a seat on any spacecraft that is bound for the Red Planet.

Hardcore scientific materialists might argue with this but I am predicting that once our hardest of hardcore astronauts arrive safely on Mars and the first flush and excitement of settling in has passed, that the humdrum business of living in a freezing cold environment, breathing manufactured air (due to the atmosphere of Mars being toxic to humans), eating "space food" all of the time (i.e. having to subsist on retortable pouches of processed comestibles and tubes of semiliquids fortified with vitamins and minerals) and just being generally confined to very small living quarters and workstations will eventually take its toll. Imagine years going by and you are only around a very small number of people. Imagine further the fact of never having access to any of the activities that most of us so take for granted: dining on delicious cuisine or junk food even, imbibing fine wine, beer, whiskey, cola, fruit juices and so on, going to movie theaters, sports facilities, rock and pop concerts, wandering for hours on end through fabulous art museums or going to ultra-sophisticated fashion shows. Or how about the privilege of just cruising around in our cars, trucks or motorcycles and going wherever we want? Or taking walks on beautiful golden beaches with the mesmerizing sound of thunderous surf cresting and ebbing? Above all, how precious is it to us to be able to visit with our beloved friends and family at will and whim?

These are all genuine concerns to which any volunteer who wishes to be taken seriously as a candidate for any mission to Mars must give earnest thought. At the end of the day, we are all human; we are not robots. We have an inner life which cannot be ignored.

In short, we are psychospiritual beings and that is a truism even if we define that complex term in a strictly humanist manner.

By the way, our Martian colonizers are going to be sitting on their backsides a lot, especially while enroute to the Red Planet, which can take upwards to a year before arrival. A spacefarer must therefore be "cool" with the inevitability of sitting in meditative repose for hours on end, day in and day out, if he or she really wishes to make such a journey.

One would be well advised, therefore, to cultivate deep states of meditation sooner rather than later if wishing to be a part of any excursion to Mars.

Yes, humanity will go to the Red Planet one day. That is a certainty. Viewing the journey as magic theater now, therefore, can make us all wiser for when we *collectively* set out on our greatest space adventure yet!

# 50

# Proof of Higher Consciousness

THE GREAT DEBATES between science and spirituality over the origins of consciousness have been raging for centuries and they show no signs of being resolved anytime soon. How is it, though, that we humans became sentient creatures capable of both conscious awareness of the immediate environment in which we find ourselves, as well as self-aware beings with a deep and abiding knowledge of our own mortal existence?

Scientific materialists, of course, postulate that consciousness is an epiphenomenon of the brain. It arises purely as a result of the biological synergy of brain chemistry and neurology.

The most widespread religious viewpoint, in contrast, postulates that "God", an infinite being inherently omniscient and self-aware, imparts a small measure of "His" macrocosmic consciousness into all living things. Among these living creatures, we are told, is a very special creature: the human being; an entity whom, unlike all other living creatures upon this planet, is self-aware just like "God Almighty Himself".

This latter exposition re the religious viewpoint is far and away the most prominent in the world today, but it is not the only theory put forward in the world. Buddhists insist that they do not know if there is a "God" or not, but they *do know* that conscious awareness is something non-material in nature. It is a phenomenon, they say, that is self-existent in a mysteriously infinite and eternal way, having arisen spontaneously and they further state that we humans derive our self-conscious awareness from this original source, one with which we are all directly interconnected.

Buddhist meditation masters and, likewise, Hindu yogis, tell us that it is entirely possible for any human being to discover the proof of this assertion by taking the time to sit in meditative repose as they do and experience this direct connection for oneself. In other words, it is entirely possible for anyone to become "aware of awareness" in its purest state.

Most scientific materialists, nevertheless, dismiss this assertion out of hand and are quite unwilling to put in the time to prove the matter one way or another for themselves. This is akin to a physicist saying that there are very decisive ways to ascertain the truth of the existence of atoms, which are invisible to the naked eye, if one is willing to put in the time to attend a university, obtain an undergraduate degree in science, then pursue a master's degree and a doctorate in physics. Along the way, at some point, they promise, one will be able to calculate all of the most significant equations this proof requires, and one will then be able to sufficiently analyze the data such that, in the end, one will be convinced of the reality of atoms!

The point here is that to prove the contention of either of these two disciplines takes *time*; time to sort through and analyze the data; time to study all aspects and parameters of the phenomenon in question; time to arrive at a meaningful answer based on knowledge and many a deeply considered insight.

The fairest question of all, however, is the one that rightly asks how anyone can offer a definitive answer to anything that one has not personally studied in great detail.

Both sides, of course, have valid arguments in their favor, which is precisely why I have personally spent a lifetime in my own way pursuing the viewpoints of both disciplines. I have done so in the spirit of scientific enquiry, where one bases one's opinion on a deep review of all the data, while keeping an open mind regarding the possibility that new data might arrive at any given moment. After all, what is true one day may be found to be false the next or vice-versa, so one must always stay open to the possibility or arrival of fresh data.

This, of course, means that the debates between science and

spirituality will most assuredly continue.

Neuroscientists, as proof of their assertion that consciousness arises owing to neurology and brain chemistry, point to the fact that pharmaceuticals obviously affect the quality of consciousness, otherwise products such as anti-depressants or even aspirin or ibuprofen simply could not work. Throbbing headaches and dangerous forms of mentality, such as schizophrenia or paranoia, have indeed been shown to be alleviated by drugs; this is indisputable. Add the effects of psychedelics or "hallucinogens" to the mix and the argument is significantly bolstered again.

What about the "proofs" that allegedly exist in terms of consciousness surviving death, however? There are certainly scores of credible books today by renowned and respected scientists that offer a great deal of data in this regard, the focus being primarily on what is known as the "Near-Death Experience". Thanks to modern day resuscitation methods the data in this field of study has grown astronomically in recent decades. The work of Doctors Raymond Moody and Kenneth Ring springs immediately to mind, but it is Doctor Ian Stevenson whose work with children comes across as most readily convincing, for young children in possession of detailed knowledge of another life cannot easily be dismissed. A great amount of follow up has gone into research of this nature in an effort to "prove" that the alleged former person really did live in a certain place and at a certain time, and that the child does indeed know details that he or she could not have made up out of thin air.

I would contend that these studies do actually qualify as a form of proof that consciousness is not a mere epiphenomenon of brain chemistry but exists independently of the body and continues to exist even after the demise of the body.

In addition to this, there is, quite possibly, an even more convincing proof that, at the very least, a form of higher consciousness does exist. That proof is based upon documented studies that have been carried out on those diagnosed as having what is known as "savant syndrome".

Daniel Tammet, for example, is an autistic savant who holds the world record for citing the numerical derivations of pi to 22, 514 decimal places. He spent five hours in this recitation in front of a professional adjudicator and perhaps only faltered finally out of sheer weariness. Most of us are lucky to memorize even ten or twenty decimal places in such an exercise. How does one carry on for over twenty-two thousand places? If this feat does not leave one thunderstruck, then one must be near death oneself!

How, we must ask, is such a feat possible without the accessing of some higher level of consciousness?

Consider the case of Leslie Lemke, a blind savant, who is able to play almost any piano song after a single hearing. He initially did so without ever having had so much as a single piano lesson. One night, it seems, he awakened his parents by launching into a perfect rendition of Tchaikovsky's *Piano Concerto No. 1* after having simply heard it for the first time earlier in the day.

Then there is the late Kim Peek. He was the inspiration for the lead character in the movie *Rain Man*, starring Dustin Hoffman and Tom Cruise. Even though he was physically without a corpus collosum to bridge the two hemispheres of his brain and could barely manage basic motor skills when he was alive, he could read a book – any book – in about an hour. His left eye would take in the left page and his right eye the right page at the same time. During the course of his life, he is said to have read around 12,000 books, all of which he committed to memory, word for word, sentence for sentence and page for page. The subjects of interest to him included history, literature, geography, sport, mathematics and music. For fun, he would memorize entire telephone books just by passing his gaze over the pages at a rapid clip.

These are but three of the many savants known to possess extraordinary mental skills and capable of a host of fantastic feats, most involving the multiplication of incredibly large numbers. Their correct answers are generally out of the reach of even the most acclaimed professors of mathematics. Even a known "genius" like Albert Einstein was never able to perform a feat of this nature, so how, we must ask, could a so-called "idiot savant" achieve such an end? Einstein at least had a background in physics and had studied it for years and years before reaching his greatest, most acclaimed achievements, which makes sense, whereas these savants have never previously pursued any academic subject to any higher level at all prior to achieving their feats. This is utterly inexplicable.

How, one must ask again, can they do it? How can they possibly do all of this without recourse to some higher level of consciousness? In my opinion, this is the only way that makes sense, and it must involve a form of telepathy that simply comes to them without too much of an effort on their part. While telepathy may sound like something out of the paranormal, millions in fact have reported experiencing this phenomenon on more than one occasion. It involves some currently inexplicable aspect of the mind in which information is quite simply received without recourse to language.

I respectfully leave it to the reader to draw his or her own conclusions as to whether savants are living proof of the existence of higher consciousness, but I challenge one and all to come up with a better explanation for how these gentle souls are able to perform their amazing mental feats. After all, most savants are not even able to look after their own most basic survival needs, never mind being capable of pursuing a standard education, making a simple meal or driving a car.

In summary, I will just say that from my perspective life is a great mystery with countless unsolved enigmas which are ceaselessly elusive and cannot be conclusively apprehended by any form of forensic analysis. Consciousness is the most evanescent phenomenon of all. Yet, without it, we would not know ourselves or our world. We would not be able to communicate with one another at any level beyond what animals, aquatic creatures and insects have achieved. We would never be able to question nor answer anything, let alone express appreciation for the life we know and love.

This is why I believe it is consciousness that is fundamental to life, not the atomic, molecular and biological processes that so enthrall our scientists.

Nevertheless, the ideal situation enjoins materiality *with* consciousness. In other words, the ideal situation is precisely the one we now happily enjoy.

# 51

# The Atom Smasher's Dreamcatcher

## *What the Quantum Physicist, the Mystic & All Seekers of Truth Have in Common*

THE EVOLUTION OF REVELATION must lead, at last, to a synthesis of science and spirituality, to an understanding of the world in which the views of mystics and physicists prove complementary as explanatory models of reality, rather than as views based on paradigms which can never be brought together in any form of harmonious unity.

Upon recently re-reading *The Tao of Physics* by Fritjof Capra, I found many of the illustrations of subatomic particles in the book quite captivating once more. Having been set loose in a collider, the particles are shown spinning off in various ways, including in elegant spirals that reminded me of the spirals carved into rock at Newgrange, the Neolithic monument which stands on a prominence near the River Boyne in County Meath here in Ireland where I am now living. No one is sure who built the megalithic edifice, but the entrance stones and the curbstones are full of engraved spirals and every year at the winter solstice the sun's rays illuminate the monument's innermost chamber and the spirals within it. At that moment, I am told, those spirals seem to almost come alive.

It would appear that whoever built the prehistoric monument – dated to around 3200 BCE and thought by archaeologists to be older than Stonehenge and the pyramids of Egypt – had a deep understanding of both the innermost forces which animate life as we know it and the astronomical forces at play in the greater cosmos. Researchers are simply unsure, therefore, if Newgrange has religious significance as a place of worship for a so-called "cult of the dead" or if it was a strictly scientifically based product of people possessing advanced levels of astronomical knowledge, a group that chose to concretize its knowledge in stone, apparently for the benefit of future generations.

Physicists, as we know, seek to discover material essences to the physical realm and what that requires is breaking matter down into smaller and smaller units. To achieve that end, the scientific community has built high-energy particle colliders which can split the atom. The largest of these facilities is the Large Hadron Collider built by CERN, the European Organization for Nuclear Research, whose headquarters are located in Meyrin in the Canton of Geneva in Switzerland.

What colliders do is accelerate particles to a very high kinetic form of energy and pit two streams of directed beams of energy against each other by sending those beams rushing in opposite directions around the circular collider. As the particles ride the beams, they attain greater and greater speeds along the way. Finally, when the two beams meet, they smash into each other head on. What is then captured by computerized sensors are the subatomic by-products of these collisions and physicists study these by-products in an effort to understand the laws of nature which govern quantum mechanics.

What prompted me to re-read *The Tao of Physics* was a dream I had that contained something like two powerful beams of energy colliding, complete with an explosion; one that stunned me.

What stunned me even further in the dream was seeing a Native American, whom I took to be a shaman, holding a dreamcatcher and leaping to my aid as if to protect me from the flying debris that was set loose by the blast.

Dreamcatchers are handmade willow hoops with leather nets stretched across them and are usually decorated with feathers and beads. The webbing is meant to capture negative energies which can assail someone in the night as the person sleeps and dreams. Most westerners, however, tend to see dreamcatchers more as magical charms for bringing one's highest and best dreams to fruition. Either way, dreams are held to be sacred by Native American wisdom masters, for they are believed to be emanations from the realm of the Great Spirit.

Neuroscientists, in contrast, have no idea how or why we humans dream at night, but they do know that dreams are vital to our cognitive functioning and, indeed, to our very survival.

The Hermetic metaphysician links dreams to the spiritual realm in the same way as Native American and Eastern wisdom masters and I can personally attest that some of my most profound insights into the nature of consciousness and the essence of life have come from dreams. Precognitive dreams have been especially telling in my view as they offer a form of paranormal insight into the nature of time and reality which is inexplicable in what we think of as normal materialist terms. How, we must ask, can the mind possibly see an event before it has occurred? In my experience, precognitive dreams can be quite vivid; so much so that when the event perceived actualizes in the "real world" it is unmistakable. In such a dream a very exact activity occurs, or a specific person appears, perhaps someone that one has never met, or someone whom one has not seen in a very long time. In either case, when the event comes to pass, it can prove quite jolting.

It is not only in dreams that such occurrences can arise, however. I was once driving home for the weekend while attending university and, at one point, happened to look in the rear-view at my own face. What I saw shocked me. It was not my face I saw looking back at me. Rather, it was the face of a man with whom my father had once been friendly; a man who had moved to California and had not been seen for many years.

It was, therefore, quite a surprise when I arrived home and discovered the man conversing with my father in the family living room. The man hadn't been back in Ohio, I heard him say, for almost ten years.

While I was full of astonishment simply by the fact of the man's presence, what subsequently occurred struck me as very strange, indeed, for the man behaved quite negatively toward me for some reason and seemed to take offense at almost everything I said. At one point, he even became quite rude about it; so rude, in fact, that I soon beat a hasty retreat from the room and left the men to themselves. Afterwards, I could only wonder why the man had behaved as he had. What I subsequently made of my "vision" of the man's presence in advance of seeing him was that my higher psyche must have processed his dark energy as a bit of an existential threat. As it transpired, once the man was gone, my father informed me that he had reeked of alcohol and had sometimes gone off on some very bizarre tangents during the course of their conversations.

Months later, the last thing we heard about this tragic figure was that he had died a horrible death in California after binge drinking alone in his home. His body, apparently, had not been discovered for a week or so and there had been so much alcohol in his system at the time that a huge quantity of gas had built up inside of him. It had built up so powerfully in his stomach and intestines, in fact, that his body had literally exploded. The man had been totally blown apart.

How tragic, how strange and how daunting the way events can sometimes play out. No matter where we look on the spectrum of life, from the subatomic realm on up to the most astronomical, there is mystery and intrigue at every level, and some of it can prove to be nothing short of astonishing. Perhaps, one might conjecture, the very purpose of life for a human being is to uncover such intrigue.

The word "uncover" here is instructive, I think. Once while camping in Tasmania, I had a dream in which I was told that the secret answer to life was to be found in the word "cover". Quite curiously, my partner and I were assailed in the night by no less a creature than the notorious Tasmanian devil. Apparently smelling the food we had at hand, one of these sizeable creatures simply began to claw its way into our tent, which made for quite a rude awakening. In my alarm, I chased off the devilish little creature with gruff words. A tent, of course, is a form of cover and clothes obviously cover us. Mystics and metaphysicians say that the world we experience is a "veil" of illusion, which is also a form of cover. Vedic yogis call this veil "maya". Furthermore, many a wisdom master has insisted that the ego-centered narrative of life as we know it is simply a "cover story" for spiritual beings undergoing life in the human dimension.

Quite interestingly, as well, the Greek word *apocalypse* actually refers to "taking off the covers" and is related semantically to another Greek word, *revelation*. Revelation essentially means *reversing that which is covered.* To reveal is to throw off the veil and so a revelation and an apocalypse were originally cuts off of the same cloth, so to speak!

Gary Zukav in his book *The Dancing Wu Li Masters*, subtitled *An Overview of the New Physics*, writes: "The Copenhagen Interpretation of Quantum Mechanics does not go so far as to say what reality is 'really like behind the scenes', but it does say that it is not like it appears. It says that what we perceive to be physical reality is actually our cognitive construction of it."

A cognitive construction is part and parcel of the mystery of consciousness, but one thing is certain: the narrative of our collective lives here on this earth is a consensus fiction that has been created over the centuries from the use of words and concepts. These lingual creations, over time, have tended to lock-in various cultural constructs with ever evolving solidity. Fritjof Capra writing in another of his books, *The Web of Life*, says, "The uniqueness of being human lies in our ability to continually weave the linguistic network in which we are embedded. To be human is to exist in language. In language we coordinate our behavior, and together in language we bring forth our world." Elsewhere in the same book, Doctor Capra explains that the original meaning of the word "maya" in Hindu mythology meant "magic creative power". The world, in this view, was brought forth by Brahman – the highest Cosmic Principle – as a divine play. Over the centuries, the original meaning broadened and came to be applied to anyone "under the spell of the magic play". That is essentially all of us.

One of the most compelling images of Brahman's divine play is known as "Shiva's dance". Shiva is a personification of Brahman, and his dance is the universe of appearances which we all mutually experience. In *The Tao of Physics*, Capra writes, "According to quantum field theory, all interactions between the constituents of matter take place through the emission and absorption of virtual particles. More than that, the dance of creation and destruction is the basis of the very existence of matter, since all material particles 'self-interact' by emitting and reabsorbing virtual particles. Modern physics has thus revealed that every subatomic particle not only performs an energy dance, but also *is* an energy dance, a pulsating process of creation and destruction. For the modern physicist, then, Shiva's dance is the dance of subatomic matter." Finally, he adds, "The metaphor of the cosmic dance thus unifies ancient mythology, religious art, and modern physics."

While I have never had the pleasure of seeing the Large Hadron Collider in Switzerland, I have stood on a mountain in that country and gazed on the most impressive alpine peak in all of Europe: the Matterhorn. It is the twelfth highest pinnacle on the continent and rises above the surrounding glaciers, with four steep faces, making it appear to the naked eye as a near-symmetric pyramidal peak of awe-inspiring perfection. Its shapely, graceful contours can summon a range of emotions, most of which felt sacred to me somehow, as if this peak should be considered nature's answer to all those cathedral spires as found in cities like Rome, Florence, Cologne, Madrid, Barcelona,

London, Paris and so many others. The thought occurred to me as I was standing there that if the Matterhorn happened to be located in the Himalayas, it would most assuredly be considered sacred in its own right and a holy abode of the gods for sure.

In the West, however, we do not ascribe spiritual qualities to nature in that way. We keep our natural sciences and our religions well separated. No physicist really expects to find the essence of God in the subatomic realm such as was implied by those who initially called the Higgs boson the "God particle" ahead of its discovery, nor do astrophysicists expect to find God somewhere "out there" in interstellar space. The idea of "God" is a mental construct to western scientists, but it is a compelling one and there are scientists who have called the quantum field itself the Mind of God. Why? Because there is inherent intelligence in the field, which is why the cosmos has generated intelligent beings such as ourselves. As Michael Talbot writes in *The Holographic Universe*, we humans have, "an evolutionary thrust toward higher consciousness". Awareness of the many in the one and the one in the many is an innate perceptual verity for humanity.

Rather than looking for God in the subatomic realm or even in the macrocosmic domain far out in interstellar space, I would recommend *feeling* the presence of that all-pervasive higher intelligence within one's own body. Gazing on a mountain like the Matterhorn can surprise us by the emotional power its presence can evoke. The same can be said about any really large and impressive structure, not only those found in the natural world, but also those built by human hands. I am thinking of some of the many wondrous edifices I have had the pleasure of seeing over the years: the Great Pyramid of Giza, the Parthenon in Athens, St Peter's Basilica in Rome, the Duomo in Florence, Notre Dame in Paris, the Oude Kerk in Amsterdam, Cologne Cathedral in Germany, Gaudi's surreal Sagrada Familia Cathedral in Barcelona, the Almudena in Madrid, Westminster

Abbey in London, Canterbury Cathedral in Kent, Stonehenge in Wiltshire, England, Newgrange in Ireland, as well as the many huge, magnificent parliaments, palaces and castles that are spread out across the continent of Europe.

To know oneself at the deepest level, the seeker of truth must explode the myths that make us human. He or she must shatter the archetypal forces that coalesce within the human psyche/soul complex so that the cross-stitching, the weave, of light which generates the material domain can be seen in all its essential, interpenetrating complexity. We who quest after truth must also explode the fictional narrative, the cover story, upon which our lives are founded, for archetypal ideas and images mediate reality. They make all that we experience coherent.

What we might well discover via this explosive approach to truth is that the fragments of our lives quickly assume their own trajectories. That which is tribal, sectarian, national or denominational will only go so far, for these are constituted of tenets which cannot escape their own preclusive boundaries, while that which is universal and applicable to all of humanity regardless of one's cultural or religious ties will sail on across the cosmos in open space and fly unimpeded.

In his Epilogue in *The Tao of Physics,* Capra states that the "significance of the parallels between the world views of physicists and mystics is beyond doubt. The interesting question, then, is not whether these parallels exist, but why; and, furthermore, what their existence implies."

The Vedic and Buddhist sages understood thousands of years ago that the world we experience is "maya', it is founded on real phenomena, but what we make of that raw sensory data is an illusory narrative that has no reality other than the one which the human mind consciously and subconsciously makes of it. Likewise, when physicists send two high-energy beams of particles smashing into each other and then decipher the result of the subsequent explosion, that is maya, as well.

What the sensors and computer images give us is a momentary snapshot of forces which, in essence, are inexplicable in ultimate terms. These images are the stuff of dreams. These computers, metaphorically speaking, are like dreamcatchers operating on a whole higher level. As Gary Zukav put it in *The Dancing Wu Li Masters*: "Our experience tells us that the physical world is solid, real, and independent of us. Quantum mechanics says, simply, this is not so."

To reframe this latter statement, therefore, one can say, based on the work of physicists (Western culture's highest arbiters of reality) that the world is not solid, it is not real, and it is not independent of the human mind.

Is that not an earth-shattering revelation?

What is amazing to physicists is that subatomic particles simply pop into and out of existence in a totally unknown way, which is why Richard Feynman famously stated, "I think I can safely say that nobody understands quantum mechanics." Physicist Max Born offered this insight: "No language which lends itself to visualizability," he said, "can describe quantum jumps." In other words, we cannot even visualize how electrons make a quantum leap from one orbit to another. What happens with electrons upon excitation is that one second they are in a particular orbit around the nucleus of the atom and the next they are in a greater orbit without having crossed the intervening space. This, among many other reasons, is why physicist Niels Bohr stated that, "Those who are not shocked when they first come across quantum theory cannot possibly have understood it."

So, life is, indeed, a great and paradoxical mystery: it is real and yet it is illusory at the same time.

As Max Planck stated, "All matter originates and exists only by virtue of a force... We must assume behind this force the existence of a conscious and intelligent Mind. This Mind is the matrix of all matter." Werner Heisenberg put it succinctly, as well, by saying that "Atoms are not things." The physicist Paul Davies in his book *God and the New Physics* offered this fascinating insight: "In the absence of observation," he said, "the atom is a ghost."

One of the most ancient of spiritual texts is *The Hermetica*. In it we find this profoundly telling statement: "For humanity, time is a destroyer, but for the Cosmos, it is an ever-turning wheel. These earthly forms that come and go are illusions." This is astonishing. The universe is both real and unreal at the same time!

This makes us free at a metaphysical level, however, which is astounding. This is so despite the fact that our bodies are subject to the laws of physics. The human mind, in stark contrast, is a boundless, transcendental wonder which one can use in any way one chooses. One of the most revealing of all possible choices is to explode the myths in which we are culturally rooted and, thereby, become – to coin a word – *metaphysicist*s. The fragments which are sent flying by this explosive mental exercise turn into something akin to subatomic units. By smashing things apart in this way, we are able to study the structures inherent in our own subset of the world and understand how powerfully we have been influenced by the archetypal forces that flow through us. One person is compelled, for example, to be like Achilles of myth and become a great warrior. Another person, under the sway of Orpheus, might become a successful singer or musician and so on.

Jung states in his book *On the Nature of the Psyche*, "The archetype as an image of instinct is a spiritual goal toward which the whole nature of man strives; it is the…prize which the hero wrests from the fight with the dragon." To know ourselves, to win that prize, we must deeply comprehend which of the archetypes compel us to act as we act and we must thoroughly understand the myths which underlie the culture into which we are born, for our archetypal, mythical roots run deep. By discovering these inner forces, we can live our lives in harmony with them and stay true to ourselves. This is what makes the human conscience a divine thing and why each soul unit is a metaphorical God particle in its own right. In other words, the mind itself is the supreme dreamcatcher and knowledge the ultimate catch. The metaphysical physicist learns this truth to the bone.

# 52

# Forever Young, Forever Old, Forever Blown Away

TO BE FOREVER YOUNG is an impossibility. Or is it? Certainly, from a common sense, down-to-earth, perspective it is indisputably that way.

Maybe, though, that is only because we are forever old from the very day we are born.

Scientists say that the atoms which make up our bodies were, by and large, already present when the Earth formed some 4.5 billion years ago.

The heavier atoms, like the carbon in our flesh and the oxygen in the water in our bodies, were made inside of stars which exploded and then spread at random across space to eventually become part of our solar system. It is estimated that such atoms were created at least seven billion years ago, quite possibly even longer. The lighter atoms in our bodies, such as hydrogen, have been around since shortly after the birth of the universe some 13.8 billion years ago.

We should all stop and think about that on occasion in order to fully understand ourselves and our world. We might begin, perhaps, by looking down at our hands and studying them. The atoms that make up those hands are billions of years old! The eyes with which we see our hands are billions of years old. The air we breathe, the water we drink, the food we consume... All of these things are billions and billions of years in age.

In other words, life as we know it is simply a structurally reconfigured ancient wonderment of spacetime.

Consider the significance of that. Once upon another day, the atoms in our bodies were a part of other things in this world. "Our" atoms were scattered across the globe and helped comprise creatures like protozoa, sea slugs and salmon. They helped form snakes, lizards, pterodactyls, brontosauri, whales and other mammals. They were in the soil, in the air, in the streams, the rivers and the oceans of the earth. They were in those "people" we call Neanderthals and then in former members of our own species, Homo Sapiens.

Yes, the atoms in our bodies were once in other people and those people lived and loved, and labored, and looked to the future the same as we do today.

The fact of the matter is our bodies – in scattered form – have been around the world many times, cycling and recycling their way through the biosphere, through vast numbers of centuries and millenniums before becoming the human body each of us happens to currently commandeer.

When this fact is considered deeply enough, even a ninety-year-old person can easily be viewed as being quite physically young! After all, what is ninety years set against ninety million or nine billion years?

To be young in spirit, of course, is down to attitude, but what is "spirit"?

Spirit is consciousness and, as bizarre as it may seem, the consciousness which facilitates our intelligence may be even older than the billions-of-years-old body that we inhabit. Certainly, that is what mystics, sages and yogis believe based on the insights so many of them claim to have directly learned in a "metaphysical" manner.

Metaphysical? Here is another word which causes confusion for so many. The word *metaphysical* means "above or beyond the physical". Metaphysical knowledge is transcendent in nature, which admittedly makes it unquantifiable and immeasurable. If there is such a thing, however, it does imply that consciousness is not only beyond physicality, it is quite possibly *timeless* in nature, for scientists agree that it is the material world's activities that create and constitute "time" as we know it.

This might mean, perhaps, that consciousness is sourced in a dimension that exists outside of time altogether. Perhaps this dimension is eternity itself.

What we can definitely state is that the manner in which we ascertain the age of all things on the Earth is based on scientific analysis. Scientific materialists do not accord the mystics, sages and yogis any measure of veracity for their conclusions, despite the fact that neuroscientists admit, straight out, that they do not know, nor fully understand, how consciousness actually arises. These scientists simply call it an "emergent property" or "epiphenomenon" of electrochemical brain activity.

Physicists do accord validity to the existence of other dimensions, however, even if that validation does come about via mathematical equations and not owing to any form of measurable materiality as such.

So that's the short and the sweet of being forever young and forever old.

Personally, I am forever blown away – awestruck – by facts such as these. What it tells me is that this universe of ours is quite simply a realm of enchantment, an enigmatic multidimensional plane of sheer wonderment; one that stretches the imagination to the stars, to distant galaxies and to the quasars. Perhaps all the way from here to eternity and beyond...

# 53

# The Recombinant Grail

TRANSMUTATION IS THE WAY of life, the world, the universe, of every living thing. Change is what there is and all there is. Nothing stays the same for long, certainly not forever. Life creates and destroys. It composes a thing, then decomposes it, so that creation and composition can go on again and again, endlessly.

The orchestration, the *show*, must always go on. It must *move* along or else, for if things stayed the same for long, stasis would set in and nothing would evolve or grow. There would be no planet, no people, no events. Nothing at all would happen.

Life does happen though. *It* happens and *we* happen. The whole universe arises from out the quantum field with such a titanic burst of energy that stellar phenomena are sent flying across the void for billions of years. Along the way, much of that stellar phenomena coils round and collapses into massive balls of fire which subsequently emit light. When those balls of fire explode, they send forth heavy metals. Life cleverly weaves lattices of light and heavy metals into planets, people and countless creatures.

Life as we humans know it, then, is basically a great light show, one brimming with morphogenetic phantasmagoria. It is a spectacle that never ceases to amaze and is *immeasurably* precious because of what it can create, for not only does life generate matter – the Earth and our very flesh and bones – but it also infuses our blood with what *feels* like a divine or numinous power, one seemingly supernatural in scope, one so powerful that it can sometimes fill us with a sense of invincibility even.

We're not invincible, though. We humans are, in fact, quite vulnerable and given to all manner of ailments, infirmities and afflictions. If none of these kill us, then we simply expire of old age one day, which is to say from an inherent form of temporal obsolescence. This is why we humans have always sought "magical" nectars, talismans, charms and amulets for ourselves as a way of fighting back against these enigmatic and frightening vulnerabilities.

Among those magical objects was one known as the Holy Grail.

According to legend, the Grail was a cup which was summoned to catch the blood of the crucified Christ when a lance was thrust into his side and the wound began to bleed. So precious was this liquid that it was said to give eternal life. It came also to symbolize what had occurred at the Last Supper when Jesus said, "Take this, all of you, and drink from it, for this is the chalice of my blood, the blood of the new and eternal covenant, which will be poured out for you and for many for the forgiveness of sins. Do this in memory of me."

To drink of the Holy Grail was to imbibe a divine elixir that would save one's soul and grant one immortality.

In the Middle Ages, many stories were told about the search for this Grail. Most of those stories revolved around tales of King Arthur and the Knights of the Round Table, but also around a character named Parsifal. Few know that there are versions of these tales in which the Grail is a stone, not a chalice. This "stone" is the "Philosopher's Stone" of the alchemists. It, too, was said to have magical properties. It was said to be luminous and to regenerate the body of the one who was lucky enough to obtain it.

In other words, the Philosopher's Stone could not only make one young again, it could reputedly make one immortal. This meant that the Philosopher's Stone had extraordinary properties, indeed, but was this thing really a stone?

The word philosophy was coined by Pythagoras, one of the most acclaimed of all the ancient sages. Noted for his mathematical skills and his deep love of wisdom, Pythagoras paid homage to his love of intuitive insight by naming his noetic pursuit after Sophia, the Goddess of Wisdom. Thus, any lover of wisdom could be a philosopher and did not need, necessarily, to be able to weave complex ideas into articulate and intricate arguments full of crafty logic and cunning existential subtlety.

What, though, could a philosopher's "stone" be? A magic crystal? A crystal ball in which one might see visions? The answer is, "No". Those who were privy to esoteric knowledge understood that "possessing" the Philosopher's Stone was simply a figure of speech. It pointed to one's ability to reach a deep level of insight into the hidden, or "occult", workings of life, allowing one to fully fathom its sacred, metaphysical nature. In other words, it was a metaphorical object, not a literal one.

Back in those days, the word "occult" only meant "hidden". It did not refer to anything devilish or satanic. The Catholic Church would later put that spin on the word in order to denigrate it, for the Church believed that "occult knowledge" undermined its authority, which was unacceptable to the institution. Having grown used to the total dictatorial level of power it had built up in the Middle Ages by dominating the lives of people across Europe, Church leaders did not take kindly to transgressions against its authority. The "Holy Inquisition" was set up specifically to mitigate against such transgressions. As a result, many scientists in their quest for truth had to do so in very clandestine ways.

So, too, did those who dared to set about questing after direct visionary epiphanies of their own. This is precisely why there was a rise in "Secret Societies" during the course of subsequent centuries. The "Great Work" of alchemy, for example, was said to be about transmuting base metals into gold, but that side of the quest was, more likely, simply a smokescreen (though there would certainly have been no objections had any of the arcane operations the alchemists performed with their alembics, beakers, potions and cauldrons worked in a literal way!).

Behind the scenes among the practitioners of the Great Art, however, there were whispers about something called "spiritual alchemy" and it was said to be a secret path to illumination. Its goal was the transmutation of elementary, or mundane, knowledge into the gold of wisdom. It was about transmuting one's profane understanding and perceptions of life into an ineffably sacred, enlightened form of insight that reached into the very deepest of levels achievable.

Sir Isaac Newton, one of the most important scientists in the history of humanity, was profoundly obsessed with alchemy and there are actual writings to prove it. His insights into transmutation were considerably influenced by the alchemists and he was much more of a mystic than people generally realize. Newton believed that every part of the universe was not only alive, but intelligent in a certain sense. Stones, minerals, plants, all possessed a degree of intelligence, he thought, and that divine intelligence was reflected in the very design and substance of any particular object. In his book *Opticks*, Newton wrote, "The changing of Bodies into Light, and Light into Bodies, is very conformable to the course of Nature, which seems delighted with Transmutation."

At a base level nowadays, most scientists subscribe to the view that every living thing that exists in the Earth's biosphere is infused with one essential substance, one *intelligent* substance: the cell. Each cell is like an individual organism and has the equivalent of a brain, lungs, hands, feet and even reproductive organs. The DNA within the cell provides the working instructions for the molecular machinery which assembles amino acids in such a way as to form proteins. Proteins, of course, build all living organic structures, the human body among them.

At an even more elementary level, every animate, as well as

inanimate, object is made up of a single substance also: atoms. Like DNA-infused cells, atoms can and do transmute and morph one thing into another. Atoms are part and parcel of a *recombinant* plenum, the quantum field, and they create all that is, ever has been or ever will be.

In a sense, atoms are God-like in their omnipresence and omnipotence.

In its deepest sense, the Holy Grail is neither a chalice nor a stone. It is the essence of life itself. It is that mysterious substance which sustains life and which streams life forward. This is why some researchers insist that the word "grail" may have come from the ancient word "*sangraal*" which possibly refers to one's bloodline. A bloodline, of course, is all about genetics. (Thus, the whole controversy about Jesus and Mary Magdalene possibly being husband and wife in books like *Holy Blood, Holy Grail* by Baigent, Leigh and Lincoln, and *The Da Vinci Code* by Dan Brown.)

Genetics, in any case, is why one might make the claim that every sentient creature is a holy grail of sorts. That is because the magical, miraculous substance of the grail is already within us. It is life itself, so there is no need to go out searching for it in far flung lands. To do so, ultimately, is therefore a fool's quest. Likewise, to seek God outside of ourselves is also unnecessary (however we may choose to define "God"). Luke 17:21 tells us in the Bible, "The kingdom of God is within." If the kingdom is within, then God is within. *Where* is God within us? In every living cell, molecule and atom.

Obviously, humans are not the only creatures comprised of cells. Virtually every living thing in the biosphere of the Earth is comprised of cells, so God is within all creatures, however sizeable or microscopic. We humans like to think that we are special, but we could not physically survive without the plant life and the creatures which populate the biosphere of our home planet. We must have the water that flows down from the skies and collects in the streams, rivers and oceans across the globe. We must have the fiery heat of the sun. We must have the air that fills our lungs.

The ancient sages knew this and insisted that there are four essential elements for life to exist as we know it: earth, air, fire and water.

Humanity is not separate from the biosphere. We, as a species, are totally dependent on it for our very sustenance. We eat, we drink, we transmute the flora and the fauna of the Earth. That flora and fauna live on in us just as we live on in the biosphere of our wondrous planet.

We should never take this fact for granted. After all, we humans emerged from out the biosphere of Planet Earth and, yes, we return to it in what is known as the life cycle. We can lament this truth or accept it as "Nature delighting in Transmutation", to use Newton's words.

According to science, energy cannot be created or destroyed, which means that the "energy body" each of us "is" does indeed go on. That may seem inexplicable in many ways, but what is even more inexplicable is why we humans foolishly poison the land and the seas of our precious home? Why, too, do we poison our own bloodstreams with carcinogenic pesticides, liquidized plastics and regularly consume the kinds of foods and oils which clog up our bloodstreams? Why do we treat the animals, marine life and the plants which sustain us with such disregard?

The lover of wisdom is a lover of life and all that sustains life. The lover of wisdom *promotes* that which makes life thrive. The true lover of wisdom sees the recombinant grail for what it is: Life in transmutation and eternal metamorphosis; sacred, precious and holy beyond words.

To *know* who we really are is the Great Quest. To understand that we are eternal immortals and co-creators of the reality we inhabit is the secret knowledge. Seeking this knowledge, it seems, is what keeps us moving forward with ceaseless curiosity and incessant fascination, a pursuit that, in metaphorical terms, is the quest for nothing less than the Holy Grail of legend.

What is the Holy Grail? As Robert Anton Wilson put it in his book *Right Where You Are Sitting Now,* "The Grail is, and always has been, and cannot be anything else but, Immortality."

## 54

# Our Garden of Earthly Delights

THE MONA LISA'S COY, enigmatic smile may be the top attraction of the Louvre Museum in Paris and, while its galleries are stuffed to the rafters with some of the most celebrated paintings and sculptures in history, I have always preferred basking in the ethereal beauty and light of the scores of Impressionist paintings at the Museum d'Orsay when I am there. The works of Monet, Manet, Gauguin, Pissarro, Renoir and their fellow artists unfailingly set my spirit soaring and keep me in a sublime state of bliss for days.

Then there are the phenomenal paintings of Vincent Van Gogh to be seen in Amsterdam, as well as in Paris and other museums in the world, including the Museum of Modern Art in New York City where the famous "Starry Night" resides. Van Gogh worked his way through Impressionism with scores of wondrous canvasses and ultimately raised his art to a level of transcendentalism that has dazzled viewers ever since. He has given us magnificent works like the "Starry Night", "Café at Night", "Cornfields and Ravens", his "Room at Arles" and those haunting self-portraits with his piercing blue eyes blazing and sparking out to daunting effect. The striking beauty, the furious riots of color and the bursting golden light in Van Gogh's work can leave one feeling as dazed as the artist himself surely must have been while lost in his exalted delirium, painting feverishly, his mind and body full of anguish at his numerous failures in life and suffering in every way possible, haunted especially, it is said, by a terrible presentiment of impending death.

Indeed, Van Gogh's works have always held me spellbound and entranced when I look on them, but on a recent trip to Madrid, I came upon a painting in the Prado by another artist that left me even more stunned. In fact, the work left me riveted and reeling, for there were scores and scores of naked bodies dancing, prancing, cartwheeling and frolicking through a bizarre surreal setting. There were women wading languidly in lake waters and men riding animals of every kind. There were people making love or engaging in every form of depravity imaginable. There was Jesus and Adam and Eve and an inferno of strange creatures on the left side of the work, while the right side was overflowing with doom, gloom and scenes of stupendous demonic debauchery.

I knew, of course, that I would be viewing famous Spanish artists in the Prado, men such as Francisco De Goya, El Greco and Diego Velazquez among others, but not this staggering masterpiece. This enormous triptych had been conjured by a Dutchman; his name Hieronymus Bosch; his famous masterpiece: *The Garden of Earthly Delights.*

What a surprise. What a painting! I had seen photographs of the work many times over the years, but to lay eyes on the real thing left me breathless.

As mentioned above, the left panel of the triptych depicts an earthly paradise with Jesus holding the hands of both Adam and Eve, while the right panel slips into deeply disturbing and gruesome scenes of hellish proportions. The center panel, however, looks like something a visionary shaman might see after ingesting a few extremely potent magic mushrooms and landing in another dimension entirely. Its depiction of earthly pleasures, especially those of a lustful nature, was supposedly meant to sound a warning note to fellow Christians, the message being that indulging in such ephemeral frolics as shown here would have dire consequences later once one's soul had "gone over to the other side".

The sheer number of naked bodies in the work must have shocked medieval observers back in the day. People are shocked even now, after all, and to think that this painting was presented to the world at roughly the outset of the 1500s beggars' belief. The detail, however, is absolutely phenomenal and I found viewers lined up five and six layers deep to stare at this fantastic masterpiece of orgiastic magnificence. It had us all absolutely mesmerized.

My impression is that Hieronymus Bosch must have been an incredibly liberated man and a true visionary. There has been speculation as to whether he was a member of any underground, secret society or not, perhaps a group such as the Brethren of the Free Spirit, but even if he was simply in a club of one, he was centuries ahead of those in his day.

More than once as I stood looking, I overheard expressions of unabashed astonishment as people stared at the bizarre beasts and monsters, the numerous depictions of dreamers indulging in the pleasures of the flesh and the countless demons who were clearly delighting in punishing every fallen soul who had so willingly given into and indulged in every conceivable version of the seven deadly sins. While those exclamations I heard were generally in Spanish or French or other European languages, I could easily interpret the breathless tones of incredulity which accompanied the words. What I most especially remember hearing was an English-speaking man loudly exclaim, "What the f**k! What the hell is that? What's that supposed to mean?" His words had burst forth in a bemused and woeful wail, but his partner had no answer for him. She had no idea the same as the rest of us and finally just frowned and shrugged her shoulders. Even the Visitor's Guide to the Prado admitted that the painting was "filled with symbolic images of unclear meaning...")

Personally, I suspect that Bosch was less a sermonizing medieval cleric-type than a man whose visionary talent was so acute that he surely must have existed in a rare dimension of his own.

The only painting that came close to *The Garden of Earthly Delights* in content and style elsewhere in the museum was

Pieter Bruegel the Elder's work entitled *The Triumph of Death*. In contrast to Bosch's delights, however, Bruegel was inspired by the literary theme known as the Dance of Death. Its imagery was macabre and gruesome from one end of the canvass to the other. "Death" in the painting – looking rather like the Grim Reaper – is mounted on a steed and he leads a vast army of skeletons across the land, destroying every man, woman and child in his path. According to the Visitor's Guide, Death is out to destroy the world of the living and the painting makes it clear that no one escapes its grisly clutches. The Guide also notes how the figures in the painting are "rendered with painstaking realism" and that is certainly true.

Of course, the Prado is rich beyond measure with paintings of painstaking realism and even a week within its walls is insufficient to take in the full bounty of Spain's most famous painters, as well as the many other European masters whose works also happen to be there: namely, Titian, Raphael, Caravaggio, Rembrandt, Rubens, Van Dyck and so many others.

Madrid has two other museums besides the Prado: the Thyssen-Bornemisza and the Reina Sofia. In these other two museums one finds modern masters such as Picasso, Van Gogh, Gauguin, Toulouse Lautrec and many others. Picasso, of course, dominates; especially his massive anti-war masterpiece, *Guernica*, in the Reina Sofia. Its size is exceptionally daunting, but the work is rendered only in shades of gray with black and white touches and so simply overwhelms due to size rather than provoking the kind of wide-eyed awe and incredulity which *The Garden of Earthly Delights* elicits.

"Earthly delights." I like that. I like that for many reasons, for the Earth is indeed a place of delights, which is why we must wage the good fight to preserve it. Only will we in the end? Bosch clearly had his doubts, for all around him in those dark days there was ignorance, vice, depravity and madness. Much of humanity was little better than animals indulging in instinctive and often cruel behaviors and fighting among themselves for whatever pleasure in which they could find comfort. The greatest among these comforts have always been food and sex and so the painter offered viewers precisely that in this painting. He gave them the feastings and the erotic splendors of physicality and did not shy away from expressing this with countless nudes. At the heart of the painting, the figures dance in a great innocent, heavenly circle and they are beautiful to behold. Bosch knew well how attractive all of this was to humanity and therefore made it the central focus of the work. It is a visionary's dream of paradise.

The problem is that the instinctual side of humanity's impulses can be utterly irrational and mad, so Bosch also offered that side of things to his viewers and in a way that no Surrealist, centuries later, could possibly top.

Is the human situation any different today?

I think not. We are still mad to eat, drink and make merry... Or to find relief in pharmaceuticals or other substances. We are still caught up in countless inexplicable, irrational and often violent activities. We are still busy fighting for objects of desire and especially the pleasures of the flesh.

"In Greek literature," Thomas Moore writes in his book *The Soul of Sex*, "eros is nothing less than the magnetism that holds the entire universe together..."

Hieronymus Bosch would broach no argument with that statement, for there is more to his work than mere carnality, especially in his painting *The Garden of Earthly Delights*. Intimacy brings people, not just body to body, but face to face, mind to mind and soul to soul. Eroticism is a force of nature in a class by itself, but it should be seen as something sacred, not just deliciously sensual and profanely salacious.

Eros is indeed an overwhelming and magnetic power, so much so, in fact, that during a shared climactic moment of intimacy the sheer physicality of it can prove so intense and electrifying that one may find one's soul rocketing off, if only briefly, into some mysterious transcendental dimension and momentarily set free.

And we do all love being set free.

The problem is that the freedom won does not last and so we must keep seeking to fly off, over and again, in ever more imaginative ways.

As Picasso once said, "You can't imagine what an everlasting need I have to break free."

Oh, we can indeed imagine it, dear Pablo... Because most of us feel the same splendid need deep, very deep, in our own beautiful, wondrous souls.

## 55

# Majestic Everest & the High Himalaya

THE STARS ABOVE DARJEELING, SIKKIM in the 3:00 a.m. darkness were mesmerizing as we made our way out onto the street and into the waiting car, but what was soon to come would prove just as sublimely mesmerizing: the sight of Mount Everest amid countless snowy Himalayan peaks in the chill scarlet dawn.

Within minutes we were gone. The driver had us bound for Tiger Hill and the sunrise to come. He had us ripping up one nameless road after the next as we made our way past many a rural home, then alongside the unfathomably vast Kanchenjunga, third highest mountain on the planet. He had us utterly wide-eyed as we wound our way up one sharp switchback after another, had us warily peering out over deep ravines and many a precipitous abyss, over silhouetted forestland wrapped in mist, over a landscape like no other on this, our beloved Earth.

We arrived on Tiger Hill just as the first luminous patches of effulgence began slowly gaining in intensity on the distant horizon.

Clambering from the Jeep, we made our way to a viewing platform and stood shivering among the scores of curious souls who had likewise come to gaze out over the pristine peaks of the mighty Himalaya. We had come for one shared purpose: to await the sovereign ascent of the Sun as it cast its magnificent golden light on Mount Everest, K2 and all of the neighboring peaks of these most famous of mountains.

Shrouded in powdery, snowy whiteness, the colossal beauty of the peaks, even in the dimness of the pre-dawn light, hinted at the incredible splendor soon to be seen. We were literally on top of the world and the scene was pure magic.

As the minutes slowly ticked by, every eye present could do little but concentrate on the boundless Milky Way above us. The sprawling, starry magnificence of it was as unfathomable as eternity itself in my mind as I stood watching it wheel its way across the sky exactly as it has done for billions of years before the existence of any human observer and will continue to do for billions of years more.

Only then, at long last, the first bold rays of sunlight came piercing upward through the darkness like beckoning beacons, climbing ever higher, stealing skyward with an intensity that was soon to leave me breathless.

The moment we were all waiting for had finally arrived.

Then there she was! The tallest mountain on Earth! Colossal, crystalline, beautiful.

Tibetans call her Chomolungma; to the Nepalese she is Sagarmatha. We westerners call her Everest, call her the Great One, call her the ultimate challenge, call her the Supreme Pinnacle of the planet.

For my part, I felt no regret that I was not climbing her, for I have never felt a need to "conquer" her steep and sacred face. For me, it was more than sufficient just to see her nestled in amid the scores of other snowy Himalayan peaks, and just that one time – yes, even from such a distance. Everest was radiant in her golden grandeur. She was stunning in her pristine perfection.

I was left staggered, left stupefied by the sight and high in my own right.

Then there was a further surprise: applause! Everyone present quite simply applauded in spontaneous unity! I was stunned. People were applauding the sunrise! This I had not expected, had never once anticipated. It was as if, inexplicably, we were all, quite suddenly, witnesses to the very glory of the gods! For the Himalayas are known as the "abode of the gods" and this was a form of confirmation. To see Mount Everest as a clear and present emanation of the gods was to seal the reality of it. Like the golden starry cosmos itself, here was an irrefutable, sublime manifestation of divine proportions and one could only revel in the wonder of it.

*How perfect,* I thought as I stood gazing. *How utterly magnificent.*

Afterwards, as the Jeep carried us swiftly back down Tiger Hill and alongside Kanchenjunga once more, as it returned us to the beautiful mountain village of Darjeeling, none of us in the vehicle spoke. We all felt as if we had been to the end of the road, to the ends of the earth itself and had witnessed the ultimate natural wonder of our enthralling, enchanted planet.

Along the way, I thought how "the road less traveled" may sound more exotic or more romantically enticing to those among us who wish an escape from the busy beaten path, desirous of excitement and adventure far from the proverbial maddening crowds, but the road *long* traveled is the one which results in wisdom.

Wisdom is what comes from the accumulation of insights into life based on personal experience.

Standing on the roof of the world and looking out over the mighty Himalaya was an unforgettable and magical experience beyond measure. In and of itself, however, such an experience cannot bring wisdom in its wake. It is not what we see in this world that makes us a greater person than we were; it is what we do. What *really* counts is how we treat others. I knew in that moment that the secret knowledge is always hiding in plain sight. Karma is our direct link to ultimate reality and the Rock of Ages is the sage within.

# 56

# The Jewel of Eternal Renewal

TO BE SANE IN A CRAZY WORLD is tricky enough, but to be wise in such a world is trickier still. Such a statement might seem an exaggeration, but for those of us who follow the daily news dispatches on the global airwaves and cable networks, the reports we encounter are generally steeped in violence and death, most of it politically, religiously or sexually motivated.

Seeing, hearing or reading such reports can make one's blood boil. The natural response is to hope that the torturers, rapists and killers among us will be brought to justice and locked away for good. We might even feel the desire for revenge and wish those persons to suffer the same fate as their victims.

Such outrage is justified, of course, but we would do well to think twice on that front and keep a certain spiritual adage in mind, namely that, "Energy flows where attention goes." In other words, if we feed energy to the idea of revenge, then that notion will grow within us and with it will come agitation. What follows on from that is stress and stress, as we know, is quite often the root cause of many, if not most, of the physical ailments with which we humans must contend. Stress weakens the immune system and that can lead to countless diseases.

While outrage in many cases is fully defensible, it is far better to realize that millions of our fellow beings have suffered terrible personal and collective injustices over the years and this cannot but have darkened their minds and hearts. In their emotional and sometimes physical pain, victims of violence often find themselves living under a cloud of distressing emotion and it narrows their openness to the light. As a result, many are driven to join in with others in an effort to right the injustices of the past. In many cases, people hand down their outrage to their own children, and those children, in turn, hand it on again in a cycle that serves only to enflame tensions in a community or a nation.

The spiritually wise do not want their children to be saddled with hand-me-down pain and anger, however. They want everyone to get beyond the atrocities and the injustices of the past, and to grow wise in their own right. The spiritually wise want every man, woman and child on the planet to become loving and compassionate, to become enlightened in some way, whether one's idea of enlightenment is defined simply as rational behavior or as some form of mystical, super conscious awakening. The spiritually wise desire peace of mind for everyone, even for perceived cultural nemeses. They want this especially for the political and religious leaders in the nations of the world and in their own societies. After all, the point of politics is to allow nations to govern its members in a fair and intelligent manner, and to prevent violence and murder, while religion is meant to keep humanity high-minded and lofty in its ideals and aspirations.

What we see and experience in today's world, however, is often almost exactly the opposite. Corruption and injustice run rampant at a governmental level in almost every nation on the planet and our major global religions are riddled with monetary fraud, exploitation of the vulnerable and prejudice against people not of the same faith.

When we see an act of foreign or domestic terrorism in the news, we cannot but realize that prejudicial violence still exists in the world. Unfortunately, it has been this way from time immemorial and we are inescapably forced to acknowledge, again and again, that it is not just one tribe, sect, religion or nation against another, but that violent outbursts can and do also happen when people within such groups turn against their very own. The storming of the U.S. Capitol on January 6, 2021 by a mob of rioters is an example of this in recent times as I write this. Here was a situation where the supporters of a president who had lost a fair and free election turned against many members of their own party, other democratically elected politicians and the police officers guarding them. They did this after being told, without a shred of evidence, that there had been massive voter fraud. The mob broke through police barriers, smashed doors and windows and went on a rampage through the Capitol edifice itself, some looking to kill certain politicians in order to stop a peaceful constitutional transfer of power. This was an act of domestic terrorism that cost people their lives and left scores of people wounded and traumatized.

Timothy Leary in his brilliant book *Neuropolitique* remarked on an event in his own day that was different from, but similarly shocking in magnitude to the Capitol riot: "America, in the past decade," he wrote, "became a spiritual Wild West with San Francisco as its Dodge City; religious gang leaders and ethical gunslingers competed for control, among them Diggers, black militants, hippie gurus, Hindu swamis, hedonic prophets, Jesus freaks, makeshift messiahs, health-food fanatics, soul pimps and hope dealers.

"Into this Byzantine situation came Manson, fresh from the academy of fear, brandishing a book that cites the highest ethical authority to justify ritual murder, a 2,000-year-old text loaded with prescription and pronunciamento designed to strike fear into nonbelievers: the book of *Revelation*."

The nine murders in four locations which Charles Manson masterminded in 1969 brought an apocalyptic end to the hippie era of peace and love. These killings shocked America as few such events ever had. With his long hair and beard (and eventually a swastika tattooed onto his forehead), this evil figure did everything in his power to start a race war in his home country. He knew that the times were like a powder keg ready to blow and he did his best to light the match that would set off the explosion he was hoping to see.

Too many among us, sadly, are consumed with fear and when such people revere and misinterpret a book like the *Revelation* of St. John the Divine, it can prove catastrophic. John was speaking of events in his own day and the Beast 666 he wrote about was a numerical reference to the Roman emperor, Nero, not Satan. The Romans, of course, had overrun the country where "John" lived and were brutal to anyone who dared to defy their authority. This is why the man expressed his anger in symbolic terms rather than saying straight out what he meant. (For a full review of this biblical text, see Bart D. Ehrman's comprehensive, scholarly tome *Heaven and Hell*.)

So entrenched are the many divisive inequities within our species that even to contemplate how we can, or should, go about changing them can seem an impossible task. Yet, for our own well-being, we must spend at least a portion of our time as individuals trying to make a positive difference in the world, however small. The best way to begin to do that is by pondering the state of our own hearts and minds, and by praying for the highest good for everyone, which I believe simply boils down to wanting everyone to equally enjoy all of the most basic of human rights.

This can be a hard thing to fight for, however, if one lives in a country that is under the sway of corrupt politicians, merciless military generals or a cold-hearted dictator. It can even be difficult in democratic countries, which the divisiveness of the political situation today once more proves.

Two truths stand out about humanity, however. One, we have an almost infinite capacity to find solutions to our problems and, two, each of us has within us something precious and eternal: a spiritual heart-essence which impels us, ever and always, toward renewal. This is true even in our darkest of hours, even when we feel as if all hope for us is lost.

To start anew again is not only possible, but life quite naturally generates such renewal. If nothing else, the healing powers of the body prove that point. Starting anew is best pursued by turning inward. Meditating even fifteen minutes a day can facilitate renewal with surprising swiftness, for we are all connected to a higher mind and a higher heart essence that is the very wellspring out of which humanity has discovered its deepest truths.

Our dreams are very revealing, as well, and can be looked at on a nightly basis for help. Emotion is the language of the soul and dreams are visual emanations of emotion, which is why they are so fluid and seemingly irrational. If we are troubled, our dreams will deliver up dark and disturbing images as a reflection of that agitation. If things are going well, our dreams will prove relatively placid. If super things are happening in our lives, our dreams might well have us soaring across an inner sky!

By opening up on a regular basis to our inner psychospiritual essence, we renew our awareness of the energy body and the soul, and it renews *us* by channeling an abundance of intelligent, emotional insights back to us. That feedback can expand our perspectives and impel us toward helpful situations via surprising synchronicities. This whole process can be intensified and accelerated if one is fortunate enough to meet a like-minded individual who shares such an approach, for two minds in concert as spiritual allies can supercharge the effort.

If any two persons happen to be physically intimate, that shared unity can even be ritualized into a form of magical praxis. I am referring here to what westerners call "sex magic" and what eastern practitioners call Tantra. Scores of books have been written on this subject and all I shall note here is what Robert Anton Wilson had to say about this topic in *Cosmic Trigger*. He writes: "It occurred to me that I finally had the secret of the Illuminati. They were not the fantasy of right-wing paranoids. 'The Illuminati' was one of the names of an underground mystical movement using sexual yoga in the

Western world. The veils of obscurity and mystery around such figures as Giordano Bruno, John Dee, Cagliostro, the original Rosicrucians (17th century), Crowley himself, and various other key figures in the 'conspiracy', had nothing to do with politics or plots to take over the world. It was a screen to protect them from persecution by the Holy Inquisition in earlier centuries and from puritanical policemen in our time." To this we might simply add that anyone who is one of the "true" Illuminati will be what the name implies: illuminated. And, if one is genuinely illuminated, this means that one has spiritually evolved to a higher stage of living where only the noblest of ideals and the most loving forms of compassion are shown to others.

By the way, fans of William Blake will be delighted to know that the renowned poet should definitely also be regarded as one of the key figures in that movement. As proof, we need only recall one of his more famous quotes: "Those who enter the gates of heaven are not beings who have no passions or who have curbed the passions, but those who have cultivated an understanding of them."

Without a doubt, there is only one way to cultivate an understanding of them: engage and indulge oneself; yes, even if it means going it alone in one's own mind should one's nearest and dearest not be inclined to so much as broach such an esoteric topic, for this is about being in control of one's own private imagery and thoughts. It's a basic human right!

How, then, can we become wise in a crazy world? By immersing ourselves as deeply as possible in the perennial wisdom of the masters and seeing the sacred in all things, even the most profane. Such mindfulness is exactly how we can help the world to become a little less crazy.

# 57

# Destination Liberation

## *A Brave New Age of Promise Is Ours for the Making*

WE ARE IN ASTRONOMICAL LUCK. According to a book entitled, *Life Beyond Death* by David Fontana, a professor of Transpersonal Psychology at Liverpool John Moores University and former president of the British Society for the Psychical Research, we are all on our way upward. While the word "upward" is metaphorical, the common understanding is that Heaven is above this Earth of ours, which is why the ancient Alchemists used to say, "As above, so below." The point is that all of us basically aspire to a "higher" way of life, and we shall have it once we pass from this planet.

This is not to denigrate how wonderful life on Earth actually is. On the contrary, according to those who have passed over and returned, this planet is a reflection of a more wondrous place existing in a parallel dimension. David Fontana is not the only researcher of near-death experiences to tell us this. The books of Doctors Raymond Moody, Kenneth Ring, Bruce Greyson and Eben Alexander, among so many others, also tell us this.

Traditionally, there are seven realms "above". The first is a hazy, shady environment much like what the Greeks called Hades. This is where a huge majority of souls go upon exiting their earthly bodies if they are not prepared mentally to pass through this region and move on to one that is filled with more light. In other words, if we spend no time in this life learning how to deepen our mental acuity, we are destined to wander about lost for a time in this murky realm. This usually passes once a soul eventually gets its bearings, however, and recognizes what has happened and asks for help, which is always available to any lost soul at any time.

Moving up and out of this dimly lit land of bewildering sights, one may pass into a land of meadows, mountains and beautiful seas, rivers and lakes. Here one may meet loved ones who will welcome us with open arms and celebratory exuberance.

After that, once we feel ready, we may move into what is known as the "Plane of Illusion", where we meet up with whatever group of souls we most resonate with and, once there, we may conjure all manner of wonders for ourselves, so long as what we magically conjure is in general congruence with those of our soul group.

In time (so to speak here, for time moves very differently in this realm), we may choose to move on to what is known as the "Plane of Color". Here the beauty is unspeakably magnificent and wonderful beyond measure. Fontana writes, "The Plane of Color seems to represent an end to sickness and suffering, a place where the power of thought replaces physical effort and where peace and love rule; and where one can follow chosen interests without the fear of failure or the stress of competition in the company of like-minded friends. In addition, the Plane of Color is attained after lengthy and demanding spiritual development on earth and in the initial levels of the afterlife. What could be more heavenly?"

Indeed! Is this not the "heaven" of our dreams? I believe that the reality of such a place has always been sensed by the more sensitive souls among us. It is most assuredly what millions of young ones in the Sixties and early Seventies sought when soaring in rapturous intoxication, believing that a New Age was dawning before their very eyes.

According to returnees who have ventured into the Great Beyond, one day we shall have that! We shall have our paradise of dreams, our divine liberation, only not here on this earth. It awaits us in a dimension to which we will have access in the future, however, if we are smart enough to navigate our way to it once we depart this world.

To do that, we need to prepare. We prepare by understanding that we are indeed living in a virtual reality, a magical matrix of phenomenal complexity, but not a technological one. Rather, we are enmeshed in a spiritually generated biological simulation of the highest magnitude and it should be seen as miraculous in the extreme. This is why we should try to make Planet Earth a better place. After all, it contains all of the environmental appearances of a paradise of dreams and serves beautifully as the perfect model for such a place. Those of us who have had the great good fortune of seeing and enjoying places like Fiji, Tahiti, Moorea and Bora Bora in the South Pacific or Caribbean islands like the Bahamas, Barbados or Jamaica know just how stunningly beautiful, perfect and paradisal such places are even though they can never actually become paradise for real. Why? Because this world is a training ground for spiritual beings, one where the stakes are life and death for a reason: the ideal challenge must be fostered by the ideal conditions. This is what makes the earth such a precious place for evolving spiritually at a personal level. When we make the effort to raise ourselves up to a greater, more expansive level of perception, we are, in effect, preparing ourselves to make the transition into a hereafter which will fulfill our highest ideal of what a heaven should be.

We best earn this privilege, it seems, by desiring to bring every soul on earth along with us, for once our hearts are this expansive, we will *deserve* the paradise of our dreams. This is not to say, however, that we will succeed in bringing even one person along with us as we aspire to such a goal. We may, but we must not assume nor expect that we will. The *intention* of hoping to do so, quite uncannily, will nevertheless work magic for us.

Others, for their part, must do the same for themselves when the time is ripe for them. It may be in this life or in one to come, for we cannot impose our will on anyone; each of us is a sovereign soul, which means that each of us must work to secure our own fate and destiny. Nevertheless, despite knowing this, we must have it in our hearts that our efforts will contribute in some way to raising humanity as a whole.

What is the best way to go about this? Prayer and meditation are certainly beneficial, but there is one thing that tops all other efforts to be made. That is by helping others. As Meher Baba, the Indian spiritual master, once put it: "No amount of prayer or meditation can do what helping others can do." This is a hugely important and significant statement.

We must help where we can, in other words, but know as we do that we can never force anyone to appreciate whatever help we freely give. We must have no expectation, in fact, that any effort we make will be appreciated in any way, shape or form. Such an attitude is what serves to keep the effort pure. It is what keeps the effort untainted by an ulterior motive.

It might, therefore, be wise to think of this planet as Boot Camp Earth. Run the obstacle courses, climb the walls, scale the mountains and cross the rivers, but by putting others ahead of ourselves as we go along, we simply become expressions of love. We gain no merit from any higher power, but at the same time, we generate the most beneficial karma for ourselves that it is possible to generate.

In brief, the truly liberated soul thrives on generating harmony instead of hard feelings and loves cooperation more than competition. Helping others is not just the right thing to do. It is the heavenly thing to do. How beautiful.

# 58

# The Phenomenal, Indomitable Human Spirit

BE INSPIRED. BE *VERY* INSPIRED. This is what we should tell ourselves every day, for this world of ours is a treasure trove of possibilities. One need only look at what we humans have brought into existence in the realms of the creative arts and scientific innovation, and one is left marveling. Clearly, the fire of desire occupies a very special place among evolution's prime directives, for otherwise, the intensity of that passion would not be so compelling. After all, if nature cared only that we survive, we humans would be as incapable of self-awareness as the insects, the animals, the birds of the air and all the creatures of the sea.

Humans do more than survive, however. We thrive.

Over the centuries, we have fought against stifling heat and the freezing cold, beasts of the wild, deadly diseases and so much more. We have organized ourselves into tribes and nations, erected great governments, cities and monetary systems, invented innumerable necessities and created fantastic cultural artworks. We have also surrounded ourselves with wondrous luxuries and technological marvels. We have triumphed in too many ways to count.

That's not all. We have tended, not only to our physical interests, but to our metaphysical intrigues, as well.

Hardcore scientific materialists doubtless believe that far too many of us delude ourselves, however, in terms of what is possible as biological entities born of sheer happenstance. Admittedly, we're great, they say, but only in a limited manner. Yes, we can dream big in certain imaginative ways. We can seek and achieve worldly fame and fortune. We can grow intellectually and thereby become acclaimed in a specific field such as business, science, politics or the arts. We can even win our ideal lover if we are charming and persistent enough.

What no hardcore scientific materialist will agree to, though, is that humanity possesses an innate ability to achieve spiritual salvation or enlightenment, or to obtain psychic powers or enjoy survival beyond this physical, material world in which we now find ourselves.

Scientific materialists, of course, believe that the brain generates consciousness, as well as the sense of self we experience as human beings and that with the demise of the body these sensate qualities simply cease.

Yet, from a certain perspective, one might say that if our consciousness and sense of self are "only" the product of a physical organ known as the brain, then the dreams that the brain conjures are still pretty spectacular.

According to polls, however, most of us believe that there is, indeed, an actual spiritual dimension and that our essential being is what we call the "soul". The soul, most say, continues on after the demise of the physical body and subsequently resides in a realm that is both boundless and eternal in nature.

Despite these major differences of ideation and perception, the one thing that can be definitively stated is that even if our sense of self is but an illusory figment of electrochemical processes, it is still phenomenal and remarkable, for even an atheist can live a robust, moral, creative and fulfilling life, despite having nothing but oblivion on his or her personal horizon.

This implies that, at the very least, the human spirit is an immaterial, evanescent "something" possessed of a numinous, transcendental quality of some nature. It is a quality that is inherent to our essential being, even if that essence is limited and given to a sense of boundlessness only within the sphere of the human imagination.

While brain activity may be the source of the self-reflexive mind, the possibility exists that the psychospiritual complex might not only be real but sourced in a supraluminal plane; a domain where energy and information actually move faster than the speed of light as we know it in this universe of ours. After all, neuroscientists admit, straight out, that they cannot prove that the brain gives rise to consciousness and a few have even argued that the brain may indeed be more like a radio or television transceiver, mediating waves of energy and information external to it, rather than being the actual generator of thought and perception. Some cutting-edge thinkers have even gone so far as to propose that the one thing that may be genuinely supraluminal within our cosmos – specifically within us – is thought itself.

Thought, of course, is an activity of the mind and if the mind is indeed sourced in a supraluminal plane, then the possibility exists that the mind may not be bound by the laws of physics as we know them. Perhaps this can account for such "impossible" phenomena as telepathy, remote viewing, psychokinesis, clairvoyance, out of body experiences, and other events of "high strangeness".

One of the most esteemed psychoanalysts of all time, Carl Jung, postulated that there may indeed be a supraluminal dimension and that dimension may be the source of the archetypal forces which shape psychic reality. Archetypes are a recurrent constellation of motifs within each of us that drive us toward a definitive destiny.

What archetypes are believed to do is propel us into acts of heroism, transform us into lovers, mothers, fathers, teachers, political or religious leaders, soldiers, police officers, merchants, artists, dramatic actors and comedic tricksters, among other roles (some of a dark nature, unfortunately, such as dictators, murderers, thieves and gangsters, for example).

In short, these recurrent forces are what motivate the human spirit.

Ideally, of course, that motivation is for noble ends, not for greedy or evil ones.

Perhaps, what drives each of us to continually reach for all that we desire in this life (both the possible and seemingly impossible) is down to the particular archetypes that dominate within each of us. We must remember, however: there are karmic implications to all that we do. As we sow, we reap.

One thing is certain: the more creative we are with our personal energetic constellation of psychic dominants, the more powerful they become.

So, yes, be inspired! Be *very* inspired (rather than "afraid, very afraid"), I say, and create in a positive manner as you desire with boundless passion. We can do that for the duration of this known lifetime or go further and choose to create as if there is *not only* tomorrow, but all of eternity in which to enrich ourselves and everyone else in this amazing world of ours.

In brief, we humans are blessed in too many ways to count and that is down to one thing: the phenomenal, indomitable spirit within.

## 59

# Intimacy with the Cosmos

THE CATHEDRAL OF STARS which fills the heavenly firmament in the night is the greatest wonder that nature has on offer. While our planet is exceptionally blessed with majestic forests, beautiful mountains, rivers and oceans, with staggering windblown deserts and gleaming, snowy white landscapes, one must remember that there are worlds numbering in the billions in the Milky Way Galaxy alone, and quite possibly numbering in the trillions in this vast universe of ours as a whole.

Whether those worlds contain life forms or not, the planets that orbit about the stellar orbs which populate the cosmos are still magnificent and spectacular.

To imagine such worlds while out under the stars at night can be about more than briefly gazing on a dazzling celestial light show, however. It can actually turn into a healing and transcendent experience if one is willing to spend more than a few cursory minutes looking up in awe, for such an experience can have genuinely regenerative and therapeutic benefits.

When we are down and out, so to speak, this state of affairs generally comes about because one is overwhelmed by the events in one's life. The mind, obsessed with a particular problem, can have us feeling as if the walls are closing in and that we are trapped. The whole world can then seem to be only about the particular problem that has us so worried. As a result, the same thoughts keep swirling round and round in our head like an agitated whirlpool, one from which there seems to be no escape.

There is an escape, however, even if one feels at "rock bottom".

Actually, rock bottom is a great place to start looking up

at the stars at night and remembering the celestial connection which unites humanity to absolutely everything in the entire cosmos.

This feeling of unity offers a constructive contrast to the isolation that can dog one when one is feeling trapped in a vortex that swirls round and round within, generating pressure and stress, and even a sense of hopelessness.

Going out under the stars at night is a positive way of escaping our problems. Once we are out in the peace of the countryside, the landscape and the sky can open us up.

Neuroscientists have discovered that the brain contains what are called "mirror neurons". These neurons mimic what is perceived by the person. When we see people struggling with difficult circumstances, for example, the mirror neurons within us fire in such a way as to trigger a sympathetic response. Or when we empathize with people when they speak to us and tell us whatever their particular issue of the day is that empathy occurs owing to neurotransmitters and electrochemical activity that cascades down through the body and suffuses it with a strong emotional reaction to the person's situation.

Obviously, there can be a positive or a negative reaction to events. On the positive front, serotonin, dopamine, oxytocin, vasopressin and endorphins can put us on a high, fill us with infatuation for someone and block pain. On the negative front, there are stress hormones, adrenaline, cytokines, histamine and cortisol, that can affect us.

Most of us, of course, desire pleasure over pain and make every effort to pursue the former and avoid the latter.

One simply cannot live in today's world and not experience an entire range of emotions, however. No one, not even the exceptionally wealthy, can avoid some level of pain, some level of disappointment, some level of agony concerning the events in their lives, even if they only listen to the news, for their mirror neurons are going to cause a reaction within. The job of these "molecules of emotion" is to trigger adrenal cascades and cause a person to feel empathy or sympathy, even though none of the problems depicted may ever be of direct concern.

The proof is easy enough to experience just by watching newsclips of people in war-torn countries trying desperately to escape the murderous and destructive ways of military and paramilitary groups.

We may frame war in today's world as a "third world" problem, but the so-called "first world" is brimming with serious mental health issues. The violence, murder and suicide rates are quite simply through the roof, so to speak, and our newspapers and news broadcasts reflect that in an all too graphic manner.

This is precisely why we all need to get out under the stars once in a while and gaze up at that awesome spangling of celestial wonder which hovers in heavenly splendor above us. That heavenly vista is there to be seen, night after night, but it is up to each of us whether we will choose to get out under it and enjoy and appreciate it or not.

No matter how it came into being, the cosmos is the source of our physicality and to be intimate with it is, far and away, the ultimate expression of appreciation for the life that we humans have been given.

## 60

# The Astonishing Nature of Ultimate Reality

THE TRUE NATURE OF REALITY has been a mystery for countless millenniums. While historians conventionally date the rise of civilization to some five thousand years ago in Sumer, more recent archaeological finds, such as at the place known as Gobekli Tepe in Turkey, have pushed that date back to at least twelve thousand years or more.

Western civilization's rise toward philosophical sophistication is generally attributed to the Greeks, although the famous Greek philosopher and mathematician Pythagoras would – if he were able to comment – definitely offer a respectful nod toward Egypt for the knowledge and wisdom which he obtained from that great nation. Egypt, of course, had a high civilization that lasted longer than any other empire in human history.

Since those days when the insights of the Greek philosophers reigned over western thought in terms of the nature of reality, we have had quite a number of European philosophers and theologians who have subsequently added their voices to the ongoing debate and in richly complex and deeply refined terms.

Has any form of absolute consensus ultimately been reached, however?

The short answer is no.

Add in all of the astonishingly complex mathematical and conceptual models on the nature of reality by 20th century physicists and surely humanity has completed the great picture, yes?

Actually, no.

Humanity is still without an absolute consensus on the ultimate nature of reality despite every effort by men like Einstein, and all of the great physicists who came after him, to delve as profoundly as possible into the realms of quantum mechanics and astrophysics.

Theologians, on the other hand, insist that the universe – "reality" in other words – is a magical, mystical, miraculous conjuration of a Supreme Being known as "God".

Only how did this "God" come into being? Theologians say that God simply "always was and always will be". They say that God is eternal and exists outside of – or beyond – time as we know it and that is what makes God the "Unmoved Mover", the timeless Creator of All That Is.

Of course, such an argument is unfathomable to virtually any and every human being, for we are entities subject to spacetime and the laws which prevail throughout the material domain. As a consequence, everything for a human being *must* have a beginning. Yes, even "God" must have had a start at *some* point. We simply cannot think otherwise or fathom how it could be any other way.

Scientific materialists, in contrast to the theologians, admit that they do not know how "something/anything" can spring from "nothing", but somehow or other that is essentially what happened. The universe burst into being with a Big Bang – a purely random explosive event – which after billions of years of evolution generated the cosmos as we know it.

Scientists, of course, are highly intelligent members of our species and their views are assuredly not to be dismissed, but purely from the point of view of sheer logic, this claim cannot be valid. Energy of such a colossal magnitude simply cannot have come into existence from nothing. That is impossible.

So, here we are then, essentially left with this great conundrum, this utterly inexplicable, mind-boggling enigma. Neither science nor religion is able to explain how we ourselves and all that we experience came to be and, in the last analysis, must admit that the first cause of "reality" is simply "unfathomable" and always will be.

Yet, "something" has indeed come from "nothing". How, we have no idea.

Curiously, according to mystics, metaphysicians and yogis, and to those who have had out-of-body or near-death experiences, the ultimate nature of reality is indeed "eternal" – meaning it exists in a state of being which lies outside of – or beyond – time as we humans conventionally know it. These claimants insist that they have actually traveled into other planes of being in some inexplicable way and have personally experienced the authenticity of these dimensions. Once there, some have even claimed to have encountered nonhuman and nonphysical beings of a higher intelligence and more than a few have even claimed to have found themselves in the presence of "God". Quite a few of these explorers of alternative dimensions even go so far as to insist that either "God", "advanced spiritual entities" or "beings of light" have actually explained the ultimate nature of reality to them.

The problem these claimants have once they return to our time-based, material domain is that human languages simply *cannot* explain reality's ultimate nature as told to them by the aforementioned nonphysical or nonhuman entities. This, they imply, is why virtually all philosophers, theologians and physicists throughout the whole of human history have never been able to reach consensus on the enigma of our origin, or the origin of the universe, not in absolute or unequivocal terms.

To our frustration, this is where the debate stands after thousands of years of pondering the great mystery of how we humans came to be.

But…

Is the answer not obvious?

Put simply, we are left in the peculiar situation of having to *infer* that the ultimate nature of reality is *not* time-based. It does not have a beginning and it will not have an end. Why? Because it is of another persuasion altogether. It exists in a completely different way than the spacetime continuum which we physically inhabit.

This is precisely why all time-based concepts, models, paradigms and words cannot elucidate the essential nature of our primary reality, the one that gave birth to the secondary reality we inhabit as human beings. The problem, therefore, is that we humans conceive – erroneously it appears – our cosmos to be primary when it is not.

To put it another way, *here* is the quantum leap in thinking which we must make. We are forced to acknowledge that we can only explain reality in *relative* terms, but not in *absolute* terms and this is why the models and paradigms which have been put forward by our theologians, philosophers and physicists over the centuries cannot and will never explain the nature of our origin.

Thus, we are left to conclude once again that reality is simply and ultimately *unfathomable*.

Perhaps, however, just perhaps, when we do die, we – like all the mystics, metaphysicians and yogis in history, and like those who have experienced out-of-body adventures and near-death experiences – will then finally be able to understand the ultimate nature of reality. We will comprehend how "reality" can actually have no beginning and no end, and we will fathom how it can be that the origin of "All That Is" simply is.

We will not, however, understand this phenomenon by stringing word-based concepts together, yet we *will* understand. We will be made to comprehend this amazing information in some manner other than via human lingual constructs, a manner which is beyond time-based words. That knowledge, in short, will be impressed upon us in some telepathic way and we will then get it. We will know, but not before then.

According to mystics, metaphysicians, yogis and those who have had out-of-body and near-death experiences, this is precisely what we *should* expect, however. We *will* have all of the answers at that point, they say, and those answers are simpler than we suppose, but words cannot and will never be able to convey the explanation we are looking for in full while we are an inhabitant of this material domain we call the universe.

So, while this is heartening on the one hand, it is frustrating on the other because we want that explanation here and now!

Still, it does give one pause to be hopeful, for it summons the possibility that virtually all of the great riddles, enigmas and mysteries of existence will be settled forever for us at some juncture, namely in the Great Beyond.

At that point, of course, if such does come to pass, we will ourselves have moved beyond time and into the timeless realm of eternity itself.

What this means, if we are willing to settle for such a view, is that we've essentially got it made *already*. After all, if this is our source, then we're already at one with it. It is already our own ultimate nature.

And so, despite the life and death struggles of the gross material world we now inhabit, we might well choose to tell ourselves that we have a very specific reason to be joyous. That reason is a time-based concept, but it *points* to an *Otherworld* which is greater than this universe – and by "greater" I mean in a sense that has nothing to do with size. I am speaking here of magnitude and scope, for spacetime as we know it here on Earth is apparently not the foundational basis of that realm.

Many of those who have visited that realm, by the way, insist that all time-based events as experienced here in this world are actually experienced in that domain in a state of simultaneity. That is past, present and future are all of a unified whole and encountered in their totality by the perceiver. Quite intriguingly, some have reported that they not only see their past life presented to them in this simultaneous fashion but experience multiple past lives at the very same moment and even see a variety of potential futures for themselves.

This, of course, confirms that we humans do live more than one life and that reincarnation is real. It does not *prove* it, but it certainly offers us a strong suggestion that this is what happens and is, therefore, very much a part of our greater reality.

By the way, it has been suggested by various metaphysicians that the reason we do not remember our past lives while experiencing this life is for a very significant reason: If we were able to experience the full scope of our existence over multiple lives it would, by necessity, require that we perceive the past, present and future simultaneously. Seeing the past is one thing, of course, and the future another. Seeing into the future means that we would see the time and place of our own death in this life and that would be detrimental to us for several reasons. It would alter all of our motivations to live spontaneously and convince us that we do not enjoy free will, for example, and instill in us a sense of dread as the year and day drew ever nearer. Uncertainty is what keeps life intriguing, and the surprise of novelty is one of life's wondrous astonishments. After all, novelty is just another word for that great open spacetime future before us in which we get to enjoy fresh streams of experience.

Those who have returned from the Great Beyond have on the rare occasion been given information about future events that have subsequently come true. There is no way that anyone in that dimension could know what will transpire in the future unless they were indeed able to experience the past, present and future in some simultaneous fashion. This tells us that such is, indeed, the reality of that domain and this "fact", if it be so, does bolster the notion that the Great Beyond does transcend time as we know it and that it exists in a timeless way.

In brief, the world as we currently experience it is a place of beginnings and endings, but such seems not to be the case in that otherworld. In that otherworld, nothing begins or ends, which means that all is birthless and deathless.

That seems incomprehensible and impossible from our

perspective here on this planet and, perhaps even too good to be true, but if the logic is valid, then such may indeed be the case, even if it is counterintuitive.

The conclusion we may, if we wish, draw from this is that we are only born and die in *this* world, *not* in that otherworld, which means: if in that realm all is birthless and deathless, then we ourselves are birthless and deathless; it means that we are eternal, even now, even here.

To my way of thinking, this is not just a fantastic revelation. It is the best revelation of any.

## 61

# A Spiritual Power of Atomic Intensity

SPIRITUALITY IN THE 21$^{ST}$ CENTURY comes – literally – in a billion different forms. For some, spirituality is about staying very down to earth, while for others spirituality is to be taken so far into the extreme that some even lash out violently against competing traditions. Others again believe that it is sufficient to stand in awe of the amazements of nature or eagerly evoke the supernatural and muse passionately about all manner of *otherworldly* powers.

In short, there are those who are very sensible about their spirituality and those who will kill for it. There are those who claim to have had "mystical" or "extraordinary" experiences and those who believe that such experiences are forms of hallucinatory lunacy.

There are also those that claim to be in contact with angels and those who assert quite the opposite: that they have daringly consorted with demons. There are those who chant mantras and those who cast spells. There are those who look to the heavens for allies from space and those who claim to channel entities from other dimensions.

Some believe that the God of Love will bring all souls safely home in the end, while others again believe in eternal damnation and argue that an Armageddon-sized battle between good and evil must one day come to pass because the prophets of yore have said so. They also say that only by following a certain prescribed belief system will anyone be saved from this all-consuming, explosive conflagration when it does come.

All of this speaks volumes about spirituality.

Clearly, it is a free-for-all.

The actions and reactions which revolve around spirituality,

I think, go on and on for a very simple reason: Every human being has a unique viewpoint as to what spirituality is and how it plays out in this life. That viewpoint is usually one based on familial and cultural traditions, which subsequently become modified over the years by whatever happens to occur at a personal level to any particular one of us.

We are all influenced by others, of course, but we do tend to resonate with those espousing viewpoints with which we are most comfortable. We also tend to read the books and articles which reinforce the views that we have gradually built up over time and only rarely do people make a radical departure from the viewpoint they have created over time, especially in their earliest years. Eventually, millions of people end up living in information bunkers of their own construction.

What are we to think about the state of humanity at this juncture in history? Are we still medieval in our spirituality or are we well on our way to a 21st century version of spirituality, one that acknowledges human equality regardless of race, religion, nationality or predilections at a personal level?

Will we yet save ourselves from self-destruction and give our children a better world when all is finally said and done, or not?

The future of humanity rides on the answers we give and the actions we take. One thing seems certain: we humans stake our very "souls" on the outcome of those answers.

Do I believe we can overcome the many challenges we now face?

I do.

Humanity's spirit is strong. In fact, I believe that it is so strong and powerful that this is the reason why the entire universe exists as it does.

We will go on, I think, and we will do so with all of the infinite, eternal power that the Source of All That Exists has bequeathed us; namely, a spirituality of atomic intensity.

We must remember the wise words found in the Bhagavad

Gita: "The soul can never be cut to pieces by any weapon, nor burned by fire, nor rotted by water, nor weathered away by wind."

The soul is unbreakable. It is indestructible. It cannot be fractured or split apart. It can even survive an atomic bomb blast.

If that isn't cause for optimism, what is?

So do not fear, but at the same time take no chances, for the flesh is fragile in the last analysis and we are in the flesh for a reason. We are here to experience duality in all its many myriad manifestations. The more we experience, the wiser we become. The wiser we become, the more enlightened we are.

What that might be worth in the next life might possibly be this: we will never, ever suffer again.

# 62

# The Light That Flies Forever

IN THE CLIMATE CHALLENGED, politically polarized environment in which we are clearly living today, we humans appear to be heading steeply toward dystopia and retreating ever further from the possibility of creating any form of utopian wonder world upon this planet of ours, which is troubling indeed.

Whether or not this is genuinely true, however, the current situation does make invoking positivity and cooperation more crucial than ever.

At a personal level, how do we stay positive when ideological belief seems to take precedence over fact by so many?

To put the dimensions of that possibility into a scenario of stark contrast, we need only look at the magnitude of challenge we faced at the dawn of the atomic era.

At some point in the early stages of that era, someone came up with the clever acronym M.A.D., which stands for Mutually Assured Destruction. In effect, it implies that if one nation sets the atomic rockets flying against another, those under attack will launch their own arsenal and then it will be, "Goodbye, world" for all of us.

In the atomic and nuclear theaters, 99% of the human race is excluded from the decision-making process as to how many bombs should be manufactured, where they should be placed and when or if a nation should use them. Considering that virtually every man, woman and child, every animal and sea creature, every plant on the entire planet will either die a swift and fiery death or a very agonizing, slow and painful one of excruciating proportions, this is indeed madness.

What is also madness is that the combined atomic bomb

power in today's world is said to be the equivalent of one million Hiroshimas.

One *million*!

Talk about a staggering fact!

Now imagine all-out war in light of that fact.

Or perhaps we better not! Perhaps we had better believe that the world's leaders, right around the globe, are all wise and fair-minded individuals who understand that Mutually Assured Destruction is to be avoided at all costs. Our hope should be that these leaders fully comprehend what J Robert Oppenheimer meant when he uttered his notorious words upon the detonation of the first atomic bomb: "Now I am become Death, the destroyer of worlds…"

If the atomic and nuclear arsenals are set loose, of course, there will not even be a dystopia left for any of us, let alone some mythical utopia of our dreams.

This is not the case, however, in terms of either a biological pandemic, climate change or the polarization of our politics. In comparison to the devastation of an all-out nuclear war, as it were, these are significantly lesser in magnitude and scope, and above all, manageable to a very high degree. Fact: action can be taken; compromise can be achieved; time is still on our side, however slight it might be! Each of us has a voice and a choice. We can take steps at a personal level to turn things around in these arenas and demand that our government, corporate and industrial leaders act decisively, at once, to relieve the ever-escalating issues we face at a collective level.

Surely, we can set our polarized, ideological beliefs aside in the name of saving the planet or in promoting economic cooperation that is to everyone's benefit. Surely any global challenge or concern which can be seen by one and all as a Mutually Assured Detriment is simply another form of M.A.D.

The Planet Earth is the only home we have, after all. We know this.

Therefore, for the love of our children and all the generations to come, why not work together to fight climate change as we globally cooperated with each other in an effort to defeat the coronavirus pandemic? What we now know from that experience is that humanity can think and act globally.

I believe that what we humans will be one day will astonish us. We have already surprised ourselves in too many ways to count and tomorrow promises to be even more astounding, for we are already living in the light that flies forever.

This is why tomorrow will take us into the heavens.

It will take us to the stars.

## 63

# Our Colossal Improbable Cosmos

HEAVENLY DELIGHTS await us in the night. They call to us with a kind of mysterious celestial telepathy that never fails to capture the enraptured imagination; not of the true lover of all things astronomical, for the cosmic spectacle that graces the night sky of this Earth is magical, it is beguiling, it is profoundly enchanting.

Those who live in the country or out in the wilderness are exposed to this spangling of wonder whenever the night sky is clear, but city dwellers get only a pale version with which they must make do at the best of times. Those who live in the city, therefore, must pursue their love of the stars when they can; be it on a holiday island, while vacationing in the desert, camping in the mountains or being out at sea on a ship that is either pressing full speed ahead into the nocturnal darkness or is anchored at bay and happily rocking with the lapping waves.

How and where it comes about, however, is purely incidental. The important consideration is whether or not one takes the time to *really* look when one can. A passing glance will only satisfy a little bit. To fully feast the eyes and mind with a fuller appreciation of the light show which dwarfs our world by a factor of trillions to one, we must break away from everyone and head off on our own. We must make a solo journey into the darkness or at least wander about in the night with someone who understands that "silence" can be "golden" in a literal, as well as a figurative, sense!

The crucial point is that an *effort* is required to fully drink in the magnitude and scope of the grandeur of the cosmos that surrounds us. Too often, unfortunately, we are so caught up in the events of our lives that we don't bother with casting so much as a glance at it. We concentrate, instead, on our troubles and worries, our hopes and dreams, while ceaselessly wracking our brains trying to figure out how we can achieve a better life for ourselves.

Such a state of affairs can render one *unappreciative* of humanity's place in the heavenly scheme of things and that is to one's detriment.

Whether we believe that a Supreme Creator conjured the staggering reality we call the universe or that the whole of it simply erupted into being purely by chance, what raises the experience to a higher, more profound, level is realizing just how *improbable* the mere existence of such a vast universe truly is and reveling in that fact.

The odds are so against it, astrophysicists tell us, that we are lucky to be here at all.

The unlikeliness of such an unfathomably great universe existing in any form can only be fully appreciated by getting out under the stars at night and deeply grasping the fact that we are not apart from this astonishing greatness. It is our eyes, our minds, our hearts that drink in this awesome phenomenal spectacle. We are the ones who attest to the actuality of it. That makes us *vital* to it.

Some astronomers have remarked that the Earth is small and insignificant in the greater scheme of things; that our planet travels along with its host star far from the center of the action at the heart of our galaxy; that our sun is not particularly substantial in size; that we really ought to be humble about our place in the cosmos. "The universe does not revolve around us," they say. "We humans are fairly trivial adjuncts to our planet, in fact, and worse, we are dangerous and destructive creatures who are collectively destroying it."

There is some truth to those assertions, of course, and being humble about our place aboard Spaceship Earth is wise, but trivial we are not. We are immensely important. We are the only known beings who can cognize and, therefore, *recognize* how unlikely and grand this universe is.

Are we driving our habitat to ruin, though? We are, but that is down to the slow arc of our evolutionary development as a species. We have proven ourselves almost too adept at surviving. We have done so with but a weak and flawed view of how fragile our host planet is.

Fortunately, human intelligence is now increasing at an exponential rate, so there is great hope that we will gain an authentically holistic perspective in time to save ourselves and our planet.

Pessimists will offer only skepticism and doubt to such a notion.

Optimists will take action and do their part.

Will it be enough to make a genuine difference, however?

Yes, it will. Count on it. Humanity is tremendously capable of sustaining itself. The biggest lesson of all revolves around a very elementary fact: to sustain ourselves we need to sustain our environment, our biosphere, the whole of our planetary home.

And we *are* central to something…

From an earthly point of view the observable universe is 46 billion light years in all directions. We are at the center of this particular sphere, this sector, of the universe. Any planet that likewise harbors sentient, self-reflective life similar to our own will see the universe in the same way we do. They, too, will be at the center of an observable sector of the whole. They, too, will be significant and vital to that region of the universe.

If such beings do exist, I hope that they have evolved enough to gaze in awe upon the spangling of unfathomable grandeur that surrounds them. I hope that they, too, understand how *improbable* such a colossal spectacle actually is and, therefore, *appreciate* how miraculous in magnitude and scope it truly is, and subsequently take care to preserve their place in it by treating their home planet with the respect it deserves.

Appreciation is a simple thing, but it is one of humanity's most remarkable of virtues. Whether one is an atheist, an agnostic or one of the religious faithful of this world, there is every reason to deeply comprehend that a virtue such as "gratitude" is a measure of the greatness of the human spirit.

I think it is a testament to humanity's evolutionary development that many "get it" about this universe of ours; they get how wondrous and majestic and colossal and improbable it truly is...

And because of that, they treat this Earth with the respect it deserves and *requires*.

There is no question on one front: We *are* lucky. Probability has come out on our side. It has favored us.

The cosmos came into being. It is here, it is real, and we are the ones who know that.

# 64

# Stardust Ever After

THE MILKY WAY GALAXY is so huge that 225 million years are required for our solar system to make a single rotation about it and that is by traveling at 514,000 miles per hour through space! This phenomenally extended voyage is known as a Galactic Year.

The orbit of the Earth, meanwhile, as it circles about the Sun on its yearly journey at 66,600 mph traces out an ellipse, as well as a spiral. The spiral movement is the result of the entire solar system racing through space at a speed that truly staggers the imagination.

As the solar system and the Earth move against the backdrop of stars that surround us, another motion is traced out. It is a flight that takes roughly 25,800 – 25,920 years. This is a trip through what is called the ecliptic. This orbit is known as a Great, or Platonic, Year and, while traversing it, we Earthlings are cycling through what we call the twelve signs of the Zodiac.

Dividing the Platonic Year by twelve, we get an average of 2160 years, which is how long it takes for the Earth to roughly pass through any particular sign of the Zodiac. There is some question at present as to whether or not we have yet moved on from the Age of Pisces and entered, fully and completely, into the Age of Aquarius. Some astrologers say yes, others say no. If not, there is certainly less than a century before we do enter into it fully.

Mark Booth in *The Secret History of the World* says that in the olden times, "The night sky was a living history, because the heavenly bodies were seen as the material bodies of spiritual beings or gods. The ancients believed that they had the ability to communicate with these beings and felt their influence."

Mercury, Venus, Mars, Saturn, Jupiter, Neptune, Uranus, these were *living* beings, not huge conglomerations of gases and matter. The Earth herself was known as Gaia. She was humanity's mother and was revered right around the globe by many names.

It was believed in olden days that these celestial "gods" were so powerful that they affected all life upon our planet. At times, when one particular god reigned over the others, a period of tranquility or war could result, depending upon whether that god promoted harmony in the world or discord.

If the gods themselves happened to be at war with one another, there could be absolute chaos unleashed in the heavens. Such chaos could wreak havoc on our planet as well.

We now know that the various planets in our solar system have a gravitational effect on each other and that, depending on their relative position to one another, the planets can have an effect on the electromagnetic field all about us. We, as electromagnetic beings in our own right, can feel this effect or, at the very least, have our moods altered by this activity.

In fact, we humans are far more influenced by "cosmic forces" than we realize. This is especially true in the realm of the mind, for once *thought* interacts with the brain, it gets swirled about in the electromagnetic fields to which the body is ceaselessly subjected.

The Moon, we know, can have a palpable effect on our planet and us, but more powerful, by far, than either the Moon or the planets is the Sun. This is why the Sun-god was always the ultimate Supreme Being. Whether that god's name was Atum, Ra, Helios, Sol, Apollo, Ahura Mazda or some other name, this god was the central focus of humanity for very obvious reasons. The life-giving rays of the Sun were indispensable to the growth and sustenance of the animal and vegetable kingdoms. Even the soil itself came from star bodies like the Sun to give us our vital minerals and elements.

Without the Sun, and without a cosmos filled with such suns, we humans would not exist. Without star power – the gods – there would be nothing.

And so the universe turns... It revolves in what we can only imagine is the "void" of space and we are the eyes that witness that revolution. The very word *universe* itself means "one turn", essentially one unified "thing", the many in the one, all things turning together, forever and anon.

To fully comprehend the interconnectedness of all things and to fully fathom how each and every living thing has an effect on every other living thing in the whole of existence is crucial to gaining a higher perspective on the human condition. As the Wisdom Master, Gungtang, says, "If you understand interdependence, you understand ultimate reality. If not, then you don't."

Jung called the "gods" archetypal forces and wrote at length about how these forces shape the human psyche. He believed that the archetypes are inherent forces that drive human behavior and compel people to act in certain ways. While every person is "constellated" with these inherent forces, certain archetypes are clearly more dominant than others within each of us. To be an indomitable warrior, a formidable leader, a fantastic mother, a prodigious intellectual, a great healer or to have any other "natural born" talent is said to be down to these forces.

We humans, however, are not mere puppets. We have free will and even though we are driven to act in a certain way, our proclivities do not ultimately determine how the archetypes will play out for us. A warrior, for example, can act for good or evil. He or she can defend life or take life. A formidable leader, likewise, can persuade people to act for the greater good or whip up the masses into a frenzy of fear and hatred. Such a person can even talk followers into marching off to war.

History is the legacy of how humanity has used its inherent proclivities in conjunction with free will for good or ill.

Highly driven people lead the way and others choose to follow or not follow.

Sometimes, of course, the freedom to choose has been denied the masses, but where true liberty exists, "freedom" refers to what we might call "sovereignty of the soul".

Quite amazingly, the whole of human history, dating from the rise of the first high civilizations on the planet, is a scant five thousand years. That is but one-fifth of a Great, or Platonic, Year. Imagine what humanity will be like in another five thousand years! Imagine what humanity will be like when this Earth has cycled the full Zodiac. Or try, if you dare, to imagine what humanity might be like when a full galactic voyage of 225 million years has passed!

I suspect that once that full revolution has occurred humanity may be little different in a physical sense than it is now. After all, paleontologists tell us that the human body has been pretty much the same for tens of thousands, if not hundreds of thousands, of years. Perhaps the human form is actually perennially perfect!

What will definitely change is the technology, the architecture that surrounds humanity, the human lifestyle and the way we perceive and fathom life.

What will we believe when we reach that future? Will we still be making war and murdering one another, or might we actually be more spiritually advanced in a collective sense than we are now? Perhaps we will have restored the Earth to a pristine condition without any pollutants in the air, on land or in the oceans. Perhaps we will be a fully harmonious species with truly illuminated minds and hearts who act with compassion toward one another.

If we do want such a future for the progeny of the Earth, then we must make every effort to move in that direction now. We must think before we act and do the kind thing, the loving thing, the thing that serves our children, our fellow inhabitants of the Earth and the Earth itself.

Time is running out. So it seems. Scientists say that we have very few years to come to grips with climate change and bring our planet back from the brink.

Only it is not the planet that faces oblivion. It is humanity.

These are strong words. Facing into the truth of our mutual situation, however, is the only positive way forward. Otherwise, the human species will meet an unfortunate end.

We will be but stardust ever after.

Personally, I believe that the climate crisis is causing millions of people to awaken as never before. As a result, millions will choose to work in concert with one another and with clarity, integrity and love for the betterment of humanity. Finally, when enough of us have made the choice to raise ourselves up and to help blaze fresh new paths toward the rejuvenation of our species and our planet, we will succeed as never before and the way forward will be clear.

It is clear even now if only we make the effort to see it.

**Afterword**

# Each to Their Soulful Own

EVERY HUMAN BEING comes into this world in a state of perfect purity, which is a beautiful thing. Mentally, we are blank slates thrust into the world without any knowledge whatsoever. We know nothing, can think nothing and can say nothing.

Not for long, however.

At the first exultant whisper of our mother's words, we begin to set down the neural imprints which will ultimately shape our perceptions of the world for virtually the duration of our lives. Those words and all of the words that follow by everyone we subsequently come to meet or know, generate the foundation upon which we make sense of this world and existence itself.

A million, billion, trillion factors come into play every single day of our lives as we come of age and the influence these dynamic stimuli exert over us is incalculable. Over time, they literally shape our perceptions, hone our considered beliefs and mold our emotional and mental intelligence. Like it or not, this is a form of indoctrination, and it persists until the day we decide that, yes, we get it; we understand. "This life is mine now and I will do with it what I want."

Unfortunately, such a declaration of independence is a rare thing in our world. Most people simply do not even begin to fully fathom how indoctrinated into a cultural mindset they are. Furthermore, our families, our friends, our teachers, our political and religious leaders all continue to pressure us to conform to a particular worldview in both overt and furtive ways. Should we resist or rebel against the agendas and paradigms of life that these people tell us we must believe there can be hell to pay, for these generally well-meaning individuals quite literally see themselves as guardians of the social order. After all, what parent doesn't want his or her child to think as he or she thinks? What society does not want its citizenry to perceive the world as it does in a collective sense? Tradition itself is at stake, they believe.

This results in serious consequences for the would-be rebel. Certain behaviors are deemed unacceptable, and this is made clear, not only in a verbal manner, but by law. To run afoul of the "authorities", of course, is illegal and can easily make one a social pariah, an outcast and an outlaw. In religious terms, the would-be rebel soul is considered an apostate, a heretic or is just otherwise ostracized by the community. In fact, with a word by any representative of the Powers That Be, the individual viewpoint, which we consider to be so absolute and precious, can be rendered invalid, irrelevant and of little or no significance or importance. For so many, to think in any way that is not conducive to conformity with the larger community is, quite simply, taboo.

Needless to say, some societies are more liberal than others in this regard and will tolerate quite a bit of dissent, while others are frighteningly repressive and will jail a person, or destroy his or her reputation in a heartbeat, for daring to express an opinion that is contrary to the prevailing mindset.

Fortunately, those of us who happen to live in liberal democracies are quite lucky and are pretty much free to say and do what we like, providing we don't stir up too much unrest and discontent among our fellow citizenry or choose to pursue our individual agendas in a violent or destructive manner.

From a spiritual perspective, freedom of thought as an expression of human rights is what keeps a society fresh and creative. Therefore, if one sees repression, one should speak out against it. If one sees forcible indoctrination into a certain belief system, one should explain why this is not in the best interest of the individual. Where there is a perceived injustice, one should call a proverbial spade a spade.

Obviously, no one has all of the answers to everything and to paraphrase yet another proverbial verity, there is more than one way to look at any particular issue. In other words, there is more than one point of view that is valid in any ongoing discussions we might have.

In the essays and personal stories presented in this book, I offered my viewpoints and spoke my truths, but I make no claim about being "right" on every topic. After all, each of us will have at the very least a slightly different perspective on any matter under debate, so no one is going to agree with anyone else one hundred percent of the time and that is actually good. Why? Because our world is the better for having billions of points of view rather than just a few or, worst of all, only one. Variety keeps life exciting and makes one's navigation through life a wondrous challenge. It forces us to grow intellectually, emotionally and spiritually.

That we all have an equally valid viewpoint and deserve the privilege of expressing that viewpoint is not just a human right, I think, but a right of the greatest consequence. We humans are not automatons, after all, we are sentient creatures with the unique ability to fathom our own existence in deep and profound ways. This ability is precisely what makes us the superior creatures we are. It means that we can take a direct hand in our own personal and collective evolution. By pursuing worldly knowledge, we can become ever more enlightened in terms of self-knowledge.

Obviously, great forms of progress have resulted from this unique ability. Our global civilizations are a wonder to behold, and our collective achievements require countless tomes to elucidate and appreciate. Of course, there have been violent and murderous setbacks along the way, but we are still here as fate would have it, alive, thriving and surviving, despite many a shameful, barbaric and savage episode in our collective human history.

In all fairness, one must admit that more than a few of humanity's tribal or ideological battles, some horribly violent, have resulted in advancements in civilization, though one could certainly argue that if humanity had become a wiser species along the way, it would have come to this point much sooner and in an infinitely less destructive way. Nevertheless, we are where we are and can only press on. There is no changing the past, only what the future may become.

Without belaboring the point, therefore, let's just say that we are most assuredly still facing some pretty terrible ongoing political and religious unrest these days, including the ever-menacing threat of war (of a conventional or a nuclear nature) and the genuine hazard of global climate change.

These are issues which I have addressed here to some degree, but in a way that I believe is ultimately positive and encouraging. After half a century of deep contemplation on all things human, I have become profoundly convinced that each and every one of us is ultimately an immortal. I believe that we are spiritual beings of the highest order and live on beyond this life in the flesh once we "slip the mortal coil".

In fact, our spirituality is so powerful, I further contend, that while our bodies are subject to the limitations of time, genetics, disease, physical trauma and events of a natural catastrophic impact, the spirit lives on far beyond our physical demise.

Whether that is true or not and whether anyone agrees with me or not, my hope is that the reader has found inspiration in these essays and many a stimulating reason to fight the good fight on humanity's behalf with positivity and a level of intelligence that will make future generations proud of us. After all, we are more alike, we humans, than we generally think. We have all experienced the good, the bad, the beautiful and the ugly. We have enjoyed happy moments and tragically sad moments. We have felt fulfillment to some degree and known the pain of broken dreams. Because of all of that we can do much better as a species and we need to for the benefit of those yet to be born into this world. Otherwise, our descendants will never enjoy, nor inherit, the staggeringly beautiful planet we, in this present moment, so enjoy; a planet so wondrous that it could, and should be, seen as a paradise of dreams, rather than as the dystopian nightmare it is fast becoming if events continue in the direction they have been going.

The choice is for each of us to make. We must ask ourselves, therefore, will we be part of the problem or part of the solution?

Indeed, virtually all that we do or say will play into the future of our beloved home.

Let us seize the moment while we may.

# Referenced Works

Alexander, Eben, *Proof of Heaven*, Simon & Shuster, New York, 2012

Alexander, John, *UFOs: Myths, Conspiracies, and Realities*, Thomas Dunne Books, NY 2011

Alexander, John, *Reality Denied*, Anomalist Books, San Antonio, 2017

Bailey & Yates, *The Near-Death Experience*, Routledge, New York, 1996

Booth, Mark, *The Secret History of the World*, The Overlook Press, Woodstock & NY, 2008

Bramley, William, *The Gods of Eden*, Dahlin Family Press, San Jose, 1990

Bruen, Ken, *The Galway Reflections*, ASAP Publishing, Mission Viejo, CA, 2021.

Budge, E.A. Wallis, *The Egyptian Book of the Dead*, Dover Publications, New York, 1967

Buhlman, William, *Adventures Beyond of the Body*, HarperOne, New York, 1996

Buhlman, William, *Secrets of the Soul*, HarperOne, New York, 2001

Burroughs, William, *Naked Lunch*, Grove Press, New York, 1959

Cave, Nick, *And the Ass Saw the Angel*, HarperCollins, New York, 1989

Capra, Fritjof, *The Tao of Physics*, Shambhala, Berkeley, 1975

Capra, Fritjof, *The Web of Life*, HarperCollins, London, 1997

Chopra, Deepak, *Life After Death*, Rider, London, 2006

Chopra, Deepak, *The Book of Secrets*, Rider, London, 2004

Currie, Ian, *Visions of Immortality*, Element, Shaftesbury, Dorset 1998

Dyer, Wayne W., *Manifest Your Destiny*, Element, London, 1997

Ehrman, Bart D., *Misquoting Jesus*, HarperCollins, New York,

2005

Ehrman, Bart D., *How Jesus Became God,* HarperOne, New York, 2014

Ehrman, Bart D., *Heaven and Hell,* OneWorld Publications, London, 2020

Evans-Wentz, W.Y., *The Tibetan Book of the Dead,* Oxford University Press, 1960

Fontana, David, *Life Beyond Death,* Watkins Publishing, 2009

Fontana, David, *Is There an Afterlife?* O Books, Hants, UK, 2007

Gibson, William, *Mona Lisa Overdrive,* Bantam Spectra Books, New York, 1988

Gibson, William, *Neuromancer,* Ace Books, New York, 1984

Ginsberg, Allen, *Howl and Other Poems,* City Lights Books, San Francisco, 1959

Hancock, Graham, *Fingerprints of the Gods,* Arrow Books, London, 1998

Harpur, Patrick, *Daimonic Reality,* Pine Winds Press, Ravensdale, WA, 2003

Hyatt, Christopher S. *Undoing Yourself with Energized Meditation,* Falcon Press, Phoenix, 1987

Hyatt, Christopher S., *Secrets of Western Tantra,* Falcon Press, Las Vegas, 1989

Jung, C.G., *Psychological Reflections,* Princeton / Bollingen Foundation, NJ 1978

Kean, Leslie, *Surviving Death,* Three Rivers Press, New York, 2017

Kean, Leslie, *UFOs,* Three Rivers Press, New York, 2010

Keel, John A., *Operation Trojan Horse,* Anomalist Books, San Antonio, 2013

Kerouac, Jack, *On the Road,* Signet Books / New American Library, New York, 1957

Kerouac, Jack, *The Dharma Bums,* Signet Books / New American Library, New York, 1958

Kesey, Ken, *One Flew Over the Cuckoo's Nest,* Signet, New York,

1962

Kesey, Ken, *The Further Inquiry*, Viking Penguin, New York, 1990

Leary, Timothy, *Neuropolitique*, Falcon Press, Las Vegas, 1988

Marrs, Jim, *Alien Agenda*, Harper Collins, New York, 1997

Marrs, Jim, *Rule by Secrecy*, Harper Collins, New York, 2000

McKenna, Terence, *The Archaic Revival*, Harper, San Francisco, 1991

McKenna, Terence, *True Hallucinations*, Harper, San Francisco, 1993

Moore, Thomas, *The Soul of Sex*, HarperPerennial, NY, 1998

Muktananda, Swami, *The Play of Consciousness*, SYDA Foundation, South Fallsberg, NY, 2000

Narby, Jeremy, *The Cosmic Serpent*, Tarcher / Putnam Books, New York, 1998

Newton, Michael, *Destiny of Souls*, Llewellyn Publications, Woodbury, MN, 2020

Newton, Michael, *Journey of Souls*, Llewellyn Publications, Woodbury, MN, 1999

Nisker, Wes "Scoop", *Crazy Wisdom*, Ten Speed Press, Berkeley, 1990

Norbu, Namkhai, *Dream Yoga*, Snow Lion Publications, New York, 1992

Powers, John, *A Concise Encyclopedia of Buddhism*, Oneworld Publications, Oxford and Boston, 2000

Reanney, Darryl, *After Death*, Avon Books, New York, 1991

Regardie, Israel, *The Golden Dawn*, Llewellyn Publications, St Paul, MN, 1988

Ring, Kenneth, *Lessons from the Light*, Insight Books, 1998

Rinpoche, Sogyal, *The Tibetan Book of Living and Dying*, Rider, 1992

Roach, Michael, *The Diamond Cutter*, Doubleday, New York, 2000

Robertson, J.M., *Pagan Christs*, University Books, New Hyde Park, NY, 1967

Saalman, Wayne, *The Dream Illuminati*, New Falcon Publications, Las Vegas, 2010

Saalman, Wayne, *The Illuminati of Immortality*, New Falcon Publications, Las Vegas, 1992

Saalman, Wayne, *Dragonfire Dreams*, JEM Books, Dallas, 2015

Saalman, Wayne, *Crimson Firestorm Mars*, JEM Books, Dallas, 2019

Strieber, Whitley, *Communion*, Beechtree Books, New York, 1987

Strieber, Whitley, *A New World*, Walker & Collier, San Antonio, 2019

Strieber, Whitley and Kripal, Jeffrey J., *The Super Natural*, Penguin Random House, NY, 2017

Talbot, Michael, *The Holographic Universe*, HarperCollins, New York, 1991

Thompson, Keith, *Angels and Aliens*, Addison-Wesley Publishing Co., Inc., 1991

Thompson, Richard L., *Alien Identities*, Govardhan Hill Publishing, Alachua, FL, 1993

Vallee, Jacques, *Dimensions*, Anomalist Books, San Antonio, 2008

Watts, Alan, *The Book on the Taboo Against Knowing Who You Are*, Collier, NY, 1969

Whitman, Walt, *Leaves of Grass*, Aventine Press, New York, 1931

Wilgus, Neil, *The Illuminoids*, Sun Publishing, Santa Fe, 1978

Wilson, Robert Anton and Shea, Robert, *The Illuminatus Trilogy*, Dell, NY, 1975

Wilson, Robert Anton, *Cosmic Trigger*, Falcon Press, Phoenix, 1977

Wilson, Robert Anton, *Right Where You Are Sitting Now*, And / Or Press, Berkeley, 1982

Wolfe, Tom, *The Electric Kool-Aid Acid Test*, Bantam Books, New York, 1968

Zukav, Gary, *The Dancing Wu Li Master*, Rider, London, 1979

Zukav, Gary, *The Seat of the Soul*, Fireside, New York, 1990

# About the Author

**Wayne Saalman** was born in Ohio in the USA and has specialized in fictional thrillers with plots centering around advanced levels of technology and spirituality. He is a novelist, poet, painter, musician and song writer. He first published with New Falcon Publications in 1988 and again in 1990. His first novel was entitled **The Dream Illuminati**. The follow up was **The Illuminati of Immortality**. Both books carried extensive introductions by **Robert Anton Wilson. The Dream Illuminati** was updated, expanded and republished in 2010.

In 2015, the author self-published a novel entitled **Dragonfire Dreams** and in 2019 one entitled **Crimson Firestorm Mars**.

His books have been lauded by **Dr Christopher S Hyatt, Robert Anton Wilson, Timothy Leary, Michael Hayes, Ken Bruen, Jason Starr** and **Colonel John B. Alexander**.

**Saalman** is a philosopher and metaphysician who has traveled the globe and has deeply studied the roots of humanity's many religions, spiritual traditions and secret societies. For decades, he has immersed himself in the writings of the world's philosophers, psychologists, mystics, yogis and wisdom masters. He has regularly posted his own metaphysical writings on Medium.com and offers additional insights on a Twitter post entitled **Quickfire Enlightenment**.

**The Journey Across Forever** is his first nonfiction work. It carries an extensive introduction by acclaimed activist author **Colonel John B. Alexander, Ph.D.**

He lives in Galway, Ireland with his wife, Karen, his son, Ciarán, and his daughter, Aisling.

# SPIRITUALITY

O is a symbol of the world, of oneness and unity; this eye represents knowledge and insight. We publish titles on general spirituality and living a spiritual life. We aim to inform and help you on your own journey in this life.

If you have enjoyed this book, why not tell other readers by posting a review on your preferred book site?

Recent bestsellers from O-Books are:

**Heart of Tantric Sex**

Diana Richardson

Revealing Eastern secrets of deep love and intimacy to Western couples.

Paperback: 978-1-90381-637-0 ebook: 978-1-84694-637-0

**Crystal Prescriptions**

The A-Z guide to over 1,200 symptoms and their healing crystals

Judy Hall

The first in the popular series of eight books, this handy little guide is packed as tight as a pill-bottle with crystal remedies for ailments.

Paperback: 978-1-90504-740-6 ebook: 978-1-84694-629-5

**Take Me To Truth**

Undoing the Ego

Nouk Sanchez, Tomas Vieira

The best-selling step-by-step book on shedding the Ego, using the teachings of *A Course In Miracles*.

Paperback: 978-1-84694-050-7 ebook: 978-1-84694-654-7

**The 7 Myths about Love...Actually!**

The Journey from your HEAD to the HEART of your SOUL

Mike George

Smashes all the myths about LOVE.

Paperback: 978-1-84694-288-4 ebook: 978-1-84694-682-0

**The Holy Spirit's Interpretation of the New Testament**

A Course in Understanding and Acceptance

Regina Dawn Akers

Following on from the strength of *A Course In Miracles*, NTI teaches us how to experience the love and oneness of God.

Paperback: 978-1-84694-085-9 ebook: 978-1-78099-083-5

**The Message of A Course In Miracles**

A translation of the Text in plain language

Elizabeth A. Cronkhite

A translation of *A Course in Miracles* into plain, everyday language for anyone seeking inner peace. The companion volume, *Practicing A Course In Miracles*, offers practical lessons and mentoring.

Paperback: 978-1-84694-319-5 ebook: 978-1-84694-642-4

**Your Simple Path**

Find Happiness in every step

Ian Tucker

A guide to helping us reconnect with what is really important in our lives.

Paperback: 978-1-78279-349-6 ebook: 978-1-78279-348-9

**365 Days of Wisdom**

Daily Messages To Inspire You Through The Year

Dadi Janki

Daily messages which cool the mind, warm the heart and guide you along your journey.

Paperback: 978-1-84694-863-3 ebook: 978-1-84694-864-0

**Body of Wisdom**

Women's Spiritual Power and How it Serves

Hilary Hart

Bringing together the dreams and experiences of women across the world with today's most visionary spiritual teachers.

Paperback: 978-1-78099-696-7 ebook: 978-1-78099-695-0

**Dying to Be Free**

From Enforced Secrecy to Near Death to True Transformation

Hannah Robinson

After an unexpected accident and near-death experience, Hannah Robinson found herself radically transforming her life, while a remarkable new insight altered her relationship with her father, a practising Catholic priest.

Paperback: 978-1-78535-254-6 ebook: 978-1-78535-255-3

**The Ecology of the Soul**
A Manual of Peace, Power and Personal Growth for Real People in the Real World
Aidan Walker
Balance your own inner Ecology of the Soul to regain your natural state of peace, power and wellbeing.
Paperback: 978-1-78279-850-7 ebook: 978-1-78279-849-1

**Not I, Not other than I**
The Life and Teachings of Russel Williams
Steve Taylor, Russel Williams
The miraculous life and inspiring teachings of one of the World's greatest living Sages.
Paperback: 978-1-78279-729-6 ebook: 978-1-78279-728-9

**On the Other Side of Love**
A woman's unconventional journey towards wisdom
Muriel Maufroy
When life has lost all meaning, what do you do?
Paperback: 978-1-78535-281-2 ebook: 978-1-78535-282-9

**Practicing A Course In Miracles**
A translation of the Workbook in plain language, with mentor's notes
Elizabeth A. Cronkhite
The practical second and third volumes of The Plain-Language *A Course In Miracles*.
Paperback: 978-1-84694-403-1 ebook: 978-1-78099-072-9

**Quantum Bliss**
The Quantum Mechanics of Happiness, Abundance, and Health
George S. Mentz
*Quantum Bliss* is the breakthrough summary of success and spirituality secrets that customers have been waiting for.
Paperback: 978-1-78535-203-4 ebook: 978-1-78535-204-1

**The Upside Down Mountain**
Mags MacKean
A must-read for anyone weary of chasing success and happiness – one woman's inspirational journey swapping the uphill slog for the downhill slope.
Paperback: 978-1-78535-171-6 ebook: 978-1-78535-172-3

**Your Personal Tuning Fork**
The Endocrine System
Deborah Bates
Discover your body's health secret, the endocrine system, and 'twang' your way to sustainable health!
Paperback: 978-1-84694-503-8 ebook: 978-1-78099-697-4

Readers of ebooks can buy or view any of these bestsellers by clicking on the live link in the title. Most titles are published in paperback and as an ebook. Paperbacks are available in traditional bookshops. Both print and ebook formats are available online.

Find more titles and sign up to our readers' newsletter at http://www.johnhuntpublishing.com/mind-body-spirit

Follow us on Facebook at https://www.facebook.com/OBooks/ and Twitter at https://twitter.com/obooks